# GRAMMAR
## EXPLORER 1

**Daphne Mackey**
Series Editors: Rob Jenkins and Staci Johnson

NATIONAL GEOGRAPHIC LEARNING | CENGAGE Learning®

Australia • Brazil • Japan • Korea • Mexico • Singapore • Spain • United Kingdom • United States

**Grammar Explorer 1**

**Daphne Mackey**

Publisher: Sherrise Roehr

Executive Editor: Laura Le Dréan

Senior Development Editor: Mary Whittemore

Assistant Editor: Vanessa Richards

Senior Technology Product Manager: Scott Rule

Director of Global Marketing: Ian Martin

Marketing Manager: Lindsey Miller

Sr. Director, ELT & World Languages:
Michael Burggren

Production Manager: Daisy Sosa

Content Project Manager: Andrea Bobotas

Senior Print Buyer: Mary Beth Hennebury

Cover Designer: 3CD, Chicago

Cover Image: George F. Herben/National
Geographic Creative

Compositor: Cenveo® Publisher Services

For product information and technology assistance, contact us at
**Cengage Learning Customer & Sales Support,**
**1-800-354-9706**

For permission to use material from this text or product,
submit all requests online at **www.cengage.com/permissions.**
Further permissions questions can be e-mailed to
**permissionrequest@cengage.com.**

Student Book 1: 978-1-111-35019-2

**National Geographic Learning**
20 Channel Center Street
Boston, MA 02210
USA

Cengage Learning is a leading provider of customized learning solutions with office locations around the globe, including Singapore, the United Kingdom, Australia, Mexico, Brazil and Japan.

Cengage Learning products are represented in Canada by Nelson Education, Ltd.

Visit National Geographic Learning online at **NGL.cengage.com**

Visit our corporate website at **www.cengage.com**

Printed in the United States of America
3 4 5 6 7 8 9 10 19 18 17 16 15

# CONTENTS

◄ A worker on top of the John Hancock skyscraper in Chicago, Illinois, USA

UNIT **3** Work

**Simple Present: Part 1**

| Lesson **1** | Lesson **2** | Lesson **3** | Lesson **4** | Review the Grammar |
|---|---|---|---|---|
| page 80 | page 88 | page 97 | page 104 | page 111 |
| Simple Present: Affirmative Statements; Irregular Verbs: Do, Go, and Have | Simple Present: Negative Statements; Prepositions of Time (part 2); Like, Need, Want | Verbs + Objects; Object Pronouns | Imperatives | Connect the Grammar to Writing page 114 |

79

**National Geographic images** introduce the unit theme—real world topics that students want to read, write, and talk about.

Units are organized in **manageable lessons**, which ensures students **explore, learn, practice**, and **apply** the grammar.

Each lesson begins with the *Explore* section, featuring a captivating National Geographic article that introduces the target grammar and builds students' knowledge in a variety of academic disciplines.

## LESSON 1 — Simple Present: Affirmative Statements

### EXPLORE

🎧 CD1-30  **1 READ** the article about Doctor Bugs. Notice the words in **bold**.

## Doctor Bugs

Most people don't like bugs, but Doctor Mark Moffett **loves** them! In fact, his nickname is Doctor Bugs. He's a photographer and an entomologist. An entomologist **studies** bugs.

Doctor Moffett's favorite bug is the ant. He **goes** all over the world to study ants. He **watches** them as they **eat**, **work**, **rest**, **sleep**, and **fight**.

He **takes** photographs of the ants. He **lies** on the ground with his camera and **waits** for the right moment. The ants and other bugs often **bite** him, but that doesn't stop Doctor Bugs. He **has** an interesting

▲ Doctor Mark Moffett

80 SIMPLE PRESENT: PART 1

## LESSON 2 — Simple Present: Negative Statements and Contractions

### EXPLORE

🎧 CD1-35  **1 READ** the article about life on the International Space Station. Notice the words in **bold**.

## Life on the Space Station

Astronauts on the International Space Station have a busy schedule. Every day they wake up at 7:00 GMT.[1] **From 7:00 to 8:00,** they wash up and eat breakfast. **At 8:00 in the morning,** they call Ground Control[2] in their countries. After they talk to Ground Control, their workday begins. The astronauts **don't do** the same thing every day. Their schedules change every week.

The astronauts **don't work** all the time. Each day they exercise for an hour **in the morning** and an hour **in the afternoon**. After dinner, they have free time. Then, it's time to go to sleep. Sometimes this isn't easy because the sun rises and sets 16 times each day on the space station.

The astronauts' work **doesn't end** on Friday. They work a half day **on Saturday** and all day **on Sunday**. Astronauts are very busy people.

[1] **GMT:** Greenwich Mean Time
[2] **Ground Control:** People on Earth who work with astronauts in space.

◄ The International Space Station (ISS)

88 SIMPLE PRESENT: PART 1

## Verbs + Objects — LESSON 3

...ephant keepers in Kenya. Notice the words in **bold**.

Kenya

...They're so cute! Where are

...keepers. They work at a place for orphan[1] elephants in ...nts, take care of **them**, and even play **soccer** with them.

...interesting job.

...ed to feed **the baby elephants** every three hours.

...o. The keepers sleep in buildings with the baby ...rom the article. One of the keepers says, "Every three ...d pull **your blankets**[2] off. The elephants are our alarms." ...nt to read **that article**.

...dead.

▼ Baby elephants and elephant keepers in Nairobi, Kenya

UNIT 3 LESSON 3  97

INSIDE A UNIT

# INSIDE A UNIT

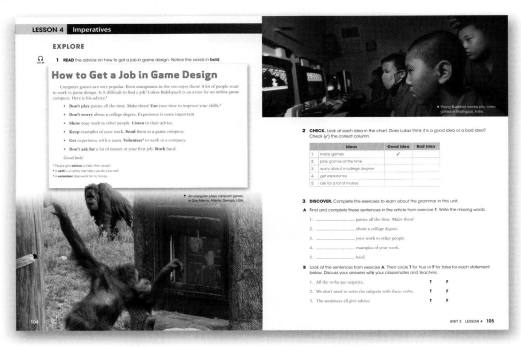

In the **Explore** section, students discover how the grammar structures are used in the readings and in real academic textbooks.

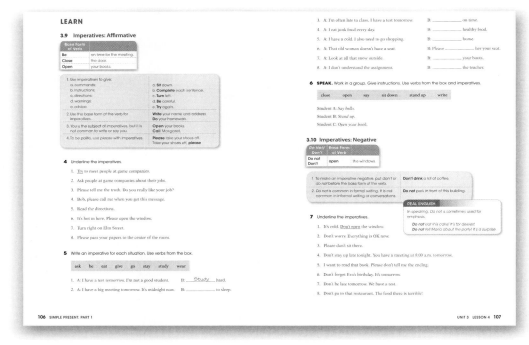

The **Learn** section features clear grammar charts and explanations followed by controlled practice of the grammar forms.

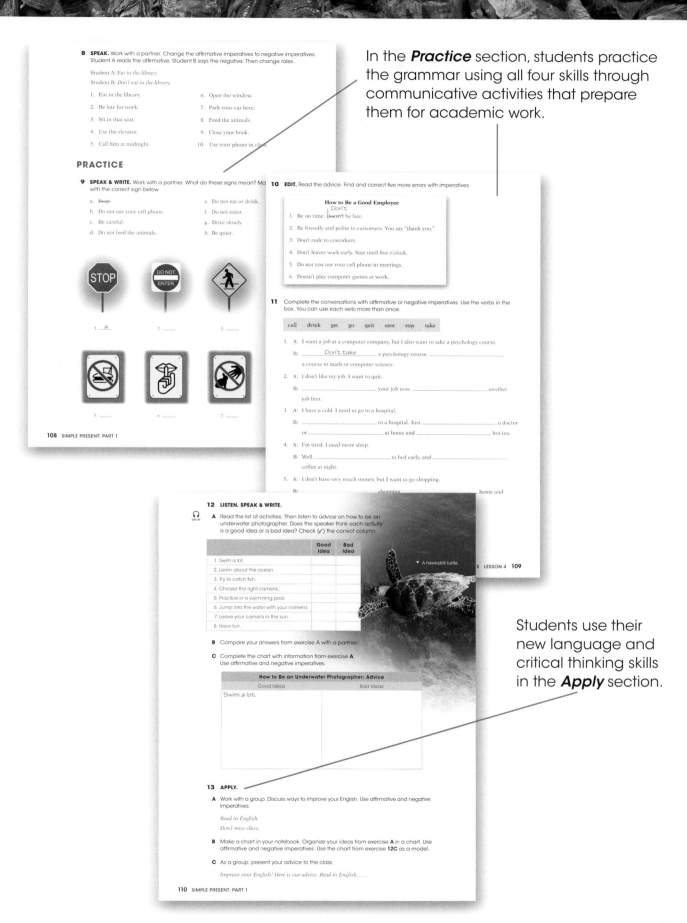

In the **Practice** section, students practice the grammar using all four skills through communicative activities that prepare them for academic work.

**8 SPEAK.** Work with a partner. Change the affirmative imperatives to negative imperatives. Student A reads the affirmative, Student B says the negative. Then change roles.

Student A: *Eat in the library.*
Student B: *Don't eat in the library.*

1. Eat in the library.
2. Be late for work.
3. Sit in that seat.
4. Use the elevator.
5. Call him at midnight.
6. Open the window.
7. Park your car here.
8. Feed the animals.
9. Close your book.
10. Use your phone in class.

## PRACTICE

**9 SPEAK & WRITE.** Work with a partner. What do these signs mean? Ma... with the correct sign below.

a. Stop.
b. Do not use your cell phone.
c. Be careful.
d. Do not feed the animals.
e. Do not eat or drink.
f. Do not enter.
g. Drive slowly.
h. Be quiet.

1. _a_   2. ____   3. ____

5. ____   6. ____   7. ____

**10 EDIT.** Read the advice. Find and correct five more errors with imperatives.

### How to Be a Good Employee
                Don't
1. Be on time. Doesn't be late.
2. Be friendly and polite to customers. You say "thank you."
3. Don't rude to coworkers.
4. Don't leaves work early. Stay until five o'clock.
5. Do not you use your cell phone in meetings.
6. Doesn't play computer games at work.

**11** Complete the conversations with affirmative or negative imperatives. Use the verbs in the box. You can use each verb more than once.

| call | drink | get | go | quit | save | stay | take |
|------|-------|-----|-----|------|------|------|------|

1. A: I want a job at a computer company, but I also want to take a psychology course.
   B: _____ Don't take _____ a psychology course. _____ a course in math or computer science.
2. A: I don't like my job. I want to quit.
   B: _____ your job now. _____ another job first.
3. A: I have a cold. I need to go to a hospital.
   B: _____ to a hospital. Just _____ a doctor or _____ at home and _____ hot tea.
4. A: I'm tired. I need more sleep.
   B: Well, _____ to bed early, and _____ coffee at night.
5. A: I don't have very much money, but I want to go shopping.
   B: _____ shopping. _____ home and

108 SIMPLE PRESENT: PART 1

3 LESSON 4 **109**

**12 LISTEN, SPEAK & WRITE.**

**A** Read the list of activities. Then listen to advice on how to be an underwater photographer. Does the speaker think each activity is a good idea or a bad idea? Check (✓) the correct column.

|  | Good Idea | Bad Idea |
|--|-----------|----------|
| 1. Swim a lot. | | |
| 2. Learn about the ocean. | | |
| 3. Try to catch fish. | | |
| 4. Choose the right camera. | | |
| 5. Practice in a swimming pool. | | |
| 6. Jump into the water with your camera. | | |
| 7. Leave your camera in the sun. | | |
| 8. Have fun. | | |

▼ A hawksbill turtle

**B** Compare your answers from exercise **A** with a partner.

**C** Complete the chart with information from exercise **A**. Use affirmative and negative imperatives.

### How to Be an Underwater Photographer: Advice
| Good Ideas | Bad Ideas |
|------------|-----------|
| Swim a lot. | |

Students use their new language and critical thinking skills in the **Apply** section.

**13 APPLY.**

**A** Work with a group. Discuss ways to improve your English. Use affirmative and negative imperatives.

*Read in English.*
*Don't miss class.*

**B** Make a chart in your notebook. Organize your ideas from exercise **A** in a chart. Use affirmative and negative imperatives. Use the chart from exercise **12C** as a model.

**C** As a group, present your advice to the class.

*Improve your English! Here is our advice. Read in English. . . .*

110 SIMPLE PRESENT: PART 1

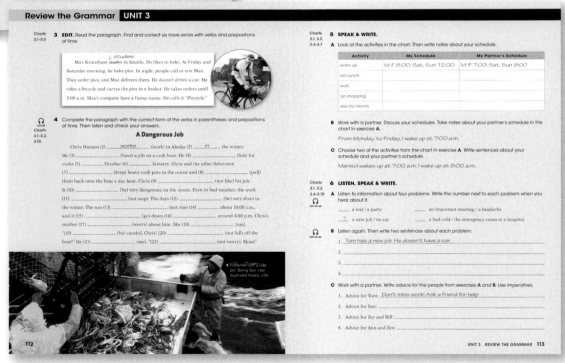

**UNIT 3** Review the Grammar

Charts
3.1, 3.4,
3.7, 3.8

**1** Change each affirmative statement to a negative statement. Then change each underlined object to an object pronoun.

1. She reads the newspaper every morning. _She doesn't read it every morning._

2. She works with Todd and Oscar. _____

3. My brother has my book. _____

4. She teaches Barbara and me. _____

5. We talk to our friends every day. _____

6. She studies biology. _____

7. He knows my sister. _____

8. He fixes cars. _____

Charts
3.1–3.5

**2** Look at the work schedule. Then complete the sentences below. Use the correct prepositions of time and the verbs in parentheses. Use the negative form when necessary.

| Name | Days | Times | Break |
|------|------|-------|-------|
| Petra | MWF | 9:00 a.m. – 5:30 p.m. | 1:00 – 1:45 p.m. |
| Ali | M-F | 3:00 a.m. – 12:00 p.m. | 8:00 – 8:45 a.m. |
| Nadia | T/Th | 11:00 p.m. – 6:00 a.m. | 2:30 – 3:00 a.m. |
| Ken | T/Th | 9:00 p.m. – 6:00 a.m. | 2:00 – 2:30 a.m. |
| Cathy | M-F | 10:00 a.m. – 6:00 p.m. | 2:00 – 2:30 p.m. |

1. Petra ___works___ (work) from 9:00 a.m. ___ 5:30 p.m.

2. Petra ___ (work) ___ Tuesday or Thursday.

3. Ali ___ (work) ___ 12:00 p.m.

4. Ali ___ (have) a break ___ 8:00 a.m.

5. Nadia ___ (work) ___ the afternoon.

6. Nadia and Ken ___ (work) ___ night.

7. Ken ___ (have) a break ___ 2:00 a.m.

8. Cathy ___ (work) ___ 10:00 a.m. ___ 6:00 p.m.

9. Cathy ___ (work) ___ Saturday and Sunday.

10. Cathy and Petra ___ (have) their breaks ___ the afternoon.

Review the Grammar **UNIT 3**

Charts
3.1–3.5

**3** EDIT. Read the paragraph. Find and correct six more errors with verbs and prepositions of time.

Max Kraushaar ~~studys~~ _studies_ in Seattle. He likes to bake. At Friday and Saturday morning, he bake pies. In night, people call or text Max. They order pies, and Max delivers them. He doesn't drives a car. He rides a bicycle and carrys the pies in a basket. He takes orders until 3:00 a.m. Max's company have a funny name. He calls it "Piecycle."

Charts
3.1–3.2,
3.10

**4** Complete the paragraph with the correct form of the verbs in parentheses and prepositions of time. Then listen and check your answers.

**A Dangerous Job**

Chris Hansen (1) ___works___ (work) in Alaska (2) ___in___ the winter. He (3) ___ (have) a job on a crab boat. He (4) ___ (fish) for crabs (5) ___ October (6) ___ January. Chris and the other fishermen (7) ___ (drop) heavy crab pots in the ocean and (8) ___ (pull) them back onto the boat a day later. Chris (9) ___ (not like) his job. It (10) ___ (be) very dangerous on the ocean. Even in bad weather, the work (11) ___ (not stop). The days (12) ___ (be) very short in the winter. The sun (13) ___ (not rise) (14) ___ about 10:00 a.m., and it (15) ___ (go) down (16) ___ around 4:00 p.m. Chris's mother (17) ___ (worry) about him. She (18) ___ (say), "(19) ___ (be) careful, Chris! (20) ___ (not fall) off the boat!" He (21) ___ (say), "(22) ___ (not worry), Mom!"

Fishermen with a crab pot, Bering Sea, near southwest Alaska, USA

112

Charts
3.1, 3.2,
3.4–3.7

**5** SPEAK & WRITE.

**A** Look at the activities in the chart. Then write notes about your schedule.

| Activity | My Schedule | My Partner's Schedule |
|----------|-------------|----------------------|
| wake up | M-F 8:00; Sat, Sun 12:00 | M-F 7:00; Sat, Sun 9:00 |
| eat lunch | | |
| work | | |
| go shopping | | |
| see my friends | | |

**B** Work with a partner. Discuss your schedules. Take notes about your partner's schedule in the chart in exercise **A**.

From Monday to Friday, I wake up at 7:00 a.m.

**C** Choose two of the activities from the chart in exercise **A**. Write sentences about your schedule and your partner's schedule.

Marisol wakes up at 7:00 a.m. I wake up at 8:00 a.m.

Charts
3.1, 3.2,
3.4–3.10

**6** LISTEN, SPEAK & WRITE.

**A** Listen to information about four problems. Write the number next to each problem when you hear about it.

___ a test / a party     ___ an important meeting / a headache

_1_ a new job / no car     ___ a bad cold / the emergency room at a hospital

**B** Listen again. Then write two sentences about each problem.

1. _Tom has a new job. He doesn't have a car._

2. _____

3. _____

4. _____

**C** Work with a partner. Write advice for the people from exercises **A** and **B**. Use imperatives.

1. Advice for Tom: _Don't miss work! Ask a friend for help._

2. Advice for Sue: _____

3. Advice for Jay and Bill: _____

4. Advice for Ann and Jim: _____

UNIT 3 REVIEW THE GRAMMAR **113**

***Review the Grammar*** gives students the opportunity to consolidate the grammar in their reading, writing, listening, and speaking.

## Connect the Grammar to Writing

**1 READ & NOTICE THE GRAMMAR.**

**A** Read the paragraph. What is the writer's advice for new teachers? Discuss with a partner.

### My Job as a Teacher

I am a teacher. I work from 8:00 a.m. to 1:30 p.m. I teach four English classes. In class, I write on the board. I ask a lot of questions. I use pictures when I teach vocabulary. I don't arrive late. At home, I plan my lessons. I correct homework and tests. My advice for new teachers – learn your students' names on the first day.

---

**GRAMMAR FOCUS**

In the paragraph in exercise **A**, the writer uses the simple present to talk about habits or routines and schedules.

I **work** from 8:00 a.m. to 1:30 p.m.
I **don't arrive** late.

---

**B** Read the paragraph in exercise A again. Underline the verbs in the simple present. Circle the imperative. Then compare your answers with a partner.

**C** Complete the chart with information from the paragraph in exercise A. What does a teacher do in class? At home?

| The Job of a Teacher | |
|---|---|
| **In Class** | **At Home** |
| She asks a lot of questions. | |

**Advice:** Learn your students' names.

### Write about a Job

**2 BEFORE YOU WRITE.** Complete the chart with information about your job as a student. What do you do in class? At home? What advice do you have for new students? Use the chart from exercise **1C** as a model.

| My Job as a Student | |
|---|---|
| **In Class** | **At Home** |
| | |

**Advice:**

**3 WRITE** a paragraph about your job as a student. Give advice for new students. Use the information from your chart in exercise **2** and the paragraph in exercise **1A** to help you.

---

**WRITING FOCUS    Indenting Paragraphs**

Good writers indent the first line of a paragraph. To indent, begin the first line of a paragraph five spaces to the right.

*I am a teacher. I work from 8:00 p.m. to 1:30 p.m. I teach four English classes. In class, I write on the board. I ask a lot of questions.*

---

**4 SELF ASSESS.** Read your paragraph. Underline the verbs in the simple present. Then use the checklist to assess your work.

- [ ] I did not put *be* in front of other verbs in the simple present. [3.1, 3.3]
- [ ] The verbs in the simple present are spelled correctly. [3.3]
- [ ] I used the base form of the verb for imperatives. [3.9, 3.10]
- [ ] The first line of my paragraph is indented. [WRITING FOCUS]

***Connect the Grammar to Writing*** provides students with a clear model and a guided writing task where they first notice and then use the target grammar in one of a variety of writing genres.

# ACKNOWLEDGMENTS

*The authors and publisher would like to thank the following reviewers and contributors:*

**Gokhan Alkanat**, Auburn University at Montgomery, Alabama; **Dorothy S. Avondstondt**, Miami Dade College, Florida; **Heather Barikmo**, The English Language Center at LaGuardia Community College, New York; **Kimberly Becker**, Nashville State Community College, Tennessee; **Lukas Bidelspack**, Corvallis, Oregon; **Grace Bishop**, Houston Community College, Texas; **Mariusz Jacek Bojarczuk**, Bunker Hill Community College, Massachusetts; **Nancy Boyer**, Golden West College, California; **Patricia Brenner**, University of Washington, Washington; **Jessica Buchsbaum**, City College of San Francisco, California; **Gabriella Cambiasso**, Harold Washington College, Illinois; **Tony Carnerie**, English Language Institute, University of California San Diego Extension, California; **Ana M. Cervantes Quequezana**, ICPNA - Instituto Cultural Peruano Norteamericano; **Whitney Clarq-Reis**, Framingham State University; **Julia A. Correia**, Henderson State University, Arkansas; **Katie Crowder**, UNT Department of Linguistics and Technical Communication, Texas; **Lin Cui**, William Rainey Harper College, Illinois; **Nora Dawkins**, Miami Dade College, Florida; **Rachel DeSanto**, English for Academic Purposes, Hillsborough Community College, Florida; **Aurea Diab**, Dillard University, Louisiana; **Marta Dmytrenko-Ahrabian**, English Language Institute, Wayne State University, Michigan; **Susan Dorrington**, Education and Language Acquisition Department, LaGuardia Community College, New York; **Ian Dreilinger**, Center for Multilingual Multicultural Studies, University of Central Florida, Florida; **Jennifer Dujat**, Education and Language Acquisition Department, LaGuardia Community College, New York; **Dr. Jane Duke**, Language & Literature Department, State College of Florida, Florida; **Anna Eddy**, University of Michigan-Flint, Michigan; **Jenifer Edens**, University of Houston, Texas; **Karen Einstein**, Santa Rosa Junior College, California; **Cynthia Etter**, International & English Language Programs, University of Washington, Washington; **Parvanak Fassihi**, SHOWA Boston Institute for Language and Culture, Massachusetts; **Katherine Fouche**, The University of Texas at Austin, Texas; **Richard Furlong**, Education and Language Acquisition Department, LaGuardia Community College, New York; **Glenn S. Gardner**, Glendale College, California; **Sally Gearhart**, Santa Rosa Junior College, California; **Alexis Giannopolulos**, SHOWA Boston Institute for Language and Culture, Massachusetts; **Nora Gold**, Baruch College, The City University of New York, New York; **Ekaterina V. Goussakova**, Seminole State College of Florida; **Lynn Grantz**, Valparaiso University, Indiana; **Tom Griffith**, SHOWA Boston Institute for Language and Culture, Massachusetts; **Christine Guro**, Hawaii English Language Program, University of Hawaii at Manoa, Hawaii; **Jessie Hayden**, Georgia Perimeter College, Georgia; **Barbara Inerfeld**, Program in American Language Studies, Rutgers University, New Jersey; **Gail Kellersberger**, University of Houston-Downtown, Texas; **David Kelley**, SHOWA Boston Institute for Language and Culture, Massachusetts; **Kathleen Kelly**, ESL Department, Passaic County Community College, New Jersey; **Dr. Hyun-Joo Kim**, Education and Language Acquisition Department, LaGuardia Community College, New York; **Linda Koffman**, College of Marin, California; **Lisa Kovacs-Morgan**, English Language Institute, University of California San Diego Extension, California; **Jerrad Langlois**, TESL Program and Office of International Programs, Northeastern Illinois University; **Janet Langon**, Glendale College, California; **Olivia Limbu**, The English Language Center at LaGuardia Community College, New York; **Devora Manier**, Nashville State Community College, Tennessee; **Susan McAlister**, Language and Culture Center, Department of English, University of Houston, Texas; **John McCarthy**, SHOWA Boston Institute for Language and Culture, Massachusetts; **Dr. Myra Medina**, Miami Dade College, Florida; **Dr. Suzanne Medina**, California State University, Dominguez Hills, California; **Nancy Megarity**, ESL & Developmental Writing, Collin College, Texas; **Joseph Montagna**, SHOWA Boston Institute for Language and Culture, Massachusetts; **Richard Moore**, University of Washington; **Monika Mulder**, Portland State University, Oregon; **Patricia Nation**, Miami Dade College, Florida; **Susan Niemeyer**, Los Angeles City College, California; **Charl Norloff**, International English Center, University of Colorado Boulder, Colorado; **Gabriella Nuttall**, Sacramento City College, California; **Dr. Karla Odenwald**, CELOP at Boston University, Massachusetts; **Ali Olson-Pacheco**, English Language Institute, University of California San Diego Extension, California; **Fernanda Ortiz**, Center for English as a Second Language, University of Arizona, Arizona; **Chuck Passentino**, Grossmont College, California; **Stephen Peridore**, College of Southern Nevada, Nevada; **Frank Quebbemann**, Miami Dade College, Florida; **Dr. Anouchka Rachelson**, Miami Dade College, Florida; **Dr. Agnieszka Rakowicz**, Education and Language Acquisition Department, LaGuardia Community College, New York; **Wendy Ramer**, Broward College, Florida; **Esther Robbins**, Prince George's Community College, Maryland; **Helen Roland**, Miami Dade College, Florida; **Debbie Sandstrom**, Tutorium in Intensive English, University of Illinois at Chicago, Illinois; **Maria Schirta**, Hudson County Community College, New Jersey; **Dr. Jennifer Scully**, Education and Language Acquisition Department, LaGuardia Community College, New York; **Jeremy Stubbs**, Tacoma, Washington; **Adrianne Thompson**, Miami Dade College, Florida; **Evelyn Trottier**, Basic and Transitional Studies Program, Seattle Central Community College, Washington; **Karen Vallejo**, University of California, Irvine, California; **Emily Young**, Auburn University at Montgomery, Alabama.

**From the Author:** It has been a pleasure to work with such talented people on this project. I would like to thank Mary Whittemore for her dedication, her sense of humor, and her wonderfully diplomatic way of giving negative feedback. I have enjoyed working with Laura Le Dréan and the team at National Geographic Learning as well as fellow authors Sammi Eckstut, Amy Cooper, and Paul Carne. Lastly, I would like to thank Daria Ruzicka for her hard work and contributions on the initial stages of the project and Diane Piniaris for her outstanding work on the final stage.

*Dedication:* With love to George and Caroline

## Text and Listening

**34:** Exercise 10. Source: "A Thing or Two about Twins" by Peter Miller: National Geographic/Features/Photo Gallery, National Geographic Magazine, January 2012. **85:** "Bush Pilots." Source: http://www.ultimathulelodge.com/people/paul-claus. **88:** Source: http://www.scienceclarified.com/scitech/Space-Stations/Living-in-Outer-Space.html. **97:** Source: "Orphans No More" by Charles Seibert: National Geographic Magazine, Sept. 2011. **129:** Exercise 9: Listen & Write. Sources: http://www.viator.com/Bangkokattractions/ Damnoen-Saduak-Floating-Market/d343-a2604; http://www.viator.com/Bangkok-tourism/Visiting-Bangkoks-Floating-Markets/d343-t11629. **136:** "52 Hikes a Year!" Source: http://52hikes52weekends.blogspot.com. **171:** Exercise 2: Listen, Write & Speak. Source: http://blogs.kqed.org/bayareabites/2012/08/07/traditional-ethiopian-coffee-ceremony-brewed-up-by-chef-marcus-samuelsson-and-cafe-colucci. **228:** Adapted from "The Hard Science, Dumb Luck, and Cowboy Nerve of Chasing Tornadoes" by Priit J. Vesilind: National Geographic Magazine, April 2004. **263:** Exercise 11: "The Inca Road." Source: http://www.nationalgeographicexpeditions.com/experts/karin-muller/detail, **270:** "Harriet Chalmers Adams." Source: http://www.squidoo.com/harrietchalmersadams. **301:** Exercise 7: "The Paralympic Games." Source: http://pri.org/stories/2012-09-06/paralympics-focus-elite-competition. **310:** "Fennec Foxes." Source: http://animals.nationalgeographic.com/animals/mammals/fennec-fox/. **318:** Exercise 13: Listen & Write. Source: http://video.nationalgeographic.com/video/photography/photographers/ocean-soul-dangerous-shark/. **320:** Source: http://news.nationalgeographic.com/news/travelnews/2011/12/111228-mountaingorillas-king-grooming-uganda-tourist-animals/. **329:** Source: http://newswatch.nationalgeographic.com/2009/09/18/iberian_lynx_conservation/. **336:** Exercise 1: "A Dangerous Situation." Sources: http://video.nationalgeographic.com/video/photography/behind-the-shot/king-cobra-klum/; http://photography.nationalgeographic.com/photography/photographers/photographermattias-klum/. **352:** "Winter the Dolphin." Source: http://www.hanger.com/prosthetics/experience/patientprofiles/winterthedolphin/Pages/WintertheDolphin.aspx. **358:** Exercise 12: Listen & Speak. Source: http://www.pbs.org/wgbh/nova/physics/sophie-germain.html. **359:** Sources: http://www.paralympic.org/news/london-2012-numbers; http://www.paralympic.org/TheIPC/HWA/HistoryoftheMovement. **365:** Exercise 12: Edit. "Aimee Mullins." Sources: http://www.paralympic.org/TheIPC/HWA/HistoryoftheMovement; http://www.ted.com/talks/aimee_mullins_the_opportunity_of_adversity.html. **381:** Exercise 14: Listen & Speak. Source: http://www.phuketland.com/phuket_links/index.htm. **382:** "Geography Trivia" Source: http://www.worldatlas.com/geoquiz/thelist.htm. **422:** Source: http://news.nationalgeographic.com/news/2003/04/0418_030418_tvmareki.html. **A7:** "Geography Trivia." Source: http://www.worldatlas.com/geoquiz/thelist.htm. **Definitions for glossed words:** Sources: *The Newbury House Dictionary plus Grammar Reference*, Fifth Edition, National Geographic Learning/Cengage Learning, 2014; *Collins Cobuild Illustrated Basic Dictionary of American English*, Cengage Learning 2010, Collins Cobuild/Harper Collins Publishers, First Edition, 2010; *Collins Cobuild School Dictionary of American English*, Cengage Learning 2009, Collins Cobuild/Harper Collins Publishers, 2008; Collins Cobuild Advanced Learner's Dictionary, 5th Edition, Harper Collins Publishers, 2006.

## Photo

**2–3:** ©Adrian Pope/Getty Images; **5:** ©James P. Blair/National Geographic Creative; **9:** ©Stephen Rees/Shutterstock; **11:** ©Beverly Joubert/National Geographic Creative; **12:** ©Beverly Joubert/National Geographic Creative; **19 top:** ©LattaPictures/iStockphoto, **middle:** ©Ingram Publishing/Thinkstock, **bottom:** © Asiaselects/Alamy; **21:** Joel Sartore/National Geographic Creative; **22:** ©Joel Sartore/National Geographic Creative; **25 top:** ©Bobby Model/National Geographic Creative, **middle:** ©Mega Pixel/Shutterstock; **26 top:** ©Andrew Rich/iStockphoto, **middle:** ©Wavebreak Media/Thinkstock, **bottom:** ©Kali Nine LLC/iStockphoto; **28:** ©Erika Larsen/Redux; **29:** ©Erika Larsen/Redux; **32:** ©Tino Soriano/National Geographic Creative; **37:** ©Richard Nowitz/National Geographic Creative; **38:** ©stevecoleimages/iStockphoto; **40-41:** ©Poras Chaudhary/Getty Images; **42–43:** ©James L. Stanfield/National Geographic Creative: **46:** ©Adalberto Ríos Szalay/age fotostock; **49:** ©luoman/iStockphoto; **50–51:** ©Neale Clark/Getty Images; **57:** ©Tyrone Turner/National Geographic Creative; **59:** ©Annie Griffiths/National Geographic Creative; **65:** ©Seregam/Shutterstock; **66:** ©Christophe Boisvieux/age fotostock; **67:** ©Keren Su/Getty Images; **71:** ©AFP/Getty Images; **72:** © epa European Pressphoto Agency creative account/Alamy; **74:** ©Lukas Hlavac/Shutterstock; **75:** ©TonyV3112/Shutterstock; **76:** ©Alistair Berg/Getty Images; **78–79:** ©Lynn Johnson/National Geographic Creative; **80 inset:** ©Minden Pictures/SuperStock; **80–81:** ©James P. Blair/National Geographic Creative; **83:** ©Joel Sartose/National Geographic Creative; **85:** ©Kate Thompson/National Geographic Creative; **87:** © YinYang/iStockphoto; **88:** ©NASA; **89:** ©NASA and The Hubble Heritage Team (STScI/AURA) Acknowledgment: N. Scoville (Caltech) and T. Rector (NOAO); **97:** ©Michael Nichols/National Geographic Creative; **98:** ©Michael Nichols/National Geographic Creative; **102:** ©J.W.Alker Image Broker/Newscom; **103 top:** ©Big Cheese/Thinkstock, **103 bottom:** © Design Pics Inc./Alamy; **104:** Peter Essick/National Geographic Creative; **105:** ©Altaf Qadri/AP Images; **110:** ©Raul touzon/National Geographic Creative; **112 inset:** ©Kelly O/The Stranger, **112 bottom:** ©AlaskaStock/Glow Images; **114:** ©Creatas Images/Thinkstock; **116–117:** ©Luca Invernizzi Tetto/age fotostock; **118–119:** ©Gianluca Colla/National Geographic Creative; **122–123:** ©Anita Stizzoli/Getty Images; **125:** ©Lonely Planet/Getty Images; **126:** ©1000 Words/Shutterstock; **129:** ©MJPrototype/Shutterstock; **131:** ©Sylvain Grandadam/Getty Images; **132:** ©Eric Albrecht/Getty Images; **136:** ©Raymond Gehman/National Geographic Creative; **138 top:** ©Jose Luis Pelaez Inc/Getty Images, **middle:** ©auremar/Shutterstock, **bottom:** ©Thorsten Rother/Getty Images; **142:** ©Richard Nowitz/National Geographic Creative; **144–145:** ©Joel Sartose/National Geographic Creative; **146–147:** ©Richard Nowitz/National Geographic Creative; **152:** ©David C. Tomlinson/Getty Images: **154–155:** ©Nando Pizzini Photography/Getty Images; **155, 1:** ©ffolas/Thinkstock, **155, 2:** ©Petr Malyshev/Shutterstock, **155, 3:** ©Jiri Hera/Shutterstock, **155, 4:** ©Eldin Muratovic/Thinkstock, **155, 5:** © wildlywise/Shutterstock, **155, 6:** ©Picsfive/Shutterstock; **159:** ©Greg Dale/National Geographic Creative; **160:** ©bitt24/Shutterstock; **161:** ©James Baigrie/Getty Images; **162:** ©Tim Hill/Alamy; **163:** ©McPHOTO/age fotostock; **164:** ©Nazzu/Shutterstock; **171:** ©Ton Koene/age fotostock; **172:** ©Stephen St. John/National Geographic Creative; **174:** ©Keri Pinzon/Getty Images; **176–177:** ©Pete Ryan/National Geographic Creative; **178, viajero:** ©zhang bo/Getty Images, **178, Chen C:** ©Asia Images Group Pte Ltd/Alamy, **178, Viet:** ©Martin Valigursky/Thinkstock; **179:** ©Hung Chung Chih/Thinkstock; **184:** ©Fran Lanting/National Geographic Creative; **185:** ©Fran Lanting/National Geographic Creative; **187:** ©tulcarion/Getty Images; **188:** ©Design Pics Inc./Alamy; **192:** © Greg Winston/National Geographic Creative; **193:** ©Boston Globe via Getty Images;

*(continued on page C1)*

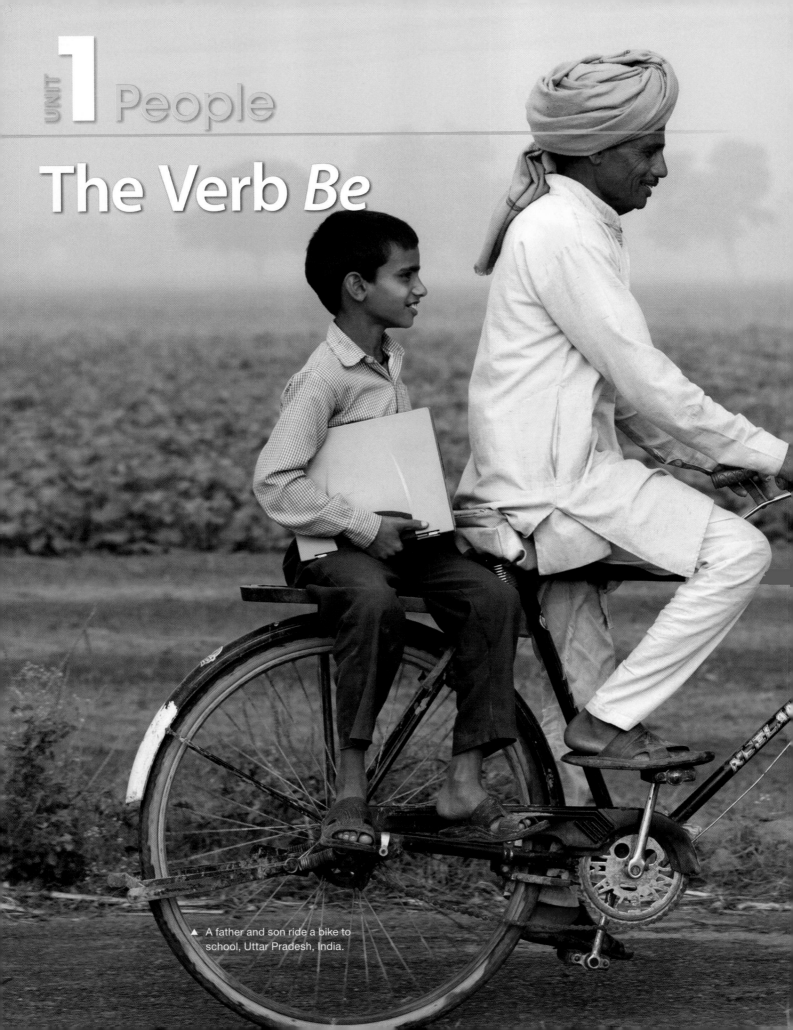

# The Verb *Be*

▲ A father and son ride a bike to school, Uttar Pradesh, India.

## EXPLORE

CD1-2

**1**   **READ** the conversation about greetings. Notice the words in **bold**.

# Say hello!

**Teacher:**    Some people bow. Some people shake hands. How do *you* say hello? Please tell us. Also, please tell us your name and country.

**Miyo:**    Hello. **My name is** Miyo. **I'm** from Japan. In Japan, people bow.

**Marie:**    Hello, everyone. **It's** nice to meet you. **I'm** Marie. **I'm** from France. In France, we shake hands and kiss two times on the cheek!

**Aran:**    **My name is** Aran. **I'm** from Thailand. We put our hands together, like this.

**Martin:**    **I'm** Martin. This is Greta. **We're** from Germany. We usually shake hands.

**David:**    Nice to meet you! **I'm** from Italy. We shake hands, too. And in my family, we hug and kiss.

**Teacher:**    **It's** nice to meet you! **You're** all from different countries, and **your customs are** very interesting!

**2**   **CHECK.** Match each name with the correct country.

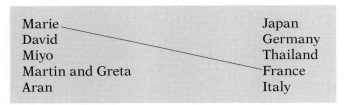

| | |
|---|---|
| Marie | Japan |
| David | Germany |
| Miyo | Thailand |
| Martin and Greta | France |
| Aran | Italy |

**3**   **DISCOVER.** Find these sentences in the conversation from exercise **1**. Write the missing words or letters. Then work with a partner and compare answers.

1. My name _____ Miyo.

2. I'_____ Marie.

3. You'_____ all from different countries, and your customs _____ very interesting.

A Sikh boy from India gives a greeting.

# LEARN

## 1.1 Simple Present of *Be*: Affirmative Statements

| Singular | | | Plural | | |
|---|---|---|---|---|---|
| Subject | *Be* | | Subject | *Be* | |
| I | am | | We<br>Dave and I | | |
| You | are | | You<br>You and Anna | | |
| He<br>Mario<br>The boy | is | from Italy. | They<br>Mario and the girl<br>The cars | are | from Italy. |
| She<br>Marie<br>The girl | | | | | |
| It<br>The car | | | | | |

| | |
|---|---|
| 1. A sentence needs a subject and a verb. | Marta   is   from Mexico.<br>Subject  Verb<br><br>✓ Jon **is** from Canada.<br>✗ Jon <u>from</u> Canada. |
| 2. The verb *be* has three forms in the present: *am, is, are.* | I **am** from Peru.<br>She **is** from Spain.<br>They **are** from Japan. |
| 3. Subject pronouns can take the place of a noun as subject. Do not use a subject pronoun after a subject noun. | Rodrigo is Brazilian. **He** is from Recife.<br><br>✓ He is from Brazil.<br>✗ Rodrigo <u>he</u> is from Brazil. |
| 4. *You* is for one person or more than one person. | Ed, **you** are late. (one person)<br>Ed and Al, **you** are late. (more than one person) |
| 5. Use *and* to join two nouns in the subject position. | <u>Lucas</u> **and** <u>Ana</u> are from Brazil.<br><u>The boy</u> **and** <u>girl</u> are from Brazil. |

**4** Circle the subject(s) in each sentences. Underline the verb *be*.

1. Hello. (My name) is Miyo.

2. Marie and Jean are from France.

3. I am from New York.

4. Chile is a country.

5. We are students.

6. Jim and Alex are teachers.

7. I am Japanese.

8. You are from Thailand.

**5** Complete each sentence with *am, is,* or *are.*

1. I <u>am</u> a student.

2. They _____ from China.

3. Toronto _____ a city.

4. My name _____ Allen.

5. We _____ friends.

6. Tom _____ from my city.

7. Anna and I _____ friends.

8. I _____ from Mexico.

9. You _____ teachers.

10. She _____ from Colombia.

**6** **SPEAK.** Work with a partner. Talk about yourself.

*Hello. My name is . . . I'm from . . .*

## 1.2 Contractions with *Be*

| Full Form | | | | Contraction | |
|---|---|---|---|---|---|
| I | am | | | I'm | |
| You | are | | | You're | |
| He | | | | He's | |
| Pierre | | | | Pierre's | |
| She | is | from Canada. | | She's | from Canada. |
| Megan | | | | Megan's | |
| It | | | | It's | |
| We | | | | We're | |
| You | are | | | You're | |
| They | | | | They're | |

| | |
|---|---|
| 1. A contraction is a short form. Contractions are used in conversation and informal writing. | A: Hello. My name's Larry.<br>B: Nice to meet you. I'm Maria. |
| 2. Use contractions with pronouns, nouns, and proper nouns. Proper nouns are names of specific people, places, and things. | **He's** from Mexico.<br>My **name's** Lisa.<br>**Yumiko's** from Japan.<br>**Montreal's** a city in Canada.<br>The **Burj Khalifa's** a building in Dubai. |
| 3. The contraction *you're* is for one person or more than one person. | Ed, **you're** late. (one person)<br>Ed and Al, **you're** late. (more than one person) |

**7** Complete the sentences. Use subject pronouns and contractions.

1. Carmela is from Italy. _She's_ Italian.

2. Tomas and Felix are from Mexico. _____ Mexican.

3. You and I are in class. _____ classmates.

4. I am from Beijing. _____ Chinese.

5. You are a student. _____ in class now.

6. The photograph is interesting. _____ on page 7.

7. Pablo is Spanish. _____ from Madrid.

8. The hotels are in Lima. _____ in Peru.

**8** Complete the conversations. Use contractions. Then listen and check your answers.

CD1-3

1. A: Hi. My name _'s_ Ali. I _'m_ from Saudi Arabia.

   B: Hi, Ali. It _____ nice to meet you. I _____ Maria.

2. A: Hello. I _____ Ted.

   B: Nice to meet you. My name _____ Chris. I'm from Vancouver.

   A: Oh, you _____ Canadian! I _____ from Canada, too. Toronto's my hometown.

3. A: Hello. We _____ in the same English class.

   B: Hi. You _____ Ricardo, right? I _____ Martin.

   A: That's right. You _____ from Germany.

   B: Yes, I am. How about you?

   A: I _____ from Mexico.

# PRACTICE

**9** Complete the sentences. Use *am, is,* or *are* in the first sentence. Use a subject pronoun and the correct contraction of *be* in the second sentence.

1. She _is_ Brazilian. _She's_ from Rio.

2. Aran and I _____ Thai. _____ from Bangkok.

3. I _____ Italian. _____ from Rome.

4. Emily _____ our teacher. _____ in class now.

5. Marc _____ from Montreal. _____ Canadian.

6. They _____ in the same class. _____ classmates.

7. He _____ Korean. _____ from Seoul.

8. You _____ my classmate. _____ in my English class.

9. My name _____ Olga. _____ Russian.

10. Quebec _____ a city. _____ in Canada.

**10** Look at the class list. Then complete the paragraph below. Use information from the class list. Use contractions when possible.

### English Conversation 101B: Class List

| | Name | Nationality | Country | City |
|---|---|---|---|---|
| 1. | Kyoko Takana | Japanese | Japan | Tokyo |
| 2. | Abdul Al Dosari | Saudi | Saudi Arabia | Jeddah |
| 3. | Marta Ramos | Mexican | Mexico | Puebla |
| 4. | Feng Chen | Chinese | China | Beijing |
| 5. | Diego Ruiz | Mexican | Mexico | Mexico City |

My (1) _____ name's _____ Kyoko. (2) _____ from Japan.

(3) _____ a student in English Conversation 101B. My classmates

(4) _____ from many different countries. Abdul is from Saudi Arabia.

He (5) _____ from Jeddah. (6) _____ Chinese. He's from

Beijing. Marta and Diego (7) _____ from Mexico. Marta's from Puebla, and

(8) _____ from Mexico City. My teacher's name is Lisa. She's Canadian.

(9) _____ from Toronto. I like my class. Lisa's a good teacher, and my classmates

(10) _____ friendly and interesting.

---

**11** **LISTEN & SPEAK.**

CD1-4

**A** Listen to students at a registration desk. Fill in the identity cards.

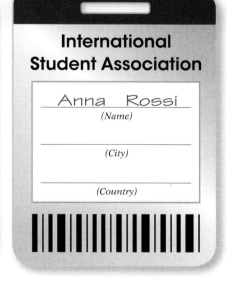
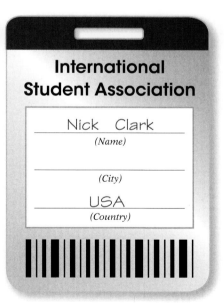

**International Student Association**

Adele  Silva
*(Name)*

Recife
*(City)*

_____
*(Country)*

**International Student Association**

Anna  Rossi
*(Name)*

_____
*(City)*

_____
*(Country)*

**International Student Association**

Nick  Clark
*(Name)*

_____
*(City)*

USA
*(Country)*

**B** Work with a partner. Say sentences about the students from exercise **A**.

*Adele is from Brazil.*

**12 EDIT.** Read the paragraph. Find and correct five more errors with subjects and *be*.

> My name *is* Adele Silva. I from Recife. Is a city in Brazil. I a student in Boston.
> It a city in the United States. Is in Massachusetts.

**13 WRITE & SPEAK.**

**A** Complete the identity card with information about yourself.

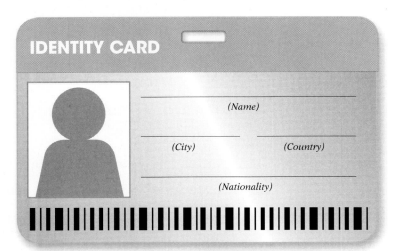

**IDENTITY CARD**

*(Name)*

*(City)*            *(Country)*

*(Nationality)*

**B** Work with a partner. Share the information on your identity card from exercise **A**.

**C** Form a group with another pair of students. Introduce your partner.

*This is Derya. She's from Turkey. . . .*

> **REAL ENGLISH**
>
> Use *This is . . .* to introduce a person.
>
> **Hana:** *Nick,* ***this is*** *my brother, Hiro.*
> **Nick:** *Nice to meet you, Hiro.*
> **Hiro:** *Nice to meet you, too.*

**14 SPEAK.** Form a group with four or five other students. Student 1 introduces himself or herself to the group. Student 2 introduces himself or herself, then introduces Student 1. The next student introduces himself or herself and Students 1 and 2. The last student in the group introduces everyone.

Student 1: *Hi. My name's Yousef.*

Student 2: *Hello. My name's Luis, and this is Yousef.*

Student 3: *Hello. My name's Leyla. This is Yousef, and this is Luis.*

Student 4: *Hi. My name's Takeshi. This is Yousef, this is Luis, and this is Leyla.*

Student 5: *Hello. My name's Barbara. This is Yousef, this is Luis, . . . .*

**15 APPLY.** Write a paragraph about yourself in your notebook. Use the corrected paragraph in exercise **12** as a model.

## EXPLORE

CD1-5

**1** **READ** the article about two National Geographic explorers. Notice the words in **bold**.

# Dereck and Beverly Joubert

Dereck and Beverly Joubert **are explorers** for National Geographic. For them, every day **is an adventure**. They explore Africa with their cameras. They **are filmmakers**. Beverly **is** also **a photographer**. They often work together. *The Last Lions* is one of their projects. It**'s a film** about a mother lion and her family. *The Last Lions* **is a book**, too. Dereck and Beverly **are authors**. They write many books about animals in Africa.

Beverly and Dereck are married. They live and work in Botswana, but they aren't from Botswana. They're from Johannesburg. It**'s a city** in South Africa.

▼ Filmmaker Dereck Joubert with his camera and a leopard

**2 CHECK.** Choose the correct information to complete each sentence about Dereck and Beverly Joubert.

1. Beverly Joubert is _____.  a. a photographer  b. a teacher

2. Johannesburg is _____.  a. a book  b. a city

3. Dereck and Beverly are from _____.  a. South Africa  b. Botswana

4. *The Last Lions* is _____.  a. a magazine  b. a film and a book

5. Beverly and Dereck are _____.  a. married  b. single

**3 DISCOVER.** Complete the exercises to learn about the grammar in this lesson.

**A** Find these sentences in the reading from exercise **1** on page 11. Write the missing words.

1. For them, every day is _____ adventure.

2. Beverly is also _____ photographer.

3. It's _____ film about a mother lion and her family.

**B** Look at the sentences from exercise **A**. Then choose the correct rule below. Discuss your answers with your classmates and teacher.

1. Rule: Use *a* or *an* before a singular noun. (singular = one)

2. Rule: Use *a* or *an* before a plural noun. (plural = more than one)

▼ Photographer Beverly Joubert takes a photo of lions.

# LEARN

## 1.3 *Be* + Singular Noun

| Subject | *Be* | Singular Noun |
|---|---|---|
| I | am | a student. |
| South Africa | is | a country. |
| A lion | is | an animal. |
| You | are | an explorer. |

| | |
|---|---|
| 1. *Singular* means *one*. Use *a* or *an* before a singular noun. | 1 student = **a student**<br>1 apple = **an apple** |
| 2. *A* and *an* have the same meaning.<br><br>Use *a* before nouns beginning with a consonant sound.<br>(Consonants = *b, c, d, f, g, h*, etc.)<br><br>Use *an* before nouns beginning with a vowel sound.<br>(Vowels = *a, e, i, o, u*) | <br><br>She is **a photographer.**<br>It is **a book.**<br><br>He is **an author.**<br>She is **an explorer.** |
| 3. Do not use *a* or *an* before proper nouns. | ✓ Lisa is **a** teacher.<br>✗ <u>A</u> Lisa is **a** teacher.<br><br>✓ Mexico is **a** country.<br>✗ <u>A</u> Mexico is **a** country. |

**4** Complete each sentence with *a* or *an*.

1. Dereck is __*a*__ filmmaker.

2. He is _____ explorer.

3. *The Last Lions* is _____ film.

4. A lion is _____ animal.

5. Botswana is _____ country.

6. Tokyo is _____ city.

7. The Pacific is _____ ocean.

8. Yale is _____ university.

9. I am _____ student.

10. You are _____ artist.

11. Photography is _____ profession.

12. Angelina is _____ author.

### REAL ENGLISH

Use *a* before nouns that begin with a vowel, but have a consonant sound.

> *a university*

Use *an* before nouns that begin with a *silent h*.

> *an hour*

**5** Use the words to write sentences. Add the correct form of *be* and *a* or *an*.

1. Beverly / photographer _____ *Beverly is a photographer.* _____

2. A leopard / animal _____

3. Africa / continent _____

4. Harvard / university _____

5. She / professor _____

6. He / student _____

7. You / engineer _____

8. Photography / profession _____

9. Carmen / author _____

10. It / article _____

## 1.4 *Be* + Plural Noun

| Subject | Be | Plural Noun |
|---|---|---|
| Beverly and Dereck | are | explorers. |
| You and Sam | are | engineers. |
| English and French | are | languages. |
| Botswana and South Africa | are | countries. |

| | |
|---|---|
| 1. Plural means *more than one*. To make most nouns plural, add *-s*. | book–book**s** <br> pen–pen**s** <br> explorer–explorer**s** |
| 2. To make nouns that end in *-ch, -sh, -ss, -x,* and *-z* plural, add *-es*. | class–class**es**, box–box**es** |
| To make nouns that end in *consonant + -y* plural, change the *-y* to *-i* and add *-es*. | city–cit**ies**, story–stor**ies** |
| 3. Some plural nouns are irregular. They do not end in *-s*. | one man–two **men** <br> one child–two **children** <br> one woman–two **women** <br> one person–two **people** |
| 4. Use *are* after nouns joined by *and*. | Ken <u>and</u> Amy **are** students. <br> Sandra <u>and</u> I **are** doctors. |

See page **A1** for a list of spelling rules for plural nouns and a list of common irregular plural nouns.

**6** Complete each sentence with *are* and the plural form of the noun in parentheses.

1. (explorer) Beverly and Dereck Joubert _____ are explorers _____ .

2. (woman) Many National Geographic explorers _____ .

3. (animal) Leopards and lions _____ .

4. (university) Oxford and Yale _____ .

5. (student) We _____ .

6. (class) English 101 and Biology 201 _____ .

7. (country) Mexico and Brazil _____ .

8. (continent) Africa and Asia _____ .

9. (city) Toronto and Montreal _____ .

10. (language) Arabic and Japanese _____ .

**7** **PRONUNCIATION.** Read the chart and listen to the examples. Then complete the exercises.

CD1-6

| PRONUNCIATION | Plural Nouns: -s and -es Endings |
|---|---|

The endings of regular plural nouns have three sounds: **/s/, /z/, /əz/.**

1. Say **/s/** after nouns that end with /f/, /k/, /p/, /t/, and /θ/ sounds.

    photographs   books   cups   students   baths

2. Say **/z/** after nouns that end with /b/, /d/, /g/, /l/, /m/, /n/, /ŋ/, /r/, /v/ sounds and vowel sounds (*a, e, i, o, u*).

    labs   beds   bags   calls   exams   pens   things   cars   gloves   shoes

3. Say **/əz/** after nouns that end with /tʃ/, /ks/, /dʒ/, /ʃ/, /s/, and /z/ sounds.

    watches   boxes   pages   dishes   classes   buzzes

See page **A4** for a guide to pronunciation symbols.

CD1-7

**A** Listen and circle the final sound you hear for each plural noun. Then listen again and repeat each word.

1. teachers   /s/ (/z/) /əz/

2. desks   /s/ /z/ /əz/

3. glasses   /s/ /z/ /əz/

4. cities   /s/ /z/ /əz/

5. languages   /s/ /z/ /əz/

6. stories   /s/ /z/ /əz/

7. things   /s/ /z/ /əz/

8. notebooks   /s/ /z/ /əz/

9. exercises   /s/ /z/ /əz/

10. universities   /s/ /z/ /əz/

11. professions   /s/ /z/ /əz/

12. photos   /s/ /z/ /əz/

CD1-7

**B** Listen again and repeat each word.

**C** Work with a partner. Student A, say a singular noun from the box. Student B, say the plural form of the noun.

| | | | | | |
|---|---|---|---|---|---|
| actor | book | city | country | man | student |
| animal | box | class | lion | pen | teacher |

Student A: *animal*

Student B: *animals*

## 1.5 Simple Present of *Be:* Negative Statements

| Full Forms | | | | Contractions | | | |
|---|---|---|---|---|---|---|---|
| I am | | | | I'm | | | |
| You are | | | | You're | | | |
| He is | | | | He's | | | |
| She is | not | from India. | | She's | not | from China. | |
| It is | | | | It's | | | |
| We are | | | | We're | | | |
| You are | | | | You're | | | |
| They are | | | | They're | | | |

| | |
|---|---|
| 1. To make a negative statement, put *not* after *be* in the present. | I **am not** a photographer. |
| 2. There are two negative contractions for *is* and *are* in the present. | **'s not = isn't**<br>He**'s not** from Argentina.<br>He **isn't** from Argentina.<br><br>**'re not = aren't**<br>They**'re not** sisters.<br>They **aren't** sisters. |
| 3. There is only one negative contraction for *am* in the present. | I**'m not** from Italy. |

**8** Complete the conversations. Use contractions and the words in parentheses. More than one negative form may be possible.

1.          A: Marc's a photographer.

   (a filmmaker) B: No, <u>he isn't a photographer. He's a filmmaker. OR</u>
                  <u>he's not a photographer. He's a filmmaker.</u>

2.          A: They're from Botswana.

   (South Africa) B: No, _____.

3.          A: Justin and Costa are brothers.

   (friends)     B: No, _____.

4.
    A: It's a book.

(film)    B: No, _____.

5.
    A: He's a teacher.

(a student)    B: No, _____.

6.
    A: Rui and Tiago are from Brazil.

(Portugal)    B: No, _____.

7.
    A: She's a doctor.

(an engineer)    B: No, _____.

8.
    A: Julia is an author.

(an artist)    B: No, _____.

9.
    A: Sylvia is Canadian.

(French)    B: No, _____.

10.
    A: London is a country.

(a city)    B: No, _____.

11.
    A: The Amazon is an ocean.

(a river)    B: No, _____.

12.
    A: Botswana is a city.

(a country)    B: No, _____.

13.
    A: Asia and Africa are countries.

(continents)    B: No, _____.

14.
    A: Spanish and Chinese are countries.

(nationalities)    B: No, _____.

# PRACTICE

**9** Use the words to write negative statements. Use contractions. Add *a* or *an* if necessary. More than one negative form may be possible.

1. Korea / city _____ Korea isn't a city. _____

2. Nora and I / explorers _____

3. Seoul and Tokyo / countries _____

4. Nick / Brazilian _____

5. I / teacher _____

6. You / from Mexico _____

7. She / filmmaker _____

8. We / actors _____

9. He / from Japan _____

10. It / film _____

**10** **EDIT.** Read the sentences. Find and correct five more errors with singular and plural nouns, *a/an*, and negatives.

1. Madrid, London, and Prague are cit̶y̶. *ⱽies*

2. Europe aren't a country. It's a continent.

3. Iceland and Ireland is islands. Water is all around them.

4. The Rhine is river in Europe. It's in Germany.

5. The Alps aren't rivers. They're mountains.

6. The Atlantic isn't a river. It's a ocean.

7. Austria and Romania are countries.

8. Lisbon isn't in Spain. It in Portugal.

**11** **SPEAK.** Work in a group. Look at the lists of words below. One word from each list does not belong. Talk about the lists of words with your group. Use the words from the box to help you. Use negative forms and *a* or *an* if necessary.

| | | | |
|---|---|---|---|
| animals | continents | foods | people |
| cities | countries | languages | school supplies |

*A teacher, an actress, and a bus driver are people. A desk isn't a person.*

1. teacher     bus driver     ~~desk~~     actress

2. banana     pencil     pen     eraser

3. Ireland     Spain     Sweden     Rome

4. egg     apple     orange     book

5. French     English     Chinese     India

6. lion     dog     horse     notebook

7. London     Romania     Paris     Berlin

8. Europe     Asia     Tokyo     Africa

**12** **SPEAK, LISTEN & WRITE.**

**A** Work with a partner. Look at the photos below and guess each person's profession.

**B** Listen to the conversations and write the correct profession for each person.

| | | |
|---|---|---|
| doctor | musicians | professor |

1. Name: <u>Larissa Santos</u>

    Profession: _____

    Country of origin: _____

2. Name: <u>Liz Stanford and Jude Wilson</u>

    Profession: _____

    Country of origin: _____

3. Name: <u>Chu Ying Liu</u>

    Profession: _____

    Country of origin: _____

**C** Listen again. Write the correct country of origin for each person.

**D** Work with a partner. Compare your answers from exercises **B** and **C**.

**E** Use the words to write correct sentences about the people in exercise **B**. Use negatives if necessary.

1. Larissa / from England  _Larissa isn't from England. She's from Brazil._

2. Chu Ying / doctor _____

3. Jude and Liz / professors _____

4. Jude / from China _____

5. Liz / professor _____

6. Chu Ying / from China _____

7. Larissa / musician _____

8. Liz / from Brazil _____

**13** **APPLY.** Write three true statements and two false sentences about students in your class. Use the verb *be*. Then read your sentences to a partner. Your partner will say "true" or "false" after each statement and correct the false statements.

Student A: *Carlos is a student.*

Student B: *True.*

Student A: *Ali is from China.*

Student B: *False. Ali isn't from China. He's from Saudi Arabia.*

## EXPLORE

CD1-11

**1 READ** the article about Tank the Bear and Doug Seus. Notice the words in **bold**.

# Tank the Bear

Tank the Bear is a **huge** grizzly bear from Utah in the United States. He is also a **famous** television and movie star. He's in a lot of television shows and movies. Tank is **huge** and **heavy**, but he's not a **typical** grizzly bear. Most grizzly bears are **wild**[1] and **dangerous**, but Tank isn't. In fact, he's **gentle** and **friendly** with his trainer Doug Seus.

Doug and his wife Lynn are animal trainers. They work with many **different** animals at their home in Utah. Doug is a **brave** man. His job is **dangerous**. It is also **difficult**, but for Doug it's **fun**. He's **patient**[2] and **kind** with Tank. Tank is a member of his family!

[1] **Wild** animals live in nature.

[2] A **patient** person is calm and does not get angry easily.

▶ Animal trainer Doug Seus with a huge grizzly bear named Bart. Bart died in 2000.

**2 CHECK.** Read the list of adjectives in the chart. Who does each adjective describe? Put a check (✓) in the correct column. Then work with a partner and compare charts.

| Adjective | Tank | Doug |
|-----------|------|------|
| brave | | ✓ |
| kind | | |
| famous | | |
| patient | | |
| friendly | | |
| huge | | |
| gentle | | |
| heavy | | |

**3 DISCOVER.** Complete the exercises to learn about the grammar in this lesson.

**A** Find these sentences in the reading from exercise **1** on page 21. Write the missing words.

1. Tank is _____ and _____ , but he's not a typical grizzly bear.

2. Doug is a _____ man.

3. His job is _____ . It is also _____ , but for Doug it's _____ .

4. He's _____ and _____ with Tank.

**B** Read the statements. Circle **T** for *true* or **F** for *false*. Then discuss your answers with your classmates and teacher.

1. Adjectives describe nouns.                    **T          F**

2. Adjectives describe pronouns.                 **T          F**

◄ Douglas Chadwick, author, with Tank the bear.

22

# LEARN

## 1.6 Descriptive Adjectives

| Subject | *Be* | Adjective |
|---------|------|-----------|
| I | am | tall. |
| He | is | strong. |
| We | are | happy. |
| They | are | late. |

| | Adjective | Noun |
|---|-----------|------|
| He is a | tall | man. |
| She is an | interesting | person. |

| | |
|---|---|
| 1. Adjectives describe nouns or pronouns. | He is **patient**.<br>They are **friendly**. |
| 2. Adjectives often come after the verb *be*. They can also come before nouns. | We are **busy**.<br>We are **busy** <u>people</u>. |
| 3. The form of an adjective does not change. An adjective is the same for singular and plural nouns and pronouns. | ✓ The room is **big**.<br>✓ The rooms are **big**.<br>✗ The rooms are <u>bigs</u>. |
| 4. Use *a* or *an* before adjectives + singular nouns.<br><br>Use *a* before an adjective beginning with a consonant sound.<br><br>Use *an* with an adjective beginning with a vowel sound. | He's **a** <u>good</u> person and **an** <u>excellent</u> <u>friend</u>.<br><br>She's **a** <u>good</u> doctor.<br><br>He's **an** <u>excellent</u> teacher. |

**REAL ENGLISH**

Two adjectives are often used to describe a noun or pronoun. Use *and* to connect two adjectives.

He is <u>tall</u> **and** <u>strong</u>.
Reika is <u>smart</u> **and** <u>funny</u>.
It's a <u>black</u> **and** <u>red</u> book.

**4** Underline the adjective in each sentence. Then draw an arrow to the nouns or pronouns they describe.

1. It is an <u>interesting</u> article.

2. Tank is famous.

3. Doug is brave.

4. They are friendly.

5. He is an excellent teacher.

6. Canada is a huge country.

7. She is funny.

8. Sandra is young.

9. I am late.

10. You are kind.

**5** Put the words in the correct order to make sentences. Add *a* or *an* if necessary.

1. Sandra / amazing / is / artist _____Sandra is an amazing artist._____

2. big / Bears / are _____

3. am / I / happy _____

4. famous / Akira Kurosawa / filmmaker / is _____

5. engineer / David / is / good _____

6. is / new / My phone _____

7. Rome / city / is / interesting _____

8. are / We / tired _____

9. is / difficult / language / Chinese _____

10. am / excellent / I / student _____

# PRACTICE

**6** Complete the exercises.

**A** Look at the adjectives in the box. Check (✓) the adjectives you know. Ask your teacher for help with the adjectives you do not know.

| ☐ big | ☐ difficult | ☐ easy | ☐ funny | ☐ nice | ☐ quiet | ☐ small |
| ☐ clean | ☐ dirty | ☐ friendly | ☐ happy | ☐ noisy | ☐ serious | ☐ smart |

**B** Use the verb *be* and adjectives from exercise **A**. Complete each sentence. Add *a/an* if necessary.

1. Our teacher _is friendly_____.

2. My classmates _____ students.

3. This exercise _____.

4. We _____.

5. I _____.

6. My friends _____ people.

7. English _____ language.

8. This classroom _____.

9. This building _____.

10. My hometown _____.

**7 EDIT.** Read the paragraph. Find and correct four more errors with adjectives and *a/an.*

### A Sherpa Climber

This is ^a^ photograph of a Sherpa climber on Mount Everest. It's a amazing photo. Mount Everest is beautiful mountain, but it's dangerous. Fura Gyaljen is Sherpa climber. He is strong. His job is difficult and dangerous. Sherpa climbers are braves people.

◄ Fura Gyaljen, a Sherpa climber, on an ice field on Mt. Everest in Nepal

**8 SPEAK, LISTEN & WRITE.**

**A** Work with a partner. Read the job advertisement. What kind of person is right for the job? Discuss with your partner. Check (✓) the adjectives in the box below.

Evening and weekend hours available. Fax application Attn: HR Dept.
Apply Today!

# WANTED

An English conversation partner for a teacher from Japan. Weekends and nights.

Call Keiko
904-555-2271

● **Sales Reps Wanted**

Self Starter with 3 Yr. Sales Exp. Necessary! Must have commercial

A perfect person for this job is . . .

| | | | |
|---|---|---|---|
| ☐ busy | ☐ funny | ☐ nice | ☐ retired |
| ☐ experienced | ☐ hardworking | ☐ old | ☐ smart |
| ☐ friendly | ☐ helpful | ☐ patient | ☐ young |

🎧 CD1-12-14

**B** Listen to the messages. Which adjectives from exercise **A** does each person use to describe himself or herself? Take notes next to each photo.

Kevin

_____ funny _____

_____

Liz

_____

_____

Jane

_____

_____

**C** Write two sentences about each person. Use your notes from exercise **B**.

Kevin: _He is funny._ _____

_____

Liz: _____

_____

Jane: _____

_____

**D** Work with a partner. Make a decision. Who is the best person for the job? Who is not good for the job? Use adjectives to talk about each person from exercise **B**.

*Kevin isn't a good person for this job. He is young. He isn't experienced.*

## 9  SPEAK & WRITE.

**A** Work with a partner. Describe yourself. Use adjectives from exercise **8A** on page 25 and your own ideas to describe yourself.

*I'm young and hardworking. . . .*

**B** Complete the Venn diagram. One partner is Student A. One partner is Student B. Write your adjectives from exercise **8A** on page 25 on the correct side of the Venn diagram.

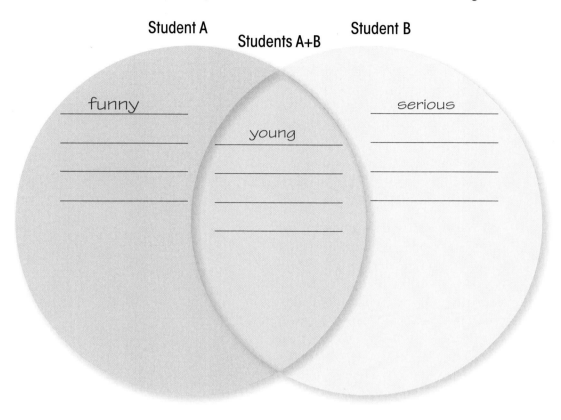

Student A        Students A+B        Student B

funny                                        serious

young

**C** Write sentences about you and your partner. Use the information from your Venn diagram in exercise **B**.

I am funny.

Alex is serious.

We are both young.

---

**REAL ENGLISH**

Use *both* when something is true about two people or two things.

*Yuri and Luisa are **both** good students.*

*Russia and Canada are **both** huge countries.*

---

## 10  APPLY.

**A** Choose a person in your class. Write a short paragraph about him or her. Do not use his or her name. Use the model below to help you. Use adjectives from exercise **8A** on page 25 and your own ideas.

She is friendly and kind. She's an excellent student. She's single. She's young. She is short and funny. Her name is _____.

**B** Read your paragraph from exercise **A** to your classmates. Do not say the person's name. Your classmates will guess.

## EXPLORE

CD1-15

**1**   **READ** the article about a family of reindeer herders. Notice the words in **bold**.

# Sami Reindeer Herders

Nils Peder Gaup is from Norway, 200 miles (almost 322 kilometers) north of the Arctic Circle. It is very cold there. Gaup is a Sami reindeer herder. He looks after large groups of reindeer and uses them for food and clothing. **Gaup's** wife is a reindeer herder, too. **Her** name is Ingrid. **Their** five children also help.

**A reindeer herder's** job is not easy. Every year Gaup and **his** family travel a long way with the reindeer to find food. They leave **their** homes and live on snowy mountains and frozen lakes for long periods of time. They sleep in special tents called *lávuts*. The Gaups take good care of the reindeer. The Gaups love **their** work, but clearly, it is not just a job. It is **their** life.

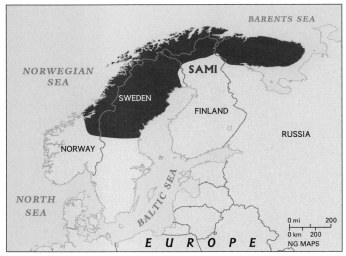

▼  Nils Peder Gaup with his reindeer

► TK

► Nils Peder Gaup's brother, Mahtta, with a herd of reindeer

**2  CHECK.** Read the statements. Circle **T** for *true* or **F** for *false*.

1.  Nils Peder Gaup is from Sweden.                        **T**        **F**

2.  Ingrid is not a reindeer herder.                       **T**        **F**

3.  The job of a reindeer herder is difficult.             **T**        **F**

4.  The Gaup children are reindeer herders, too.           **T**        **F**

**3  DISCOVER.** Complete the exercise to learn about the grammar in this lesson.

**A**  Find these sentences in the reading from exercise **1**. Write the missing words.

1.  Gaup's wife is a reindeer herder, too. _____ name is Ingrid.

2.  Every year Gaup and _____ family travel a long way with the reindeer to find food.

3.  The Gaups love _____ work, but clearly, it is not just a job. It is _____ life.

**B**  Look at the sentences from exercise **A**. Who does *her* refer to? Who does *his* refer to? Who does *their* refer to? Discuss with your classmates and teacher.

# LEARN

## 1.7 Possessive Adjectives

| Subject Pronouns | Possessive Adjectives | Example Sentences |
|---|---|---|
| I | my | I am from India. **My** name is Manik. |
| you | your | You are a student. **Your** class is in Room 209. |
| he | his | He is from Norway. **His** name's Lars. |
| she | her | She is married. **Her** husband is a scientist. |
| it | its | It is a friendly dog. **Its** name is Nanook. |
| we | our | We are French. **Our** home is in Paris. |
| you | your | You are great photographers. **Your** photos are beautiful. |
| they | their | They are actors. **Their** movie is funny. |

| | |
|---|---|
| 1. Possessive adjectives show possession or relationships. | **Our** apartment is small. <br> **My** brother is funny and smart. |
| 2. Possessive adjectives come before nouns. | **His** eyes are brown. <br> Nora is a scientist. **Her** job is very interesting. |
| 3. Use *your* for one person or more than one person. | Max, **your** friend is here. <br> Max and Jesse, **your** friend is here. |

**4** Underline the subject pronouns. Then complete each sentence with the correct possessive adjective.

1. <u>They</u> are reindeer herders. _Their_ children are reindeer herders, too.

2. We are Spanish. Toledo is _____ hometown.

3. He is from India, but _____ home is in the United States.

4. You are a good cook, Maria. _____ soup is delicious!

5. I am a grandfather. _____ grandson is three years old.

6. We are students. _____ class is in Room 206.

7. She is tall. _____ brothers are tall, too.

8. You are good teachers. _____ students are very lucky.

9. She is married. _____ husband is Russian.

10. I am from Portugal. _____ name's Carlos.

11. He is an author. _____ books are interesting.

12. They are students. _____ teacher's name is Paula.

13. You are late. _____ seat is over there.

14. It's a nice car. _____ seats are comfortable.

## 1.8 Possessive Nouns

| Singular | Plural |
| --- | --- |
| The **student's** last name is Ming. | The **students'** last names are Ming and Diaz. |
| My **neighbor's** house is small. | My **neighbors'** houses are small. |

| | |
| --- | --- |
| 1. To make a singular noun possessive, add an apostrophe (') + -s to the end of the noun. | The **baby's** room is small.<br>**Lisa's** car is green. |
| 2. To make most plural nouns possessive, add an apostrophe (') after the -s. | The **babies'** room is small.<br>My **brothers'** names are Ted and Jeremy. |
| 3. To make an irregular plural noun possessive, add an apostrophe (') + -s to the end of the noun. | The **children's** room is small. |

**5** Circle the correct possessive form to complete each sentence.

1. Susan is **Ken's** / **Kens'** wife.

2. A **doctors'** / **doctor's** job is not easy.

3. My uncle Mike is my **fathers'** / **father's** brother.

4. My **sons'** / **son's** names are Sam and Leo.

5. The **girl's** / **girls'** dress is yellow.

6. My **mother's** / **mothers'** name is Lenka.

7. The **children's** / **childrens'** room is messy.

8. **Italys'** / **Italy's** flag is green, white, and red.

**6** Write the correct possessive form of the word in parentheses to complete each conversation.

1. A: What's _____Aileen's_____ (Aileen) last name?

   B: It's Peterson.

2. A: Is this the _____ (women) room?

   B: No, it's the _____ (men) room!

3. A: Where is _____ (Kim) coat?

   B: It's over there.

4. A: Your _____ (roommates) names are Carl and Matt, right?

   B: No, their names are Kevin and Mike.

5. A: My _____ (husband) hometown is Prague.

   B: Oh, Prague is a beautiful city!

6. A: Where is your _____ (children) school?

   B: It's on Elm Street.

## PRACTICE

**7** Rewrite each sentence. Replace each possessive noun with a possessive adjective.

1. Nils Peder's job is dangerous. _His job is dangerous._

2. Ingrid's children are herders, too. _____

3. The workers' company is successful. _____

4. The children's grandfather is famous. _____

5. Elena's office is huge. _____

6. David's house is beautiful. _____

7. Maria's grandmother is 89 years old. _____

8. The hotel's rooms are small. _____

**8** **EDIT.** Read the paragraph. Find and correct five more errors with possessive nouns and possessive adjectives.

> Teresa Pereira is from Portugal. She's Portuguese. Óbidos is ~~his~~ ↓her hometown.
> Her father name is Antonio, and her mother's name is Fatima. They are teachers.
> Teresas brother is an engineer. He name is Pedro. His wife name is Luisa. She's a
> doctor. They children's names are Rui and Eduardo.

◄ Óbidos, Portugal

## 9  SPEAK & WRITE.

**A**  Look at the words for family members in the box. Check (✓) the words you know. Ask your teacher about any words you do not know.

| | | |
|---|---|---|
| ☐ aunt | ☐ grandparents | ☐ sister-in-law |
| ☐ brother | ☐ husband | ☐ son |
| ☐ brother-in-law | ☐ nephew | ☐ uncle |
| ☐ cousin | ☐ niece | ☐ wife |
| ☐ daughter | ☐ sister | |

**B**  Look at the Perez family tree. Then complete the sentences that follow with the correct possessive adjectives and possessive nouns.

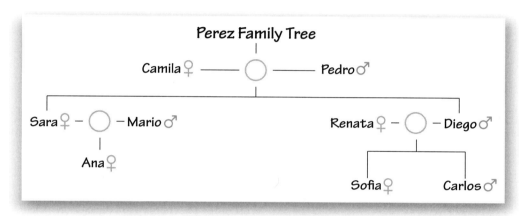

Perez Family Tree

Camila ♀ —— ◯ —— Pedro ♂

Sara ♀ – ◯ – Mario ♂          Renata ♀ – ◯ – Diego ♂

Ana ♀                              Sofia ♀        Carlos ♂

1. Camila and Pedro are married. _____Their_____ daughter's name is Sara. _____ son's name is Diego.

2. Diego is _____ brother.

3. Diego is married. _____ wife's name is Renata.

4. Sara is married, too. _____ husband's name is Mario.

5. Mario is not Diego's brother. He's _____ brother-in-law. He's _____ brother-in-law, too.

6. Sofia is Sara's niece, and Carlos is _____ nephew.

7. Carlos and Sofia are _____ cousins.

8. Diego is _____ uncle, and Renata is _____ aunt.

9. Renata is not Pedro's daughter. She's _____ daughter-in-law.

10. Camila and Pedro are not Ana's parents. They are _____ grandparents.

**C** Write two sentences about each person. Use possessive nouns and possessive adjectives. Use the Perez family tree from exercise **B** and the words from exercise **A** to help you.

Camila: _____Camila is Pedro's wife._____

_____

Mario: _____

_____

Carlos: _____

_____


**10  LISTEN & SPEAK.**

CD1-16

**A** Listen to the information about another family and complete the family tree. Use the names from the box.

| Jena | Rylie | Tim | Doug |
|------|-------|-----|------|

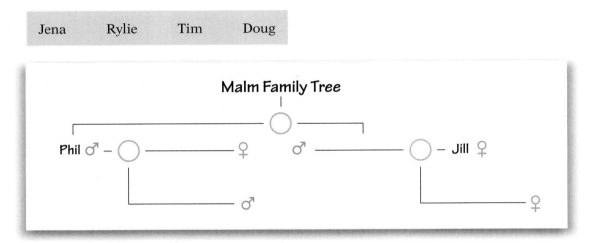

**B** Compare your answers from exercise **A** with a partner. Then make sentences about the Malm Family Tree.


**11  APPLY.**

**A** Draw your family tree in your notebook and include your family members' names. Use the Perez family tree from exercise **9B** on page 33 as a model.

**B** Work with a partner. Talk about your family tree. Talk about your family members' jobs and where they are from.

*My father Alvaro is a farmer. His father is a farmer, too. They are from Venezuela. . . .*

**Charts**
**1.1–1.8**

**1** Put the words and contractions in the correct order to make sentences.

1. Pat / 'm / I _____ I'm Pat. _____

2. name / My / Jim / is _____

3. sister / She / Pat's / is _____

4. parents / are / We / Carl's _____

5. Ken's / is / brother / tall _____

6. isn't / My / dangerous / job _____

7. friend / person / is / an / interesting / My _____

8. an / It / easy / 's / exercise _____

**CD1-17**

**Charts**
**1.1–1.8**

**2** **LISTEN** and write the sentences you hear.

1. I'm a teacher. _____    5. _____

2. _____    6. _____

3. _____    7. _____

4. _____    8. _____

**Charts**
**1.1, 1.3**
**1.4, 1.6**

**3** **WRITE & SPEAK.**

**A** Write sentences. Use one of the adjectives in parentheses and your own ideas. Use the correct form of *be*. Add *a* or *an* if necessary.

1. (famous / small) university _Harvard is a famous university._ _____

2. (good / terrible) actor _____

3. (kind / funny) people _____

4. (great / scary / funny) movie _____

5. (excellent / terrible) cars _____

6. (small / huge / beautiful) country _____

7. (good / great) soccer player _____

8. (safe / dangerous / interesting) city _____

**B** Share your sentences from exercise **A** with a partner.

Charts
1.1–1.8

**4** Write a negative and then an affirmative statement. Use the words in parentheses and the correct form of *be*. Use a pronoun in the second sentence.

1. (Ed / funny / serious) _Ed's not funny. He's serious._

2. (You / late / early) _____

3. (My / car / old / new) _____

4. (She / from Mexico / from Chile) _____

5. (They / engineers / explorers) _____

6. (I / photographer / student) _____

7. (We / lazy students / hardworking students) _____

   _____

8. (My mother's father / my uncle / my grandfather) _____

Charts
1.1–1.7

**5** Complete each sentence with *is/isn't* or *are/aren't* and the singular or plural form of words from the box.

| dangerous animal | easy language | interesting profession | small city |
|---|---|---|---|
| difficult class | good student | large country | warm continent |

1. Lions and bears _are dangerous animals_ .

2. You and I _____ .

3. Tokyo _____ .

4. Geometry and Biology 101 _____ .

5. French _____ .

6. Actor and artist _____ .

7. Belgium and Costa Rica _____ .

8. Antarctica _____ .

Charts
1.1–1.8

**6** **EDIT.** Read the conversation. Find and correct five more errors with the verb *be* and *a/an*.

      I'm from Brazil. Brazil is ~~an~~ ^a^ big country. It's a beautiful country. My family's home are in Rio. We are all in different cities now. My mother and father is at our home in Rio. My sister and I aren't in Rio. We am students in London. My brother is in Boston. He's a architect. He is married with two children. My nephews are twins. They is six years old.

**7** Complete the conversation with affirmative or negative forms of *be*. Add *a* or *an* if necessary.

**Sally:** This photo _is_ interesting.

**Jim:** Yes, it _____. He's /an amazing gymnast.

**Sally:** He _____ gymnast. He's acrobat.

**Jim:** Oh, right.

**Sally:** Chinese acrobats _____ famous.

**Jim:** That' _____ true. They' _____ very good.

▲ A juggler with dishes, Beijing, People's Republic of China

**8 LISTEN & WRITE.**

**A** Listen and choose the best name for the school.

a. Ling High School
b. Ling School of Art
c. Ling School for Acrobats

**B** Listen again. Write each name from the box next to the correct person in the picture.

| Jing | Li | Min | Sheng | Wu |
|------|----|----|-------|----|

**C** Write five sentences about the people in the picture. Use the words in the box and information from exercises **A** and **B**.

| Sheng | wife | grandmother | father | children |
|-------|------|-------------|--------|----------|

1. _____

2. _____

3. _____

4. _____

5. _____

# Connect the Grammar to Writing

## 1 READ & NOTICE THE GRAMMAR.

**A** Read the paragraph. Who are the writer's family members? Discuss with a partner.

## JAY AND HAYLEY

My brother's name <u>is</u> Jay. He's 29. He's married. Hayley is his wife. She's my sister-in-law. They're in Scotland. Jay is a teacher. Hayley isn't a teacher. She's a salesclerk. They're very kind.

### GRAMMAR FOCUS

In the paragraph in exercise **A**, the writer uses the verb *be* to give information about family members.

**Remember:** Use *is* when the subject is singular. Use *are* when the subject is plural.

*My brother's name **is** Jay.*
*She**'s** my sister-in-law.*
*They**'re** very kind.*

**B** Read the paragraph in exercise **A** again. Underline affirmative and negative forms of the verb *be*. Then work with a partner and compare answers.

**C** Complete the chart with information about the writer's family members in exercise **A**.

| Family Members | | |
|---|---|---|
| Name | Jay | Hayley |
| Family member | Brother | |
| Age | | X |
| Married / Single | | |
| Job | | |
| Other information | | |

**2 BEFORE YOU WRITE.** Complete the chart with information about two of your family members. Use the chart in exercise **1C** as a model.

| Family Members | | |
|---|---|---|
| Name | | |
| Family member | | |
| Age | | |
| Married / Single | | |
| Job | | |
| Other information | | |

**3 WRITE** a paragraph. Use the information from your chart in exercise **2** and the paragraph in exercise **1A** to help you.

> **WRITING FOCUS**   Capital Letters and Periods
>
> A statement begins with a capital letter and ends with a period.
>
> *H*e's 29.
> *S*he's a sales clerk.

**4 SELF ASSESS.** Read your paragraph. Underline the verb *be* in your paragraph. Then use the checklist to assess your work.

- ☐ I used the correct form of *be*. [1.3, 1.4, 1.5]
- ☐ I used the correct possessive nouns and adjectives. [1.7, 1.8]
- ☐ I used a capital letter at the beginning of each statement. [WRITING FOCUS]
- ☐ I put a period at the end of each statement. [WRITING FOCUS]

# The Verb *Be:* Questions

▶ People celebrating Holi (the Festival of Colors), India

## EXPLORE

 **1 READ** the interview about name days. Notice the sentences in **bold**.

Greece

# HAPPY NAME DAY!

| | |
|---|---|
| **TV host:** | Welcome to the show, Dimitris. **Are you from Greece?** |
| **Dimitris:** | Yes, **I'm from Athens**. |
| **TV host:** | Great. Well, today our show is about celebrations.[1] Tell us about a celebration in Greece. |
| **Dimitris:** | OK. My favorite celebration is my name day. |
| **TV host:** | **Is your name day your birthday?** |
| **Dimitris:** | No, **my name day isn't my birthday**. It's different. My birthday is in September, but my name day is in October. Everyone with the name Dimitris celebrates on October 26. |
| **TV host:** | Really? That's interesting! **Are name days common all over Europe?** |
| **Dimitris:** | Yes, **they're common in many European countries**. They're also common in Latin America. |
| **TV host:** | And how do you celebrate your name day? |
| **Dimitris:** | Well, we have five Dimitrises in my family, so we have a big party. It's a lot of fun. |
| **TV host:** | Five Dimitrises!? Wow! |

[1] A **celebration** is a party or activity for a special day or occasion.

▶ The Acropolis, Athens, Greece

**2 CHECK.** Read the statements. Circle **T** for *true* or **F** for *false*.

1. Dimitris is from Greece.      **(T)**      **F**

2. The TV show is about celebrations.      **T**      **F**

3. Dimitris's name day is his birthday.      **T**      **F**

4. Dimitris's name day is in November.      **T**      **F**

5. Name days are common in other countries.      **T**      **F**

**3 DISCOVER.** Complete the exercises to learn about the grammar in this lesson.

**A** Find these questions and answers in the interview from exercise **1**. Write the missing words. Then underline the verb *be* and circle the subject in each question and answer.

| Yes/No Questions | Answers (Statements) |
|---|---|
| 1. <u>Are</u> (you) from Greece? | 1. Yes, _____ from Athens. |
| 2. _____ your birthday? | 2. No, _____ my birthday. It's different. |
| 3. _____ common all over Europe? | 3. Yes, _____ common in many European countries. |

**B** Look at the questions and answers from exercise **A**. Choose the correct answer to complete the statement below. Then discuss your answer with your classmates and teacher.

The word order is _____ in questions and statements.     a. the same     b. different

# LEARN

## 2.1   Simple Present of *Be*: Yes/No Questions

| Statements | | |
| --- | --- | --- |
| Subject | *Be* | |
| I | **am** | late. |
| He<br>She<br>It | **is** | from Greece. |
| You<br>We<br>You<br>They | **are** | from Greece. |

| Yes/No Questions | | |
| --- | --- | --- |
| *Be* | Subject | |
| **Am** | I | late? |
| **Is** | he<br>she<br>it | from Greece? |
| **Are** | you<br>we<br>you<br>they | from Greece? |

| | |
| --- | --- |
| 1. The subject comes before the verb in a statement. A statement ends with a period (.). | The festival **is** in February.<br>They **are** from Athens.<br>I **am** from Greece. |
| 2. The verb comes before the subject in a *Yes/No* question with *be*. A question ends with a question mark (?). | **Is** the festival in February?<br>**Are** they from Athens?<br>**Is** your name day in April? |

**4**   Underline the subject and circle the verb *be* in each statement. Then complete each *Yes/No* question with *be* + subject.

**Statements**

1. Eleni (is) from Patras.
2. Alex is from Athens.
3. Athens and Patras are in Greece.
4. Eleni and Alex are married.
5. They are happy.
6. Costas is their last name.
7. Eleni and Alex are popular Greek names.
8. Eleni's name day is on May 21.

**Yes/No Questions**

1. __Is__ __Eleni__ from Patras?
2. ____ ____ from Athens?
3. ____ ____ in Greece?
4. ____ ____ married?
5. ____ ____ happy?
6. ____ ____ their last name?
7. ____ ____ popular Greek names?
8. ____ ____ on May 21?

**5** Put the words in the correct order to make *Yes/No* questions.

1. you / Are / from Mexico _Are you from Mexico?_

2. in / Mexico city / Mexico / Is _____

3. common / name days / Are / in Latin America _____

4. they / from Brazil / Are _____

5. your birthday / in November / Is _____

6. you / a / student / Are _____

7. she / a / teacher / Is _____

8. Korean / Is / he _____

## 2.2 Simple Present of *Be:* Short Answers

| *Yes/No* Questions | | | Affirmative Short Answers | | | | Negative Short Answers | |
|---|---|---|---|---|---|---|---|---|
| *Be* | Subject | | | Subject | *Be* | | Subject + *Be* + *Not* | |
| **Am** | I | late? | | you | are. | | you're not. | |
| **Are** | you | from Athens? | | I | am. | | I'm not. | |
| **Is** | he she it | in Europe? | Yes, | he she it | is. | No, | he's not. she's not. it's not. | |
| **Are** | we you they | happy? | | we you they | are. | | we're not. you're not. they're not. | |

| | |
|---|---|
| 1. Do not use contractions in affirmative short answers. | ✓ Yes, she **is**.<br>✗ Yes, she's.<br><br>✓ Yes, they **are**.<br>✗ Yes, they're. |
| 2. There are two forms of negative contractions for *is* and *are* in the present. | No, he's **not** / she's **not** / it's **not**.<br>No, he **isn't** / she **isn't** / it **isn't**.<br><br>No, we're **not** / you're **not** / they're **not**.<br>No, we **aren't** / you **aren't** / they **aren't**. |
| 3. There is only one negative contraction for *am* in the present. | No, I'm **not**. |

**6** Complete the short answer to each *Yes/No* question. Use contractions when possible.

1. Are name days common in Europe?    Yes, _they are_____.

2. Is today Bill's birthday?    No, _____.

3. Is he from Mexico?    No, _____.

4. Is Madrid in Spain?    Yes, _____.

5. Are we late?    No, _____.

6. Is she a student?    No, _____.

7. Am I in Room 207?    Yes, _____.

8. Are they in the cafeteria?    No, _____.

# PRACTICE

**7** Complete each *Yes/No* question with the correct form of *be*. Then write the correct short answer to each question. Use the photo and the photo caption to help you.

1. A: _Is_ Argentina in North America?

   B: _No, it isn't._____

2. A: _____ Rio in Argentina?

   B: _____

3. A: _____ the man and the woman in Brazil?

   B: _____

4. A: _____ the tango a dance?

   B: _____

5. A: _____ they dancers?

   B: _____

6. A: _____ they in Argentina?

   B: _____

7. A: _____ our teacher from Argentina?

   B: _____

8. A: _____ you a good dancer?

   B: _____

▲ Tango dancers in Buenos Aires, Argentina

**8** Complete the *Yes/No* questions and short answers in each conversation. Use only one word or contraction for each blank. Use contractions when possible. Then listen and check your answers.

1. A: It's noisy. (1) __Are__ __you__ at a party?

   B: No, (2) _____ _____. (3) _____ at a wedding.

   A: (4) _____ _____ fun?

   B: Yes, (5) _____ _____! (6) _____ a lot of fun!

2. A: (7) _____ our meeting at nine o'clock?

   B: Yes, (8) _____ _____. (9) _____ we late?

   A: No, (10) _____ _____. (11) _____ early. It's only 8:45.

3. A: Hi. (12) _____ you at home?

   B: No, (13) _____ _____. (14) _____ at school. Carol and Ann say hello.

   A: Oh, (15) _____ _____ with you?

   B: Yes, they (16) _____.

**9 SPEAK.** Work with a partner. Practice the conversations from exercise **8**.

**10 LISTEN & SPEAK.**

**A** Read the questions. Then listen to the information about a special celebration for a girl named Isabel. Check (✓) *Yes* or *No* for each question.

| | Yes | No |
|---|---|---|
| 1. Is *quinceañera* an English word? | ☐ | ✓ |
| 2. Is it a celebration for boys? | ☐ | ☐ |
| 3. Is it popular in Latin America? | ☐ | ☐ |
| 4. Is Isabel in Miami, Florida? | ☐ | ☐ |
| 5. Is she 16 years old? | ☐ | ☐ |
| 6. Is her dress white? | ☐ | ☐ |

**B** Work with a partner. Ask and answer the questions from exercise **A**.

Student A: *Is* quinceañera *an English word?*

Student B: *No, it isn't.*

**11** **EDIT.** Read the conversation. Find and correct six more errors with *Yes/No* questions and short answers.

                           *Are you*

**Ken:**       Hi. ~~You are~~ at the hotel now?

**Molly:**    Yes, I'm. I'm in the hotel restaurant.

**Ken:**       Is it a nice hotel?

**Molly:**    Yes, it is. It's beautiful! It's very busy here, too.

**Ken:**       It is a business meeting?

**Molly:**    No, it not. The women here are in long dresses.

**Ken:**       Is they at the hotel for a wedding?

**Molly:**    No, they aren't. The party is for a young girl.

**Ken:**       It is a *quinceañera*?

**Molly:**    Yes, it's.

**12** **READ, WRITE & SPEAK.**

**A** Read the e-mail message. Then write *Yes/No* questions.

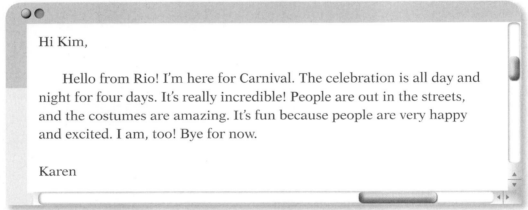

Hi Kim,

   Hello from Rio! I'm here for Carnival. The celebration is all day and night for four days. It's really incredible! People are out in the streets, and the costumes are amazing. It's fun because people are very happy and excited. I am, too! Bye for now.

Karen

1.   Is Karen in New York? _____

2.   _____

3.   _____

4.   _____

5.   _____

6.   _____

**B** Work with a partner. Ask and answer your questions from exercise **A**.

Student A: *Is Karen in New York?*

Student B: *No, she isn't.*

▶ A Samba School Parade during Carnival in Rio de Janiero, Brazil

## 13 APPLY.

**A** Work with a partner. Get ready to role-play a phone conversation about a celebration. First, choose a celebration from the box or your own idea.

| | | |
|---|---|---|
| a birthday party | a name day celebration | a wedding |
| a graduation party | a *quinceañera* party | your idea: _____ |

**B** Read the model conversation. Then complete the conversation below for your role-play. Student B is at the celebration. Student A asks Student B questions about the celebration.

Student A: *Hi, Mario. Are you at home?*

Student B: *No, I'm not. I'm at my sister's graduation party.*

Student A: *Oh. Is it her high school graduation?*

Student B: *No, it's not. It's her college graduation.*

Student A: *Is it a fun party?*

Student B: *Yes, it is! My sister and her classmates are really happy and excited.*

> **REAL ENGLISH**
>
> *Really* is often used in conversation. It means *very*.
>
> A: *This is a **really** fun party.*
> B: *Yeah, it is!*

Student A: Hi, _____. Are you _____?

Student B: No, _____. I'm _____.

Student A: _____?

Student B: _____.

Student A: _____?

Student B: _____.

**C** Role-play your conversation from exercise **B** for the class.

## EXPLORE

CD1-22

**1** **READ** the advertisement for a tour of the Eiffel Tower in Paris, France. Notice the words in **bold**.

# Eiffel Tower Tour

Paris, France

Visit the Eiffel Tower! Gustave Eiffel built it for the 1889 World's Fair and to celebrate the 100-year anniversary[1] of the French Revolution.

Take our exciting tour! Our first stop is for a photo of *you* **in front of** the Eiffel Tower. Next, we go to a secret room **under** the tower to learn about its history.

Our last stop is the top of the tower. The view **over** the city is amazing! The Seine River is **below**, and the beautiful Trocadero Park is **across** the river.

**FAQs[2]**

**Where is the meeting place for the tour?**

Meet the tour guide **next to** the statue[3] of Gustave Eiffel.

**Where is the ticket office?**

The ticket counter is **next to** the elevator.

See you **in** Paris!

---

[1] **anniversary:** a date that is remembered because something special happened on that day in an earlier year

[2] **FAQs:** Frequently Asked Questions

[3] **statue:** a large model made of stone or metal

▶ The Eiffel Tower, Paris, France

**2  CHECK.** Read the statements. Circle **T** for *True* or **F** for *False*.

1.  The ad is for a bus tour of Paris.                    **T**      **F**

2.  The Eiffel Tower is 100 years old.                    **T**      **F**

3.  The first stop is a secret room.                      **T**      **F**

4.  Trocadero is a river.                                 **T**      **F**

5.  The last stop is the top of the tower.                **T**      **F**


**3  DISCOVER.** Complete the exercises to learn about the grammar in this lesson.

**A** Find these sentences in the advertisement from exercise **1**. Write the missing words.

1.  Our first stop is for a photo of *you* _____ the Eiffel Tower.

2.  The view _____ the city is amazing!

3.  Meet the tour guide _____ the statue of Gustave Eiffel.

**B** Look at the sentences from exercise **A**. Then choose the correct word to complete the statement below. Discuss your answer with your classmates and teacher.

We use *in front of, over, below, across from, under,* and *next to* to talk about _____.

a. time      b. place      c. people

# LEARN

## 2.3 Prepositions of Place

The pen is **in** the glass.

The pen is **on** the book.

The pen is **next to** the glass.

The pen is **near** the glass.

The pen is **in front of** the glass.

The pen is **in back of / behind** the glass.

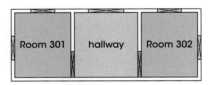

Room 301 is **across from** Room 302.

The pen is **between** the glasses.

The pen is **under / below** the chair.

The pen is **over / above** the glass.

| | |
|---|---|
| 1. Phrases with prepositions tell where something is. | Our class is **in** <u>Room 502</u>.<br>My book is **on** <u>my desk</u>. |
| 2. Use *at* with specific addresses and with places we visit in daily life. | She lives **at** <u>39 Main Street</u>.<br>He's **at** <u>the supermarket</u>.<br>They're **at** <u>the library</u>. |
| 3. Use *on* with streets, roads, avenues, and floors of a building. | Their office is **on** <u>Park Street</u>.<br>We live **on** <u>Maple Road</u>.<br>Her office is **on** <u>the second floor</u>. |
| 4. Use *in* with cities, countries, and rooms. | The Eiffel Tower is **in** <u>Paris</u>.<br>Paris is a city **in** <u>France</u>.<br>Our class is **in** <u>Room 215</u>. |

**4** Complete each sentence with the correct preposition from the box.

| above   across from   behind   between   in   in front of   near   next to   on   under |

1. The light is _____*above*_____ the table.

6. The keys are _____ the table.

2. The keys are _____ the books.

7. The pen is _____ the glass.

3. The pen is _____ the book.

8. The backpack is _____ the table.

4. The pen is _____ the glass.

9. The keys are _____ the book.

5. The pen is _____ the book.

10. The red chair is _____ the green chair.

**5** Complete each sentence with *at*, *in*, or *on*.

1. Paris is __in__ France.

2. The Eiffel Tower is _____ Paris.

3. Beijing is a city _____ China.

4. The doctor's office is _____ 21 Palmer Street.

5. The supermarket is _____ Mountain Avenue.

6. The Statue of Liberty is _____ New York City.

7. Our new house is _____ 141 Hillview Road.

8. Our meeting is _____ Room 210.

## 2.4 Questions with *Where* + *Be*

| Questions | | | Answers |
|---|---|---|---|
| *Where* | *Be* | Subject | |
| Where | is | the exit? | **Next to** the stairs. <br> It's **next to** the stairs. |
| Where | is | the post office? | **On** Park Street. <br> It's **on** Park Street. |
| Where | are | Ben and Louisa? | **In** the park. <br> They're **in** the park. |

| | |
|---|---|
| 1. Use *Where* to ask questions about place. | A: **Where** is the library? <br> B: It's next to the Science Building. |
| 2. Put the verb before the subject in questions with *Where*. | ✓ Where **is** the park? <br> ✗ Where the park is? |
| 3. *Where's* is the contraction of *Where* and *is*. <br><br> Do not contract *Where* and *are*. | **Where's** the bus stop? <br><br> ✓ **Where are** the books? <br> ✗ Where're the books? |

**REAL ENGLISH**

Use *Where* alone to clarify or get more information.

A: *They're in the park.*
B: ***Where?***
A: *Over by the bridge.*
B: *Oh, OK. Now I see them.*

**6** Put the words in the correct order to make questions.

1. our class / is / Where <u>Where is our class?</u>

2. is / the bathroom / Where _____

3. teacher / Where's / our _____

4. are / Where / our / books _____

5. your / home / Where / is _____

6. our / classmates / are / Where _____

7. classroom / our / Where's _____

8. you / are / Where _____

9. Chan and Meg / are / Where _____

10. your / Where's / office _____

**7** **SPEAK.** Work with a partner. Ask and answer questions 1-8 from exercise **6**.

Student A: *Where's our class?*

Student B: *It's in Room 205.*

# PRACTICE

**8 READ & SPEAK.**

**A** Look at the floor plan of an office building. Then choose the correct preposition of place to complete each statement.

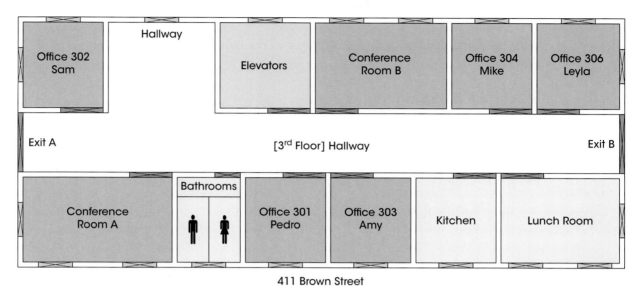

1. The office building is _____ 411 Brown Street.  (a.) at  b. in  c. on

2. The office building is _____ Brown Street.  a. in  b. at  c. on

3. These offices are _____ the third floor.  a. in  b. on  c. at

4. The elevators are _____ Conference Room B.  a. next to  b. between  c. in

5. Pedro's office is _____ Amy's office.  a. in front of  b. behind  c. next to

6. The lunch room is _____ the kitchen.  a. between  b. next to  c. behind

7. The parking lot is _____ the building.  a. between  b. near  c. in

8. Mike is _____ Office 304.  a. on  b. in  c. at

9. Leyla's office is _____ the lunch room.  a. across from  b. behind  c. between

10. The kitchen is _____ Office 303 and the lunch room.  a. between  b. across from  c. in front of

**B** Work with a partner. Ask and answer questions about the office building floor plan from exercise **A** on page 55. Use prepositions of place, *Yes/No* questions, and questions with *where + be*.

Student A: *Is Leyla's office next to Mike's office?*

Student B: *Yes, it is.*

Student A: *Where's Amy's office?*

Student B: *It's between Pedro's office and the kitchen.*

**9 LISTEN & SPEAK.**

CD1-23

**A** Look at the list of places in New Orleans. Then listen to a tour guide describe each place. Write the number of each place on the map.

~~1.~~ The Cabildo Museum

2. The Cathedral

3. Jackson Square

4. The Pontalba Buildings (two places)

5. Statue of Andrew Jackson

6. The Café du Monde

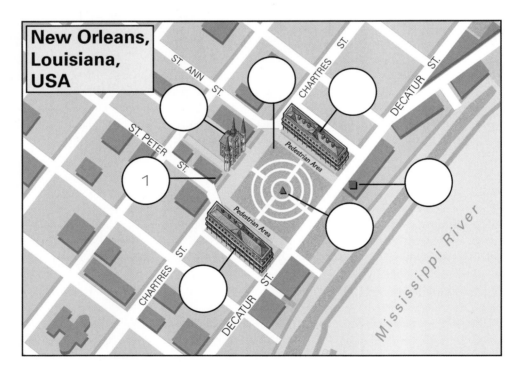

**B** Work with a partner. Ask and answer questions about the map from exercise **A**.

Student A: *Where is Jackson Square?*

Student B: *It's between the Pontalba Buildings.*

**10 EDIT.** Read the information about New Orleans. Find and correct six more errors with prepositions of place. Use the map in exercise **9A** to help you.

## New Orleans

New Orleans is a city ∨<sup>in</sup> ~~on~~ the United States. It is in the state of Louisiana. The French Quarter is a very old part of New Orleans. It is between the Mississippi River. Jackson Square is under Decatur Street and Chartres Street. The Café du Monde is in Decatur Street. It is across of Jackson Square. The Cathedral is on Chartres Street. It is above the Cabildo Museum. Apartments are under the stores and restaurants in the Pontalba Buildings.

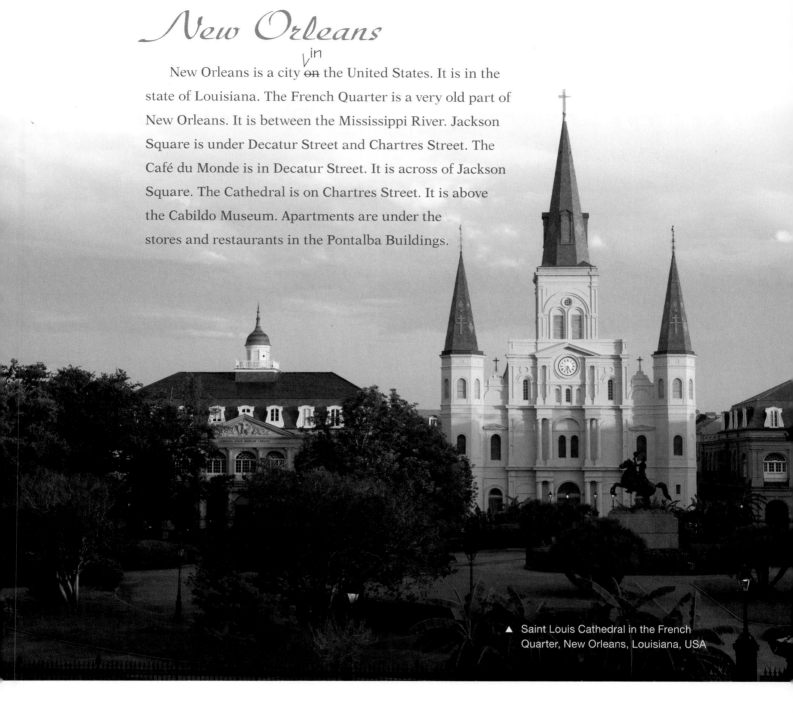

▲ Saint Louis Cathedral in the French Quarter, New Orleans, Louisiana, USA

## 11 APPLY.

**A** In your notebook, draw a map of a place you know with stores, parks, and interesting buildings (for example: a post office, a school, a library, a supermarket, a bank, etc). Then write a few sentences about it. Describe the location of the different buildings. Use prepositions of place.

My apartment is at 51 Garden Street. It is between a park and a school . . .

**B** Work with a partner. Talk about places on your map from exercise **A**.

*The park is on Garden Street. It's next to the shopping center.*

## EXPLORE

CD1-24

**1** **READ** the news report. Notice the words in **bold**.

# New Year's Celebrations around the World

**Reporter 1:** 5, 4, 3, 2, 1 . . . Happy New Year, London! **It's midnight on New Year's Eve!** This is Emily Michaels. I have our reporter[1] Philip Jones in New York on the line. Hi, Philip. Happy New Year!

**Reporter 2:** Hello, Emily. Happy New Year to you, too! **How's the weather in London?**

**Reporter 1:** **It's cool and rainy**, but people are in the streets. Everyone is very excited. **How is it in New York?**

**Reporter 2:** **It's freezing[2] here! It's cold and snowy** . . . It's terrible!

**Reporter 1:** That's too bad! **What time is it there?**

**Reporter 2:** **It's seven o'clock in the evening**.

**Reporter 1:** OK, thank you, Philip. Keep warm! Now, let's check in with our reporter in Sydney, Australia. Nicole, are you there?

**Reporter 3:** Yes, hello. Happy New Year, everyone! **It's sunny and warm here!**

**Reporter 2:** That's right—it's summer in Australia. **What time is it there?**

**Reporter 3:** **It's eleven o'clock in the morning**.

**Reporter 1:** Thanks, Nicole. Happy New Year! Now back to our celebration in London!

[1] **reporter:** someone who tells or writes about news          [2] **freezing:** very cold

**2** **CHECK.** Complete the chart with information from the news report in exercise **1**.

|  | Time | Weather |
|---|---|---|
| London |  | *cool* and rainy |
| New York | *seven o'clock* |  |
| Sydney |  |  |

**3** **DISCOVER.** Complete the exercises to learn about the grammar in this lesson.

**A** Find and underline statements and questions with *it* in the news report from exercise **1**. Are they about time or weather? In the margin, write **T** for *time* and **W** for *weather*.

It's midnight on New Year's Eve.   T          It's cool and rainy.   W

**B** Work with a partner. Compare your answers from exercise **A**. Then discuss your answers with your classmates and teacher.

▲ Fireworks explode over Sydney Harbor, Sydney, Australia, January 1, 2000,

# LEARN

## 2.5 Questions about Time

| Questions | | | | Answers | |
|---|---|---|---|---|---|
| What time | is | it? | | | two o'clock. |
| What day | | | | | Monday. |
| What month | | | | It's | February. |
| What year | | | | It is | 2017. |
| What | is<br>'s | the date today?<br>today's date? | | | May 3rd. |

| | |
|---|---|
| 1. Use *it* in questions with *What* + a time word. | **What time** is it?<br>**What year** is it? |
| 2. Do not use *it* in time questions with *What is/What's*. | ✓ **What is** the time?<br>✗ What is <u>it</u> the time? |
| 3. Put the verb *is* before the subject in questions about time. | ✓ What time **is** <u>it</u>?<br>✗ What time <u>it is</u>?<br>✓ What **is** <u>the date</u> today?<br>✗ What <u>the date is</u> today? |
| 4. Use *it* to answer questions about time. | **It**'s five-thirty.<br>**It**'s Thursday. |

**4** Write the correct question for each answer. More than one answer may be possible.

1. A: <u>What month is it?</u>

   B: It's April.

2. A: _____

   B: It's two o'clock.

3. A: _____

   B: It's Saturday.

4. A: _____

   B: It's April 5th.

5. A: _____

   B: It's Monday.

6. A: _____

   B: It's November.

7. A: _____

   B: It's 2017.

8. A: _____

   B: It's nine-thirty.

**5** Choose the correct answer for each question.

1. What time is it?          a. It's April 9th.          (b.) It's four o'clock.

2. What day is it?           a. It's Monday.             b. It's March.

3. What year is it?          a. It's September.          b. It's 2017.

4. What time is it?          a. It's ten-thirty.         b. It's 2017.

5. What month is it?         a. It's January.            b. It's Friday.

6. What's today's date?      a. It's October 14th.       b. It's Wednesday.

7. What day is it?           a. It's 2017.               b. It's Thursday.

8. What is the date today?   a. It's December.           b. It's December 2nd.

**6** **SPEAK.** Work with a partner. Ask and answer the questions from exercise **5**.

Student A: *What time is it?*          Student B: *It's eleven-thirty.*

## 2.6 Questions with *When*; Prepositions of Time (Part 1)*

| Questions | | Answers | | |
|---|---|---|---|---|
| | | | Preposition of Time | |
| **When is** **When's** | your class? | My class is It's | **at** | two o'clock. |
| | | | **on** | Monday night. |
| | | | **in** | the morning. |

| | |
|---|---|
| 1. Use *When* to ask questions about time. | **When** is our meeting? **When's** your birthday? |
| 2. *When's* is the contraction of *When* and *is*. | A: **When's** your soccer game? B: It's on Saturday afternoon. |
| 3. Put the verb *is* before the subject in questions with *When*. | ✓ When **is** <u>the test</u>? ✗ When <u>the test is</u>? |
| 4. Phrases with prepositions tell when something happens. | The party is **on Saturday**. |
| 5. Use *at* with clock times. | **at** <u>three-thirty</u> **at** <u>one o'clock</u> **at** <u>midnight</u> |
| 6. Use *in* with years, months, seasons of the year, and times of the day (exception: *at night*). | **in** <u>2015</u> **in** <u>May</u> **in** <u>the summer</u> **in** <u>the morning</u> / <u>afternoon</u> / <u>evening</u> |
| 7. Use *on* with dates and days of the week. *On* is also used with *the weekend*. | **on** June 29 **on** Sunday **on** the weekend |

*For Prepositions of Time (Part 2), see Unit 3, Lesson 2.

**7** Use the words in parentheses to write questions with *When*. Then complete the answers with *in*, *at*, or *on*.

1. (New Year's Eve)  A: ___When's New Year's Eve?_____

   B: It's _____ December 31st.

2. (her 21st birthday)  A: _____

   B: It's _____ 2020.

3. (your birthday)  A: _____

   B: My birthday's _____ June.

4. (St. Patrick's Day)  A: _____

   B: It's _____ March 17th.

5. (our English class)  A: _____

   B: It's _____ two o'clock.

6. (the party)  A: _____

   B: It's _____ Tuesday night.

7. (the exam)  A: _____

   B: It's _____ Monday.

8. (the winter festival)  A: _____

   B: The winter festival is _____ December.

**8** Complete the conversations with the correct prepositions of time.

1. A: When's Mother's Day in the United States?

   B: It's _in_ May. It's always _____ Sunday.

2. A: When's your name day?

   B: It's _____ September.

3. A: Is the party _____ Friday?

   B: No, it's not. It's _____ Thursday.

4. A: When's the music festival?

   B: It's _____ the summer.

5. A: When's his birthday?

   B: It's _____ December 3rd.

6. A: My class is _____ seven-thirty.

   B: Is it _____ the morning?

   A: No, it's _____ night.

**9** **SPEAK.** Work with a partner. Ask questions about special days, holidays, and celebrations. Use the ideas from the box below or your own ideas.

| your birthday | Mother's Day in your country | New Year's Day | your class |

Student A: *When's your birthday?*    Student B: *It's on August 9th.*

## 2.7 Questions about the Weather

| Questions | Answers | |
|---|---|---|
| | It's cool / cold / freezing. | |
| | It's mild / warm / hot. | |
| **How is** / **How's** the weather? | It's cloudy. | |
| | It's rainy. | |
| | It's snowy. | |
| | It's sunny. | |
| | It's windy. | |

| | |
|---|---|
| 1. Use questions with *how* and answers with *it to* talk about the weather. | A: **How** is the weather in Madrid today?<br>B: **It's** warm and sunny. |
| 2. *How's* is the contraction of *How* and *is*. | A: **How's** the weather in London?<br>B: It's cool and rainy. |
| 3. *What's the weather like* is also used to ask about weather. | A: **What's the weather like** in Chicago in the winter?<br>B: It's cold and windy. |
| 4. Use adjectives to describe the weather. | It's **hot** and **sunny**.<br>It's **freezing**. |

**10** Complete each question. Then write the correct answer to each question.

1. A: _____How's_____ the weather?     B: (cold and windy) ___It's cold and windy.___

2. A: _____ the weather?     B: (warm and sunny) _____

3. A: _____ the weather like?     B: (rainy) _____

4. A: _____ the weather?     B: (cold and snowy) _____

5. A: _____ the weather?     B: (hot and sunny) _____

6. A: _____ the weather like?     B: (cool and cloudy) _____

7. A: _____ the weather?     B: (sunny and mild) _____

8: A: _____ the weather like?     B: (freezing) _____

**11** **SPEAK.** Work with a partner. Ask and answer questions about different places.

Student A: *What's the weather like in Hawaii?*     Student B: *It's hot and sunny.*

# PRACTICE

**12** Complete each conversation. Use contractions when possible. Then listen and check your answers.

CD1-25

1. A: (1) _____What_____ _____time_____ is it?

   B: (2) _____It's_____ one o'clock.

   A: Oh no! Are we late for the meeting?

   B: No, it's (3) _____ two o'clock.

2. A: Hi, Peter. (4) _____ the weather in Miami today?

   B: (5) _____ warm and sunny.

   A: You're lucky! (6) _____ cold and rainy here in Toronto.

3. A: Hmmm. (7) _____ the (8) _____ today?

   B: (9) _____ July 9th.

   A: Thank you.

4. A: (10) _____ the game?

   B: It's (11) _____ Saturday.

   A: Is it (12) _____ the morning?

   B: No, it's (13) _____ the afternoon. It's (14) _____ three o'clock.

**13** **EDIT.** Read the conversations. Find and correct six more errors with questions about time and prepositions of time.

1. **Sam:** Hi, Mel. What time ~~it is~~? *(is it)*

   **Mel:** It's nine-thirty.

   **Sam:** Oh no! I'm late!

2. **Ben:** When is your birthday?

   **Mika:** It's on June.

   **Ben:** Really? My birthday's in June, too. It's in June 24th.

3. **Nora:** What time is it?

   **Chan:** It seven o'clock.

   **Nora:** Oh, good! The movie is on 7:30.

4. **Toshi:** When Steve's graduation party?

   **Maria:** It's on Friday.

   **Toshi:** Is it in the afternoon?

   **Maria:** No, it's in night.

## 14 LISTEN & WRITE.

 **A** Listen to the news report. Circle the holiday you hear.

    a. Mother's Day     b. Valentine's Day     c. a name day

 **B** Read the questions. Then listen to the news report again and write the answer to each question.

1. What time is it? _____

2. What day is it? _____

3. What month is it? _____

4. What's the date? _____

5. How's the weather? _____

## 15 APPLY.

**A** Choose a holiday or festival from your country. Then write notes for a news report below. Use the model to help you.

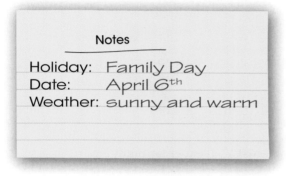

Notes
Holiday: Family Day
Date: April 6th
Weather: sunny and warm

Notes
Holiday:
Date:
Weather:

**B** Role-play your weather report for the class. Use your notes from exercise **A** and the model below to help you.

*Good morning, Cape Town. It's nine o'clock on Monday, April 6.*

*It's Family Day today, and it's beautiful outside. It's sunny and warm.*

*Have a great day, families!*

### EXPLORE

CD1-27

**1 READ** the conversation about the Holi Festival. Notice the words in **bold**.

# Holi Festival

**Scott:** Hi, Dan. **Is this seat** free?

**Dan:** Oh, hi, Scott. Yeah, **it is**. Have a seat. How are you doing?

**Scott:** Good. **Is that** your new laptop?

**Dan:** Yes, **it is**. I'm really happy with it so far.

**Scott:** **What's that** on your screen? **Is that** your photo, or is it from the Internet?

**Dan:** Oh, **it's** a photo from my trip to India last month. **It's** the Holi festival of colors.

**Scott:** The Holi festival. **What's that?**

**Dan:** **It's** a Hindu holiday to celebrate spring. People of all ages are in the streets. They throw paint and water on each other.

**Scott:** Interesting. It looks like fun . . . Wow. Look at **those colors**. **Is that** paint in the air?

**Dan:** Yes. **It** was everywhere. Do you see **these people** here?

**Scott:** Yeah?

**Dan:** I was completely yellow thanks to them . . . Look, here are a few more photos of the Holi festival.

**Scott:** Wow! **Those are** amazing photos! You're a great photographer.

**Dan:** Thanks. **Is this** your stop?

**Scott:** Oh, yes, **it is**. See you, Dan.

**Dan:** OK. See you later, Scott.

◀ The Holi Festival, Mathura, Uttar Pradesh, India

▲ People throw paint and water at the Holi Festival, Mathura, Uttar Pradesh, India.

**2 CHECK.** Choose the correct word(s) to complete each sentence about the conversation.

1. This photograph is from _____.      a. Hollywood     b. India

2. Holi is the festival of _____.     a. paint     b. colors

3. On this holiday, people dance in _____.     a. the streets     b. their houses

4. _____ is a great photographer.     a. Dan     b. Scott

**3 DISCOVER.** Complete the exercises to learn about the grammar in this lesson.

**A** Find these statements and questions in the conversation from exercise **1**. Write the missing words.

1. Is _____ your new laptop?

2. Look at _____ colors.

3. Do you see _____ people here?

4. _____ are amazing photos!

5. Is _____ your stop?

**B** Circle the correct word to complete each statement. Then discuss your answers with your classmates and teacher.

1. We use *this* and *that* with **singular / plural** nouns.

2. We use *these* and *those* with **singular / plural** nouns.

# LEARN

## 2.8 This, That, These, Those

| Singular | | |
|---|---|---|
| Subject | Verb | |
| This<br>That | is | a great photo. |
| This<br>That laptop | is | great. |

| Plural | | |
|---|---|---|
| Subject | Verb | |
| These<br>Those | are | great photos. |
| These<br>Those laptops | are | great. |

| | |
|---|---|
| 1. *This, that, these,* and *those* can be pronouns or adjectives. | **This** is a great photo. (pronoun)<br>**This** photo is great. (adjective) |
| 2. Use *this* and *that* with singular nouns.<br><br>Use *these* and *those* with plural nouns. | **This** exercise is easy.<br>**That** is Miguel's coat.<br><br>**These** cookies are delicious.<br>**Those** are expensive shoes. |
| 3. Use *this, that, these,* and *those* to identify people or things. | **This** is my grammar book.<br>**That**'s my house across the street.<br>**Those** women are my classmates. |
| 4. Use *this* and *these* for people or things that are near.<br><br>Use *that* and *those* for people or things that are not near. | **This** is my wife, Erika. **These** are our children, Anna and Jason.<br><br>**That** is my car over there.<br>**Those** are my keys on the table. |

**REAL ENGLISH**

Use *this* to introduce people. After you introduce the person, use a personal pronoun.

***This** is Arlene. **She's** my wife.*

**4** Circle the correct word to complete each sentence.

1. **This** / (**These**) photos are from my trip to India.

2. **That** / **Those** is an interesting photo.

3. **This** / **These** festival is a lot of fun!

4. **This** / **These** is my new camera.

5. **That** / **Those** men over there are teachers at my school.

6. **This** / **These** are Miguel's books.

7. **This** / **These** flowers are beautiful.

8. **That** / **Those** laptops are very expensive.

9. **This** / **Those** is my sister, Yoko.

10. **Those** / **That** is Hamid's backpack.

**5** Complete each sentence with *this, that, these,* or *those.* Look at the information in parentheses (*near/not near*).

1. _____These_____ are photos of the festival. (*near*)

2. _____ man is from India. (*not near*)

3. _____ is a beautiful building. (*not near*)

4. _____ is my new phone. (*near*)

5. _____ students are in our class. (*not near*)

6. _____ classroom is cold! (*near*)

7. _____ books are heavy. (*near*)

8. _____ are Greg's parents. (*not near*)

## 2.9 Questions and Answers with *This, That, These, Those*

| Yes/No Questions | |
|---|---|
| **Is** | **this** your notebook? **that** boy your son? |
| **Are** | **these** scarves **those** people from India? |

| Affirmative Short Answers | Negative Short Answer | |
|---|---|---|
| Yes, **it is.** | No, | it isn't. it's not. |
| Yes, **they are.** | No, | they aren't. they're not. |

| Questions with *What* | |
|---|---|
| What **is** | this? |
| | that? |
| What **are** | these? |
| | those? |

| Answers | |
|---|---|
| **It's** | a phone. |
| | my new camera. |
| **They're** | glasses. |
| | apartment buildings. |

| | |
|---|---|
| 1. For *Yes/No* questions with *this* and *that,* use *it* in the short answer. | A: Is **this** your notebook? B: Yes, **it** is. A: Is **that** building a museum? B: No, **it** isn't. **It's** a high school. |
| 2. For *Yes/No* questions with *these* and *those,* use *they* in the short answer. | A: Are **these** your sunglasses? B: No, **they're** not. They're Mary's. A: Are **those** students from China? B: Yes, **they** are. |
| 3. Use *What* to ask questions about things. | A: **What's** that? B: It's my <u>homework assignment</u>. A: **What** are these? B: They're <u>photographs</u> from my trip. |

**6** Put the words in order to make questions. Then write the correct answer for each question.

1. your camera / Is / that

A: Is that your camera?

B: Yes, it is .

2. Are / Bob's sons / those

A: _____

B: Yes, _____ .

3. those cars / Are / expensive

A: _____

B: No, _____ .

4. this / your jacket / Is

A: _____

B: Yes, _____ .

5. Are / Cho's books / these

A: _____

B: No, _____ .

6. Is / our bus / that

A: _____

B: No, _____ .

7. is / What / that

A: _____

B: _____ my backpack.

8. those / What / are

A: _____

B: _____ notebooks.

9. these / are / What

A: _____

B: _____ earrings.

10. is / What / this

A: _____

B: _____ a scarf.

**7** **LISTEN** and choose the correct answer for each question.

CD1-28

1. (a.) Yes, it is.        b. Yes, they are.

2. a. No, they aren't.        b. No, it isn't.

3. a. No, it isn't.        b. No, they're not.

4. a. Yes, it is.        b. Yes, they are.

5. a. Yes, they are.        b. Yes, it is.

6. a. No, they're not.        b. No, it's not.

7. a. Yes, they are.        b. Yes, it is.

8. a. Yes, they are.        b. Yes, it is.

# PRACTICE

**8** Circle the correct word(s) to complete each conversation.

1. A: Happy Birthday, Alberto! (1) **This** / These is a fun party.

   B: Thanks, Roberto.

   A: Alberto, (2) **this** / these is my wife, Amelia.

   B: Nice to meet you, Amelia.

2. A: (3) **That** / **Those** are amazing photos.

   B: Thank you. They're from Trocadero Park.

   A: Is (4) **that** / **those** in Belgium?

   B: No, (5) **it's** / **they're** not. (6) **It's** / **They're** in Paris, France.

3. A: Excuse me, is (7) **this** / **these** the Language Lab?

   B: No, (8) **it's** / **they're** not. (9) **It's** / **They're** in Room 410.

   A: Is (10) **that** / **those** on the fourth floor?

   B: Yes, (11) **it is** / **they are**.

4. A: (12) **That** / **Those** is a beautiful scarf. (13) **Is** / **Are** it from India?

   B: Yes, (14) **it is** / **that is**. (15) **This** / **These** earrings are from India, too.

**9 EDIT.** Read the conversation. Find and correct six more errors with *this, that, these,* or *those*.

## THE MEDELLÍN FLOWER FESTIVAL

▶ The Medellín flower festival, Medellín, Colombia

**Alicia:** Wow! ~~These~~ *This* festival is amazing!

**Ima:** Yeah, it is. All of this flowers are beautiful.

**Alicia:** Are that roses over there?

**Ima:** Yes, it is.

**Alicia:** They're so colorful.

**Ima:** This big yellow flowers here are beautiful, too. I think they're sunflowers.

**Alicia:** Are that people over there farmers?

**Ima:** Yes, they are. They grow the flowers for these festival every year.

**10  SPEAK.** Work with a partner. Practice saying sentences and asking and answering questions about things in your classroom. Use *this, that, these, those, Yes/No* questions, and questions with *What*.

Student A: *That's a beautiful sweater.*

Student B: *Thanks.*

Student A: *What's that?*

Student B: *It's my phone.*

Student A: *Is that your backpack?*

Student B: *Yes, it is.*

**11  APPLY.**

**A**  Work with a partner. Write a conversation about a party, festival, or celebration. Use the conversation from exercise **9** on page 71 to help you.

A: _____

B: _____

A: _____

B: _____

A: _____

B: _____

**B**  Role-play your conversation from exercise **A** for the class.

▼ People with lanterns at the Kratong festival, Chiang Mai, Thailand

CD1-29

Charts
2.1–2.9

**1 LISTEN** and choose the correct answer for each question.

1.  a. No, I'm not.            ⓑ Yes, she is.

2.  a. Yes, they are.         b. Yes, you are.

3.  a. No, they're not.       b. No, it's not.

4.  a. It's in the morning.   b. It's in Conference Room B.

5.  a. It's at 9 a.m.          b. It's 9:00 a.m.

6.  a. It's in Room 203.      b. It's at 10:30.

7.  a. They're flowers.       b. It's a flower.

8.  a. Yes, it is.             b. It's cool and cloudy.

Charts
2.1–2.7

**2 WRITE & SPEAK.**

**A** Look at Angela's calendar. Then write four questions about the information.

| February | | | | | | |
| Sunday | Monday | Tuesday | Wednesday | Thursday | Friday | Saturday |
| 12 | 13 | 14 | 15 | 16 | 17 | 18 |
| | Meeting Boston 10:00 a.m. | Jack's party 7:00 p.m. 21 Baker Street | Soccer game 5:30 p.m. | Meeting Room 206 2:00 p.m. | Concert 21 Park Street 7:00 p.m. | Street fair 8th Street |
| | | Valentine's Day | | Marta's Birthday | | Alma and Ted's Wedding 4:00 |

_Is Marta's birthday on Wednesday?_

_____

_____

_____

_____

**B** Work with a partner. Ask and answer your questions from exercise **A**.

Student A: _Is Marta's birthday on Wednesday?_

Student B: _No, it's not. It's on Thursday._

Charts
2.1–2.6

**3  EDIT.** Read the conversation. Find and correct six more errors with questions and prepositions of time and prepositions of place.

| | |
|---|---|
| **Delma:** | Hello? |
| **Sara:** | Hi, Delma. Are you in Madrid now? |
| **Delma:** | Yes, I am. It's beautiful here. |
| **Sara:** | Where *is* your hotel ~~is~~? |
| **Delma:** | It's near to the Prado Museum. |
| **Sara:** | Is it nice? |
| **Delma:** | Yes, it is. It's really nice. What time is it at Boston now? |
| **Sara:** | It's eight o'clock at the morning. What time it there? |
| **Delma:** | It's at two o'clock at the afternoon here. It's time for lunch. I'm hungry! |
| **Sara:** | OK. Well, enjoy your vacation! |
| **Delma:** | Thanks! Bye. |
| **Sara:** | Bye. |

Charts
2.1–2.6

**4  READ, WRITE & SPEAK.**

**A**  Read about the Harbin International Ice Festival. Then ask *Yes/No* questions and questions with *When, Where,* and *How.*

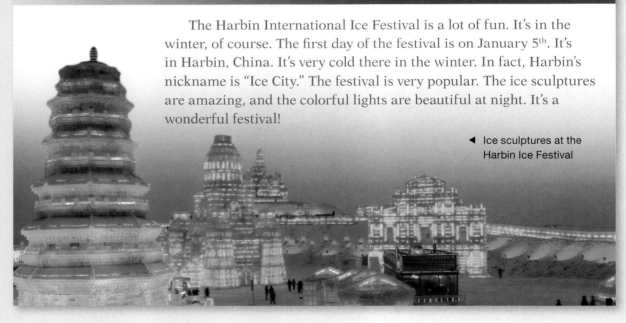

# The Harbin Ice Festival

The Harbin International Ice Festival is a lot of fun. It's in the winter, of course. The first day of the festival is on January 5th. It's in Harbin, China. It's very cold there in the winter. In fact, Harbin's nickname is "Ice City." The festival is very popular. The ice sculptures are amazing, and the colorful lights are beautiful at night. It's a wonderful festival!

◀ Ice sculptures at the Harbin Ice Festival

Student A: *Is Harbin in China?*     Student B: *Yes, it is.*

◄ Buildings of ice at the Harbin Ice Festival, Harbin, China

**B** Think of a festival or celebration in your country or a country you know. Write sentences about the festival or celebration.

It's in Harbin, China.

It's in the winter.

_____

_____

_____

_____

_____

**C** Work with a partner. Share your sentences from exercise **B**. Ask and answer questions.

Student A: *The festival is in China.*

Student B: *Is it in the summer?*

Student A: *No, it's not. It's in the winter.*

# Connect the Grammar to Writing

## 1 READ & NOTICE THE GRAMMAR.

**A** Read the paragraph. What is the grandfather's favorite celebration? Discuss with a partner.

### A Favorite Celebration

My grandfather's favorite celebration is his birthday. It's in September. His party isn't at a restaurant. It's at our home. The weather is often warm and sunny in September, so the party is outside in our yard. My grandfather is very happy on September 3rd. It's his special day, and it's a lot of fun!

> **GRAMMAR FOCUS**
>
> In the paragraph in exercise **A**, the writer uses phrases with prepositions to give information about time and place.
>
> It's **in September.**
> His party isn't **at a restaurant.**

**B** Read the paragraph in exercise **A** again. Underline the prepositions of time and place. Then work with a partner and compare answers.

**C** Complete the chart with questions and answers about the celebration in the paragraph in exercise **A**.

| A Favorite Celebration | | |
|---|---|---|
| | Questions | Answers |
| What | What is the grandfather's favorite celebration? | His birthday. |
| When | | |
| Yes/No question | Is his party at a restaurant? | |
| How | | |
| Yes/No question | | |

## 2 BEFORE YOU WRITE.

**A** Write interview questions in the chart to ask someone about his or her favorite celebration. Use the chart from exercise **1C** as a model.

| _____'s Favorite Celebration | | |
|---|---|---|
| | Questions | Answers |
| What | What is your favorite celebration? | |
| When | | |
| *Yes/No* question | | |
| How | | |
| *Yes/No* question | | |

**B** Choose a person to interview. Ask him or her your interview questions from exercise **2A**. Take notes on his or her answers in your chart.

## 3 WRITE a paragraph. Use the information from your chart in exercise **2A** and the paragraph in exercise **1A** to help you.

> **WRITING FOCUS**    Paragraph Format
>
> A paragraph is not a list of sentences. It has a special format.
>
> **A List of Sentences:**
> *My favorite celebration is the Kite Festival.*
> *It is a celebration in Shirone, Japan.*
> *It's in June.*
> *It's warm and sunny then.*
>
> **A Paragraph:**
> *My favorite celebration is the Kite Festival. It is a celebration in Shirone, Japan. It's in June. It's warm and sunny then.*

## 4 SELF ASSESS. Read your paragraph. Underline the prepositions of time and place. Then use the checklist to assess your work.

- [ ] I used the correct form of *be*. [1.3–1.5]
- [ ] I used the correct prepositions of time. [2.6]
- [ ] I used the correct prepositions of place. [2.3]
- [ ] I used the correct format for my paragraph. [WRITING FOCUS]

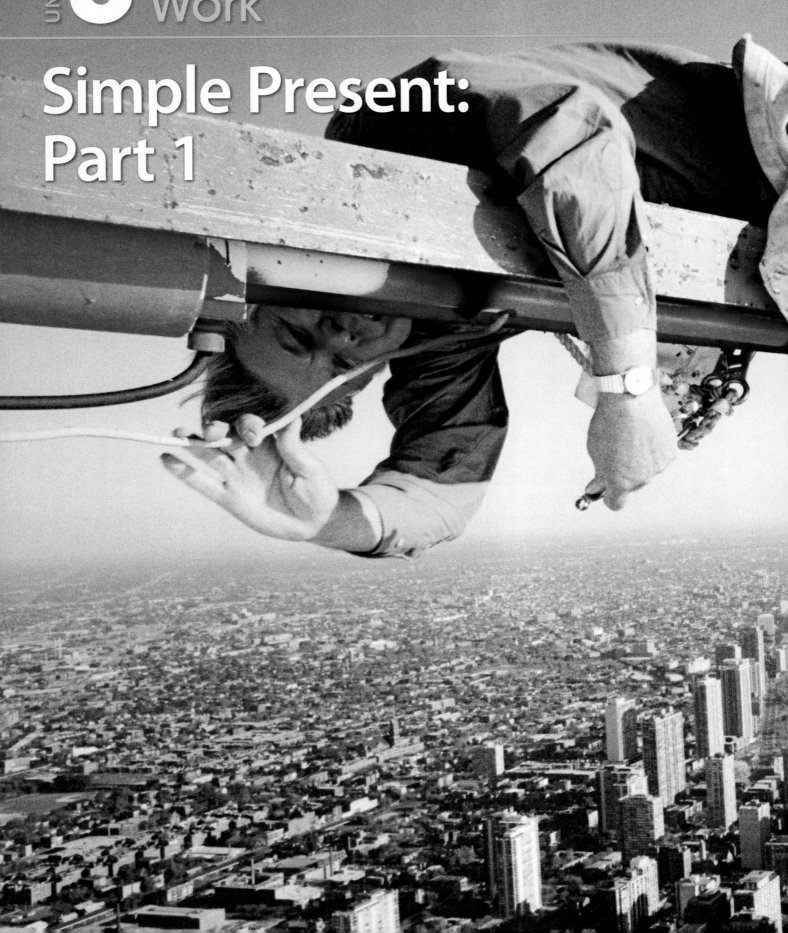

# Simple Present: Part 1

◀ A worker on top of the John Hancock skyscraper in Chicago, Illinois, USA

## EXPLORE

**1 READ** the article about Doctor Bugs. Notice the words in **bold**.

# Doctor Bugs

Most people don't like bugs, but Doctor Mark Moffett **loves** them! In fact, his nickname is Doctor Bugs. He's a photographer and an entomologist. An entomologist **studies** bugs.

Doctor Moffett's favorite bug is the ant. He **goes** all over the world to study ants. He **watches** them as they **eat**, **work**, **rest**, **sleep**, and **fight**.

He **takes** photographs of the ants. He **lies** on the ground with his camera and **waits** for the right moment. The ants and other bugs often **bite** him, but that doesn't stop Doctor Bugs. He **has** an interesting and unusual job, and he **loves** it!

▲ Doctor Mark Moffett

**2  CHECK.** Read the list of verbs in the chart. Who does each action? Check (✓) the correct column.

| Verbs | Doctor Moffett | Ants |
|---|---|---|
| 1. studies | | |
| 2. fight | | |
| 3. waits | | |
| 4. bite | | |

**3  DISCOVER.** Complete the exercises to learn about the grammar in this lesson.

**A**  Look at the list of verbs in exercise **2**. Then find other verbs in the article from exercise **1**. Who does each action? Write each verb in the correct column.

| Doctor Moffett | Ants |
|---|---|
| goes | eat |

**B**  Look at the charts from exercise **2** and exercise **A**. Choose the correct answer to complete each statement. Then discuss your answers with your classmates and teacher.

1.  The verbs under *Doctor Moffett* **end in -s / do not end in -s.**

2.  The verbs under *Ants* **end in -s / do not end in -s.**

◄ Leaf cutter ants

# LEARN

## 3.1 Simple Present: Affirmative Statements

| Subject | Verb | | Subject | Verb | |
|---|---|---|---|---|---|
| I<br>You<br>We<br>You<br>They<br>Tom and Sue | **work** | every day. | He<br>She<br>It<br>My brother | **works** | every day. |

| | |
|---|---|
| 1. Use the simple present to talk about habits or routines, schedules, and facts. | Habit or Routine: I **exercise** every day.<br>Schedule: She **starts** work at eight.<br>Fact: It **rains** a lot in April. |
| 2. Add -s to the verb for *he, she, it,* and singular subjects. | He **drives** to work.<br>She **works** in an office.<br>The bank **opens** at 9:00 a.m. |
| 3. Do not put *be* in front of another verb in the simple present. | ✓ He works at a bank.<br>✗ He <u>is work</u> at a bank. |

**4** Circle the correct form of the verb to complete each sentence.

1. Doctor Moffett **love** / (**loves**) his job.

2. He **study** / **studies** ants.

3. A salesperson **sell** / **sells** products for a company.

4. You and Anita **work** / **works** on weekends.

5. Nurses **help** / **helps** people.

6. We **write** / **writes** science books.

7. Our office **close** / **closes** at 7:00 p.m.

8. She **take** / **takes** classes at the business school.

9. You **walk** / **walks** to work every day.

10. I **start** / **starts** work at 8:00 a.m. every morning.

**5** **WRITE & SPEAK.** List three activities you do often. Share your sentences with a partner. Then tell the class about your partner.

Student A: *I study. I play games. I talk with my friends.*

Student B: *Maria studies. She plays games. She talks with her friends.*

**6** Complete each sentence with the correct form of the verb in parentheses.

1. A zookeeper _____feeds_____ (feed) animals.

2. Computer programmers _____ (write) software.

3. Photographers _____ (take) photos.

4. A chef _____ (cook) food.

5. A firefighter _____ (fight) fires.

6. Musicians _____ (play) instruments.

7. A farmer _____ (work) on a farm.

8. A dancer _____ (dance).

▼ A zookeeper feeds a rhino at the Sedgwick County Zoo in Wichita, Kansas, USA.

## 3.2 Simple Present Spelling Rules: -s and -es Endings

| 1. Add -s to most verbs. | close–close**s** | love–love**s** | stop–stop**s** |
|---|---|---|---|
| | dance–dance**s** | open–open**s** | take–take**s** |
| | exercise–exercise**s** | play–play**s** | write–write**s** |
| | feed–feed**s** | put–put**s** | work–work**s** |
| 2. Add -es to verbs ending in -sh, -ch, -s, -x, and -z. | wash–wash**es** | dress–dress**es** | buzz–buzz**es** |
| | teach–teach**es** | relax–relax**es** | |
| 3. Change -y to -i and add -es to verbs ending in a consonant + y. | carry–carri**es** | copy–copi**es** | study–studi**es** |

See page **A2** for additional spelling rules for -s, -es, and -ies endings.

**7** Write each verb with the correct *-s, -es,* or *-ies* ending.

1. study _____studies_____
2. fish _____
3. pass _____
4. worry _____
5. explore _____
6. bite _____
7. buy _____

8. help _____
9. miss _____
10. fly _____
11. fix _____
12. watch _____
13. like _____
14. pay _____

## 3.3 Irregular Verbs: *Do, Go,* and *Have*

| Subject | Verb | | Subject | Verb | |
|---------|------|--|---------|------|--|
| I<br>You | **do** | the dishes every day. | He | **does** | the dishes every day. |
| We<br>You | **go** | to work at 7:00 a.m. | She<br>It | **goes** | to work at 7:00 a.m. |
| They | **have** | dinner at 6:00 a.m. | | **has** | dinner at 6:00 a.m. |

The verbs *do, go,* and *have* are irregular for *he, she, it,* and singular subjects.

She **goes** home at six-thirty.
He **has** a meeting at two-thirty.
John **does** the laundry on Sunday night.

**8** Complete the paragraphs with the correct form of the verbs in parentheses.

## Manuel and Lila Vega

Manuel and Lila Vega (1) _____have_____ (have) a busy lifestyle. Manuel is a doctor at a hospital. He works at night, so he (2) _____ (go) to work at 7:00 p.m. and comes home at 7:00 a.m. His wife Lila works at a bank. She (3) _____ (go) to work at 8:00 a.m. and comes home at 6:00 p.m. They don't see each other a lot during the week.

Manuel and Lila also (4) _____ (have) two children, Luis and Carla. Every morning they all (5) _____ (have) breakfast together at 7:30. Then, Luis and Carla (6) _____ (go) to school, and Lila (7) _____ (go) to work. Manuel (8) _____ (do) the dishes, and then (9) _____ (go) to bed. Carla usually (10) _____ (do) her homework at a friend's house in the afternoon, and Luis (11) _____ (have) soccer practice. Manuel gets up at 4:00 p.m. At 6:00 p.m., he (12) _____ (have) dinner with Lila, Luis, and Carla. After dinner, he (13) _____ (go) to work. Manuel and Lila (14) _____ (have) a busy schedule during the week, but on weekends they relax.

# PRACTICE

CD1-31

**9** Complete the paragraphs with the correct form of the verbs in parentheses. Then listen and check your answers.

## Bush Pilots

Bush pilots (1) _____ have _____ (have) interesting jobs. They (2) _____ (fly) special planes to Alaska's bush country. (This is a wild area, far away from cities with airports.) Bush pilots (3) _____ (carry) people or supplies in their bush planes. They also (4) _____ (help) rescue people.

Paul Claus is a famous bush pilot. He (5) _____ (have) a lot of experience, and he is an excellent pilot. Paul also (6) _____ (own) a hotel in Alaska. He (7) _____ (fly) customers to his hotel and (8) _____ (take) them on adventures. He (9) _____ (go) to interesting places with them. It's an exciting job!

▲ Bush planes on a glacier in Denali National Park, Alaska, USA

**10 EDIT.** Read the paragraph. Find and correct five more errors with the simple present.

Bill is a mechanic. He know ˢ a lot about cars. He work at a garage. He fix cars and talks to customers. They asks questions about their cars. Bill works from 8:00 a.m. to 6:00 p.m. every day. He haves a busy schedule, but he like his job very much.

**11 PRONUNCIATION.** Read the chart and listen to the examples. Then complete the exercises.

CD1-32

| PRONUNCIATION | Simple Present -*s* and –*es* Endings | | |
|---|---|---|---|
| The ending of third-person singular verbs has three sounds: /s/, /z/, /əz/ | **/s/** walks | **/z/** pays | **/əz/** fixes |
| 1. Say **/s/** after /p/, /t/, /k/, and /f/ sounds. | stop-stops | put-puts | work-works    laugh-laughs |
| 2. Say **/z/** after /b/, /d/, /g/, /l/, /m/, /n/, /ŋ/, /r/, /v/, and /ð/ sounds, and after vowel sounds. | rub-rubs read-reads bag-bags feel-feels | come-comes spin-spins sing-sings hear-hears | love-loves bathe-bathes pay-pays go-goes |
| 3. Say **/əz/** after verbs that end in /s/, /z/, /ʃ/, /tʃ/, /dʒ/, and /ks/. | kiss-kisses buzz-buzzes | wash-washes watch-watches | judge-judges relax-relaxes |

See page **A4** for a guide to pronunciation symbols.

**A** Read the sentences about Rick's schedule. Then listen and circle the sound you hear for the verb in each sentence.

**Rick's Schedule**

| | | /s/ | /z/ | /əz/ |
|---|---|---|---|---|
| 1. | Rick **wakes** up at 6:15 a.m. every morning. | (/s/) | /z/ | /əz/ |
| 2. | He **jogs** for an hour in the park. | /s/ | /z/ | /əz/ |
| 3. | Then he **takes** a shower. | /s/ | /z/ | /əz/ |
| 4. | He **brushes** his teeth. | /s/ | /z/ | /əz/ |
| 5. | He **eats** breakfast at 7:45. | /s/ | /z/ | /əz/ |
| 6. | He **reads** the newspaper. | /s/ | /z/ | /əz/ |
| 7. | He **washes** the dishes. | /s/ | /z/ | /əz/ |
| 8. | Then he **drives** to work. | /s/ | /z/ | /əz/ |
| 9. | He **starts** work at 8:30. | /s/ | /z/ | /əz/ |
| 10. | He **goes** home at 5:30. | /s/ | /z/ | /əz/ |
| 11. | He **relaxes** on Saturday and Sunday. | /s/ | /z/ | /əz/ |
| 12. | He **loves** weekends! | /s/ | /z/ | /əz/ |

**B** Work with a partner. Practice reading the sentences from exercise **A**. Pay attention to the pronunciation of the –s and -es endings.

## 12 LISTEN & SPEAK.

**A** Look at the list of activities in the chart. Then listen to the conversation between two teachers. Who does each activity? Check (✓) the correct column(s).

| | Alvaro | Galina |
|---|---|---|
| 1. lives in Ecuador | ✓ | |
| 2. lives in Russia | | |
| 3. teaches at a university | | |
| 4. teaches at a high school | | |
| 5. teaches biology | | |
| 6. gets up early | | |
| 7. goes home at 3:00 p.m. | | |
| 8. goes home at 6:00 p.m. | | |
| 9. meets with students after class | | |
| 10. relaxes on Saturday | | |

**B** Compare your answers from exercise **A** with a partner. Then practice saying sentences about Alvaro and Galina. Use the information from the chart.

*Alvaro lives in Ecuador.*

**C** In your notebook, write sentences about Alvaro and Galina. Use the chart from exercise **A** to help you.

Alvaro lives in Ecuador.

## 13 READ, SPEAK & WRITE.

**A** Read the e-mail about Rosa's new job. Guess her job. Then discuss your idea with a partner.

To: Sato, Akiko
Subject: New Job!

Hi Akiko,

Good news! I have a new job. I work for an office supply company. I have a busy schedule, but I love the work. On Monday, I go to the office. I meet with my boss and plan my schedule for the week. I visit customers and sell our products during the week. I drive to different cities here in New York. I also fly to California every month. I work really hard, but the job pays well, so I'm happy.

See you soon!

Rosa

**B** Write five sentences about Rosa's new job. Use the information from the e-mail in exercise **A**.

Rosa goes to the office on Monday.

▶ A ballet dancer

## 14 APPLY. In your notebook, write a paragraph about a friend's or family member's job. Do not write the name of his or her job. Use the model to help you.

My cousin Maya has an interesting job. She has ballet class every morning. Then, she goes to the gym and exercises for two hours. She has a short break after lunch, and then she practices her dances. She gives performances on the weekends.

**B** Work with a partner. Exchange paragraphs and try to guess the person's job.

### EXPLORE

CD1-35

**1** **READ** the article about life on the International Space Station. Notice the words in **bold**.

# Life on the Space Station

Astronauts on the International Space Station have a busy schedule. Every day they wake up at 7:00 GMT.[1] **From 7:00 to 8:00,** they wash up and eat breakfast. **At 8:00 in the morning,** they call Ground Control[2] in their countries. After they talk to Ground Control, their workday begins. The astronauts **don't do** the same thing every day. Their schedules change every week.

The astronauts **don't work** all the time. Each day they exercise for an hour **in the morning** and an hour **in the afternoon**. After dinner, they have free time. Then, it's time to go to sleep. Sometimes this isn't easy because the sun rises and sets 16 times each day on the space station.

The astronauts' work **doesn't end** on Friday. They work a half day **on Saturday** and all day **on Sunday**. Astronauts are very busy people.

[1] **GMT:** Greenwich Mean Time
[2] **Ground Control:** People on Earth who work with astronauts in space.

◄ The International Space Station (ISS)

**2 CHECK.** Match each of the astonauts' activities with the correct time.

1. They wash up and have breakfast. __d__    a. at 8:00 in the morning

2. They talk to Ground Control. _____    b. after dinner

3. They exercise. _____    c. on Saturday

4. They have some free time. _____    d̶. from 7:00 to 8:00 in the morning

5. They need to work a half day. _____    e. for an hour in the morning and an hour in the afternoon

**3 DISCOVER.** Complete the exercises to learn about the grammar in this lesson.

**A** Find these sentences in the article from exercise **1**. Write the missing words.

1. The astronauts don't _____ the same thing every day.

2. Astronauts don't _____ all the time.

3. The astronauts' work doesn't _____ on Friday.

**B** Look at the sentences from exercise **A**. Then circle **T** for *true* or **F** for *false* for each statement below. Discuss your answers with your classmates and teacher.

1. Use the base form of the verb after *don't*.    **T**    **F**

2. Add an *-s* to the base form of the verb after *doesn't*.    **T**    **F**

# LEARN

## 3.4 Simple Present: Negative Statements

| Subject | Do Not/ Don't | Base Form of Verb | Subject | Does Not/ Doesn't | Base Form of Verb |
|---|---|---|---|---|---|
| I<br>You<br>We<br>You<br>They | do not<br>don't | work. | He<br>She<br>It | does not<br>doesn't | work. |

**Be careful!** In negative statements with *does not* or *doesn't*, do not add *-s* to the base form of the verb.

✓ She **doesn't exercise** every day.
✗ She doesn't exercise<u>s</u> every day.

**4** Circle *doesn't* or *don't* to complete each sentence.

1. An astronaut on the International Space Station (**doesn't**) / **don't** have a lot of free time.

2. Astronauts **doesn't** / **don't** work all day on Saturday.

3. An astronaut **doesn't** / **don't** have the same schedule every day.

4. We **doesn't** / **don't** work on weekends.

5. I **doesn't** / **don't** work in an office.

6. My office **doesn't** / **don't** have a window.

7. She **doesn't** / **don't** travel for her job.

8. You **doesn't** / **don't** have a busy schedule.

**5** Change each affirmative statement to a negative statement.

1. My brother has a job. _My brother doesn't have a job._

2. I drive to work. _____

3. Pilots fix planes. _____

4. Our teacher does homework. _____

5. I go to the gym in the morning. _____

6. We have class on Sunday. _____

7. You teach biology. _____

8. We have an exam on Saturday night. _____

**6 SPEAK.** Work with a partner. Make negative statements with the words below.

| | |
|---|---|
| I ... | work |
| My mother ... | study |
| My father ... | exercise |
| My ... | drive to class/work |

Student A: *I don't drive to class.*     Student B: *My mother doesn't study.*

## 3.5  Prepositions of Time (Part 2)

| | |
|---|---|
| 1. Many time expressions are prepositional phrases. A prepositional phrase is a preposition + a noun. | Preposition Noun<br>**at** three-thirty<br>**in** the afternoon<br>**at** night<br>**on** Sunday |
| 2. Remember: Use *at* with specific times and in the phrase *at night*.<br><br>Use *in* with *morning, afternoon,* and *evening*.<br><br>Use *on* with days of the week and specific dates. | The bank opens **at** nine o'clock.<br>We relax **at** night.<br><br>We go to work **in** the morning.<br>We eat dinner **in** the evening.<br><br>I don't work **on** Saturday.<br>The meeting is **on** Monday afternoon.<br>His birthday is on November 25th. |
| 3. To show when an activity begins and ends, use *from . . . to*. | She works **from** nine **to** five-thirty. |
| 4. Use *until* to talk about an activity that continues up to a specific time. | The bank is open **until** four o'clock. |
| 5. A sentence can have more than one prepositional phrase. | He wakes up at five-thirty in the morning. |

For Prepositions of Time (Part 1), see Unit 2, Lesson 3.

**REAL ENGLISH**

To be less specific, we use *around* and *about*.

> *We usually eat dinner at **about** 8:00. (We don't eat exactly at 8:00 every night.)*

> *I usually leave work at **around** 6:00. (I don't leave work at exactly 6:00 every night.)*

**7** Underline the prepositional phrases in these sentences.

1. We have class <u>from 9:40 to 10:50</u>.

2. On Wednesday, I have class until 3:30.

3. The party is on Saturday night.

4. The meeting doesn't end until 3:00.

5. My workweek is from Monday to Friday.

6. I work from 9:00 to 7:00 on Tuesday and Wednesday.

7. I don't work on weekends.

8. She doesn't get home until 4:00 in the afternoon.

**8** Complete each sentence with the correct preposition(s).

1. She works ____at____ night.

2. The meeting is _____ Wednesday afternoon.

3. I sleep _____ 9:30 _____ the morning _____ Saturday.

4. I work _____ Monday _____ Friday.

5. Class starts _____ 8:30 _____ the morning.

6. We study _____ night.

7. The library is open _____ eleven o'clock _____ night.

8. I have lunch _____ 12:00 _____ 1:00 every day.

9. She goes to bed _____ 1:00 a.m. _____ Friday and Saturday.

10. We have a break _____ 10:30 _____ 10:45 _____ the morning.

**9** **WRITE & SPEAK.** Complete the sentences with prepositional phrases of time. Use the prepositions from chart **3.5** on page 91. Then share your sentences with a partner.

1. I have breakfast _____at 7:00._____

2. English class starts _____

3. We have class from _____

4. I have lunch _____

5. I have dinner _____

## 3.6  *Like, Need,* and *Want* + Infinitive

| Subject | Verb | Infinitive | |
|---------|------|-----------|---|
| I | like | to exercise | in the morning. |
| He | likes | | |
| We | need | to relax | today. |
| She | needs | | |
| They | want | to meet | every week. |
| He | wants | | |

| | |
|---|---|
| 1. An infinitive is *to* + the base form of the verb. | He likes **to play** soccer. |
| 2. Some verbs are followed by infinitives. | We <u>want</u> **to play** soccer.<br>She <u>needs</u> **to call** her boss.<br>I <u>like</u> **to read**.<br><br>✓ We **want to leave**.<br>✗ We <u>want leave</u>. |

**10** Put the words in the correct order to make sentences.

1. Saturday / to / work / They / need / on ___They need to work on Saturday.___

2. He / have / lunch / wants / at / 1:00 / to _____

3. tonight / to / need / work / until / 7:00 / You _____

4. need / buy / I / to / computer / a / new _____

5. She / play / to / likes / tennis _____

6. want / watch / to / the game / We _____

7. to / He / study / in the library / likes _____

8. need / I / do / my homework / to _____

9. need / I / my / call / mother / to _____

10. ask / to / wants / a / She / question _____

# PRACTICE

**11 SPEAK.**

**A** Work with a partner. Complete the sentences with information about yourself. Use prepositional phrases, the simple present, and infinitives.

| | |
|---|---|
| I get up . . . | I like . . . on weekends. |
| I have breakfast . . . | I need . . . today. |
| On weekends, I sleep until . . . | I do my homework . . . |
| I go to bed . . . | I want to . . . |

Student A: *I go to bed at midnight.*

Student B: *I do my homework in the morning.*

**B** Work in a group. Say three sentences about your partner. Use the information from exercise **A**.

Student A: *Sun-hee does her homework in the afternoon.*

Student B: *Walid goes to bed at midnight.*

Student C: *Maria likes to relax on Sundays.*

**REAL ENGLISH**

Use *on weekends* to talk about activities that happen every weekend or on most weekends.

*We relax on weekends.*
*She doesn't work on weekends.*

## 12 READ, WRITE & SPEAK.

**A** Read the information about Lia. Then complete the sentences in the chart below with the correct form of the verbs in parentheses and the correct prepositions of time.

> Lia is from Indonesia. She works in Toronto, Canada. This is her first time away from home, and she misses her life in Indonesia. Her life is very different in Canada!

| In Indonesia |
| --- |
| 1. Lia's mother _____cooks_____ (cook) breakfast for her. |
| 2. Lia _____ (have) classes _____ 9:30 _____ 12:30 from Monday to Saturday. |
| 3. Lia _____ (go) out with her friends _____ weekends. |

| In Canada |
| --- |
| 4. Lia's mother _____ (not cook) breakfast for her. |
| 5. Lia _____ (have) breakfast at a coffee shop _____ about 7:15 _____ the morning. |
| 6. Lia _____ (not have) classes _____ the morning. |
| 7. She _____ (work) _____ 9:00 _____ 5:00 _____ Monday _____ Friday. |
| 8. She also _____ (study) at a business school because she _____ (want to) start a business in Indonesia someday. |
| 9. She _____ (have) a class _____ 6:00 _____ 9:00 _____ night _____ Tuesday and Thursday. |
| 10. Lia _____ (not have) many friends in Toronto. |
| 11. She _____ (not go) out _____ weekends. |
| 12. She _____ (be) lonely. |
| 13. She _____ (miss) her friends in Indonesia. |

**B** Is your life similar to Lia's life, or is it different? Complete the sentences with information about your life.

1. My life is (similar to / different from) Lia's life. In the morning, I

   _____ .

2. During the day, I _____ from _____ to _____ .

3. At night, I _____ .

4. I _____ friends in _____ .

5. On weekends, I _____ .

6. I _____ lonely.

**C** Work with a partner. Share your sentences from exercise **B**.

*My life is different from Lia's life. In the morning, I have breakfast at home.*

**13 EDIT.** Read the paragraph. Find and correct six more errors with negatives and prepositions of time.

> Iris is a reporter. She works for a newspaper. She asks questions and writes articles.
> doesn't
> She ~~don't~~ drive to work. She walks. She don't work in the morning. She works from 2:00 p.m.
> in 11:00 p.m. She doesn't goes to bed early. She goes to bed on 1:00 a.m. She doesn't work at
> Saturday and Sunday. She relaxes in weekends.

**CD1-36**

**14** Complete the conversation below. Use words from the box. You can use some words more than once. Then listen and check your answers.

| work | have | from | at | to | in | on |
|------|------|------|----|----|----|----|

**Ted:** Hi, Jana!

**Jana:** Hey, Ted! How about coffee sometime? (1) I'm free ____in____ the morning ____on____ Thursday.

**Ted:** (2) I _____ class in the morning.
(3) How about _____ 2:00?

**Jana:** Sorry. I'm not free then. (4) I _____ soccer practice _____ 2:00 _____ 4:00. How about Saturday?

**Ted:** I'm sorry. (5) I _____ on Saturday _____ 9:00 _____ 5:00. How about Sunday afternoon?

**Jana:** Sure. That sounds good. (6) How about _____ 2:00?

**Ted:** Great. See you then!

**REAL ENGLISH**

Use *How about . . .?* to make suggestions.

A: *Hi. How about coffee this afternoon? I'm free at 4:00.*

B: *Sorry. I work from 9:00 to 5:00. How about Saturday afternoon?*

**15 SPEAK.** Work with a partner. Partner A, look at the schedule on this page. Partner B, look at the schedule on page **A5**. Do not show each other your schedules. Find a time to meet for coffee. Use the suggestions and answers from the chart below.

Partner A's Schedule

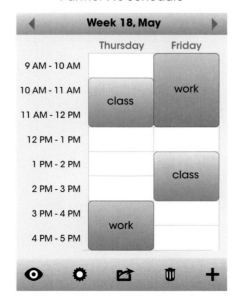

| Suggestions | Answers |
|-------------|---------|
| How about coffee sometime? | Sure. That sounds good. |
| How about (*time of day*)? | I'm sorry. I have <u>(class / practice / work / a meeting)</u>. |
| How about (*time*)? | |
| OK. See you then. | Great. |

## 16  LISTEN & SPEAK.

CD1-37

**A** Listen to the information about workweeks around the world. Check (✓) the workdays for each country in the chart.

| | M | T | W | Th | F | Sat | Sun |
|---|---|---|---|---|---|---|---|
| Canada | | | | | | | |
| United States | | | | | | | |
| Thailand | | | | | | | |
| Austria | | | | | | | |
| Saudi Arabia | | | | | | | |
| United Arab Emirates | | | | | | | |
| Japan | | | | | | | |
| India | | | | | | | |

**B** Work with a partner. Use the information in your chart from exercise **A** to make true and false statements. Say a statement. Your partner will say "true" or "false" and correct your false statements.

Student A: *People in Canada don't work on Monday.*

Student B: *That's false. People in Canada work on Monday.*

**C** Tell your partner about the workweek in your country or a country you know about.

*People in my country work from Monday to Friday. They don't work on Saturday and Sunday.*

## 17  APPLY. Write six sentences about the workweeks in different countries. You can write about countries from exercise **16A** or use your own ideas.

_People in Canada work from Monday to Friday._

_____

_____

_____

_____

_____

## EXPLORE

**1**   **READ** the conversation about the elephant keepers in Kenya. Notice the words in **bold**.

# Elephant Keepers

**Bill:**   Wow! This is an interesting article.

**Sue:**   Oh, baby elephants! Look at **them**! They're so cute! Where are their mothers?

**Bill:**   Hunters killed **them**.

**Sue:**   That's terrible!

**Bill:**   Yeah, it is. These men are elephant keepers. They work at a place for orphan[1] elephants in Kenya. They feed **the baby elephants**, take care of **them**, and even play **soccer** with them.

**Sue:**   Hmmm. Elephant keeper. That's an interesting job.

**Bill:**   Yes, but it isn't easy. The keepers need to feed **the baby elephants** every three hours.

**Sue:**   Really? What about at night?

**Bill:**   They need to feed **them** at night, too. The keepers sleep in buildings with the baby elephants. . . . Listen to this quote from the article. One of the keepers says, "Every three hours you feel **a trunk** reach up and pull **your blankets[2]** off. The elephants are our alarms."

**Sue:**   That's funny. Smart elephants! I want to read **that article**.

[1] An **orphan** is a child or baby animal whose parents are dead.

[2] People use **blankets** in bed at night to stay warm.

▼ Baby elephants and elephant keepers in Nairobi, Kenya

▲ Baby elephants play with their keeper in a wildlife refuge in Nairobi, Kenya.

**2 CHECK.** Read the false statements about elephant keepers. Then correct each statement to make it true.

                                          ↓ elephants
1. The keepers feed the ~~baby~~.

2. Hunters killed the baby elephants.

3. The keepers work in Botswana.

4. The keepers sleep in houses with their families.

**3 DISCOVER.** Complete the exercises to learn about the grammar in this lesson.

**A** Look at these sentences from the conversation from exercise **1** on page 97. Notice the words in **bold**. Then choose the correct word to complete the statement below.

1. They feed **the baby elephants** . . .

2. I want to read **that article.**

The words in bold in these sentences are _____ .

a. subjects          b. objects of the verb

**B** Discuss your answer from exercise **A** with your classmates and teacher.

# LEARN

## 3.7 Verb + Object / Verb + Preposition + Object

| Subject | Verb/Verb + Preposition | Object | |
|---------|-------------------------|--------|---|
| I | teach | children. | |
| He | drives | a bus | every day. |
| We | listen to | music | a lot. |
| She | looks at | magazines | in her free time. |

1. Many verbs take an object. The object receives the action of the verb. It can be a person or thing.

   Doctors <u>help</u> **people.**
   We <u>study</u> **English.**
   She <u>needs</u> **a new car.**

2. Some verbs are followed by a preposition. Verb + preposition combinations also take an object.

   Many people <u>listen to</u> **music.**
   I <u>worry about</u> **my grades** a lot.
   He <u>waits for</u> **his sister** every day after class.

**4** Circle the verb and underline the object in each sentence.

1. He (helps) <u>baby elephants</u>.

2. They play soccer.

3. He likes his job.

4. She writes articles.

5. We visit customers every day.

6. You need a new computer.

7. I ride my bike every day.

8. Makiko loves weekends.

**5** Put the words in the correct order to make sentences.

1. has / a / new / job / He ___He has a new job.___

2. A / cars / mechanic / fixes _____

3. has / huge / office / a / Jasmin _____

4. feed / Zookeepers / animals _____

5. her boss / Deanna / every day / talks to _____

6. beautiful / photographs / takes / Jay _____

7. music / listen to / I / at night _____

8. misses / Katrina / her friends _____

**6** **WRITE & SPEAK.** Complete each sentence with an object. Then share your statements with a partner.

1. I speak _____ .

2. I talk to _____ every day.

3. I watch _____ on TV.

4. I listen to _____ .

5. I like _____ .

6. I love _____ .

Student A: *I watch movies on TV.*

Student B: *I love my children.*

## 3.8 Object Pronouns

| Subject Pronouns | Example Sentences |
|---|---|
| I | **I** like Tina. |
| he | **He** likes Tina. |
| she | **She** is nice. |
| it | **It** is fun. |
| we | **We** know Al and Eva. |
| you | **You** are friends with Al and Eva. |
| they | **They** are your friends. |

| Object Pronouns | Example Sentences |
|---|---|
| me | Tina likes **me**. |
| him | She likes **him**. |
| her | I like **her**. |
| it | We like **it**. |
| us | They know **us**. |
| you | They like **you**. |
| them | You like **them**. |

| | |
|---|---|
| 1. Object pronouns replace object nouns. | He rides <u>the bus</u>. → He rides **it** every day.<br>I talk to <u>my parents</u> a lot. → I talk to **them** a lot. |
| 2. Pronouns refer back to an earlier person or thing. | George loves <u>pizza</u>. He eats **it** every night.<br><br>My sister's <u>son and daughter</u> are cute. I love **them**. |

**7** Complete the exercises.

**A** Circle the object pronoun in each pair of sentences.

1. Angel has a new job. He likes (it) a lot.

2. I'm Cory's boss. He works for me.

3. Sally is Joe's employee. She works for him.

4. My sister lives in Australia. I miss her a lot.

5. It's an excellent newspaper. I read it every day.

6. You are in my class. I sit behind you.

7. We go to the park on weekends. Henri sometimes comes with us.

8. Paulina has two dogs. She walks them in the park every morning.

**B**  Work with a partner. Look at each sentence in exercise **A** again. What word or phrase does the object pronoun refer back to? Draw an arrow back to it.

1.  Angel has a new job. He likes it a lot.

**8**  Complete each sentence with the correct object pronoun.

1.  Nico's sister is in town this week. I want to meet _____her_____.

2.  It's my father's birthday today. I need to call _____.

3.  She lives near her grandparents. She visits _____ on weekends.

4.  Alexa has a difficult job, but she likes _____.

5.  Are those students in our class? I don't know _____.

6.  The teacher wants to meet with _____. She has a question about your homework.

7.  Nadia and Jen want to attend the meeting. Please invite _____.

8.  Fumiko is my best friend. She calls _____ every day.

9.  Ron and Ella are our neighbors. They live near _____.

10. Spinach is my brother's favorite vegetable. He loves _____!

# PRACTICE

**9**  Complete the exercises.

**A**  Put the words in the correct order to make sentences.

1.  thinks / about / He / Linda / every day  ___He thinks about Linda every day.___

2.  sometimes / Mr. and Mrs. Lee / visit / We _____

3.  my parents / don't call / I / every day _____

4.  her sister / Kate / loves _____

5.  Fiona and Ken / He / sees / at work _____

6.  music / doesn't / listen to / He / every night _____

7.  my bike / I / ride / weekends / on _____

8.  like / doesn't / his job / He _____

**B**  Look at the sentences in exercise **A**. Replace each object with an object pronoun.

　　　　　　　　　　　　*her*
He thinks about ~~Linda~~ every day.

## 10 LISTEN, WRITE & SPEAK.

**CD1-39**

**A** Listen to the information about three jobs. Match the jobs with the correct names. Write the letter on the line.

> a. pet food taster   b. crocodile hunters   c. golf ball diver

1. Kelly _____   2. Tim _____   3. Max and Jackson _____

**CD1-39**

**B** Read each statement. Then listen again. Circle **T** for *true* and **F** for *false*.

| | | |
|---|---|---|
| 1. Kelly likes her job a lot. | **T** | **F** |
| 2. The company pays Kelly a lot of money. | **T** | **F** |
| 3. Tim sells balls at a golf course. | **T** | **F** |
| 4. Tim doesn't wear scuba gear. | **T** | **F** |
| 5. An alligator lives in the lake. | **T** | **F** |
| 6. Max and Jackson live in South Africa. | **T** | **F** |
| 7. Max and Jackson kill crocodiles. | **T** | **F** |
| 8. Max and Jackson are very careful. | **T** | **F** |

▲ Golf ball divers

**C** All of the statements below are false. Change each statement to make it true. Use a pronoun to replace the words in **bold**.

1. Tim looks for **golf balls** in the ocean.
   _He doesn't look for them in the ocean. OR He looks for them in a lake._

2. Tim sells **used golf balls**. _____

3. Tim doesn't like **his job**. _____

4. Tim doesn't watch for **the alligator**. _____

5. Kelly likes **her job**. _____

6. People want **Kelly's job**. _____

7. Kelly eats **animal food**. _____

8. The pet food company doesn't pay **Kelly**. _____

9. An animal park pays **Max** and **Jackson**. _____

10. Most people don't worry about **crocodiles**. _____

**D** Work with a partner. Rank the jobs. Write 1, 2, or 3 for each category. (1 is the highest rank, and 3 is the lowest rank.)

|  | danger | difficulty | excitement | fun |
|---|---|---|---|---|
| pet food taster |  |  |  |  |
| crocodile hunter |  |  |  |  |
| golf ball diver |  |  |  |  |

*Pet food taster is number 1 for difficulty.*

**11 READ & SPEAK.** Work with a partner. Read about one of the people below. Then close your book. Tell your partner about the person from your paragraph. Use the *-s* form of the simple present and object pronouns.

Student A: *His name is Dan. He loves dogs and they love him.*

## Dan

My name is Dan. I love dogs and they love me. I'm a professional dog walker. People pay me, and I take their dogs for walks. Sometimes I take the dogs to the park and run with them. The dogs are very fast, so it's good exercise for me. I have an unusual job, but I love it.

## Clara

My name is Clara. I'm a bus driver. I drive a school bus. I take children to school in the morning and take them home in the afternoon. They say hello to me every morning, and sometimes they bring cookies or flowers. I love children, so it's a good job for me.

**12 APPLY.**

**A** Write five sentences about your work, your studies, or your family. Use objects and object pronouns.

I am a nurse. I help patients.

_____

_____

_____

_____

_____

**B** Work with a partner. Share your sentences from exercise **A**.

## EXPLORE

**1** **READ** the advice on how to get a job in game design. Notice the words in **bold**.

# How to Get a Job in Game Design

Computer games are very popular. Even orangutans in the zoo enjoy them! A lot of people want to work in game design. Is it difficult to find a job? Lukas Bidelspach is an artist for an online game company. Here is his advice.[1]

- **Don't play** games all the time. Make them! **Use** your time to improve your skills.[2]

- **Don't worry** about a college degree. Experience is more important.

- **Show** your work to other people. **Listen** to their advice.

- **Keep** examples of your work. **Send** them to a game company.

- **Get** experience with a team. **Volunteer**[3] to work at a company.

- **Don't ask for** a lot of money at your first job. **Work** hard.

Good luck!

[1] People give **advice** to help other people.
[2] A **skill** is an ability that helps you do a job well.
[3] A **volunteer** does work for no money.

▼ An orangutan plays computer games in Zoo Atlanta, Atlanta, Georgia, USA.

▲ Young Buddhist monks play video games in Bodhgaya, India.

**2  CHECK.** Look at each idea in the chart. Does Lukas think it is a good idea or a bad idea? Check (✓) the correct column.

| | Ideas | Good Idea | Bad Idea |
|---|---|---|---|
| 1. | make games | ✓ | |
| 2. | play games all the time | | |
| 3. | worry about a college degree | | |
| 4. | get experience | | |
| 5. | ask for a lot of money | | |

**3  DISCOVER.** Complete the exercises to learn about the grammar in this unit.

**A**  Find and complete these sentences in the article from exercise **1**. Write the missing words.

1. _____ games all the time. Make them!

2. _____ about a college degree.

3. _____ your work to other people.

4. _____ examples of your work.

5. _____ hard.

**B**  Look at the sentences from exercise **A**. Then circle **T** for *true* or **F** for *false* for each statement below. Discuss your answers with your classsmates and teachers.

1.  All the verbs are negative.                          **T**      **F**

2.  We don't need to write the subjects with these verbs.   **T**      **F**

3.  The sentences all give advice.                       **T**      **F**

# LEARN

## 3.9 Imperatives: Affirmative

| Base Form of Verb | |
|---|---|
| **Be** | on time for the meeting. |
| **Close** | the door. |
| **Open** | your books. |

| | |
|---|---|
| 1. Use imperatives to give:<br>   a. commands;<br>   b. instructions;<br>   c. directions;<br>   d. warnings;<br>   e. advice. | a. **Sit** down.<br>b. **Complete** each sentence.<br>c. **Turn** left.<br>d. **Be** careful.<br>e. **Try** again. |
| 2. Use the base form of the verb for imperatives. | **Write** your name and address.<br>**Do** your homework. |
| 3. *You* is the subject of imperatives, but it is not common to write or say *you*. | **Open** your books.<br>**Call** Margaret. |
| 4. To be polite, use *please* with imperatives. | **Please** take your shoes off.<br>Take your shoes off, **please**. |

**4** Underline the imperatives.

1. <u>Try</u> to meet people at game companies.

2. Ask people at game companies about their jobs.

3. Please tell me the truth. Do you really like your job?

4. Bob, please call me when you get this message.

5. Read the directions.

6. It's hot in here. Please open the window.

7. Turn right on Elm Street.

8. Please pass your papers to the center of the room.

**5** Write an imperative for each situation. Use verbs from the box.

| ask | be | eat | give | go | stay | study | wear |
|---|---|---|---|---|---|---|---|

1. A: I have a test tomorrow. I'm not a good student.   B: ____Study____ hard.

2. A: I have a big meeting tomorrow. It's midnight now.   B: _____ to sleep.

3. A: I'm often late to class. I have a test tomorrow.

B: _____ on time.

4. A: I eat junk food every day.

B: _____ healthy food.

5. A: I have a cold. I also need to go shopping.

B: _____ home.

6. A: That old woman doesn't have a seat.

B: Please _____ her your seat.

7. A: Look at all that snow outside.

B: _____ your boots.

8. A: I don't understand the assignment.

B: _____ the teacher.

**6 SPEAK.** Work in a group. Give instructions. Use verbs from the box and imperatives.

| close | open | say | sit down | stand up | write |
|-------|------|-----|----------|----------|-------|

Student A: *Say hello.*

Student B: *Stand up.*

Student C: *Open your book.*

## 3.10 Imperatives: Negative

| Do Not/ Don't | Base Form of Verb | |
|---------------|-------------------|---|
| Do not Don't | **open** | the windows. |

| 1. To make an imperative negative, put *don't* or *do not* before the base form of the verb. | **Don't drink** a lot of coffee. |
|---|---|
| 2. *Do not* is common in formal writing. It is not common in informal writing or conversations. | **Do not** park in front of this building. |

**REAL ENGLISH**

In speaking, *Do not* is sometimes used for emphasis.

> **Do not** *eat this cake! It's for dessert.*
> **Do not** *tell Maria about the party! It's a surprise.*

**7** Underline the imperatives.

1. It's cold. <u>Don't open</u> the window.

2. Don't worry. Everything is OK now.

3. Please don't sit there.

4. Don't stay up late tonight. You have a meeting at 8:00 a.m. tomorrow.

5. I want to read that book. Please don't tell me the ending.

6. Don't forget Eva's birthday. It's tomorrow.

7. Don't be late tomorrow. We have a test.

8. Don't go to that restaurant. The food there is terrible!

**8 SPEAK.** Work with a partner. Change the affirmative imperatives to negative imperatives. Student A reads the affirmative, Student B says the negative. Then change roles.

Student A: *Eat in the library.*

Student B: *Don't eat in the library.*

1. Eat in the library.
2. Be late for work.
3. Sit in that seat.
4. Use the elevator.
5. Call him at midnight.

6. Open the window.
7. Park your car here.
8. Feed the animals.
9. Close your book.
10. Use your phone in class.

# PRACTICE

**9 SPEAK & WRITE.** Work with a partner. What do these signs mean? Match each imperative with the correct sign below.

a. ~~Stop.~~
b. Do not use your cell phone.
c. Be careful.
d. Do not feed the animals.

e. Do not eat or drink.
f. Do not enter.
g. Drive slowly.
h. Be quiet.

1. ___a___     2. _____     3. _____     4. _____

5. _____     6. _____     7. _____     8. _____

**10 EDIT.** Read the advice. Find and correct five more errors with imperatives.

> ### How to Be a Good Employee
>
> _Don't_
> 1. Be on time. ~~Doesn't~~ be late.
>
> 2. Be friendly and polite to customers. You say "thank you."
>
> 3. Don't rude to coworkers.
>
> 4. Don't leaves work early. Stay until five o'clock.
>
> 5. Do not you use your cell phone in meetings.
>
> 6. Doesn't play computer games at work.

**11** Complete the conversations with affirmative or negative imperatives. Use the verbs in the box. You can use each verb more than once.

| call | drink | get | go | quit | save | stay | take |
|------|-------|-----|-----|------|------|------|------|

1. A: I want a job at a computer company, but I also want to take a psychology course.

   B: _____ Don't take _____ a psychology course. _____
   a course in math or computer science.

2. A: I don't like my job. I want to quit.

   B: _____ your job now. _____ another
   job first.

3. A: I have a cold. I need to go to a hospital.

   B: _____ to a hospital. Just _____ a doctor
   or _____ at home and _____ hot tea.

4. A: I'm tired. I need more sleep.

   B: Well, _____ to bed early, and _____
   coffee at night.

5. A: I don't have very much money, but I want to go shopping.

   B: _____ shopping. _____ home and
   _____ your money.

## 12 LISTEN, SPEAK & WRITE.

CD1-41

**A** Read the list of activities. Then listen to advice on how to be an underwater photographer. Does the speaker think each activity is a good idea or a bad idea? Check (✓) the correct column.

|  | Good Idea | Bad Idea |
|---|---|---|
| 1. Swim a lot. |  |  |
| 2. Learn about the ocean. |  |  |
| 3. Try to catch fish. |  |  |
| 4. Choose the right camera. |  |  |
| 5. Practice in a swimming pool. |  |  |
| 6. Jump into the water with your camera. |  |  |
| 7. Leave your camera in the sun. |  |  |
| 8. Have fun. |  |  |

▼ A hawksbill turtle

**B** Compare your answers from exercise A with a partner.

**C** Complete the chart with information from exercise **A**. Use affirmative and negative imperatives.

| How to Be an Underwater Photographer: Advice | |
|---|---|
| Good Ideas | Bad Ideas |
| Swim a lot. |  |

## 13 APPLY.

**A** Work with a group. Discuss ways to improve your English. Use affirmative and negative imperatives.

*Read in English.*

*Don't miss class.*

**B** Make a chart in your notebook. Organize your ideas from exercise **A** in a chart. Use affirmative and negative imperatives. Use the chart from exercise **12C** as a model.

**C** As a group, present your advice to the class.

*Improve your English! Here is our advice. Read in English. . . .*

**Charts
3.1, 3.4,
3.7, 3.8**

**1** Change each affirmative statement to a negative statement. Then change each underlined object to an object pronoun.

1. She reads <u>the newspaper</u> every morning. _____ *She doesn't read it every morning.* _____

2. She works with <u>Todd and Oscar</u>. _____

3. My brother has <u>my book</u>. _____

4. She teaches <u>Barbara and me</u>. _____

5. We talk to <u>our friends</u> every day. _____

6. She studies <u>biology</u>. _____

7. He knows <u>my sister</u>. _____

8. He fixes <u>cars</u>. _____

**Charts
3.1–3.5**

**2** Look at the work schedule. Then complete the sentences below. Use the correct prepositions of time and the verbs in parentheses. Use the negative form when necessary.

| Name | Days | Times | Break |
|------|------|-------|-------|
| Petra | MWF | 9:00 a.m. – 5:30 p.m. | 1:00 – 1:45 p.m. |
| Ali | M–F | 3:00 a.m. – 12:00 p.m. | 8:00 – 8:45 a.m. |
| Nadia | T/Th | 11:00 p.m. – 6:00 a.m. | 2:30 – 3:00 a.m. |
| Ken | T/Th | 9:00 p.m. – 6:00 a.m. | 2:00 – 2:30 a.m. |
| Cathy | M–F | 10:00 a.m. – 6:00 p.m. | 2:00 – 2:30 p.m. |

1. Petra _____ *works* _____ (work) from 9:00 a.m. _____ 5:30 p.m.

2. Petra _____ (work) _____ Tuesday or Thursday.

3. Ali _____ (work) _____ 12:00 p.m.

4. Ali _____ (have) a break _____ 8:00 a.m.

5. Nadia _____ (work) _____ the afternoon.

6. Nadia and Ken _____ (work) _____ night.

7. Ken _____ (have) a break _____ 2:00 a.m.

8. Cathy _____ (work) _____ 10:00 a.m. _____ 6:00 p.m.

9. Cathy _____ (work) _____ Saturday and Sunday.

10. Cathy and Petra _____ (have) their breaks _____ the afternoon.

Charts
3.1–3.5

**3 EDIT.** Read the paragraph. Find and correct six more errors with verbs and prepositions of time.

_studies_
Max Kraushaar ~~studys~~ in Seattle. He likes to bake. At Friday and Saturday morning, he bake pies. In night, people call or text Max. They order pies, and Max delivers them. He doesn't drives a car. He rides a bicycle and carrys the pies in a basket. He takes orders until 3:00 a.m. Max's company have a funny name. He calls it "Piecycle."

CD1-42
Charts
3.1–3.2,
3.10

**4** Complete the paragraph with the correct form of the verbs in parentheses and prepositions of time. Then listen and check your answers.

## A Dangerous Job

Chris Hansen (1) _____ _works_ _____ (work) in Alaska (2) ____ _in_ ____ the winter. He (3) _____ (have) a job on a crab boat. He (4) _____ (fish) for crabs (5) _____ October (6) _____ January. Chris and the other fishermen (7) _____ (drop) heavy crab pots in the ocean and (8) _____ (pull) them back onto the boat a day later. Chris (9) _____ (not like) his job. It (10) _____ (be) very dangerous on the ocean. Even in bad weather, the work (11) _____ (not stop). The days (12) _____ (be) very short in the winter. The sun (13) _____ (not rise) (14) _____ about 10:00 a.m., and it (15) _____ (go) down (16) _____ around 4:00 p.m. Chris's mother (17) _____ (worry) about him. She (18) _____ (say), "(19) _____ (be) careful, Chris! (20) _____ (not fall) off the boat!" He (21) _____ (say), "(22) _____ (not worry), Mom!"

◀ Fishermen with a crab pot, Bering Sea, near southwest Alaska, USA

**5 SPEAK & WRITE.**

**A** Look at the activities in the chart. Then write notes about your schedule.

| Activity | My Schedule | My Partner's Schedule |
|---|---|---|
| wake up | M-F 8:00; Sat, Sun 12:00 | M-F 7:00; Sat, Sun 9:00 |
| eat lunch | | |
| work | | |
| go shopping | | |
| see my friends | | |

**B** Work with a partner. Discuss your schedules. Take notes about your partner's schedule in the chart in exercise **A**.

From Monday to Friday, I wake up at 7:00 a.m.

**C** Choose two of the activities from the chart in exercise **A**. Write sentences about your schedule and your partner's schedule.

Marisol wakes up at 7:00 a.m. I wake up at 8:00 a.m.

**6 LISTEN, SPEAK & WRITE.**

CD1-43–46

**A** Listen to information about four problems. Write the number next to each problem when you hear about it.

_____ a test / a party          _____ an important meeting / a headache

__1__ a new job / no car          _____ a bad cold / the emergency room at a hospital

CD1-43–46

**B** Listen again. Then write two sentences about each problem.

1. _Tom has a new job. He doesn't have a car._____

2. _____

3. _____

4. _____

**C** Work with a partner. Write advice for the people from exercises **A** and **B**. Use imperatives.

1. Advice for Tom:  _Don't miss work! Ask a friend for help._____

2. Advice for Sue: _____

3. Advice for Jay and Bill: _____

4. Advice for Ann and Jim: _____

## 1 READ & NOTICE THE GRAMMAR.

**A** Read the paragraph. What is the writer's advice for new teachers? Discuss with a partner.

# My Job as a Teacher

I am a teacher. I work from 8:00 a.m. to 1:30 p.m. I teach four English classes. In class, I write on the board. I ask a lot of questions. I use pictures when I teach vocabulary. I don't arrive late. At home, I plan my lessons. I correct homework and tests. My advice for new teachers—learn your students' names on the first day.

---

### GRAMMAR FOCUS

In the paragraph in exercise **A**, the writer uses the simple present to talk about habits or routines and schedules.

I **work** from 8:00 a.m. to 1:30 p.m.
I **don't arrive** late.

---

**B** Read the paragraph in exercise **A** again. Underline the verbs in the simple present. Circle the imperative. Then compare your answers with a partner.

**C** Complete the chart with information from the paragraph in exercise **A**. What does a teacher do in class? At home?

| The Job of a Teacher | |
| --- | --- |
| In Class | At Home |
| She asks a lot of questions. | |
| **Advice:** Learn your students' names. | |

**2 BEFORE YOU WRITE.** Complete the chart with information about your job as a student. What do you do in class? At home? What advice do you have for new students? Use the chart from exercise **1C** as a model.

| My Job as a Student | |
| --- | --- |
| In Class | At Home |
| | |

Advice:

**3 WRITE** a paragraph about your job as a student. Give advice for new students. Use the information from your chart in exercise **2** and the paragraph in exercise **1A** to help you.

> **WRITING FOCUS**  Indenting Paragraphs
>
> Good writers indent the first line of a paragraph. To indent, begin the first line of a paragraph five spaces to the right.
>
> *I am a teacher. I work from 8:00 a.m. to 1:30 p.m. I teach four English classes. In class, I write on the board. I ask a lot of questions.*

**4 SELF ASSESS.** Read your paragraph. Underline the verbs in the simple present. Then use the checklist to assess your work.

☐ I did not put *be* in front of other verbs in the simple present. [3.1, 3.3]

☐ The verbs in the simple present are spelled correctly. [3.3]

☐ I used the base form of the verb for imperatives. [3.9, 3.10]

☐ The first line of my paragraph is indented. [WRITING FOCUS]

# Simple Present: Part 2

▲ Food sellers at a floating market
in Damnoen Saduak, Thailand

## EXPLORE

CD1-47

**1  READ** the conversation about the people from the Nicoya Peninsula. Notice the words in **bold**.

# The People from the Nicoya Peninsula

*Nicoya—
Peninsula,
Costa Rica*

**Mari:**  This is an interesting article.

**Ben:**  Really? What's it about?

**Mari:**  It's about the Nicoya Peninsula in Costa Rica. A lot of people there live to be 90 or 100.

**Ben:**  Interesting. What's their secret? **Do they have a healthy diet?**

**Mari:**  **Yes, they do!** They eat a lot of fruit, vegetables, beans, and rice. They also drink a lot of water.

**Ben:**  Well, that sounds healthy. **Do they eat a lot of meat?**

**Mari:**  **No, they don't.** They only eat meat about once a week.

**Ben:**  **Does the article talk about exercise?**

**Mari:**  Hmmm. Let's see. . . **Yes, it does.** It says the people there walk a lot and work outside—even the old people. . . Hey, listen to this—one woman there, Abuela Panchita, is over 100 years old, and she still walks everywhere!

**Ben:**  Wow! That's amazing!

**Mari:**  Yeah, it is. Also, many old people there live with their families. This makes them happy and helps them live longer.

**Ben:**  Hmmm. That makes sense.

▶ A 96-year-old Costa Rican *sabanero* (or cowboy) still works hard.

118

**2 CHECK.** Read the statements. Circle **T** for *true* or **F** for *false*.

1. A lot of people from the Nicoya Peninsula live a long time.  (T)  F

2. They eat a lot of meat.  T  F

3. Abuela Panchita doesn't exercise.  T  F

4. A lot of old people from the Nicoya Peninsula live with their families.  T  F

**3 DISCOVER.** Complete the exercises to learn about the grammar in this lesson.

**A** Find three questions and answers in the conversation from exercise **1**. Write them in the chart.

| Questions | Answers |
|---|---|
| Do they have a healthy diet? | |

**B** Look at the questions and answers in your chart from exercise **A**. When do we use *Do*? When do we use *Does*? Discuss with your classmates and teacher.

# LEARN

## 4.1 Simple Present: Yes/No Questions

| Do/ Does | Subject | Base Form of Verb |
|---|---|---|
| Do | I you we you they | work? |
| Does | he she it | |

1. Use the base form of the verb after the subject in *Yes/No* questions in the simple present.

✓ Does she **walk** a lot?
✗ Does she <u>walks</u> a lot?

2. Do not use *do* or *does* in *Yes/No* questions with *be*.

✓ Are you healthy?
✗ <u>Do</u> you <u>be</u> healthy?

### REAL ENGLISH

When the main verb is *do*, we still use *do* to start *Yes/No* questions.

A: **Do** you **do** your homework in the morning?
B: *No, I* **do** *it in the afternoon.*

A: **Does** he **do** the dishes at night?
B: *No, he* **does** *them in the morning.*

**4** Circle the correct word to complete each question.

1. (**Do**) / **Does** people from the Nicoya Peninsula live a long time?

2. **Do** / **Does** they drink a lot of water?

3. **Do** / **Does** Abuela Panchita exercise?

4. **Do** / **Does** she have a healthy diet?

5. **Do** / **Does** they live with their families?

6. **Do** / **Does** they work outside?

7. **Do** / **Does** he eat a lot of vegetables?

8. **Do** / **Does** the article talk about exercise?

**5** Change each statement to a *Yes/No* question.

1. Abuela Panchita walks every day. _Does Abuela Panchita walk every day?_

2. People from the Nicoya Peninsula eat beans and rice. _____

3. They live in Costa Rica. _____

4. He has a big family. _____

5. We have a healthy lifestyle. _____

6. You live with your grandparents. _____

7. She hikes six miles every day. _____

8. He is healthy and happy. _____

## 4.2 Simple Present: Short Answers to *Yes/No* Questions

| Yes/No Questions | | | Short Answers | | | | | | | |
|---|---|---|---|---|---|---|---|---|---|---|
| Do/ Does | Subject | Base Form of Verb | | Affirmative | | | | Negative | | |
| Do | I you we you they | work? | Yes, | I you we you they | do. | | No, | I you we you they | don't. | |
| Does | he she it | | | he she it | does. | | | he she it | doesn't. | |

**6** Complete the short answer for each *Yes/No* question.

1. A: Do healthy people exercise every day?

   B: Yes, _they do_____ .

2. A: Does she live with her family?

   B: Yes, _____ .

3. A: Do they go on vacation every year?

   B: No, _____ .

4. A: Does she have a healthy diet?

   B: No, _____ .

5. A: Does he have a big family?

   B: No, _____ .

6. A: Do you live in a small town?

   B: No, _____ .

7. A: Do Juan and you travel a lot?

   B: Yes, _____ .

8. A: Do I need to eat more vegetables?

   B: Yes, _____ .

**7 SPEAK.** Work with a partner. Ask and answer the questions in exercise **6**. Use *Do you . . . ?*

Student A: *Do you exercise every day?*     Student B: *No, I don't.*

# PRACTICE

**8 WRITE, LISTEN & SPEAK.**

CD1-48

**A** Complete the conversation with *Yes/No* questions and short answers. Then listen and check your answers.

**Nora:** Lucia, hi! How are you? (1) _____Do you like_____ (you / like) Miami?

**Lucia:** (2) _____Yes, I do_____ . I love the university and the people, but the American lifestyle is so different from my lifestyle at home.

**Nora:** Really? (3) _____ (you / miss) Italy?

**Lucia:** (4) _____ . I miss my family and friends—and the food.

**Nora:** (5) _____ (you / like) the food here?

**Lucia:** (6) _____ . American food is terrible!

**Nora:** Well, I like it. (7) _____ (you / eat) different food in Italy?

**Lucia:** (8) _____ . I don't eat fast food, and I eat fresh vegetables from our garden every day. We have a huge vegetable garden.

**Nora:** Well, that sounds healthy. (9) _____ (you / help) with the garden?

**Lucia:** (10) _____ . It's a lot of work, but I enjoy it.

**Nora:** (11) _____ (your parents / speak) English?

**Lucia:** (12) _____ . They only speak Italian and German.

**Nora:** (13) _____ (you / have) a big family?

**Lucia:** (14) _____ . I have four brothers and three sisters.

**Nora:** Wow! That *is* a big family! (15) _____ (you all / live ) in one house?

**Lucia:** (16) _____ . My grandparents live with us, too. It's noisy, but I love it!

▼ The Dolomites, Val di Fassa, Italian Alps

**B** Work with a partner. Ask and answer questions (1), (5), (11), and (13) from the conversation in exercise **A**. Use your own answers, not the answers in the book.

Student A: *Do you like _____ (place) _____?*

Student B: *No, I don't. It's very cold. I miss my city.*

**9** **EDIT.** Read the conversations. Find and correct five more errors with *Yes/No* questions and short answers.

1. A: Does Fabian have a big family?
   B: No, he ~~hasn't~~. He only has one brother.
   *(doesn't)*

2. A: Do you work in an office?

   B: Yes, I do.

   A: You live in Toronto?

   B: No, I don't. I live in Montreal.

3. A: Does Richard likes his job?

   B: Yes, he does.

4. A: Does it rain a lot here?

   B: No, it don't. Does it rain a lot in London?

   A: Yes, it does.

5. A: Do you from Italy?

   B: Yes, I am. I live in Rome.

6. A: Do you eat meat?

   B: Yes, I eat.

   A: Do you like fish?

   B: No, I don't.

## 10  LISTEN & SPEAK.

CD1-49

**A**  Read each statement in the chart. Then listen to Kate and Rena talk about their lifestyles. Is the statement true for Kate, Rena, or both? Put a check (✓) in the correct column(s).

|  | Kate | Rena |
|---|---|---|
| 1.  She has a job. | ✓ | ✓ |
| 2.  She cooks every day. |  |  |
| 3.  She takes care of her family. |  |  |
| 4.  She eats fast food. |  |  |
| 5.  She drinks a lot of coffee. |  |  |
| 6.  She sleeps every afternoon. |  |  |
| 7.  She sleeps 4–5 hours every night. |  |  |
| 8.  She needs a vacation. |  |  |
| 9.  She has a healthy lifestyle. |  |  |
| 10.  She has a stressful lifestyle. |  |  |

**B**  Work with a partner. Ask and answer questions about Kate and Rena's lifestyles. Use the information from the chart in exercise **A**.

Student A:  *Does Kate have a job?*

Student B:  *Yes, she does.*

## 11  APPLY.

**A**  Write six interview questions in the chart below to ask a classmate about his or her lifestyle.

| Lifestyle Survey | Yes, I do. | No, I don't. |
|---|---|---|
| 1.  Do you walk a lot? |  |  |
| 2. |  |  |
| 3. |  |  |
| 4. |  |  |
| 5. |  |  |
| 6. |  |  |

**B**  Work with a partner. Ask your questions from exercise **A**. Check your partner's answers.

Student A: *Do you walk a lot?*

Student B: *Yes, I do.*

## EXPLORE

CD1-50

**1  READ** the article about night markets. Notice the words in **bold**.

# Night Markets

Most people go to a market in the daytime. They go to buy food, but in some cities in Asia people **often** go to special street markets at night.

These night markets are very busy places. They're also interesting and fun. People **usually** go to night markets with friends. They walk around and look at the things for sale. They **often** buy special snacks[1] at the market. Some night markets are famous for unusual kinds of food. In Taipei, stinky[2] tofu is a popular snack. It has a very strong smell and taste. In Beijing, night markets sell fried insects.

Night markets aren't open **every night.** Some night markets are only open on weekends, and some night markets are only open **once a year** at New Year's. Night markets are **always** interesting. They are great places to go for food and entertainment.

[1] **snack:** a small serving of food
[2] **stinky:** an informal way to describe something with a bad smell

▲ A night market in Kaifeng, China

**2 CHECK.** Read the statements. Circle **T** for *true* or **F** for *false*.

1. Markets are usually open in the daytime.     (T)     F

2. Night markets are special street markets.     T     F

3. Stinky tofu has a nice smell.     T     F

4. Night markets are open every night.     T     F

5. Night markets are interesting places.     T     F

**3 DISCOVER.** Complete the exercises to learn about the grammar in this lesson.

**A** Find these sentences in the article from exercise **1** on page 125. Write the missing words.

1. People _____ go to night markets with friends.

2. They _____ buy special snacks at the market.

3. Night markets are _____ interesting.

**B** Look at your answers from exercise **A**. What do these words tell us? Choose the correct word(s) to complete the statement below. Then discuss your answer with your classmates and teacher.

These words tell us _____ .

a. where     b. what time     c. how often

▶ A street vendor cooks at a night market in Bangkok, Thailand.

126

# LEARN

## 4.3 Frequency Adverbs

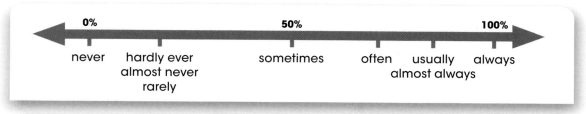

| | |
|---|---|
| 1. Frequency adverbs tell you how often something happens. | She **always** eats eggs for breakfast. I **sometimes** drink coffee at night. |
| 2. Frequency adverbs usually come before other verbs. | ✓ They **usually** <u>go</u> to the park. ✗ They <u>go</u> **never** to the park. |
| 3. *Sometimes, often,* and *usually* can also come at the beginning or end of a statement. | **Sometimes** we go to the park. We go to the park **sometimes**. |
| 4. *Rarely, almost never,* and *never* are negative in meaning. Do not use them with *don't* or *doesn't*. | ✓ I **never** see Jack. ✗ I <u>don't</u> **never** see Jack. |
| 5. Put frequency adverbs after the verb *be*. | ✓ I'm **usually** late. ✗ I <u>usually am</u> late. |

**4** Put the frequency adverb in the correct place in each sentence.

1. (usually) The night market is <sup>usually</sup>open on weekends.

2. (always) We go to the market with friends.

3. (usually) I buy a snack at the night market.

4. (rarely) The market is open in the morning.

5. (almost always) She goes shopping on Saturday afternoon.

6. (never) He buys groceries.

7. (sometimes) I eat dinner at ten o'clock.

8. (almost never) Marta eats dessert.

**5** Put the words in parentheses in the correct order to complete each sentence.

1. I _____usually shop_____ (shop / usually) in the afternoon.

2. The grocery store _____ (always / busy / is).

3. Anna _____ (shops / rarely) at a market.

4. I _____ (am / never / hungry) in the morning.

5. We _____ (buy / always) snacks at the night market.

6. Night markets _____ (open / often / are) late at night.

7. Jim _____ (walks / almost never) to the store.

8. The farmer's market _____ (never / open / is) in the winter.

**6 SPEAK.** Work with a partner. Use frequency adverbs and the activities from the box to make sentences.

| buy snacks | shop at a grocery store | shop at an outdoor market |
|---|---|---|

Student A: *I rarely shop at a grocery store.*

Student B: *I usually buy snacks at the movie theater.*

## 4.4 Frequency Expressions

| | every day. |
|---|---|
| | every Monday. |
| | every week. |
| We go to the market | once a week. |
| | twice a month. |
| | three times a day. |
| | four times a year. |

| 1. Frequency expressions tell how often something happens. | We buy bread **twice a week**.<br>He eats meat **every day**. |
|---|---|
| 2. Frequency expressions can come at the beginning or end of a statement. | They go shopping **every Saturday**.<br>**Every Saturday** they go shopping. |
| 3. *once* = one time<br>*twice* = two times<br>*Once* is more common than *one time*. | The market is only open **once a year**.<br>I go to the grocery store **twice** a week. |
| 4. Use a singular noun after *every*. Use a plural noun after *every* + number. | We go there **every** <u>month</u>.<br>We go there **every two** <u>weeks</u>. |

**7** Circle the correct word(s) to complete each sentence.

1. Mary goes to the market every **Saturdays** /(**Saturday**).

2. Kara buys flowers **once** / **one** a week.

3. Every **night** / **nights** we eat Italian food.

4. Ben buys clothes **twice** / **two** times a year.

5. Once **week** / **a week** they go to the grocery store.

6. The store has a special sale three **time** / **times** a year.

7. I go to the bakery every **day** / **days**.

8. We usually go to the mall two times **month** / **a month**.

9. My mother buys bread every **day** / **days**.

10. Every three **day** / **days** Carl buys vegetables at the market.

**8 SPEAK.** Work with a partner. Use the activities from the box and different frequency expressions to make sentences.

| | | |
|---|---|---|
| exercise | go to a store | go to a restaurant |

Student A: *I exercise every day.*    Student B: *Really? I exercise twice a week.*

# PRACTICE

**9 LISTEN & WRITE.**

CD1-51

**A** Listen to the information from a travel blog. Write the missing words.

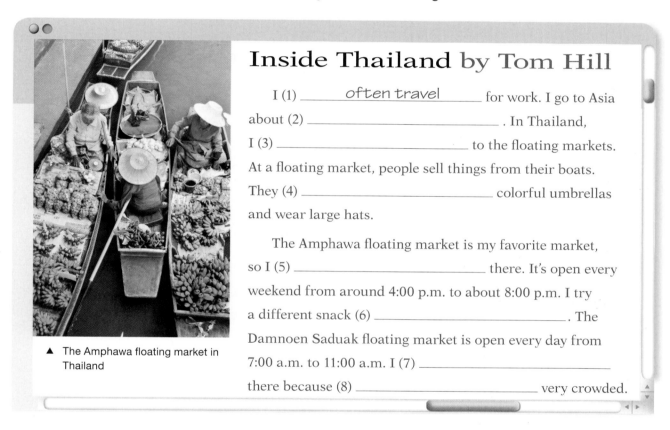

## Inside Thailand by Tom Hill

I (1) _____ often travel _____ for work. I go to Asia about (2) _____ . In Thailand, I (3) _____ to the floating markets. At a floating market, people sell things from their boats. They (4) _____ colorful umbrellas and wear large hats.

The Amphawa floating market is my favorite market, so I (5) _____ there. It's open every weekend from around 4:00 p.m. to about 8:00 p.m. I try a different snack (6) _____ . The Damnoen Saduak floating market is open every day from 7:00 a.m. to 11:00 a.m. I (7) _____ there because (8) _____ very crowded.

▲ The Amphawa floating market in Thailand

**B** Choose the correct word(s) to complete each sentence. Use the information from Tom Hill's travel blog in exercise **A** to help you.

1. Tom _____ travels for work.                                    a. almost never      b. often
2. _____ he goes to Asia.                                          a. Sometimes         b. Always
3. He goes there every _____ .                                     a. week              b. six months
4. He _____ goes to a floating market on his visits to Thailand.   a. usually           b. sometimes
5. Tom _____ goes to the Amphawa market.                           a. almost always     b. every time
6. He _____ tries new snacks there.                                a. sometimes         b. always
7. He _____ goes to the Damnoen Saduak floating market.            a. rarely            b. never
8. The Damnoen Saduak market is _____ crowded.                     a. often             b. rarely

**C** Write sentences about the floating markets. Use the information from Tom Hill's travel blog in exercise **A** on page 129 and the words below.

1. (always) ___People always sell things from their boats___ at the floating markets.

2. (almost always) They _____ .

3. (every weekend) The Amphawa market _____ .

4. (always) The Damnoen Suduak market _____ .

5. (almost always) It _____ .

**10** **LISTEN** to a phone conversation about Sophie's lifestyle in Canada and France. Complete the notes.

CD1-52

| In Canada |
| --- |
| Sophie ___almost never___ cooks. |
| She _____ goes to the grocery store. |

| In France |
| --- |
| Sophie walks to the market _____ . |
| She buys bread or pastries _____ . |
| She cooks dinner _____ . |

**11** **APPLY.** Work with a partner. Talk about how often you do each of the activities from the box. Use frequency expressions.

| | |
| --- | --- |
| buy clothes on sale | go to a museum |
| eat candy | shop for clothes |
| exercise | shop for groceries |
| get a hair cut | take a bus |

Student A: *I shop for food once a week. How about you?*

Student B: *Me, too. / I never shop for food! / I shop for food every day.*

**REAL ENGLISH**

Use *Me, too* and *Me neither* to show you share a feeling or an experience with someone.

Use *Me, too* after an affirmative statement.

  A: *I like shopping.*
  B: **Me, too.**

Use *Me neither* after a negative statement.

  A: *I don't exercise every day.*
  B: **Me neither.**

## EXPLORE

CD1-53

**1 READ** the article about the Amish. Notice the words in **bold**.

Pennsylvania
Ohio

# The Amish

**Who are the Amish and where do they live?** Over 250,000 Amish people live in North America. Many live in Pennsylvania and Ohio in the United States. The Amish have a very traditional lifestyle. For example, most Amish people don't own cars or trucks. They own horses and ride in buggies.[1] Many Amish don't have electricity[2] in their houses.

**Why do they live this way?** The Amish believe in a simple lifestyle. Most Amish people live on farms near small towns. They don't want a lot of contact with the "outside" world.

It is easy to recognize the Amish. The men wear hats, dark pants and jackets, and white shirts. Amish women wear plain[3] dresses and white caps on their heads.

People often ask, "**What do they do for fun? What do they enjoy?**" They sometimes go to restaurants, and young people often play baseball or other games. The Amish enjoy their families, their community, and visits with other Amish families.

[1] **buggy:** a small carriage pulled by a horse
[2] **electricity:** energy used for power
[3] **plain:** simple, not fancy

▼ An Amish family rides in a buggy in Pennsylvania, USA.

131

**2 CHECK.** Choose the correct information to complete each statement.

1. Many Amish people live in ____.
   (a.) North America    b. South America

2. Amish people own ____.
   a. cars and trucks    b. horses and buggies

3. Their farms are ____.
   a. near cities    b. near small towns

4. Amish women wear ____.
   a. plain pants    b. white caps

5. Amish people ____ for fun.
   a. visit other families    b. go to the movies

**3 DISCOVER.** Complete the exercises to learn about the grammar in this lesson.

**A** Find these questions in the article from exercise **1** on page 131. Write the missing words.

1. _____ do they live?

2. _____ do they live this way?

3. _____ do they do for fun?

4. _____ do they enjoy?

**B** Look at the questions from exercise **A**. Are the answers to these questions *Yes, No,* or other information? Discuss with your classmates and teacher.

◀ An Amish boy sits on a fence in New Bedford, Ohio, USA.

# LEARN

## 4.5 Simple Present: *Wh-* Questions

| *Wh-* Word | Do/<br>Does | Subject | | Answers |
|---|---|---|---|---|
| Who | do | you | see? | Ted and Amy. |
| What | do | the women | wear? | Plain dresses. |
| When | do | they | work? | From Monday to Friday. |
| Where | do | you | live? | In Berlin. |
| Why | does | he | live in Miami? | Because he likes the weather. |
| How | does | she | get to work? | She takes the subway. |
| How often | does | it | happen? | A lot. |

| | |
|---|---|
| 1. Use *Wh-* questions to ask for specific information. | A: **What** do they do for fun?<br>B: They <u>play baseball</u>.<br><br>A: **When** do you get up?<br>B: <u>At six-thirty</u>. |
| 2. Notice the difference between questions with *be* and questions with other verbs. | *Be:* When **is** your class?<br><br>Other Verbs: When **does** your class **start**? |

> **REAL ENGLISH**
>
> *Wh-* words are often used alone as questions in conversation.
>
> A: *I only sleep four hours a night.*
> B: **Why?**
> A: *I have two jobs.*

**4** Add *do* or *does* to each question.

                *do*

1. Where 〡many Amish people live?

2. How often they visit other families?

3. What an Amish woman wear?

4. Why they live on farms?

5. What an Amish child do for fun?

6. How often they go to big cities?

7. What *cap* mean?

8. When they go to restaurants?

**5** Look at each sentence. Write a *Wh-* question about the underlined word or phrase.

1. We live <u>in Ohio</u>. <u>  Where do you live?  </u>

2. She visits <u>her grandparents</u>. _____

3. I exercise <u>at the gym</u>. _____

4. He plays baseball <u>because it's fun</u>. _____

5. She teaches <u>Spanish</u>. _____

6. They <u>play soccer</u> in their free time. _____

7. I visit my parents <u>once a week</u>. _____

8. They eat dinner <u>at eight o'clock</u>. _____

## 4.6 *Who* Questions about a Subject

| *Who* | Verb | |
|------|------|------|
| **Who** | lives | here? |
| **Who** | is | our teacher? |

| | |
|---|---|
| 1. *Wh-* questions with *Who* are sometimes about a subject. | A: **Who** speaks Spanish? <br> B: <u>Mr. Lopez</u> does. |
| 2. Always use the *-s/-es* form of the verb in *Who* questions about a subject. The answer can be singular or plural. | A: Who **has** my book? <br> B: <u>Rita</u> does. <br><br> A: Who **knows** the answer? <br> B: <u>We</u> all do! |
| 3. Do not use *do* or *does* + base form of verb when a *Who* question is about a subject. | ✓ Who **lives** on that farm? <br> ✗ Who <u>does live</u> on that farm? |

**6** Put the words in the correct order to make questions.

1. lives / Who / that / farm / on _____Who lives on that farm?_____

2. has / a traditional lifestyle / Who _____

3. plays / baseball / Who _____

4. wants / Who / coffee _____

5. absent / today / Who / is _____

6. Who / your laundry / does _____

7. speaks / Who / Japanese _____

8. drives / to class / Who _____

**7** **SPEAK.** Work with a partner. Ask and answer questions 5–8 from exercise **6**.

Student A: *Who speaks Japanese?*     Student B: *Takeshi does.*

# PRACTICE

CD1-54

**8  WRITE, LISTEN & SPEAK.**

**A**  Complete the survey. Use *Who, What, When, Where, Why, How,* and *How often.* Then listen and check your answers.

**Scott:** Hello. Excuse me. Do you have time to answer some questions for a short survey?

**Camila:** Um . . . Yeah, OK.

**Scott:** Great! So, here's the first question. (1) _____Where_____ do you live?

**Camila:** Here in Mexico. I'm from Puebla.

**Scott:** OK, thanks. (2) _____ do you live with?

**Camila:** My family—my husband and our two daughters. My mother lives with us, too.

**Scott:** Do you work?

**Camila:** Yeah, I do. I'm a nurse.

**Scott:** (3) _____ do you work?

**Camila:** At the Hospital Betania in Puebla.

**Scott:** (4) _____ do you get to work?

**Camila:** Well, I usually drive, but sometimes I take the bus.

**Scott:** (5) _____ do you start work?

**Camila:** Early. I usually start work at seven o'clock in the morning.

> **REAL ENGLISH**
>
> *Well* is often used to begin the answer to a question.
>
> A: *When do you usually get up in the morning?*
> B: ***Well,*** *I usually wake up at 7:00, but on weekends I get up at around 9:00.*
>
> A: *Do you drive to work?*
> B: ***Well,*** *yes, but sometimes I ride my bike.*

**Scott:** Wow! That *is* early! (6) _____ do you do for fun?

**Camila:** Well, I shop, and I listen to music.

**Scott:** Really? (7) _____'s your favorite musician?

**Camila:** Hmmm. Carla Morrison.

**Scott:** I like her music, too. Next question: (8) _____ do you take a vacation?

**Camila:** Twice a year.

**Scott:** Thanks. (9) _____ do you usually go on vacation?

**Camila:** Well, we usually go to the beach, but this year we want to see the mountains.

**Scott:** Nice! (10) _____ do you like the beach?

**Camila:** I love the sun and water! Who doesn't love the beach?

**Scott:** Well, those are all of my survey questions. Thank you very much!

**Camila:** No problem. Good luck with your survey!

**B**  Work with a partner. Ask and answer questions about Camila.

Student A: *Where does she live?*

Student B: *In Puebla, Mexico.*

**9** **LISTEN** and choose the correct answer to each question.

1. (a.) In the morning.　　b. At school.

2. a. The Amish.　　b. A small hat.

3. a. With her family.　　b. In Puebla.

4. a. In France.　　b. Marie.

5. a. In September.　　b. Because traffic is terrible this morning.

6. a. Every day for lunch.　　b. With Nancy.

7. a. At the coffee shop.　　b. A sandwich.

8. a. I walk.　　b. At 7:00 a.m.

**10** **READ, WRITE & SPEAK.**

**A** Read the story about Jeremy Stubbs. Underline the verbs in each sentence.

# 52 Hikes a Year!

Jeremy Stubbs <u>lives</u> in Tacoma, Washington. He teaches math at a high school. On weekends, he likes to go on hikes. In fact, he goes on a hike every weekend, 52 times a year!

In the winter, Jeremy sometimes climbs a mountain trail in snowshoes[1] and carries his skis[2]. Then he has a fast trip back down the mountain on the skis!

Jeremy sometimes goes on hikes alone, but other teachers and students usually go with him. Sometimes he writes and posts photos on his blog, "52 Hikes 52 Weekends."

[1] People use **snowshoes** to walk on top of deep snow.
[2] People use **skis** to move quickly across snow, especially downhill.

▼ Mount Rainier National Park, Washington, USA

**B** Complete the questions about the story from exercise **A**.

1. Where _does Jeremy_ live?

2. What _____ at a high school?

3. When _____ to go on hikes?

4. How often _____ on hikes?

5. What _____ sometimes
   _____ in the winter?

6. Why _____ his skis?

7. Who usually _____ with him?

8. What _____
   sometimes _____ alone?

**C** Work with a partner. Ask and answer the questions from exercise **B**.

Student A: *Where does Jeremy live?*

Student B: *In Tacoma, Washington.*

**11** **EDIT.** Read the conversations. Find and correct four more errors with *Wh*- questions.

1. A: Where he does live?

   B: In Tacoma, Washington.

2. A: When he goes on hikes?

   B: He goes on weekends.

3. A: When have a vacation?

   B: In the summer.

4. A: How often does he go on hikes?

   B: Almost every weekend.

5. A: Who does goes on hikes with him?

   B: His students and other teachers.

6. A: Where he teaches?

   B: At a high school.

## 12 LISTEN, WRITE & SPEAK.

CD1-56-58

**A** These people have very different lifestyles. Listen and take notes about their daily activities.

Sara and Max

*exercise in the morning*

Kai

Julie

**B** How many questions can you write about the people from exercise **A?** Use *Who, Where, When, What,* and *How often.*

Who has a job in a store?

**C** Work with a partner. Ask and answer your questions from exercise **B**.

Student A: *Who has a job in a store?*      Student B: *Kai does.*

## 13 APPLY.

**A** Write three *Wh-* questions for a classmate about his or her lifestyle.

What do you do in your free time?

**B** Work with a partner. Ask your questions from exercise **A**.

Charts
4.1, 4.2,
4.4–4.6

**1** Complete the exercises.

**A** Complete each conversation with the correct question word(s).

1. A: _____What_____ does he do?      B: He's a professor.

2. A: _____ Mateus live in Costa Rica?      B: No, he doesn't.

3. A: _____ do you live?      B: I live on Livingston.

4. A: _____ do you travel to China?      B: Twice a year.

5. A: _____ do the night market open?      B: At 9:00 p.m.

6. A: _____ you miss your family?      B: Yes, I do.

7. A: _____ does he usually buy at the market?      B: Special snacks.

8. A: _____ wants a snack?      B: I do!

9. A: _____ do you get to work?      B: I take the subway.

10. A: _____ do you live in a small town?      B: Because I like the peace and quiet.

**B** Work with a partner. Practice the conversations from exercise **A**.

**2** **LISTEN** and choose the correct answer for each question.

CD1-59

Charts
4.1, 4.2,
4.4–4.6

1. a. Yes, I do.      ⓑ Twice a week.

2. a. Because it's fun.      b. No, I don't.

3. a. Yes, it does.      b. It means *very big*.

4. a. Because it's good exercise.      b. Every day.

5. a. They live in Italy.      b. No, she doesn't.

6. a. Dora and I do.      b. Never.

7. a. To the beach.      b. Twice a year.

8. a. On Saturday.      b. At the market.

9. a. At 9:00 a.m.      b. She takes a bus.

10. a. My sister.      b. In an apartment.

Charts
4.1–4.6

**3  EDIT & SPEAK.**

**A**  Read the conversations. Find and correct six more errors with simple present questions and answers and frequency adverbs and expressions.

1.  A:  Who's that?

    B:  That's my sister Katie.

    A:  Does she ~~visits~~ ^visit you often?

    B:  No, she doesn't. She comes rarely to California.

2.  A:  How often do you travel for your job?

    B:  Once a month.

    A:  Wow, that's a lot. You do like it?

    B:  Yes, I like, but sometimes it's difficult. I miss my family.

3.  A:  Where you do live?

    B:  I live on River Road.

    A:  How you get to class?

    B:  I usually take the subway.

4.  A:  Do you exercise every day?

    B:  Yes, I go to the gym every days.

**B**  Work with a partner. Ask and answer the questions from conversations 3 and 4 from exercise **A**. Use your own answers, not the answers in the book.

Student A: *Do you exercise every day?*            Student B: *Yes, I do.*

Charts
4.1–4.6

CD1-60

**4  LISTEN & SPEAK.**

**A**  Look at the Internet activities in the chart. Ask your teacher about any words or activities you don't know. Then listen to the conversation. Check (✓) the Internet activities you hear.

| Internet Activity | How Often |
|---|---|
| ✓ Sends or reads e-mail | Three times a week |
| ☐ Watches videos online | |
| ☐ Uses a social networking site | |
| ☐ Banks online | |
| ☐ Plays online games | |
| ☐ Shops online | |
| ☐ Reads the news online | |

CD1-60

**B** Look at the Internet activities you checked in exercise **A**. Listen again. How often does Lena do each activity? Take notes in the chart.

**C** Work with a partner. Ask and answer questions about how often Lena does the Internet activities in exercise **A**.

Student A: *How often does Lena read or send e-mail?*　　　Student B: *Three times a week.*

Charts
4.1–4.6

**5 WRITE & SPEAK.**

**A** Write five interview questions in the chart for a classmate about his or her Internet activities. Write *Yes/No* and *Wh-* questions.

| Interview Questions | Answers |
|---|---|
| Do you watch videos online? | |
| | |
| | |
| | |
| | |

**B** Work with a partner. Ask your questions from exercise **A**. Take notes on your partner's answers in your chart.

**C** In your notebook, write five sentences about your partner's Internet activities.

*Juliana watches videos online every day.*

# Connect the Grammar to Writing

**1  READ & NOTICE THE GRAMMAR.**

**A**  Read the paragraph. Is Pradit's daily life similar to your life? Discuss with a partner.

▶ Bangkok, Thailand

## PRADIT'S DAILY LIFE

   Pradit lives in Bangkok, Thailand. He works in a trading company. He often travels because of his job. Every night he goes out with his friends. They usually go to a restaurant. Sometimes they go to the movies. On weekends, he usually visits his parents or goes to the beach. He enjoys his life in Bangkok.

### GRAMMAR FOCUS

In the paragraph in exercise **A,** the writer uses frequency adverbs and frequency expressions to talk about how often certain activities happen.

> He **often** travels because of his job.
> **Every night** he goes out with his friends.

**B**  Read the paragraph in exercise **A** again. Underline the frequency adverbs and fequency expressions. Then work with a partner and compare answers.

**C**  Complete the chart with questions and answers about Pradit's lifestyle.

| Information about Pradit | | |
|---|---|---|
| | Questions | Answers |
| Where | Where does Pradit live? | In Bangkok. |
| What | | |
| Why | | |
| How often | | |
| Who | | |
| Yes/No | | |

## 2 BEFORE YOU WRITE.

**A** Write questions in the chart below to ask someone about his or her daily life. Use the chart from exercise **1C** as a model.

| Information about _____ | | |
| --- | --- | --- |
| | Questions | Answers |
| Where | | |
| What | | |
| Why | | |
| How often | | |
| Who | | |
| *Yes/No* | | |

**B** Choose a person to interview. Ask him or her your interview questions from exercise **A**. Take notes in your chart.

## 3 WRITE a paragraph. Use the information from your chart from exercise **2A** and the model paragraph in exercise **1A** to help you.

> **WRITING FOCUS**    Subject-Verb Agreement
>
> Subject-verb agreement is important for good writing. Subject-verb agreement means the verb agrees with the subject.
>
> **Remember:** In the simple present, add *-s* to the verb for *he, she, it,* and subjects that are the name of a person or a singular noun.
>
> *Pradit* **lives** *in Bangkok, Thailand.*
> *He* **works** *in a trading company.*
> *He* **enjoys** *his life in Bangkok.*

## 4 SELF ASSESS. Read your paragraph. Underline the adverbs of frequency and expressions of frequency. Then use the checklist to assess your work.

- [ ] I put the frequency adverbs in the correct place. [4.3]
- [ ] I put the frequency expressions in the correct place. [4.4]
- [ ] I used a singular noun after *every*. [4.4]
- [ ] The forms of the verbs agree with the subjects. [WRITING FOCUS]

# Count and Non-Count Nouns

▶ Weaverbirds stand on a lunch table in Queen Elizabeth National Park, Uganda.

## EXPLORE

CD2-2

**1  READ** the conversation. Notice the words in **bold**.

# At the Grand Hotel

| | |
|---|---|
| **Front Desk Clerk:** | Good afternoon, sir. Welcome to **the Grand Hotel**. Do you have **a reservation**? |
| **Mike Martin:** | Yes, my **last name**'s Martin. |
| **Front Desk Clerk:** | Yes, Mr. Martin. I see **the reservation**. It's for **a double room** for **two nights**. |
| **Mike Martin:** | That's right. |
| **Front Desk Clerk:** | All right. Just **a minute**, please. . . . OK, here's **information** about **the fitness center,**[1] and here's **the key** for your **room**. Do you need any **help** with **luggage**? |
| **Mike Martin:** | No, thanks. I only have **one bag**. |
| **Front Desk Clerk:** | All right. **The coffee shop** is on this **floor**. It's open every **morning** from six-thirty to ten-thirty for **breakfast**. We also have **vending machines**[2] near **the elevators** on each **floor**. |
| **Mike Martin:** | OK, thank you. Are there any good **restaurants** nearby? |
| **Front Desk Clerk:** | Oh, yes! There's **an** excellent Italian **restaurant** just around **the corner**. It's called Little Venice, and **the food** there is very good. |
| **Mike Martin:** | Great. Thanks. |

[1] **fitness center:** a gym
[2] **vending machine:** a machine that give snacks or drinks after money is put in it

**2 CHECK.** Look at the statements and questions from the conversation in exercise **1**. Who says each? Put a check (✓) in the correct column.

| | Front Desk Clerk | Mike Martin |
|---|:---:|:---:|
| 1. Do you have a reservation? | ✓ | ☐ |
| 2. Just a minute, please. | ☐ | ☐ |
| 3. Do you need any help with luggage? | ☐ | ☐ |
| 4. I only have one bag. | ☐ | ☐ |
| 5. Are there any good restaurants nearby? | ☐ | ☐ |

**3 DISCOVER.** Look at the question and statement from the conversation. Notice the words in **bold**. Why do we say *one bag* but not *one luggage*? Discuss with your classmates and teacher.

1. Do you need any help with **luggage**?

2. No, thanks. I only have **one bag**.

▼ Negril Beach, Jamaica, West Indies

# LEARN

## 5.1 Count and Non-Count Nouns

| | |
|---|---|
| 1. Count nouns are things we can count. They have a singular and plural form. | I eat an **apple** every morning.<br>Andrea eats two **apples** every day. |
| 2. Non-count nouns are things we cannot count. | **Sugar** is sweet.<br>A: *Do we have **homework** tonight?*<br>B: *Yes, we have two grammar exercises.* |
| 3. Non-count nouns do not have a plural form. | ✓ This **information** is important.<br>✗ These informations are important. |

### Some Common Non-Count Nouns

| Foods | Liquids | Activities | Category Nouns | Abstract Nouns |
|---|---|---|---|---|
| bread<br>butter<br>cheese<br>chicken<br>fish<br>flour<br>meat<br>pasta<br>rice<br>salad<br>salt<br>sugar<br>yogurt | coffee<br>gasoline<br>milk<br>oil<br>soup<br>tea<br>water | baseball<br>basketball<br>golf<br>hockey<br>soccer<br>tennis<br>yoga | clothing (dresses, pants, shoes)<br>furniture (chairs, tables)<br>fruit (apples, oranges)<br>homework (assignments, exercises)<br>jewelry (earrings, necklaces, rings)<br>luggage (backpacks, bags, suitcases)<br>money (coins, dollars)<br>time (hours, minutes)<br>traffic (buses, cars)<br>weather (hurricanes, showers, storms) | advice<br>fun<br>help<br>information<br>love<br>work |

**REAL ENGLISH**

Some nouns can be count and non-count.

I like **pizza**. (non-count noun)
We need five **pizzas** for the party. (count noun)

**4** Look at the underlined noun in each sentence. Is it a count noun or a non-count noun? Put a check (✓) in the correct column.

| | Count Noun | Non-Count Noun |
|---|:---:|:---:|
| 1. I don't need any help with <u>luggage</u>. | ☐ | ✓ |
| 2. I only have a small <u>bag</u>. | ☐ | ☐ |
| 3. I need a <u>room</u> with a double bed. | ☐ | ☐ |
| 4. She has two <u>suitcases</u>. | ☐ | ☐ |
| 5. He needs some <u>information</u> about restaurants. | ☐ | ☐ |
| 6. That restaurant has very good <u>pasta</u>. | ☐ | ☐ |
| 7. Let's get some <u>coffee</u> at the coffee shop. | ☐ | ☐ |
| 8. I need <u>coins</u> for the vending machine. | ☐ | ☐ |
| 9. Our hotel room has two <u>beds</u>. | ☐ | ☐ |
| 10. I don't need <u>help</u> with anything. | ☐ | ☐ |

**5** Complete each sentence with the correct category from the box.

| clothing | furniture | jewelry | money | ~~traffic~~ |
| fruit | homework | luggage | time | weather |

1. Cars and buses are examples of _____ traffic _____.

2. A grammar exercise is an example of _____.

3. Minutes and hours are examples of _____.

4. A suitcase is an example of _____.

5. Rings and watches are examples of _____.

6. Beds and chairs are examples of _____.

7. Dollars and cents are examples of _____.

8. A storm is an example of _____.

9. Oranges and bananas are examples of _____.

10. A shirt is an example of _____.

## 5.2   Using *A/An* with Count Nouns

| | Singular | Plural |
|---|---|---|
| 1. **Remember:** Use *a* or *an* before singular count nouns or before an adjective + singular count noun. | **a** suitcase **an** old suitcase | suitcases |
| | **an** orange **a** big orange | oranges |
| Don't use *a* or *an* with plural nouns. | ✓ That store sells suitcases. ✗ That store sells <u>a</u> suitcases. | |
| 2. Do not use *a* or *an* with non-count nouns. | ✓ Look online for information. ✗ Look online for <u>an</u> information. | |
| 3. **Remember:** Use *a* before a consonant sound. Use *an* before a vowel sound. | He usually has **a sandwich** and **an apple** for lunch. It is **a hard exercise**. He's **an honest man**. | |

**6** Complete each sentence with *a*, *an*, or Ø for no article.

1. He works for _a_ hotel.

2. This is _____ excellent restaurant.

3. Cindy needs _____ new suitcase for her trip.

4. That vending machine doesn't take _____ coins.

5. That store sells _____ luggage.

6. It's _____ old hotel.

7. The gift shop sells _____ jewelry.

8. Do we have _____ time for breakfast?

**7** Write *a*, *an*, or Ø for no article.

1. __Ø__ sugar
2. _____ sandwich
3. _____ jacket
4. _____ information
5. _____ minute

6. _____ people
7. _____ egg
8. _____ old furniture
9. _____ hour
10. _____ difficult exercise

11. _____ traffic
12. _____ earring
13. _____ help
14. _____ assignment
15. _____ rain

**8** **SPEAK.** Work with a partner. Look around the classroom and in your bags. Which things are count nouns? Which things are non-count nouns? Write each noun in the correct column of the chart.

| Count Nouns | Non-Count Nouns |
| --- | --- |
| a desk | money |
| | |

## 5.3   *A/An* vs. *The*

| | |
| --- | --- |
| 1. *A* and *an* are indefinite articles. Use *a* or *an* when the person, place, or thing is not specific.<br><br>**Remember:** Do not use *a* or *an* before plural nouns. | I usually have **a** sandwich and **an** apple for lunch. |
| 2. *The* is the definite article. Use *the* before count and non-count nouns when: | |
|   a. there is only one of something; |   a. **The** earth is round. |
|   b. the person, place, or thing is specific and something both the speaker and listener know about; |   b. Do you have **the** suitcases? (The speaker and listener are on a trip together.) |
|   c. you refer to a person, place, or thing a second time. |   c. I always stay at a hotel downtown. **The** hotel is very nice. |

**9** Circle the correct article to complete each statement or question.

1. What's **a** /(**the**) number of our hotel room?

2. My room's on **a** / **the** sixth floor.

3. Do you need Ø / **the** help with your luggage?

4. Do you have **the** / Ø key to our hotel room?

5. Do you have **a / Ø** reservation, sir?

6. Do you know **an / the** address of our hotel?

7. **Ø / The** restaurant in the hotel is very good.

8. Do you like **a / Ø** pasta? **A / The** pasta at that restaurant is excellent.

9. What time does **a / the** fitness center close?

10. **A / The** people in this hotel are very friendly.

11. Our hotel room has **a / the** great view of **a / the** city.

12. Wow! Look at **a / the** moon! It's beautiful.

## PRACTICE

**10** Write *a, an, the,* or *Ø* for no article to complete each conversation.

1. A: Hello. Welcome to <u>the</u> Pacific Hotel.

   B: Hi. I have _____ reservation. My name is Sims.

2: A: Excuse me. Is there _____ fitness center in the hotel?

   B: Yes. It's on _____ second floor next to _____ elevators.

3. A: Do you have _____ restaurant here in the hotel?

   B: Yes, we do. It's on _____ first floor.

4. A: I'm hungry. Let's look for _____ restaurant.

   B: OK. I like _____ restaurant at the hotel. Do you want to go there?

5. A: We need to buy _____ fruit.

   B: Right. We need _____ apples, oranges, and bananas.

6. A: OK, we have all _____ food for the party. Let's go buy _____ flowers.

   B: Good idea. Let's go to Vinny's Farm. _____ flowers there are always very pretty.

7. A: It's really nice today. _____ sky is very blue.

   B: It really is! _____ weather is perfect. Let's have a picnic.

8. A: I have _____ question about _____ homework.

   B: Ask _____ teacher.

> **REAL ENGLISH**
>
> Use *Let's* + verb to make suggestions. *Let's* includes you and your listener(s).
>
> A: **Let's have** lunch.
>
> B: *Good idea. I'm hungry.*
>
> A: **Let's not go** to the deli. *The food there isn't very good.*
>
> B: *OK.*

**11  EDIT.** Read the paragraph. Put five more articles in the correct place.

## Barney's

We have $\overset{a}{\vee}$ big hotel in our city. name of hotel is Barney's. It's expensive, but many people like to stay there. It has pool. It also has restaurant with very good food. restaurant's name is Martindale by the Sea. Sometimes my family goes there for special celebrations.

**12  SPEAK.** Work with a partner. Discuss these questions.

1. Does your city have a famous hotel? What is special about it?

2. Do you know any good restaurants? Why do you like it / them?

▶ Customers enjoy the view at a popular village restaurant, Oia, Santorini, Greece.

**13  LISTEN.**

CD2-3-6

**A** Listen to the conversations. Write the number of the conversation next to the word(s) you hear in each conversation.

a. _____ radio    b. __1__ front desk    c. _____ job    d. _____ train

CD2-3-6

**B** Read the questions about the conversations from exercise **A**. Then listen again and choose the correct answer for each question.

1. What does the caller in Conversation 1 need?

   a. a new computer    b. help with the TV    c. information

2. What does the traveler in Conversation 2 ask for?

   a. a map    b. information    c. a ticket

3. What is the problem in Conversation 3?

    a. traffic                           b. cars at the airport          c. the news

4. What advice does the worker's friend give in Conversation 4?

    a. Work late.                        b. Get a new job.             c. Have some dinner.

🎧 CD2-3-6

**C**   Work with a partner. Read the sentences from the conversations. Complete the sentences with the words you remember. Then listen again and write any missing words.

### Conversation 1

**Hotel Clerk:**     Hello. Front desk. May I help you?

**Guest:**     Yes, I need _____ . I have _____ problem with

                 _____ in my room.

**Hotel Clerk:**     I'm sorry to hear that.

### Conversation 2

**Woman:**     Good afternoon. Welcome to the Philadelphia airport. Would you like

                 _____ of _____ ?

**Traveler:**     Yes, I would. Thanks. I'd also like _____

                 about _____ into the city.

**Woman:**     Sure. No problem. It's really easy to take _____ downtown.

### Conversation 3

**Mike:**     Do you drive to _____ ? Well,

                 don't get stuck in _____ !

**Mary:**     Right now _____ is very slow on

                 all of our _____ .

### Conversation 4

**Karen:**     Hey, sorry. I'm still at _____ .

                 I have about _____ of

                 _____ here.

**Berta:**     I think you need _____ !

> **REAL ENGLISH**
>
> *Would like* means *want*, but *would like* is more polite.
>
>     A: **Would you like** coffee or tea?
>
>     B: *I'd like* tea. Thanks.
>
> In a short answer, do not use the contraction.
>
>     A: **Would you like** a cup of coffee?
>
>     B: Yes, I **would**.

## 14   APPLY.

**A**   Work with a partner. Write a short conversation. Use at least two of the words in the box.

| | | | |
|---|---|---|---|
| assignment | information | restaurant | test |
| exercise | jewelry | rice | watch |
| food | job | ring | weather |
| help | necklace | snow | wind |
| homework | rain | soup | work |

**B**   Role-play your conversation for your classmates.

## EXPLORE

CD2-7

**1** **READ** the blog entry. Notice the words in **bold**.

Budapest, Hungary

# ERIK'S FOOD BLOG
WELCOME FOOD LOVERS!
Enjoy! Share your recipes.

SUNDAY, JANUARY 28

Every summer I travel home to Budapest. My grandmother lives downtown. When I arrive, she always gives me **some** coffee and **a piece of** honey[1] cake. She's a wonderful cook!

Unfortunately, my grandmother doesn't have **any** recipes[2] on paper. She never writes them down, and she doesn't have **any** cookbooks. She doesn't need them. "How do you make goulash,[3] Grandma?" I asked. "Oh, that's simple," she answered. "You need **some** meat, onions, oil, flour, paprika, salt, and a green pepper. Then cook everything for two to three hours."

That *is* an easy recipe, but my first goulash was *not* very successful. I need exact directions, so now I watch her in her kitchen and write down every step and every ingredient[4] in her goulash recipe. She cooks, and I write down the ingredients: **2 pounds of** meat, 2 onions, **1/2 cup of** flour, **1 teaspoon of** paprika, 1 green pepper, and **2 teaspoons of** salt.

For the full recipe, click below and enjoy!

GOULASH RECIPE
OTHER HUNGARIAN FOOD

[1] **honey:** a sweet, sticky food made by bees

[2] **recipe:** a set of directions that tells you how to make something to eat

[3] **goulash:** a favorite Hungarian dish

[4] **ingredient:** one of the things you use to make a particular food

POSTED BY ERIK AT 10:56 PM
**2 COMMENTS:**

Nick Burke said . . .
Great goulash recipe. Thank you!
February 5, 5:21 PM

**POST A COMMENT**

**2 CHECK.** Match each measurement or number in the box with the ingredient from the goulash recipe in exercise **1**. Write the letter.

| a. 1 | b. 1/2 cup | c. 2 pounds | d. 1 teaspoon | e. 2 teaspoons | f. 2 |

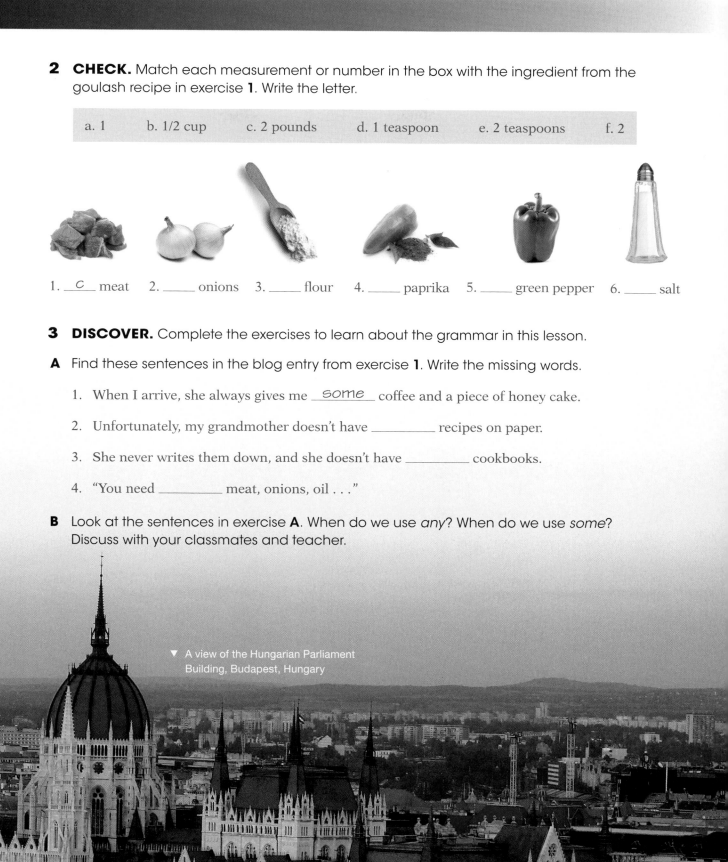

1. __c__ meat    2. ____ onions   3. ____ flour   4. ____ paprika   5. ____ green pepper   6. ____ salt

**3 DISCOVER.** Complete the exercises to learn about the grammar in this lesson.

**A** Find these sentences in the blog entry from exercise **1**. Write the missing words.

1. When I arrive, she always gives me __some__ coffee and a piece of honey cake.

2. Unfortunately, my grandmother doesn't have _____ recipes on paper.

3. She never writes them down, and she doesn't have _____ cookbooks.

4. "You need _____ meat, onions, oil . . ."

**B** Look at the sentences in exercise **A**. When do we use *any*? When do we use *some*? Discuss with your classmates and teacher.

▼ A view of the Hungarian Parliament Building, Budapest, Hungary

# LEARN

## 5.4 Measurement Words

| 1. Use measurement words + *of* to talk about specific quantities. | We need a **bag of** rice. <br> Please get a **pound of** meat at the market. <br> Would you like a **cup of** coffee? |
| --- | --- |
| 2. **Be careful!** Make a count noun plural after a measurement word + *of*. | ✓ We need a carton of eggs. <br> ✗ We need a carton of egg. |

### Some Common Measurement Words

| Containers | Portions | Specific Measurements | Other |
| --- | --- | --- | --- |
| a **bag** of rice | a **bowl** of soup | a **cup** of sugar | a **bar** of soap |
| a **bottle** of shampoo | a **cup** of coffee | a **gallon** of gasoline | a **bunch** of bananas |
| a **box** of cookies | a **glass** of juice | a **liter** of water | a **head** of lettuce |
| a **carton** of eggs | a **piece** of fruit | a **pound** of meat | a **loaf** of bread |
| a **can** of soup | a **slice** of bread | a **tablespoon** of honey | a **sheet** of paper |
| a **carton** of milk | | a **teaspoon** of salt | a **stick** of butter |
| a **jar** of honey | | | a **tube** of toothpaste |

**4** Complete each sentence with the correct measurement word from the box.

| | | | |
| --- | --- | --- | --- |
| bowl | cup | jar | piece |
| ~~carton~~ | glass | loaf | stick |

1. Please get a ___carton___ of milk at the grocery store.

2. We need a _____ of butter for the recipe.

3. She drinks a _____ of orange juice every morning.

4. Would you like a _____ of pizza?

5. She usually has a _____ of soup and a sandwich for lunch.

6. He always has a _____ of tea after dinner.

7. We need a _____ of jam. How about strawberry?

8. I buy a _____ of bread at that bakery every morning.

**5** Choose the correct word to complete each sentence.

1. I'd like a glass of _____ , please.

   a. flour          (b.) water          c. honey

2. I'd like a bunch of _____ and three apples, please.

   a. lettuce          b. bananas          c. bread

3. My family drinks a gallon of _____ each week.

   a. meat        b. bread        c. milk

4. Would you like a cup of _____ ?

   a. pizza        b. coffee        c. cereal

5. Please buy a box of _____ at the grocery store.

   a. cookies        b. bread        c. eggs

6. We need a teaspoon of _____ for the recipe.

   a. sugar        b. eggs        c. bread

7. I always order a bowl of _____ here. It's delicious!

   a. cake        b. soup        c. juice

8. I buy two pounds of _____ every week.

   a. juice        b. gasoline        c. meat

**6** **WRITE & SPEAK.** Complete the sentences. Include measurement words. Then share your sentences with a partner.

I drink ___six glasses of water___ every day.

I have _____ in the morning.

I usually buy _____ every week.

Student A: *I drink six glasses of water every day.*

Student B: *I have a bowl of cereal in the morning.*

## 5.5   Some, Any

|  | Non-Count Nouns | Plural Count Nouns |
| --- | --- | --- |
| Affirmative Statements | I have **some** food at home. | I have **some** onions. |
| Questions | Do you have **any** paper?<br>Do you have **some** paper? | Do we need **any** cups?<br>Do we have **some** cups? |
| Negative Statements | We don't have **any** homework. | We don't need **any** onions. |

1. Use *some* in affirmative statements.

2. Use *any* in negative statements.

3. Use *some* and *any* in questions.

**REAL ENGLISH**

*Some* is often used to make offers.

*Would you like* **some** *coffee?*
*Do you need* **some** *help?*

**7** Circle *some* or *any* to complete each sentence.

1. I don't have **some** / (**any**) green peppers for the recipe.

2. We need **some** / **any** orange juice.

3. She doesn't eat **some** / **any** meat.

4. Add **some** / **any** water to the soup.

5. We don't have **some** / **any** bread.

6. My aunt knows **some** / **any** great recipes.

7. She doesn't use **some** / **any** salt in her cooking.

8. Adam doesn't want **some** / **any** soup.

9. I need **some** / **any** money for groceries.

10. He doesn't need **some** / **any** help.

**8** **WRITE & SPEAK.** Complete the sentences. Then share your sentences with a partner.

I usually eat some _____*rice*_____ every day.

I don't eat any _____ .

I'd like _____ right now.

I want some _____ .

*I usually eat some rice every day.*

# PRACTICE

**9** Complete the conversations. Use the words from the box. You can use some words more than once. Then listen and check your answers.

| any | bowl | box | glass | jar | pieces | slice | some |
|-----|------|-----|-------|-----|--------|-------|------|

1. **Server:**  Are you ready to order?

   **Customer:**  Yes, I'd like a (1) _____*glass*_____ of lemonade.

   **Server:**  I'm sorry. We don't have (2) _____ lemonade. Would you like (3) _____ iced tea or juice?

   **Customer:**  Hm. No, thank you. I'd just like a (4) _____ of water.

   **Server:**  Would you like something to eat?

   **Customer:**  Yes, I'd like a (5) _____ of tomato soup.

2. **Dalia:** You look great, Mila. What's your secret?

   **Mila:** Thanks. I just eat healthy food. I don't eat (6) _____ meat, and I eat a lot of vegetables. I also have about six (7) _____ of fruit each day.

   **Dalia:** Wow! Do you eat (8) _____ bread or sweets?

   **Mila:** I don't eat sweets, but every morning I have a (9) _____ of bread with (10) _____ butter on it! I love butter!

3. **Andy:** Do you have (11) _____ easy recipes for dinner?

   **Tasha:** Sure. I have a very easy recipe for spaghetti. For four people, you need a (12) _____ of pasta, a (13) _____ of pasta sauce, and (14) _____ cheese.

   **Andy:** Great! Thank you!

---

**REAL ENGLISH**

*Or* is often used to talk about choices.

> A: *Would you like soup **or** salad?*
> B: *Soup, please.*

*Also* is often used to show an addition.

> *I'd **also** like some salad.*

---

**10  EDIT.** Find and correct five more errors with *some, any,* and measurement words.

## Fried Rice

This is an easy recipe for fried rice. You need two or three eggs, four cup of rice, any green onions, and some oil. Any people also use some small piece of chicken or shrimp. First, chop the onions and mix the eggs. Then, cook the eggs in two tablespoon of oil, and add some salt. Next, fry the rice in some oil. Add the eggs and onions. This is also delicious with a cup of vegetable such as peas.

A woman prepares a meal in a kitchen in Pematangsiantar, Sumatra, Indonesia.

## 11   LISTEN, SPEAK & WRITE.

**A**   Listen to the conversation about a recipe. Circle the ingredients the speakers have at home.

|  | Some | A carton | 2 tablespoons | A large bag | 2 cups | 1 |
|---|---|---|---|---|---|---|
| Potatoes |  |  |  | ✓ |  |  |
| Eggs |  |  |  |  |  |  |
| Onions |  |  |  |  |  |  |
| Flour |  |  |  |  |  |  |
| Oil |  |  |  |  |  |  |
| Salt |  |  |  |  |  |  |

▲ Potato pancakes

**B**   Listen again. In the chart in exercise **A**, check the amount you hear for each ingredient.

**C**   Work with a partner. Ask and answer *Yes/No* questions about the conversation from exercises **A** and **B**. Use the information from the chart in exercise **A** to help you.

Student A: *Do they have any potatoes?*      Student B: *Yes, they do.*

**D**   **WRITE** affirmative and negative statements about the conversation from exercises **A** and **B**. Use the information from the chart to help you.

1. <u>They have a large bag of potatoes.</u>

2. _____

3. _____

4. _____

5. _____

6. _____

## 12 READ, SPEAK & WRITE.

**A** Work with a partner. Read the recipe. Notice the underlined verbs. Which verbs do you know? Ask your teacher about any verbs you do not know.

### Spaghetti Sauce Recipe

### Directions

<u>Chop</u> the onion and the green pepper.
<u>Slice</u> the garlic.
<u>Heat</u> two tablespoons of olive oil in a sauce pan.
<u>Fry</u> the onion and the green pepper in the olive oil for 5-10 minutes.
<u>Stir</u> the onion and green pepper every one to two minutes.
<u>Add</u> the garlic, ground beef, salt, and Italian seasoning.
<u>Mix</u> the tomato sauce, tomatoes, and tomato paste and add them to the pot.
<u>Add</u> the sugar.
<u>Boil</u> water in a large pot.
<u>Add</u> the spaghetti to the water and <u>cook</u> it for 12-15 minutes.
<u>Heat</u> a loaf of garlic bread in the oven.
<u>Serve</u> the spaghetti with garlic bread and some salad.

**B** Work with a partner. Partner A, look at this page. Partner B, look at page A6.

Partner A, look at the ingredients in the recipe. Ask your partner questions about the ingredients. Put a check (✓) next to the food you have. Write the amount of each ingredient you need to buy.

Partner A: *Do we have **one and a half pounds of ground beef**?*

Partner B: *No, we don't. We have **one pound**.*

### Spaghetti Sauce

### Ingredients

- 1½ pounds of ground beef
- 2 tablespoons of olive oil
- 1 large onion
- 1 green pepper
- 2 tablespoons of garlic
- 2 cans of tomato paste
- 1 can of tomato sauce
- 1 large can of cooked tomatoes
- 1 tablespoon of Italian seasoning
- 1 teaspoon of salt
- 2 tablespoons of sugar

**Shopping List**

½ pound of ground beef

**C** Compare your shopping list with your partner's. Are your shopping lists the same?

**13 APPLY.** Complete the exercises.

**A** Do you know any easy recipes? What ingredients do you need? Write the name of the ingredients and the amount you need of each. Use the recipe below as a model.

## Hot Chocolate Recipe

### Ingredients

- 1 cup of milk_____
- 2 tablespoons of sugar_____
- 1 tablespoon of cocoa_____

### Directions

Heat the milk in a pan, and slowly add the sugar and cocoa. Stir well, and then pour the hot chocolate into your favorite mug.

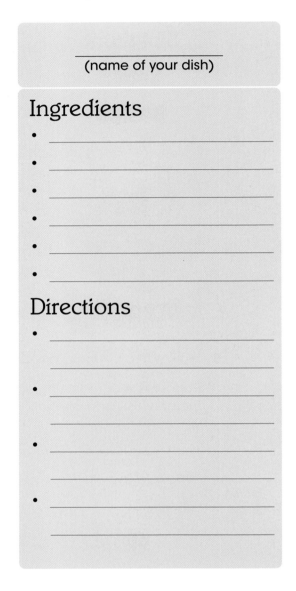

_____
(name of your dish)

### Ingredients

- _____
- _____
- _____
- _____
- _____
- _____

### Directions

- _____
  _____
- _____
  _____
- _____
  _____
- _____
  _____

**B** Work with a partner. Talk about how to make your recipes. Use the verbs in the box to help you. Then write the directions for your recipe in exercise **A**.

| | | |
|---|---|---|
| add | chop | mix |
| bake | fry | slice |
| boil | heat | stir |

**C** Discuss these questions.

1. Are you a good cook?

2. What do you usually make?

## EXPLORE

CD2-10

**1   READ** the article about the Hadza people. Notice the words in **bold**.

# The Hadza People

The Hadza people live in northern Tanzania around Lake Eyasi. **Many** Hadza people are hunters and gatherers. In other words, they move from place to place to find food. They don't live in towns or cities, and they don't have permanent[1] homes. Instead, they build small, simple shelters.[2] This usually takes just **a few** hours.

The Hadza people don't buy their food. The women gather food from plants and trees. The Hadza eat **a lot of** berries. They also eat **a lot of** fruit from a tree called the *baobab*. Baobab fruit has **a lot of** vitamins, so it's an important part of the Hadza diet. The men hunt animals, but the Hadza people don't eat **much** meat. Most of their diet comes from plants. Honey is also an important part of the Hadza diet. It's sweet and delicious, and just **a little** honey has **a lot of** calories.[3]

The Hadza people have a very interesting, traditional lifestyle.

For more information about the Hadza's traditional lifestyle, look at the links below.

How many Hadza people live in Tanzania today?

How much land do the Hadza people own?

What language do the Hadza people speak?

Facts about Lake Eyasi

[1] **permanent:** lasting for a long time or forever
[2] **shelter:** a building or covering that gives protection
[3] **calorie:** a unit used to measure the amount of energy in food

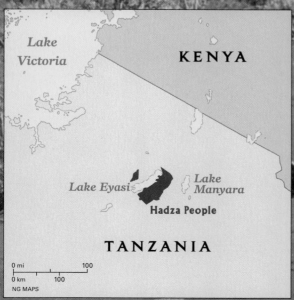

Lake Victoria
KENYA
Lake Eyasi
Lake Manyara
**Hadza People**
TANZANIA
0 mi          100
0 km      100
NG MAPS

▲ Hadza hunters, Lake Eyasi, Tanzania

**2 CHECK.** Read each statement about the Hadza people. Then circle **T** for *true* or **F** for *false*.

1. The Hadza people don't eat a lot of berries.          **T**     (**F**)

2. They eat a lot of fruit from the baobab tree.          **T**       **F**

3. Baobab fruit doesn't have a lot of vitamins.          **T**       **F**

4. The Hadza people don't eat a lot of meat.          **T**       **F**

5. Honey doesn't have a lot of calories.          **T**       **F**

**3 DISCOVER.** Complete the exercises to learn about the grammar in this lesson.

**A** Find and complete these sentences in the article from exercise **1** on page 163.

1. _____ Hadza people are hunters and gatherers.

2. They also eat _____ fruit from a tree called the *baobab*.

3. Baobab fruit has _____ vitamins, so it's an important part of the Hadza diet.

4. The Hadza people don't eat _____ meat.

**B** Look at the sentences in exercise **A**. Then circle **T** for *true* or **F** for *false* for each statement below. Discuss your answers with your classmates and teacher.

1. We use *many* with non-count nouns.          **T**       **F**

2. We use *a lot of* with non-count nouns.          **T**       **F**

3. We use *a lot of* with plural count nouns.          **T**       **F**

4. We use *much* in negative statements with non-count nouns.          **T**       **F**

▶ Baobab trees in Morondava, Madagascar

# LEARN

## 5.6 Much, Many, A Lot Of

| | Non-Count Nouns | Plural Count Nouns |
|---|---|---|
| Affirmative Statements | I eat **a lot of** honey. | We eat **a lot of** vegetables. <br> **Many** people drink tea in the morning. |
| Negative Statements | They don't eat **much** meat. <br> She doesn't drink **a lot of** coffee. | They don't grow **many** vegetables. <br> We don't eat **a lot of** potatoes. |
| Questions | Does he drink **much** coffee? <br> Do they grow **a lot of** fruit? | Do you eat **many** snacks? <br> Does the menu have **a lot of** choices? |

1. Use *much, many,* or *a lot of* to talk about large quantities.

2. Use *much* with non-count nouns in negative statements and questions.

3. Use *many* with plural count nouns in affirmative statements, negative statements, and questions.

4. Use *a lot of* with plural count nouns or non-count nouns in affirmative and negative statements and questions.

**4** Look at the underlined noun in each sentence. Then circle the correct word(s) to complete each statement or question.

1. The Hadza people eat **much** / (**a lot of**) <u>fruit</u>.

2. They don't drink **many** / **much** <u>milk</u>.

3. The women collect **a lot of** / **much** <u>berries</u>.

4. Does honey have **many** / **much** <u>calories</u>?

5. The article has **a lot of** / **many** interesting <u>information</u> about the Hadza people.

6. We have **a lot of** / **much** <u>questions</u> about the article.

7. I read **a lot of** / **much** <u>articles</u> about food and healthy lifestyles.

8. **Many** / **Much** <u>people</u> in my country eat cereal for breakfast.

9. Do people in your country drink **many** / **much** <u>coffee</u>?

10. Do people in your country eat **much** / **many** <u>potatoes</u>?

11. Are **much** / **many** <u>people</u> in your country vegetarians?

12. Do you eat **many** / **much** <u>junk food</u>?

### REAL ENGLISH

In informal situations, some people use *lots of* instead of *a lot of*.

A: *We have* ***lots of*** *homework tonight.*

B: *Yeah, we do.*

**5** **SPEAK.** Work with a partner. Ask and answer questions 9–12 from exercise **4**.

Student A: *Do people in your country drink much coffee?*

Student B: *Yes, the coffee in my country is delicious!*

## 5.7 A Few, A Little

| 1. Use *a few* and *a little* to talk about small quantities. | I drink **a few** cups of tea every day.<br>I usually put **a little** milk in my tea. |
| 2. Use *a few* with plural count nouns. | I have **a few** pencils in my bag.<br>She has **a few** questions. |
| 3. Use *a little* with non-count nouns. | He drinks **a little** orange juice every morning.<br>We have **a little** time before class. |

**6** Complete each sentence with *a few* or *a little*.

1. She drinks _____ a few _____ cups of tea every day.

2. I'm not a vegetarian. I usually have _____ meat for dinner.

3. A healthy diet includes _____ pieces of fruit every day.

4. People in my country eat _____ junk food, but not a lot.

5. I always buy _____ bananas when I go to the market.

6. I like _____ sugar in my coffee.

7. _____ students in our class are vegetarians.

8. The article has _____ new words.

9. I need _____ help with my homework.

10. We only have _____ minutes before class.

## 5.8 Questions with *How Much* and *How Many*

| Questions | | | Answers |
|---|---|---|---|
| How Much/<br>How Many | Non-Count Noun | | |
| **How much** | time<br>homework | do we have? | A lot.<br>Not much.<br>A little. |
| | Plural Count Noun | | |
| **How many** | oranges<br>chairs | do we need? | A lot.<br>Not many.<br>A few. |

**REAL ENGLISH**

The noun after *how much* or *how many* is not necessary when the listener knows what the speaker is referring to.

A: *We need some oranges.*
B: **How many** *do we need?*
A: *Six.*
B: **How much** *do they cost?*
A: *Seventy-five cents each.*

| 1. Use *how much* and *how many* for questions about quantity. | **How much** milk is in the refrigerator?<br>**How many** bottles of water do we need? |
| 2. Use *how much* with non-count nouns. | ✓ **How much** money does it cost?<br>✗ How <u>much</u> dollars does it cost? |
| 3. Use *how many* with plural count nouns. | ✓ **How many** bags do you have?<br>✗ How <u>many</u> luggage do you have? |

**7** Use the words in parentheses to write questions with *How much/How many.*

1. (cups of coffee / you / drink / every day)

   <u>How many cups of coffee do you drink every day?</u>

2. (meat / you / eat / every day)

   _____

3. (meals / you / have / every day)

   _____

4. (junk food / you / eat)

   _____

5. (money / you / spend / on food / every week)

   _____

6. (free time / you / have / every day)

   _____

7. (hours / you / sleep / every night)

   _____

8. (brothers / you / have)

   _____

9. (homework / our teacher / give)

   _____

10. (hours / you / spend on homework / every day)

    _____

11. (English / you / know)

    _____

12. (languages / you / speak)

    _____

**8 SPEAK.** Work with a partner. Ask and answer the questions from exercise **7.**

Student A: *How many cups of coffee do you drink every day?*

Student B: *Two.* OR *I don't drink coffee.*

# PRACTICE

**9** Circle the correct word(s) to complete each statement. Then write a *How much/How many* question about the underlined noun in each statement.

1. She puts (a lot of)/ **much** / **many** <u>honey</u> in her tea.

   _How much honey does she put in her tea?_

2. Yogurt doesn't have **many** / **a few** / **much** <u>calories</u>. It's a healthy food.

   _____

3. She eats **much** / **a few** / **a little** <u>pieces</u> of fruit every day.

   _____

4. I don't use **much** / **a little** / **a few** <u>sugar</u>. I don't like my coffee very sweet.

   _____

5. Samir doesn't use **much** / **many** / **a few** <u>salt</u>.

   _____

6. We don't need **many** / **much** / **a little** <u>flour</u> for the recipe.

   _____

7. My daughter drinks **a lot of** / **much** / **a few** <u>milk</u>. It's her favorite drink.

   _____

8. Hilda has **a lot of** / **a little** / **a few** <u>homework</u>. She has seven assignments for tomorrow.

   _____

9. **A few** / **A little** / **Much** <u>students</u> are absent today.

   _____

10. Marco speaks **a little** / **a few** / **much** <u>languages</u>. He speaks French, Italian, and Arabic.

    _____

11. Pedro knows **much** / **many** / **a lot of** <u>English</u>. He lives in Toronto.

    _____

12. I'm new here. I don't know **much** / **many** / **a few** <u>people</u> in this city.

    _____

13. I don't have **a little** / **a lot of** / **a few** <u>time</u> these days. I'm very busy at work.

    _____

14. These flowers cost **many** / **much** / **a lot of** <u>money</u>. They're very expensive!

    _____

**10  EDIT.** Read the information about the Mediterranean Diet Food Pyramid. Find and correct six more errors with *much*, *many*, *a lot of*, *a few*, and *a little*. There is more than one way to correct some errors.

# The Mediterranean Diet Food Pyramid

This food pyramid shows the Mediterranean diet. In general, Mediterranean people eat
~~many~~ *a lot of* brown rice and pasta. They eat much vegetables. They eat a lot of fruit and nuts. They eat a few cheese and yogurt. They also eat fish a little times every week, but they don't eat many meat. They also don't eat much sweets. They usually have fresh fruit for dessert. They drink a lot of water—six to eight glasses a day.

The Mediterranean lifestyle is also very healthy. Mediterranean people get a lot of exercise, and they spend much time with their families. This is the Mediterranean secret to a long and happy life!

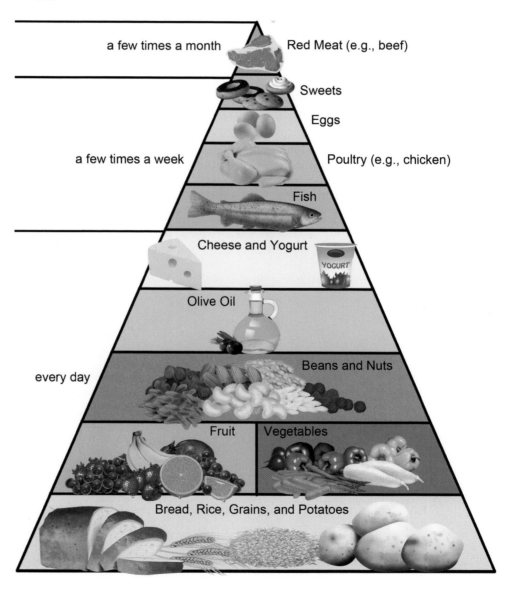

a few times a month — Red Meat (e.g., beef)

Sweets

Eggs

a few times a week — Poultry (e.g., chicken)

Fish

Cheese and Yogurt

Olive Oil

every day — Beans and Nuts

Fruit   Vegetables

Bread, Rice, Grains, and Potatoes

## 11 LISTEN & SPEAK.

**A** Read each statement in the chart. Then listen to Sunil and Henry talk about their diets. Is the statement true for Sunil, Henry, or both? Put a check (✓) in the correct column(s).

| | Sunil | Henry |
|---|---|---|
| 1. He's from India. | ✓ | |
| 2. He eats a lot of rice. | | |
| 3. He eats a lot of beef. | | |
| 4. He eats a lot of fruit. | | |
| 5. He eats a lot of vegetables. | | |
| 6. He eats a little fruit. | | |
| 7. He doesn't eat any beef. | | |
| 8. He eats a lot of potatoes. | | |
| 9. He eats a lot of ice cream. | | |
| 10. He only eats a few sweets. | | |
| 11. He follows the Mediterranean diet. | | |
| 12. He follows the Mediterranean lifestyle. | | |

**B** Work with a partner. Ask and answer questions about Sunil and Henry's diets. Use the information from exercise **A**.

Student A: *Does Henry eat much rice?*       Student B: *No, he doesn't.*

## 12 APPLY.

**A** Work with a partner. What do you eat? Ask and answer *How much/How many* questions about the food in the box below. Add three of your own ideas. Use *much, many, a lot of, a few,* or *a little*. Put a check (✓) next to the things your partner eats a lot of. Put **X** next to the things your partner only eats a little of.

Student A: *How much rice do you eat?*       Student B: *A lot. How about you?*

| | | |
|---|---|---|
| 1. rice _____ | 6. fish _____ | 11. potatoes _____ |
| 2. fruit _____ | 7. vegetables _____ | 12. yogurt _____ |
| 3. cheese _____ | 8. ice cream _____ | 13. (your idea) _____ |
| 4. eggs _____ | 9. sweets _____ | 14. (your idea) _____ |
| 5. meat _____ | 10. bread _____ | 15. (your idea) _____ |

**B** Discuss your answers. Do you or your partner follow the Mediterranean diet? Report to your classmates.

**C** Now write a paragraph about your partner. Does he or she follow the Mediterranean diet? Use your information from the chart in exercise **A**.

*Barbara doesn't follow the Mediterranean diet. She eats a lot of ice cream and sweets. She doesn't eat many vegetables. She doesn't eat a lot of fruit . . .*

Charts
5.1–5.3,
5.5–5.7

**1** Circle the correct words to complete the paragraph.

## Potluck Dinners

Do you have (1) **a / an /Ø/ the** potluck dinners in your country? (2) **Many / Much** people have this kind of dinner in the United States. At a potluck dinner, everyone brings (3) **some / any** food to share. At many potluck dinners, (4) **a / an / Ø** people usually bring (5) **a / an / Ø / the** dish for eight to twelve people. (6) **Some / Any** people bring (7) **a lot of / a few / much** food. Other people don't bring (8) **some / much**. (9) **A / An / Ø / The** potluck dinners are always (10) **a lot of / a few** fun.

Charts
5.1, 5.4–5.8

**2  LISTEN, WRITE & SPEAK.**

CD2-12

**A** Listen and circle the correct word(s) to complete each sentence.

1. This story is about a **coffee / tea** ceremony in **England / Ethiopia**.

2. The ceremony takes a few **minutes / hours**.

3. **Many / A few** people come in the open door of the house.

4. People sometimes have **a lot of / a few** salty snacks.

5. The ceremony takes **a little / a lot of** time.

▲ An Ethiopian woman pours coffee.

**B** Use the words in parentheses to write *How much/How many* questions about the Ethiopian coffee ceremony.

1. (time / people / usually / spend) ___How much time do people usually spend___ with their morning coffee?

2. (time / the coffee ceremony / take) _____ in Ethiopia?

3. (neighbors / come) _____ in the open door?

4. (minutes / she / boil / the coffee) _____ with the water?

5. (cups of coffee / they / usually / have) _____ ?

**C** Work with a partner. Ask and answer the questions from exercise **B**.

**D** Do you have any customs such as the coffee ceremony in Ethiopia? Discuss with your classmates and teacher.

*In Argentina, we drink yerba mate. We drink it with friends or family members. The first person drinks and then gives the mate to the next person. We often drink mate in the park. It's not a ceremony, but it's a very nice custom.*

▲ Typical gourds used for yerba mate, San Telmo District, Buenos Aires, Argentina

Charts
5.1–5.3,
5.5

**3 EDIT.** Read the information about barbecues. Add the missing articles in the correct places. There are five more errors.

## Barbecues

The definition of *barbecue* is "to cook meat or other food over ∨<sup>an</sup> open fire, usually outside."

It's common all over world. In many countries, people barbecue on grill. Other people use a spit. spit turns to cook the meat. It's great idea for party!

Charts
5.1, 5.2,
5.5

CD2-13

**4 LISTEN & SPEAK.**

**A** Listen to the conversation about a barbecue dinner. What do the speakers plan to serve? Write the correct word for each category.

1. Main dish: _____  3. Dessert: _____

2. Vegetable: _____

CD2-13

**B** Listen again. Check the items on their shopping list.

---

### Shopping List

☐ steak
☑ hamburger meat
☐ tomatoes
☐ onions
☐ broccoli
☐ green beans
☐ corn
☐ apple pie
☐ vanilla ice cream
☐ hamburger rolls

---

**C** Work with a partner. Look at the items on the shopping list in exercise **B**. What amount of each item do you think they need for eight hungry people? Ask each other questions and discuss.

Student A: *How much hamburger meat do they need?*     Student B: *Two pounds.*

Charts
5.1–5.8

### 5  SPEAK & WRITE.

**A** Plan a picnic for your class. What food do you like? What food is good for a picnic? Look at and discuss the items in the box and discuss them with your group.

Student A: *I like apples. I don't like broccoli.*

Student B: *Me neither, and broccoli isn't good for a picnic.*

| | | | | |
|---|---|---|---|---|
| apples | chicken | juice | pears | soda |
| bananas | coffee | lemonade | peppers | soup |
| beans | cookies | milk | pie | steak |
| beef | cucumbers | noodles | pizza | strawberries |
| bread/rolls | eggs | nuts | potatoes | tea |
| broccoli | fish | olives | rice | tomatoes |
| cake | grapes | onions | salad | water |
| carrots | hamburgers | oranges | sandwiches | |
| cheese | ice cream | pasta | shrimp | |

**B** Decide on the menu for your picnic. Choose a main dish, a vegetable, a dessert, drinks, and other items. Then make a shopping list.

Student A: *Let's have hamburgers.*

Student B: *I don't like hamburgers. How about sandwiches?*

Student C: *Good idea. How much bread do we need?*

# Connect the Grammar to Writing

**1  READ & NOTICE THE GRAMMAR.**

**A**  Read the paragraph. What kind of event is it? Discuss with a partner.

## How to Plan a Potluck Dinner

It's very easy to plan a potluck dinner. Here are some things you need to do. First, choose the date and the time. Next, invite some friends. Prepare or buy some food. Put some plates and glasses on a table. Leave some space on the table for a lot of other dishes. Last, put on some music. Have a great party!

◀ A potluck dinner

### GRAMMAR FOCUS

In the paragraph in exercise **A**, the writer uses *a, the, a lot of*, and *some* before count and non-count nouns.

**Remember:** Use *a* before count nouns that begin with a consonant sound. Use *an* before count nouns that begin with a vowel sound. Use *the* before specific nouns when there is only one of something or when you want to refer to a person, place, or thing for a second time.

*It's very easy to plan **a** potluck party.*

*First, choose **the** date and **the** time.*

**B**  Read the paragraph in exercise **A** again. Underline the nouns and circle the articles. Why does the writer use *a* and *the*? Discuss your answers with a partner.

**C**  Complete the chart with information from the paragraph in exercise **A**. How many steps does the writer list? Write them in the chart.

| How to Plan a Potluck |
|---|
| 1. Choose the date and the time. |

**2** **BEFORE YOU WRITE.** Think of an event; for example, a party, a wedding, or a trip. What do you need to do to prepare for this event? Write the steps in the chart. Use the chart in exercise **1C** as a model.

| How to Plan a _____ |
| --- |
| |

**3** **WRITE** a paragraph about how to plan your event. Use the information in your chart from exercise **2** and the paragraph in exercise **1A** to help you.

> **WRITING FOCUS**    Using Transition Words
>
> Writers use transition words to explain the steps in a process. Use transition words at the beginning of a sentence. These transition words are often used to explain a process: *first, second, then, next, after that, last,* and *finally.*
>
> **First,** choose the date and the time.
> **Next,** invite some friends.
> **Last,** put on some music.

**4** **SELF ASSESS.** Read your paragraph. Underline the articles *a, an,* and *the.* Then use the checklist to assess your work.

- [ ] I used an article before each singular count noun. [5.1–5.3]
- [ ] I used a plural ending at the end of each plural count noun. [5.1, 5.4–5.7]
- [ ] I used singular verbs with non-count nouns. [5.1]
- [ ] I used transition words at the beginning of sentences. [WRITING FOCUS]

# *There Is/There Are*

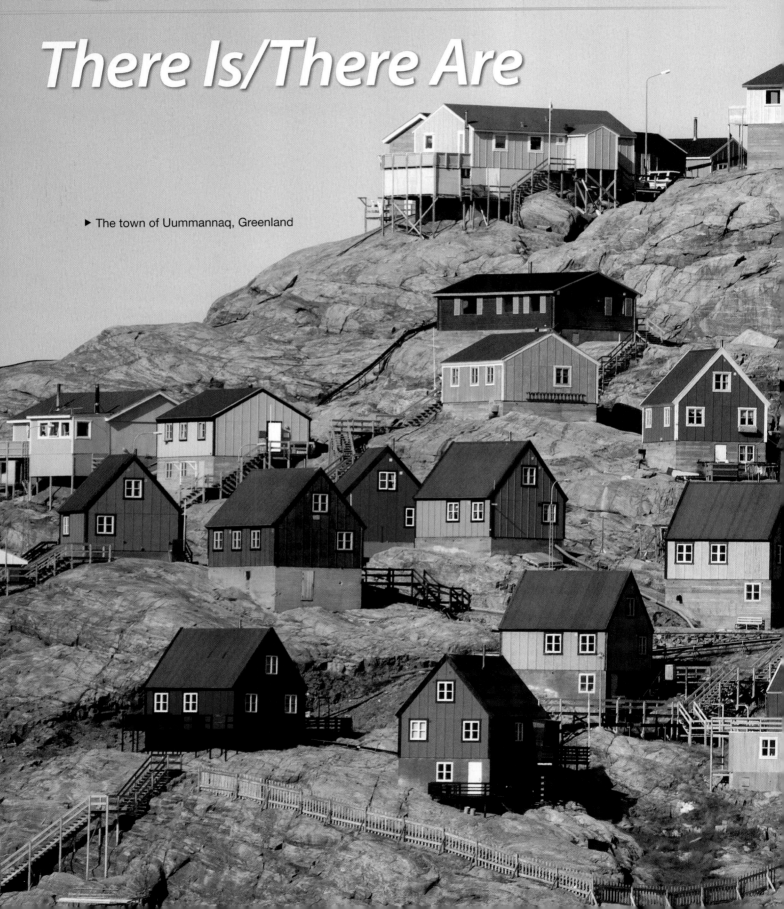

▶ The town of Uummannaq, Greenland

### EXPLORE

CD2-14

**1 READ** the online forum about side trips from Shanghai, China. Notice the words in **bold**.

## Side Trips from Shanghai

**VIAJERO**
**Madrid, Spain**

I have three free days during a business trip to Shanghai. Any ideas for side trips[1]?
I'm interested in historic places. Thanks.

**CHEN C**
**Qingdao, China**

**There are** a lot of interesting places near Shanghai. Suzhou is on the Grand
Canal. It's famous for its gardens. Near Suzhou, **there are** a lot of ancient water
towns. Tongli is my favorite. It has 15 canals, and **there are** 49 bridges. It's
beautiful.

**VIAJERO**
**Madrid, Spain**

Thanks. **Is there** a bus from Shanghai to Tongli? And how much time do I need
to see the city? **Are there** many tourists there?

**VIET**
**Da Nang, Vietnam**

**There's no** bus, but **there's** a train to Suzhou and a bus from Suzhou to Tongli.
One day is enough time to see Tongli. Go early in the day when **there aren't** a
lot of tourists.

**VIAJERO**
**Madrid, Spain**

Thanks, everyone!

[1] **side trip:** a short trip during a longer visit

Yangzhou
Zhenjiang
Nanjing
Wuxi
*Yangtze*
Suzhou
Luzhi
Shanghai
*Tai Hu*
Tongli
Zhouzhuang
Nanxun
Xitang
Wuzhen
Hangzhou
Shaoxing
Ningbo

*East
China
Sea*

Canal
Dark blue type represents a
water town near Shanghai.

0 km    40
0 mi        40

**2 CHECK.** Read the false statements. Then correct each statement to make it true.

1. There are ~~not~~ a lot of places to visit near Shanghai.

2. There are 25 canals in Tongli.

3. There are 49 roads in Tongli.

4. There is no train from Shanghai to Suzhou.

5. There are a lot of tourists in Tongli early in the day.

**3 DISCOVER.** Complete the exercises to learn about the grammar in this lesson.

**A** Find these sentences in the online forum from exercise **1**. Write the missing words.

1. _____ a lot of interesting places near Shanghai.

2. It has 15 canals, and _____ 49 bridges.

3. _____ bus, but _____ a train to Suzhou and a bus from Suzhou to Tongli.

4. Go early in the day when _____ a lot of tourists.

**B** Look at the sentences in exercise **A**. Then choose the correct words to complete each statement below. Discuss your answers with your classmates and teacher.

1. We use **there is** / **there are** with singular nouns.

2. We use **there is** / **there are** with plural nouns.

▼ A water town near Suzhou, China

# LEARN

## 6.1 *There Is/There Are*: Statements

| | | Affirmative | | |
|---|---|---|---|---|
| *There* | *Be* | Subject | | |
| There | is<br>'s | a hospital<br>a lot of traffic | on Main Street. | |
| | are | two elevators | in this building. | |

| | | Negative | | |
|---|---|---|---|---|
| *There* | *Be + Not* | Subject | | |
| There | is not<br>isn't | a hospital<br>a lot of traffic | on Elm<br>Street. | |
| | are not<br>aren't | any classes | at night | |

| | |
|---|---|
| 1. Use *There is/There are* to refer to things or people for the first time and to emphasize that they exist. Sometimes we include additional information about when or where these things or people exist. | **There are** two students from Peru in my class.<br>**There is** a post office near my house.<br>**There's** a class from 9:30–12:30 on Monday. |
| 2. Use *There is*, *There's*, and *There isn't* with a singular count noun or a non-count noun*. | **There is** a <u>lamp</u> on the table.<br>**There isn't** a lot of <u>noise</u> on my street. |
| 3. Use *There are*, *There are not*, and *There aren't* with plural count nouns*. | **There are** a few <u>students</u> in the hallway.<br>**There aren't** any <u>classes</u> tomorrow. |
| 4. These contractions are used in conversation or informal writing: *There's*, *There isn't*, and *There aren't*. *There're* is used in conversation, but it is not common in writing. | A: **There's** a test on Monday.<br>B: *Really? I need to study this weekend!*<br><br>**There aren't** any students absent today. |
| 5. When *There is/are* is followed by two or more nouns, the verb usually agrees with the first noun. | **There's** a <u>book</u> and a <u>pen</u> on my desk.<br>**There's** <u>coffee</u> and <u>tea</u>.<br><br>**There are** some <u>cookies</u>, <u>milk</u>, and <u>juice</u> in the kitchen. |
| 6. *There is no* and *there are no* are often used in negative statements. They mean the same as *There isn't any* and *There aren't any*. | **There is no** homework tonight.<br>**There are no** classes on Sunday. |

*See 5.1 in Unit 5 for more information on count and non-count nouns.

**4** Complete each sentence with *There is* or *There are*.

1. _____There are_____ 49 bridges in Tongli.

2. _____ a bus to the town.

3. _____ some beautiful gardens in the city.

4. _____ two trains every morning.

5. _____ a lot of tourists in the summer.

6. _____ three buses and a train in the afternoon.

7. _____ a coffee shop and two restaurants in the train station.

8. _____ a lot of water towns in China.

9. _____ a park near my apartment.

10. _____ no museums in my city.

11. _____ a bus stop on my street.

12. _____ a lot of traffic in the morning.

**5  SPEAK.** Work with a partner. Make sentences with *There is/isn't, There are/aren't,* or *There is/are no.* Use the words in the box.

| in our classroom | in this building | in this city | in my family |
| --- | --- | --- | --- |

*There's a cafeteria in this building.*

*There aren't any vending machines in this building.*

## 6.2  *There Is/There Are*: Yes/No Questions and Short Answers

| Yes/No Questions | | | | Short Answers | |
| --- | --- | --- | --- | --- | --- |
| Be | There | Subject | | Affirmative | Negative |
| Is | there | an entrance a lot of traffic | on Main Street? | Yes, there is. | No, there isn't. |
| Are | | two elevators | in this building? | Yes, there are. | No, there aren't. |

| *Be* comes before *there* in Yes/No questions. | ✓ **Is there** a bus stop on Park Street? <br> ✗ There is a bus stop on Park Street? |
| --- | --- |

**6**  Underline the verb in each statement. Then change the statement to a *Yes/No* question.

| **Statements** | **Yes/No Question** |
| --- | --- |
| 1.  There <u>aren't</u> a lot of tourists in the summer. | <u>Are there</u> a lot of tourists in the summer? |
| 2.  There isn't much traffic. | _____ much traffic? |
| 3.  There's no parking. | _____ any parking? |
| 4.  There's a coffee shop near here. | _____ a coffee shop near here? |
| 5.  There aren't any more cookies. | _____ any more cookies? |
| 6.  There are no students absent today. | _____ any students absent today? |
| 7.  There's a lot of homework. | _____ a lot of homework? |
| 8.  There's a test today. | _____ a test today? |

**7** **SPEAK.** Work with a partner. Ask and answer *Yes/No* questions with *Is there* and *Are there*. Use a word or phrase from each column.

| a/an<br>any | bus stop<br>subway station<br>Indian restaurant<br>coffee shops<br>post office<br>parking<br>student(s) from Japan /<br>Germany / Brazil, etc. | near here<br>in this class |
|---|---|---|

Student A: *Is there a bus stop near here?*

Student B: *Yes, there's one on the next block.*

Student A: *Thanks!*

---

**REAL ENGLISH**

*There's one* is often used in answers to *Yes/No* questions with *Is there/Are there*.

A: *Is there a post office near here?*

B: *Yes, **there's one** across the street.*
  (one = a post office)

---

## 6.3 How Much ... Is There? / How Many ... Are There?

| How Much/<br>How Many | Subject | Be | There | | Answers |
|---|---|---|---|---|---|
| **How much** | homework | is | | tonight? | There's a little.<br>A little.<br>A lot.<br>Not much. |
| **How many** | computers | are | there | in the library? | There are six.<br>Six.<br>A lot.<br>A few.<br>Not many. |

| 1. **Remember:** Use *How much* and *How many* for questions about quantity. | **How much** time **is there?**<br>**How many** Brazilian students **are there** in our class? |
|---|---|
| 2. **Remember:** Use *How much* with non-count* nouns. | ✓ **How much** space **is there?**<br>✗ **How <u>much</u>** windows **are there?** |
| 3. **Remember:** Use *How many* with plural count* nouns. | ✓ **How many** windows **are there?**<br>✗ **How <u>many</u>** space **is there?** |

*See 5.1 in Unit 5 for more information on count and non-count nouns.

**8** Complete each question with *much* or *many* and the correct form of *be*.

1. How _____many_____ buses _____are_____ there in the morning?

2. How _____ traffic _____ there at 5:00 p.m.?

3. How _____ tourists _____ there every summer?

4. How _____ information _____ there on the website?

5. How _____ universities _____ there in your city?

6. How _____ classrooms _____ there in this building?

7. How _____ teachers _____ there in this program?

8. How _____ snow _____ there in the winter?

9. How _____ desks _____ there in his room?

10. How _____ questions _____ there in this exercise?

# PRACTICE

**9 WRITE & SPEAK.**

**A** Use the words in parentheses to write questions with *How much . . . is there?* and *How many . . . are there?*

1. (students / in this class) __How many students are there in this class?__

2. (tables / in this room) _____

3. (floors / in this building) _____

4. (windows / in our classroom) _____

5. (homework / tonight) _____

6. (money / in your wallet) _____

7. (train stations / in your city) _____

8. (furniture / in your home) _____

**B** Work with a partner. Ask and answer the questions from exercise **A**.

Student A: *How many students are there in this class?*

Student B: *There are sixteen. / Sixteen.*

**C** Ask your partner other questions with *How much . . . is there?* and *How many . . . are there?* Use your own ideas.

Student A: *How many people are there in your family?*

Student B: *Three. / There are three. / Just one.*

**10 EDIT.** Read the conversation between two people on an airplane. Find and correct five more errors with *there is/there are.*

**Al:** Wow! Look at the islands. They're incredible.

**Dan:** They sure are. That's Santa Cruz Island over there.

**Al:** It looks like there ~~is~~ *are* some boats down there.

**Dan:** They're probably tour boats. There is a lot of tourists at this time of year.

**Al:** Is this your first time in the Galápagos Islands?

**Dan:** No. I'm actually from here. I live on San Cristóbal. It's that island over there.

**Al:** Really? Have there a town on the island?

**Dan:** Yes, there are a small town and a few thousand people on the island. They live there.

**Al:** How about hotels? There are any hotels on the island?

**Dan:** Yes, a few small ones, but there haven't any big hotels on the island.

**Al:** Do people live on all of the islands?

**Dan:** No, only on four of them.

**Al:** Interesting.

▶ Puerto Ayora harbor, Galápagos Islands

**11 READ, WRITE & SPEAK.**

CD2-15

**A** Read about the Galápagos Islands.

## The Galápagos Islands: Not Just Home to Animals

The Galápagos Islands belong to Ecuador and are about 600 miles (1000 kilometers) off the coast of South America. They are home to many different kinds of unusual animals, such as giant tortoises[1] and land iguanas. The islands are also home to over 25,000 people. There are permanent[2] residents on four of the islands. There are airports on two of the islands, Santa Cruz and San Cristóbal.

The island of Santa Cruz has the largest population. Many of the people there live in Puerto Ayora, a busy town with hotels, restaurants, banks, shops, scuba diving schools, and one of the Galápagos' two airports. It's an important tourist stop, so there are a lot of tourists in the town. The island has beautiful beaches, and, of course, a lot of interesting wildlife. The Charles Darwin Research Center is also on this island.

[1] **tortoise:** a land turtle
[2] **permanent:** lasting a long time

**B** Rewrite each false statement to make it true.

1. There aren't any unusual animals on the Galápagos Islands.

   <u>There are many unusual animals on the Galápagos Islands.</u>

2. There aren't any giant tortoises on the islands. _____

3. There are about 10,000 people on the islands. _____

4. There are four airports. _____

5. There isn't an airport on Santa Cruz. _____

6. There aren't any hotels in Puerto Ayora. _____

7. There aren't many tourists on Santa Cruz. _____

8. There's no wildlife on Santa Cruz. _____

**C** Write five or six quiz questions to find out how much a classmate remembers about the article from exercise **A**. Begin your questions with *Is there, Are there, How much,* and *How many.*

   <u>Are there any unusual animals on the Galápagos Islands?</u>

   _____

   _____

   _____

   _____

   _____

   _____

**D** Work with a partner. Ask and answer your quiz questions from exercise **C**.

Student A: *Are there any unusual animals on the Galápagos Islands?*

Student B: *Yes, there are.*

◄ A giant tortoise, Isabela Island, Galápagos Islands

## 12  LISTEN & SPEAK.

CD2-16

**A**  Listen to a man talk about Vancouver, Canada. Check (✓) the topics you hear.

| | | | |
|---|---|---|---|
| ✓ | fun activities | ☐ | water |
| ☐ | clubs and restaurants | ☐ | scenery |
| ☐ | cost of activities | ☐ | rain |
| ☐ | movies | ☐ | snow |
| ☐ | open space | ☐ | canals |
| ☐ | parks | ☐ | highway |
| ☐ | mountains | ☐ | bridges |
| ☐ | fishing | ☐ | traffic |

> **REAL ENGLISH**
>
> *There* sounds the same as *they're* and *their*. Be careful about the spelling when you write these.
>
> **There** is a man in the boat.
> I see Ted and Amy. **They're** in the park.
> **Their** house is on Pine Street.

CD2-16

**B**  The speaker does not like some things about Vancouver. Listen again and circle the things in exercise **A** he doesn't like.

**C**  Work with a partner. What does the speaker like about Vancouver? What doesn't he like about it? Use the topics from exercise **A** to help you.

*There are a lot of things to do. They're expensive.*

## 13  APPLY.

**A**  Think of a city or town. Do you like it? Why or why not? Complete the chart with your ideas.

| Things I like about _____ | Things I don't like about _____ |
|---|---|
| There are a lot of good restaurants. | There is a lot of traffic. |
| | |

**B**  Work with a partner. Tell your partner about your city or town. Talk about the things you like and do not like about it. Use the information from your chart in exercise **A**. Use affirmative and negative forms of *There is* and *There are*.

Student A: *My city is Lisbon in Portugal. There are a lot of good restaurants. Are there good restaurants in your city?*

Student B: *No. I'm from a small town. There aren't many restaurants. There are a lot of beautiful parks. Are there many parks in Lisbon?*

## EXPLORE

**1** **READ** the advertisement about home design. Notice the words in **bold**.

# Home Design

▼ A living room with straight lines, basic colors, and lots of empty space

What color are the walls? How much furniture do we need? Do we need a sofa? Where do we put it? Is there **enough art** on the walls? Do we have **too many things** on the tables? These are some common question about home design. There are many different ideas and opinions!

Some people like a very simple design. They like straight lines and basic colors such as white or black. In their opinions, most people have **too much furniture** in their homes. They like empty space. For them, "the right amount" of furniture is one or two pieces.

Other people prefer round edges and soft colors such as blue and beige. They like comfortable furniture, and they like to have **enough furniture** so that people can sit close together and talk. They like **enough tables** and **shelves** for their books, lamps, and photographs.

How about you? What do you like? What questions about home design do you have? Ask us! We're experts[1] in home design. <u>Contact us</u> today!

[1] **expert:** a person who knows a lot about a particular subject

**2 CHECK.** People have different ideas about home design. Write these words from the advertisement from exercise **1** on page 187 in the correct column of the chart.

basic colors       empty space       ~~simple design~~       straight lines
comfortable furniture       ~~round edges~~       soft colors

| Some people like . . . | Other people like . . . |
|---|---|
| simple design | round edges |
|  |  |
|  |  |
|  |  |

**3 DISCOVER.** Complete the exercises to learn about the grammar in this lesson.

**A** Find these sentences in the reading from exercise **1** on page 187. Write the missing words.

1. Do we have **too many** _____ on the tables?

2. In their opinions, most people have **too much** _____ in their homes.

**B** Look at the sentences in exercise **A**. Then choose the correct answer to complete each statement below. Discuss your answers with your classmates and teacher.

1. *Too much* and *too many* have a _____ meaning.

    a. positive

    b. negative

2. We use *too much* with _____ .

    a. plural count nouns

    b. non-count nouns

3. We use *too many* with _____ .

    a. plural count nouns

    b. non-count nouns

◄ A living room with soft colors and comfortable furniture

# LEARN

## 6.4 Too Much/Too Many + Noun

| | Too Much | Non-Count Noun | | Too Many | Plural Count Noun |
|---|---|---|---|---|---|
| We have | | homework. | We have | | chairs. |
| There is | too much | traffic. | There are | too many | tourists. |
| He drinks | | coffee. | He eats | | sweets. |

| | |
|---|---|
| 1. *Too much* and *too many* mean "more than necessary." They have a negative meaning. | There is **too much** noise. (We aren't happy about the noise.) There are **too many** people here. (We aren't happy about it.) |
| 2. Use *too much* with non-count nouns. | ✓ There is **too much** traffic. ✗ There are <u>too much</u> cars. |
| 3. Use *too many* with plural count nouns. | ✓ We have **too many** chairs. ✗ We have <u>too many</u> furniture. |

**4** Complete each sentence with *too much* or *too many*.

1. I don't like Marco's apartment. There's ___too much___ space with nothing in it.

2. There are _____ lamps in this room. Let's put one in the bedroom.

3. I don't like that wallpaper. It has _____ different colors.

4. Jill prefers a simple style. In her opinion, my house has _____ furniture.

5. My sister spends _____ money on furniture. She needs to save more money.

6. It's always difficult to find my keys. I have _____ things in my bag.

7. I don't like Seattle in the winter. It gets _____ rain.

8. There's no place to park. There are _____ cars here today.

9. I drink _____ soda. I need to stop.

10. _____ coffee keeps me awake at night.

**5** **WRITE & SPEAK.** Complete the sentences. Then share your ideas with a partner.

1. There's too much ___furniture___ in my home.

2. There are too many _____ in my home.

3. I eat too much _____ .

4. I eat too many _____ .

## 6.5  *Enough/Not Enough* + Noun

| | *Enough* | Non-Count Noun |
|---|---|---|
| We have | | time. |
| We don't have | enough | information. |
| There's | | furniture. |
| There isn't | | space. |

| | *Enough* | Plural Count Noun |
|---|---|---|
| We have | | desks. |
| We don't have | enough | chairs. |
| There are | | cups. |
| There aren't | | plates. |

| | |
|---|---|
| 1. *Enough* means "the necessary amount." | There is **enough** furniture. We don't need more furniture. |
| 2. *Not enough* means "less than the necessary amount." | There are **not enough** chairs. We need more chairs. |
| 3. Do not use *enough* with singular count nouns. | ✓ We have **enough** chairs in our classroom.<br>✗ We have **enough** <u>teacher</u> in our classroom. |

### 6  LISTEN.

**A**  Listen to each sentence. Is the amount *enough* or *not enough*? Put a check (✓) in the correct column.

| | Enough | Not Enough | | Enough | Not Enough |
|---|---|---|---|---|---|
| 1. | ☐ | ✓ | 5. | ☐ | ☐ |
| 2. | ☐ | ☐ | 6. | ☐ | ☐ |
| 3. | ☐ | ☐ | 7. | ☐ | ☐ |
| 4. | ☐ | ☐ | 8. | ☐ | ☐ |

**B**  Listen again. Complete the sentences from exercise **A**.

1. _There isn't enough_ furniture in the room.

2. _____ empty space.

3. _____ chairs.

4. _____ books for everyone.

5. We _____ money.

6. _____ time.

7. We _____ food for dinner.

8. _____ light in the kitchen.

# PRACTICE

**7** Read the statements. Then complete the sentence(s). Use *enough, not enough, too much,* and *too many.*

1. My apartment is very small. There are two sofas, three tables, and ten chairs in it.
   I have _too much furniture. There isn't enough space._

2. I need more shelves in my office. I have a lot of books. There isn't a place for all of them.
   I have _____. My office doesn't have
   _____.

3. I like my apartment. It has one bedroom, a living room, and a kitchen. It's perfect for me.
   My apartment has _____.

4. The sofa costs $600. I have $600. It's perfect.
   I have _____.

5. This classroom has 15 chairs. There are 18 students.
   This is a big problem. We don't have _____.

6. We have 25 books and 15 students.
   We have _____.

7. I don't want to drive to Ed's house. There are a lot of cars and buses on the roads today.
   There _____. Let's take the subway.

8. The apartment building has 12 parking spaces, and 20 people have cars.
   It's a big problem. There _____.

## 8 LISTEN & SPEAK.

CD2-19

**A** Listen to the conversation. Then choose the correct answer to complete each sentence.

1. They are talking about _____ .

   a. some friends' apartment          b. a hotel          c. their home

2. The two speakers are _____ .

   a. coworkers          b. a married couple          c. a mother and her son

CD2-19

**B** Listen again. Are the man and woman's opinions positive or negative? Write **P** for *positive* and **N** for *negative.*

|              | Man | Woman |
|--------------|-----|-------|
| Neighborhood | N   | P     |
| Stairs       |     |       |
| Windows      |     |       |
| Size         |     |       |
| Decor        |     |       |

**C** What are the problems with their friends' neighborhood and apartment? Use *too many/much* or *enough* with the words in the box.

| | | | | |
|---|---|---|---|---|
| flowers | nightclubs | parking | stairs | windows |
| light in the room | noise | space | things on tables | |

*There are too many nightclubs in the neighborhood.*

**9** **WRITE** sentences in your notebook about the photograph below. Use the words in parentheses and *too much/many* or *enough*.

1. (He / work)

   He has *too* much work.

2. (He / space on his desk to work)

3. (He / things on his desk)

4. (He / space for his coffee cup)

5. (There / papers in his office)

6. (He / furniture)

7. (His office / space)

8. (He / time to clean his office)

▲ A busy author and filmmaker at work in his messy office

**10** **APPLY.**

**A** Think about the positive and negative things about your own room, office, or home. In the chart, put a check (✓) to show your opinion about each item.

| | Too Much | Too Many | Enough | Not Enough |
|---|---|---|---|---|
| Space | ☐ | ☐ | ☐ | ☐ |
| Bookshelves | ☐ | ☐ | ☐ | ☐ |
| Furniture | ☐ | ☐ | ☐ | ☐ |
| Places for papers, books, furniture, windows, etc. | ☐ | ☐ | ☐ | ☐ |
| *Your idea* _____ | ☐ | ☐ | ☐ | ☐ |

**B** Work with a partner. Talk about your room, office, or home. Use the information from your chart in exercise **A**.

*My room is similar to the room in the photograph. I don't have enough space for . . .*

## EXPLORE

**1** **READ** the online forum about dune shacks. Notice the words in **bold**.

Cape Cod,
Massachusetts

# Dune Shacks

**Li592** Does **anyone** know **anything** about dune shacks[1] on the beach on Cape Cod,
Massachusetts?

**BW** Yes. Don't stay in one! They are very, very small, and they don't have any water or
electricity.[2] There's **nothing** to do there. **Someone** told me about them, so we stayed in
one last summer. Big mistake.

**BeachBunny** That's the best thing about them. There isn't **anything** to do! Actually,
that's not true. There's always **something** to do—walk on the beach, swim in the
ocean, and enjoy nature. I love the dune shacks.

**Traveler212** These little houses are very special, but they're not for **everyone**. Take
warm clothes and **something** to read. Don't take **anything** that uses electricity. They're
a great place to go and just relax!

**Birdy** The dune shacks are fine in warm, sunny weather. On a rainy day, **no one** wants
to stay out there. Believe me. I know! I love the beach, but now I stay in town at a hotel.
There's always **something** to do in town, even when it rains.

[1] **dune shack:** a small house on the sand dunes of a beach
[2] **electricity:** energy used for heat or light, or to power machines

▶ A dune shack, Cape Cod,
Massachusetts, USA

**2 CHECK.** Are the writers' opinions from the online forum on page 193 positive or negative? Write **P** for *positive* and **N** for *negative*.

|  | Opinion |
|---|---|
| 1. BW | N |
| 2. BeachBunny |  |
| 3. Traveler212 |  |
| 4. Birdy |  |

**3 DISCOVER.** Complete the exercises to learn about the grammar in this lesson.

**A** Find these sentences from the online forum in exercise **1** on page 193. Write the missing words.

1. _____ told me about them, so we stayed in one last summer.

2. That's the best thing about them. There isn't _____ to do.

3. There's always _____ to do.

4. Take warm clothes and _____ to read.

5. Don't take _____ that uses electricity.

**B** Look at the sentences in exercise **A**. Then choose the correct word to complete each statement below. Discuss your answers with your classmates and teacher.

1. We use *anything* and *something* for _____ .

    a. people          b. things

2. We use *anyone* and *someone* for _____ .

    a. people          b. things

3. We use _____ for negative statements.

    a. *something*          b. *anything*

▼ A beach cottage in Truro, Cape Cod, Massachusetts, USA

# LEARN

## 6.6 Indefinite Pronouns: *Nothing, Anything, Something, Everything*

| Affirmative Statements | |
| --- | --- |
| Indefinite Pronoun | |
| Something Nothing Everything | is on your desk. |

| Negative Statements | | |
| --- | --- | --- |
| | Indefinite Pronoun | |
| There isn't | anything | in the kitchen. |
| I don't need | | from the store. |

| Yes/No Questions |
| --- |
| Do you want **anything** from the store? |
| Is there **something** wrong? |
| Do we have **everything?** |

| | |
| --- | --- |
| 1. Use the indefinite pronouns *nothing, anything, something,* and *everything* to refer to things that are not specific or are not known. | There's **nothing** in the box.<br>**Everything** in that store is expensive. |
| 2. *Nothing* has a negative meaning. Use it with an affirmative verb form, not a negative verb. | ✓ He <u>knows</u> **nothing** about Cape Cod.<br>✗ He <u>doesn't know</u> nothing about Cape Cod. |
| 3. Use *anything* in negative statements. | I don't see **anything** under the table.<br>There isn't **anything** for homework tonight. |
| 4. Use *anything, something,* and *everything* in questions. | Is there **anything** in that bag?<br>Would you like **something** to drink?<br>Is **everything** ready? |
| 5. Use the singular form of the verb when an indefinite pronoun is the subject. | ✓ **Nothing** <u>is</u> wrong with my computer.<br>✗ **Nothing** <u>are</u> wrong with my computer. |

### REAL ENGLISH

Indefinite pronouns are often used with infinitives.

*There's always **something** <u>to do</u> on Cape Cod.*
*I want **something** <u>to eat</u>.*
*There's **nothing** <u>to do</u> there.*

**4** Choose the correct word to complete each sentence.

1. I don't know _____ about dune shacks.　　a. nothing　　ⓑ anything

2. I love Cape Cod. There's always _____ to do there.　　a. something　　b. anything

3. Don't stay in a dune shack. There's _____ to do!　　a. nothing　　b. anything

4. Do you know _____ about Cape Cod?　　a. nothing　　b. anything

5. This is a very boring town. There's _____ to do here!　　a. nothing　　b. anything

6. Take _____ warm to wear. It gets cold at night.　　a. something　　b. nothing

7. I don't have _____ warm to wear.

    a. anything      b. nothing

8. The hotel is very nice. _____ is perfect.

    a. Everything      b. Anything

9. I'm hungry. Let's get _____ to eat.

    a. something      b. nothing

10. I'm not thirsty. I don't want _____ to drink.

    a. nothing      b. anything

**5** Complete the sentences with *nothing, anything, something,* or *everything.* For some sentences, more than one answer is possible.

1. I don't know _____anything_____ about Boston, Massachusetts. I want to learn about it.

2. Boston is an interesting city. There's always _____ to do there.

3. Let's get up early and walk around town. I want to see _____.

4. The city has _____ : interesting museums, great restaurants, shops, and beautiful parks.

5. Does Jackie know _____ about buses from Boston to Cape Cod?

6. I know _____ about the history of Boston. I want to learn about it.

7. Do you know _____ about Boston or Cape Cod?

8. Tell me _____ about your hometown.

▼ Boston, Massachusetts, USA

## 6.7 Indefinite Pronouns: *No One, Nobody, Anyone, Anybody, Someone, Somebody, Everyone, Everybody*

| Affirmative Statements | |
| --- | --- |
| Indefinite Pronoun | |
| **No one/Nobody**<br>**Someone/Somebody**<br>**Everyone/Everybody** | is absent today. |
| | knows the answer. |

| Negative Statements | | |
| --- | --- | --- |
| | Indefinite Pronoun | |
| There isn't | **anyone/anybody** | in the kitchen. |
| I don't know | | in your class. |

| Yes/No Questions |
| --- |
| Is **anyone/anybody** home? |
| Does **everyone/everybody** understand the problem? |
| Is there **someone/somebody** at the door? |

| | |
| --- | --- |
| 1. The indefinite pronouns *no one, nobody, someone, somebody, everyone,* and *everybody* are used to refer to people that are not specific or are not known. | **Nobody** lives in that house.<br>There's **someone** in the office. |
| 2. *No one* and *nobody* have a negative meaning. Use them with affirmative verb forms, not negative verb forms. | ✓ I <u>know</u> **nobody** from Spain.<br>✗ I <u>don't know nobody</u> from Spain. |
| 3. Use *anyone* and *anybody* in negative statements. | I don't know **anyone** from Spain.<br>There isn't **anybody** from Norway in our class. |
| 4. Use *anyone, anybody, someone, somebody, everyone,* and *everybody* in questions. | Does **anybody** live in that house?<br>Is there **someone** at the door?<br>Is **everybody** ready? |
| 5. **Remember:** Indefinite pronouns are always singular, not plural. They take the same form of the verb as *he, she,* and *it.* However, we often use a plural pronoun to refer back to *everyone.* | ✓ **Everybody loves** ice cream.<br>✗ **Everybody** <u>love</u> ice cream.<br><br>A: *Where **is everyone?***<br>B: ***They're** all in the coffee shop.* |

**6** Choose the correct indefinite pronoun to complete each sentence.

1. Do you know **no one** / (**anyone**) from Cape Cod?

2. Is **someone** / **everyone** ready to go? We're late!

3. I work with **someone** / **anyone** from Boston.

4. I see **somebody** / **anybody** in the yard. Who is it?

5. **Anyone** / **Everyone** likes the beach. Let's go there on Saturday.

6. **Anyone** / **Someone** in our building plays loud music every night.

7. I don't know **anybody** / **nobody** from Thailand.

8. **Anyone** / **No one** is in the office. Let's come back later.

**7** Complete each sentence with *no one, anyone, someone,* or *everyone.* For some sentences, more than one answer is possible.

1. It's rainy today. _____No one_____ is on the beach.

2. Listen! _____ is at the door.

3. Does _____ speak Italian?

4. I don't know _____ from Iceland.

5. _____ knows Alice. She has a lot of friends.

6. Our classroom is empty. Where is _____?

7. Does _____ have an extra pencil? I need one for the test.

8. _____ is absent. We're all here.

# PRACTICE

**8** Complete each conversation with the correct indefinite pronouns. In some sentences, more than one answer is possible.

1. A: Let's do ___*something*___ different on vacation this winter. How about camping?

   B: What? Are you serious? _____ goes camping in the winter!

2. A: Is _____ wrong?

   B: No, _____ is wrong. I'm fine.

3. A: Knock on the door again. There's always _____ home.

   B: Well, there's _____ there now.

4. A: Do we need more chairs?

   B: No, we have enough for _____ .

5. A: There's _____ wrong with my camera.

   B: I'd like to help you, but I don't know _____ about cameras.

## 9 LISTEN & SPEAK.

CD2-21

**A** Read each statement. Then listen to a conversation about camping and glamping (a new form of camping). Circle **T** for *true* or **F** for *false*.

1. Someone wants to go camping.     (**T**)    **F**

2. Everyone likes to go camping.     **T**    **F**

3. Camping is a relaxing vacation.     **T**    **F**

4. Everyone gets enough sleep.     **T**    **F**

5. Glamping is a lot of work.     **T**    **F**

6. In glamping, someone else gets wood for the fire.     **T**    **F**

7. In glamping, someone cooks for you.     **T**    **F**

8. No one likes the idea of glamping.     **T**    **F**

> **REAL ENGLISH**
>
> *Someone else* means another person or a different person.
>
> *Jack doesn't know anything about cameras. Let's ask* **someone else**.
>
> A: *Who's at the door? Is it Lucy?*
>
> B: *No, it's* **someone else**.

CD2-21

**B** Listen again. Complete the sentences from the conversation with the correct indefinite pronouns. Then listen again and check your answers.

1. What does _____*everyone*_____ want to do for vacation?

2. Does _____ want to go camping?

3. On vacation, I don't want to do _____ .

4. I want to relax and do _____ .

5. You don't do any work or _____ .

▲ A luxury tent

6. _____ else does _____ for you.

7. _____ else gets the wood for the fire.

8. _____ good is ever free, right?

**C** Work with a partner. Discuss these questions.

1. Is camping a relaxing vacation? Why or why not?

2. Do you want to try glamping? Why or why not?

**10** Complete the conversation with *everyone, everything, no one, nothing, anyone,* or *anything*. Then listen and check your answers.

CD2-22

**Alex:** Hey, (1) _____*everyone*_____! Let's talk about our camping trip.

First, (2) _____ needs to bring a sleeping bag.

**Matt:** Right. We also need a tent or (3) _____ to put over our sleeping bags.

Does (4) _____ have one?

**Jim:** I have a tent.

**Alex:** Great. Next, it gets cold at night. Does (5) _____ have warm clothes?

**Matt:** No. I don't have (6) _____ warm to wear. Does (7) _____

have an extra jacket or something?

**Jim:** Yeah, I do. Now, how about food? We need eggs or (8) _____ for breakfast. How about pancakes? They're easy to make.

**Alex:** Sure. That's fine. There's a store near the campground. It sells (9) _____ : food, maps, bug spray . . .

**Jim:** Great. Let's go there tomorrow.

> **REAL ENGLISH**
>
> We often use *or something* in speaking to add another possibility.
>
> A: *Where's Pamela?*
> B: *I don't know. Maybe her bus is late **or something**.*

**11 APPLY.** Work in a small group. Follow the directions below.

**A** Decide on a type of trip to take (e.g., an overnight camping trip, a visit to a city with an overnight stay in a hotel, or a tour, etc.). Decide on a place to go (e.g., Paris, the Galápagos Islands, a national park, etc.). Write three sentences about the reasons for your decision.

*There's always something to do there. Someone makes all the arrangements. No one needs to . . .*

**B** Make a list of things you need to do to prepare for the trip. Then write a conversation about your plans. Use the conversation from exercise **10** as a model. Use indefinite pronouns.

*Everyone needs to bring something warm to wear.*

**C** Role-play your conversation for your classmates.

Charts
6.1–6.7

CD2-23

**1  LISTEN.** Complete the conversation about a beach house. Use the words in the box. You can use some words more than once. Then listen and check your answers.

| | | | |
|---|---|---|---|
| anyone | there's | is there | enough |
| anything | there isn't | are there | much |
| nobody | there are | | too much |
| something | there aren't | | |

**Luisa:** I'm so excited about our little beach house. Let's go this weekend and figure out the furniture.

**Carmen:** We don't need (1) _____ much _____ furniture. (2) _____ much space.

**Rosa:** True. We don't want to have (3) _____ furniture. What do we need?

**Luisa:** Well, we need (4) _____ to sit on, so we need some chairs.

**Rosa:** (5) _____ a few chairs in my garage. Let's use those.

**Carmen:** OK, good. Does (6) _____ have a small table?

**Luisa:** I do. (7) _____ one in my bedroom at home.

**Rosa:** Great! (8) _____ space for a sofa?

**Luisa:** Yes, (9) _____ space for a small one.

**Carmen:** How about the kitchen?

**Rosa:** It's really small. It doesn't have (10) _____ space.

(11) _____ many cabinets or shelves.

**Luisa:** That's OK. Do you want to cook on vacation? I don't!

**Carmen:** Me neither. (12) _____ wants to cook on vacation.

**Rosa:** True! After all, it is a vacation house.

▼ A small cottage near the ocean in Wellfleet, Cape Cod, Massachusetts, USA

Charts
6.1–6.3

**2 EDIT.** Find and correct six more errors with *There is/There are*, *Yes/No* questions, and questions with *How much/How many . . . is/are there.*

> _There are_

**Reporter:** Welcome back to *WZCZ News*. Listen to this everyone! ~~There's~~ great white sharks near the beach in Cape Cod, Massachusetts. We're on the phone now with Tom Hardy. He's in our traffic helicopter over the beach. Tom, tell us, how much sharks are there? There is any danger?

**Tom:** Yes! There are a shark right below me. I see a lot more nearby. I'm glad I'm in a helicopter!

**Reporter:** Right. Are there many people in the water?

**Tom:** No, there isn't. There's a shark warning, and everyone knows about the danger.

**Reporter:** OK, Tom. Thanks. How many traffic is there today?

**Tom:** Usually, there aren't a lot of traffic out here, but today there are a lot of cars on the roads. Everyone wants to see the sharks!

Charts
6.1–6.7

🎧
CD2-24

**3 LISTEN, SPEAK & WRITE.**

**A** Listen to the conversation about an apartment. What does the apartment have? Check (✓) the items on the list below.

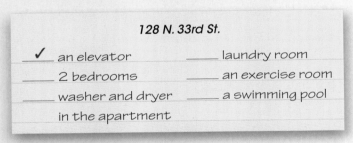

> **128 N. 33rd St.**
>
> ✓ an elevator      _____ laundry room
> _____ 2 bedrooms      _____ an exercise room
> _____ washer and dryer    _____ a swimming pool
> _____ in the apartment

**B** Write questions about the apartment.

1. (How many / bedrooms )
   _How many bedrooms are there?_

2. (a washer and dryer)
   _____

3. (enough / laundry rooms)
   _____

4. (How many / units)
   _____

5. (How many / buildings)
   _____

6. (an exercise room)
   _____

7. (have / a swimming pool)
   _____

8. (anyone / in the apartment / now)
   _____

**C** Work with a partner. Use your questions from exercise **B** to practice the conversation about an apartment.

Charts
6.1–6.7

**4 SPEAK.** Partner A, look at the picture. Partner B, look at the picture on page A6. Ask and answer questions to find eight differences between the two pictures.

*How many sofas does it have?*     *Is there a table?*     *Is there anything on the table?*

**5 SPEAK.** Work with a partner. Discuss the room in the photo. Ask and answer questions with *enough, too many,* and *too much.*

Student A: *Do you like the room design?*

Student B: *No, I don't. There's too much empty space.*

# Connect the Grammar to Writing

## 1 READ & NOTICE THE GRAMMAR.

**A** Read the paragraph. Does the writer like the college? Discuss with a partner.

# My College

I like my college. It has a beautiful campus. There are about 1500 students. Everyone is very friendly. There is always someone to talk to. The classes are small. There are no large lectures, and the professors know all of their students' names. In my opinion, there is only one problem. There is too much homework!

Unfortunately, the college is in a very small town. There is only one restaurant. There are only two small stores. There are no movie theaters, and there is nothing to do on weekends. After college, I want to live in a big city.

---

**GRAMMAR FOCUS**

In the paragraph in exercise **A**, the writer uses affirmative and negative forms of *there is/there are* to express her opinion about a place.

... **there is** nothing to do on weekends.
**There is** too much homework!

---

**B** Read the paragraph in exercise **A** again. Underline the sentences with *There is* and *There are* (affirmative and negative). Then work with a partner and compare answers.

**C** Complete the chart with information from the paragraph in exercise **A**. What does the writer like about her college? What doesn't she like about it?

| My College | |
|---|---|
| Positive Things | Negative Things |
| It has a beautiful campus. | |

**2 BEFORE YOU WRITE.** Think of a place or a community. What do you like about it? What don't you like about it? Write notes in the chart. Use the chart from exercise **1C** as a model.

| _____ (your place or community) | |
|---|---|
| Positive Things | Negative Things |
| | |

**3 WRITE** a paragraph about your place or community. Use the information from your chart in exercise **2** and the paragraph in exercise **1A** to help you.

> **WRITING FOCUS**     Expressing Opinions
>
> An opinion is how someone feels about something. It can be positive or negative. These introductory phrases are commonly used to introduce an opinion: _fortunately, unfortunately, in my opinion, personally_, and so on.
>
> **In my opinion**, there is only one problem.
> **Unfortunately**, the college is in a very small town.

**4 SELF ASSESS.** Read your paragraph. Underline _there is_ and _there are_ (negative and affirmative). Then use the checklist to assess your work.

- [ ] I used a singular count noun or non-count noun after _there is_. [6.1]
- [ ] I used a plural count noun after _there are_. [6.1]
- [ ] I used a non-count noun after _too much_. [6.4]
- [ ] I used a plural count noun after _too many_. [6.4]
- [ ] I used introductory phrases to introduce the opinions in my paragraph. [WRITING FOCUS]

# Present Progressive

▲ A climber in an ice cave, Myrdalsjokull Glacier, Iceland

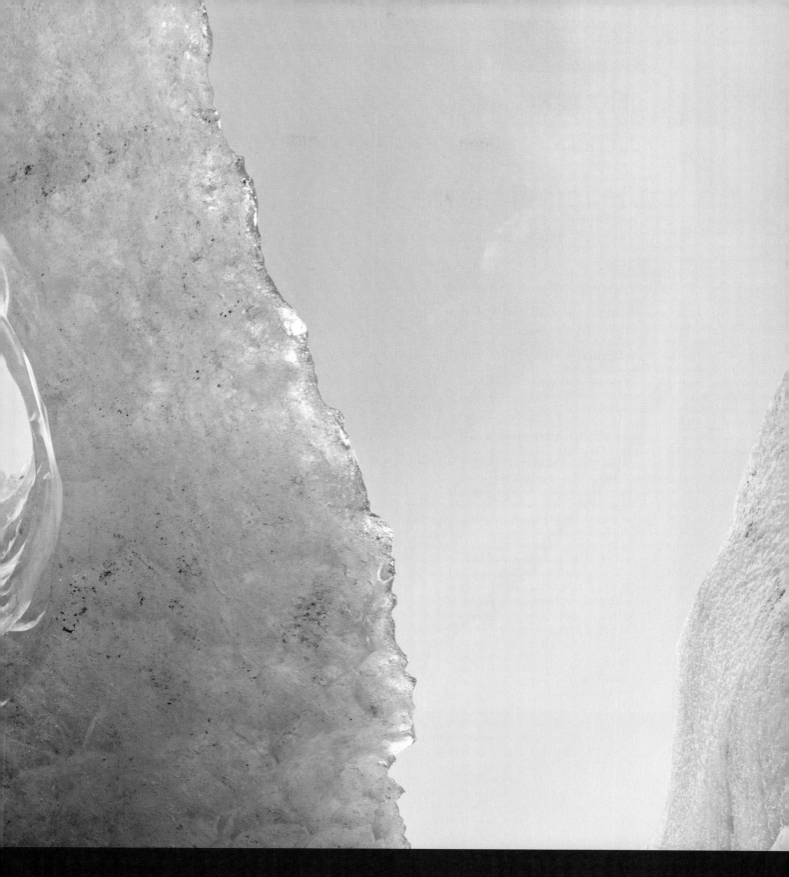

### EXPLORE

CD2-25

**1 READ** the conversation about highliners. Notice the words in **bold**.

Norway

# Highliners

**Angie:** Hey, Cary. What are you doing?

**Cary:** Oh, hi, Angie. **I'm looking** at photos of extreme sports.[1] Look at this one!

**Angie:** Oh, wow. That's scary! How high are they?

**Cary:** 3600 feet. The article says they**'re walking** toward Troll Wall. It's the highest cliff in Europe. It's in Norway.

**Angie:** That's really extreme—it's incredible!

**Cary:** Yeah, it's called "highlining." See. They**'re balancing**[2] on lines. They**'re not wearing** shoes. I guess that helps them balance. It says they're tied to the lines. They**'re wearing** belts[3] or something for safety.

**Angie:** That's good, but I'm glad **I'm not doing** that. I don't like heights.[4]

**Cary:** Me neither. Listen. Here's a quote from the photographer. His name's Branislav Beliancin. He**'s standing** really close to the edge[5] of the mountain. He says, "You need to be careful because you are directly on the mountain's edge. One bad step and bye-bye."

**Angie:** He**'s not joking**. That's true for the highliners, too!

[1] **extreme sport:** a sport that is physically dangerous such as bungee jumping
[2] **balance:** the ability to stand, walk, etc., without falling down
[3] **belt:** a piece of leather, plastic, etc., worn around the waist
[4] **heights:** high places
[5] **edge:** the place or line where something ends

**2 CHECK.** Read each statement about the highliners. Then circle **T** for *true* or **F** for *false*.

1. The highliners are in Norway.                                  (T)        F

2. The highliners are wearing shoes.                        T          F

3. Angie wants to try highlining.                               T          F

4. Cary doesn't like heights.                                      T          F

5. Beliancin is walking on a highline in this photo.    T          F

**3 DISCOVER.** Complete the exercises to learn about the grammar in this lesson.

**A** Find these sentences in the conversation from exercise **1**. Write the missing words.

1. I _____ at photos of extreme sports.

2. The article says they_____ toward Troll Wall.

3. They_____ shoes.

4. He_____ very close to the edge of the mountain.

**B** Look at the sentences in exercise **A**. Notice the verbs. Then choose the correct answer to complete the statement below. Discuss your answer with your classmates and teacher.

The verb after *be* _____ .     a. ends with an -s

                                                  b. is the base form

                                                  c. has -*ing* at the end

◄ Highliners Alexander
Lauterbach and Julien Miller
walk on lines of nylon webbing
in the mountains of Norway.

# LEARN

## 7.1 Present Progressive: Affirmative Statements

| Subject | Be | Verb + -ing |
|---|---|---|
| I | am<br>'m | writing. |
| You | are<br>'re | teaching. |
| He<br>She<br>It | is<br>'s | working. |
| We<br>You<br>They | are<br>'re | reading. |

| | |
|---|---|
| 1. Use the present progressive* to talk about actions that are in progress now. The actions are not completed. | A: Are you busy?<br>B: Yes, **I'm reading** this book for homework. |
| 2. Use the present progressive to talk about actions that are in progress at the present time but maybe not at this moment. | She**'s taking** three classes this semester.<br>He**'s teaching** in Japan this year. |
| 3. When the subject is doing two actions, do not repeat the subject and the verb *be*. | ✓ **I'm studying** and **living** in Chicago.<br>✗ I'm studying and <u>am</u> living in Chicago. |
| 4. **Remember:** Contractions are usually used in conversation and informal writing. | A: My brother**'s studying** in Italy this semester.<br>B: Interesting!<br><br>A: Are you busy right now?<br>B: Yes. **I'm doing** my homework. |

*The *present progressive* is sometimes called the *present continuous*.

**4** Underline the present progressive in each sentence.

1. They<u>'re walking</u> on lines above a valley.

2. They're wearing safety belts.

3. The photographer is standing on the cliff.

4. He's taking photos.

5. He's watching the highliners.

6. They're doing this in Norway.

7. We're talking about extreme sports.

8. She's looking at the photo and asking about the highliners.

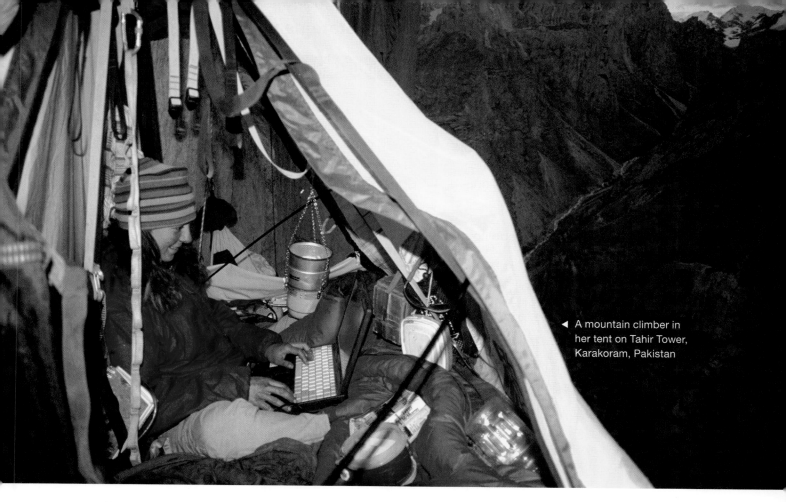

◄ A mountain climber in her tent on Tahir Tower, Karakoram, Pakistan

**5** Look at the photo of the mountain climber above. Then complete each sentence with the present progressive form of the verb in parentheses.

1. The mountain climber _____is relaxing_____ (relax) in her tent.

2. She _____ (climb) a mountain in Pakistan.

3. She _____ (wear) warm clothing.

4. She _____ (check) her e-mail.

5. Her tent _____ (hang) from the cliff.

6. The photographer _____ (look) at her through his camera.

7. He _____ (think) about the photo.

8. The other climbers _____ (camp) on the mountain.

9. They _____ (rest) in their tents.

10. Everyone _____ (wait) to continue the climb the next day.

**6** **SPEAK.** Work with a partner. Make three more sentences about the photo at the top of the page. Use the present progressive and the verbs from the box.

| hang | read | wear |
|------|------|------|

*She's wearing a red jacket.*

## 7.2 Present Progressive: Negative Statements

| Subject | Be Not | Verb + -ing |
|---|---|---|
| I | am not<br>'m not | writing. |
| You | are not<br>'re not<br>aren't | teaching. |
| He<br>She<br>It | is not<br>'s not<br>isn't | working. |
| We<br>You<br>They | are not<br>'re not<br>aren't | reading. |

**REAL ENGLISH**

When the subject is a noun that ends in an *-s, -z, -ch, -sh,* or soft *-g* sound, use the contraction with the verb. Do not use the contraction with the noun.

✓ *Marge isn't watching TV.*
   *She's studying.*
✗ *Marge's not watching TV.*
   *She's studying.*

To make a negative statement in the present progressive, put *not* after *be*.

He*'s not studying.* He's watching TV.

---

**7**  Change each affirmative statement to a negative statement.

1. We're doing an exercise right now. *We're not doing an exercise right now.*

2. I'm changing the sentences to questions. _____

3. She's taking a test. _____

4. Our teacher is wearing a jacket. _____

5. We're eating lunch. _____

6. He's checking his e-mail. _____

7. Tom's reading a book in class. _____

8. My parents are working right now. _____

9. You're teaching math. _____

10. They're taking Greek this semester. _____

**8  SPEAK.** Work with a partner. Say two things you are doing. Say two things you are not doing. Use the present progressive of the verbs in the box or your own ideas.

| sit | speak | stand | study | talk | wear |
|---|---|---|---|---|---|

*I'm speaking English.*

*We're not studying Spanish.*

## 7.3  Spelling Rules: -ing Forms

| | | |
|---|---|---|
| 1. Add -ing to the base form of most verbs. | talk-talk**ing** | study-study**ing** |
| 2. Verbs that end in a consonant and silent e: drop the -e and add -ing. | hike-hik**ing** | make-mak**ing** |
| 3. One-syllable verbs that end in CVC*: double the final consonant and add -ing. | shop-sho**pping** | sit-si**tting** |
| 4. Two-syllable verbs that end in CVC and have the stress on the first syllable: add -ing, but do not double the final consonant. | enter-enter**ing** | listen-listen**ing** |
| 5. Two-syllable verbs that end in CVC and have the stress on the second syllable: double the final consonant and add -ing. | begin-be**ginning** | |
| 6. Verbs that end in -w, -x, or -y: add -ing, but do not double the final consonant. | grow-grow**ing** | fix-fix**ing**   play-play**ing** |
| 7. Verbs ending in –ie: change the ie to y and add -ing. | tie-**tying** | die-d**ying** |

*consonant + vowel + consonant

**9**  Write the -ing form of each verb.

1. play _____
2. plan _____
3. try _____
4. make _____
5. practice _____

6. hit _____
7. exercise _____
8. climb _____
9. show _____
10. enter _____

**10**  **LISTEN** and complete the sentences.

CD2-26

1. The ice climber ___is using___ special equipment.

2. She _____ special boots.

▼ A female ice climber in British Columbia, Canada

3. The kiteboarder _____ in the air.

4. He _____ on his kiteboard.

5. The skier _____ to win the race.

6. She _____ very fast.

7. The hang glider _____ over the valley.

8. He _____ at the camera.

9. These people _____ interesting things.

10. They _____ fun.

▲ A professional kiteboarder

▲ A skier in a race

▲ A hang glider

# PRACTICE

**11** Complete the e-mail with the present progressive form of the verbs in parentheses. Use contractions where possible.

Greetings from Austria! (1) <u>I'm not spending</u> (I / not spending) this semester on campus. (2) _____ (I / study) here in Austria. (3) _____ (I / not live) in a dormitory. (4) _____ (I / stay) with a family in Salzburg. They're very nice. (5) _____ (They / help) me with my German. (6) _____ (I / do) a lot of interesting things here. (7) _____ (I / take) a hang gliding class on Saturdays. It's a little scary, but I like it! My class has four people, and our teacher is great. (8) _____ (We / learn) a lot. Right now (9) _____ (I / sit) outside and (10) _____ (enjoy) the scenery. (11) Some _____ (children / play) games and (12) _____ (have) a lot of fun. I miss you. Write soon!

Amanda

**12** Put the words in the correct order to make sentences about the photo on this page. Use the present progressive form of the verbs in bold.

1. this / **climb** / not / Andy / photo / in ___Andy is not climbing in this photo.___

2. He / dangerous / **do** / very / something _____

3. **jump** / from a cliff / He / to a rock _____

4. rope / a / **carry** / He _____

5. safety / belt / He / **wear** / a / not _____

6. He / right now / in the air / **fly** _____

7. The / **watch** / photographer / him _____

8. photos / He / great / **take** / some _____

◄ Andy Marquardt is a rock climber in Sedona, Arizona in the United States.

**13 EDIT.** Read the text message. Find and correct six more errors with the present progressive form and spelling.

>           *I'm*
> I texting you from Arizona. I'm visitting my sister Carol. Right now I'm siting near a huge cliff. I enjoying the scenery. Carol is takeing lessons. She's climbing the cliff with her teacher today. I waiting for her. They no are climbing very high, but it's dangerous!

**14 SPEAK & WRITE.** Complete the exercises.

**A** Work with a partner. Look at the words in the chart. Check (✓) the words you know. Ask your teacher about any words you do not know.

| Nouns | Verbs |
|---|---|
| bathing suit | feel scared/happy |
| belt | fly (in the air) |
| board | hold (onto) |
| father | kiteboard |
| hat | ride |
| kite | teach |
| ocean | learn |
| son | smile |
| water | stand |

**B** Look at the photos. Say a sentence in the present progressive about one of the photos. Use the words in exercise **14A** and your own ideas. Your partner says, "Photo A" or "Photo B."

Student A: *The father is wearing a hat.*        Student B: *Photo A.*

▲ A father and son kiteboard together in Nags Head, North Carolina, USA.

▲ A father teaches his six-year-old son to kiteboard in Nags Head, North Carolina, USA.

**C** Work with a partner. Complete the Venn diagram with information about the photos from exercise **B**. Use the words from exercise **A** and your own ideas. Use the present progressive.

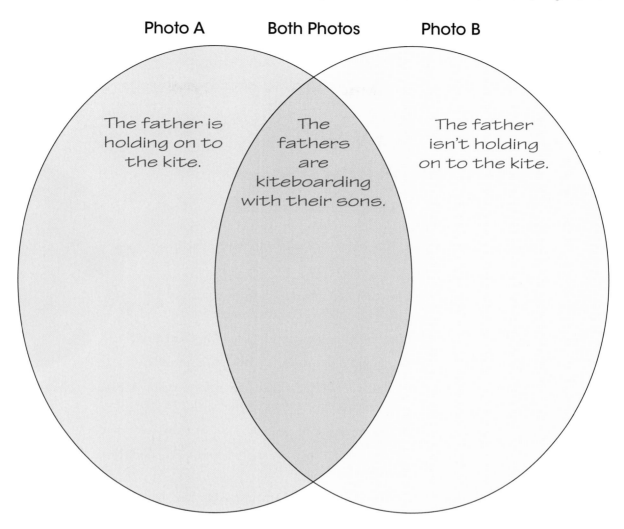

Photo A — The father is holding on to the kite.

Both Photos — The fathers are kiteboarding with their sons.

Photo B — The father isn't holding on to the kite.

**D** Form a group with another pair of students. Compare your Venn diagrams from exercise **C**.

**15 APPLY.** Work with a partner. Describe a classmate to your partner. Use affirmative and negative statements in the present progressive. Who is it?

Student A: *This student is wearing a white shirt. This student isn't talking right now.*

Student B: *Is it Layla?*

Student A: *Yes, it is. / No, it isn't.*

## EXPLORE

CD2-27

**1** **READ** the interview with a National Geographic photographer. Notice the words in **bold**.

# An Interview with Stephen Alvarez

Stephen Alvarez is a photographer for National Geographic. He travels to interesting places around the world and takes amazing photographs. His job is very exciting, but sometimes it's dangerous, too.

**Interviewer:** So, Stephen, please tell us about this photograph. Where are you exactly?

**Stephen Alvarez:** I'm in Oman at a cave[1] called Majlis al Jinn.

**Interviewer:** How high up are you in this photograph?

**Stephen Alvarez:** I'm about 700 feet off the cave floor. Below me, the rock opens up into one of the largest cave rooms in the world.

**Interviewer:** Are you afraid of heights? Do you ever look down?

**Stephen Alvarez:** No, I'm not afraid of heights, and it's a good thing. I have to look down to see where I am!

**Interviewer:** Are you hanging from ropes? Oh, yes, I see you are. What are the ropes attached to?

**Stephen Alvarez:** They're attached to steel[2] anchors.[3] I drilled the anchors into the rock.

**Interviewer:** **What are you taking a photograph of?**

**Stephen Alvarez:** I'm taking a photograph of Dr. Louise Hose. She's a geologist.[4]

**Interviewer:** **What's she doing?**

**Stephen Alvarez:** She's climbing out of the cave.

**Interviewer:** **Who's taking the photograph of you?**

**Stephen Alvarez:** My assistant, Ben.

**Interviewer:** Were you afraid?

**Stephen Alvarez:** No, I wasn't afraid. When I take photographs, I don't think about anything except the photograph.

**Interviewer:** How often do you do things like this? Is this kind of risk normal in your job?

**Stephen Alvarez:** I do things like this all the time. It's part of my job.

Oman

---

[1] **cave:** a large space or hole under the ground or in a mountain

[2] **steel:** a hard metal

[3] **anchor:** a device to keep something in place

[4] **geologist:** a person who studies the earth

**2 CHECK.** Choose the correct answer for each question about the interview from exercise **1**.

1. What is Stephen Alvarez's job?     a. He's a geologist.     b. He's a photographer.

2. Where is he?     a. At a cave.     b. On a mountain.

3. Is he afraid of heights?     a. Yes.     b. No.

4. What is Dr. Hose's job?     a. She's a climber.     b. She's a geologist.

5. How often does Alvarez do things like this?     a. Rarely.     b. All the time.

**3 DISCOVER.** Complete these exercises to learn about the grammar in this lesson.

**A** Look at the sentences from the interview in exercise **1**. Notice the words in **bold**. Then choose the correct word to complete the rule below.

1. What **are you taking** a photograph of?

2. What**'s she doing?**

**Rule:** The subject usually comes **before** / **after** the verb *be* in questions.

**B** Discuss your answer from exercise **A** with your classmates and teacher.

▶ Stephen Alvarez
and Dr. Louise Hose
at the top of Majlis
al Jinn in Oman

# LEARN

## 7.4 Present Progressive: *Yes/No* Questions and Short Answers

| Be | Subject | Verb + *-ing* |
|---|---|---|
| Am | I | |
| Are | you | |
| Is | he she it | working? |
| Are | we you they | |

**Yes/No Questions**

**Short Answers**

| | Affirmative | | | Negative | |
|---|---|---|---|---|---|
| | you | are. | | you're | |
| | I | am. | | I'm | |
| Yes, | he she it | is. | No, | he's she's it's | not. |
| | you we they | are. | | you're we're they're | |

| | |
|---|---|
| 1. The verb *be* goes before the subject in a *Yes/No* question. | Statement: Sam **is taking** the photograph. Question: **Is** Sam **taking** the photograph? |
| 2. Use the verb *be* in short answers to *Yes/No* questions. Do not use *do* or *does*. | A: **Is** she **sleeping?** ✓ B: Yes, she **is**. ✗ B: Yes, she <u>does</u>. |
| 3. **Remember:** There are two forms of contractions for negative short answers with *is* and *are*. | A: Is it working? B: No, it**'s not**. B: No, it **isn't**. A: Are they climbing? B: No, they **aren't**. B: No, **they're** not. |
| 4. **Remember:** Do not use contractions in affirmative short answers. | A: Is she checking her e-mail? ✓ B: Yes, she **is**. ✗ B: Yes, <u>she's</u>. |

**4** Read each question. Then choose the correct answer.

1. Is Stephen taking a photograph?           a. Yes, he is.           b. Yes, they are.

2. Is Dr. Hose climbing out of the cave?           a. Yes, she is.           b. Yes, she does.

3. Are they sitting in a tent?           a. No, they don't.           b. No, they aren't.

4. Are they working?           a. Yes, they're.           b. Yes, they are.

5. Is Stephen wearing a jacket?           a. No, he isn't.           b. No, he doesn't.

6. Is the interviewer asking questions?           a. Yes, she is.           b. Yes, they are.

7. Is Stephen answering the questions?           a. Yes, he's.           b. Yes, he is.

8. Are you looking at the photograph?           a. Yes, I'm.           b. Yes, I am.

9. Are they listening to the interview?           a. No, they're not.           b. No, we're not.

10. Are we studying English?           a. Yes, we are.           b. Yes, we do.

**5** Look at the photo and read the information. Then use the words in parentheses to write *Yes/No* questions in the present progressive.

The scientist in this photo is studying sharks. He's putting tags on them. The tags help him find the same sharks later and collect information about them. In this photo, he's standing inside a shark cage in the Bahamas. There's a boat above him.

1. ___Is the scientist studying___ (the scientist / study) sharks?

2. _____ (he / work) in the Bahamas now?

3. _____ (he / stand) in a shark cage?

4. _____ (the shark / swim) near the cage?

5. _____ (the shark / look) at him?

6. _____ (the scientist / do) something dangerous?

7. _____ (he / put) a tag on the shark?

8. _____ (he / wear) special clothing?

9. _____ (the people in the boat / help) him?

10. _____ (they / watch) him?

**6 SPEAK.** Work with a partner. Ask and answer the questions from exercise **5**.

Student A: *Is the scientist studying sharks?*　　　Student B: *Yes, he is.*

## 7.5 Present Progressive: *Wh-* Questions

| Wh- Word | Be | Subject | Verb + -ing | Answers |
|---|---|---|---|---|
| Who | are | you | calling? | I'm calling Alma. |
| What | is | she | studying? | She's studying Spanish. |
| Where | are | they | going? | They're going to the market. |
| Why | are | you | running? | We're late. Because we're late. |
| Why | aren't | you | eating? | I'm not hungry. Because I'm not hungry. |

| | |
|---|---|
| 1. **Remember:** *Wh-* questions ask for specific information. | A: **What** are you reading? B: An article about sharks. |
| 2. *Why* is often used with negative questions. | A: **Why** aren't you playing in the game? B: Because I have a cold. |
| 3. The contracted form of the verb *be* is usually used in negative questions. | Common: Why isn't she coming? Not Common: Why is she not coming? |

**7** Look at each sentence. Write a *Wh-* question about the underlined word or phrase.

1. I'm calling Ned. ___What are you doing?___

2. I'm crying <u>because this story is very sad</u>.

   _____

3. She's calling <u>her daughter</u>.

   _____

4. They're living <u>in Hong Kong</u>. _____

5. We're watching <u>a movie about sharks</u>. _____

6. He's working <u>at his father's company</u>. _____

7. She's teaching <u>English 101</u> this semester. _____

8. I'm not working today <u>because it's a holiday</u>. _____

> **REAL ENGLISH**
>
> In informal conversation, many common questions are in the present progressive.
>
> *How are you doing? (How're you doing?)*
> *How is it going? (How's it going?)*
>
> These questions are often used as greetings, and the speaker does not expect a specific answer.
>
> A: *How's it going?*
> B: *Oh, hey, Bob. How're you doing?*

**8 SPEAK.** Work with a partner. Ask and answer *Wh-* questions in the present progressive. Use the verbs in the box or your own ideas.

| do | live | sit | study | wear |
|---|---|---|---|---|

Student A: *Why are you wearing your jacket in class?*
Student B: *Because I'm cold.*

## 7.6 Wh- Questions with Who

| Questions about a Subject | | |
|---|---|---|
| Who | Be | Verb + -ing |
| Who | is | calling? |

| Answers |
|---|
| Hector. |
| Hector is. |
| Hector is calling. |

| Questions about an Object | | | |
|---|---|---|---|
| Who | Be | Subject | Verb + -ing |
| Who | is | he | calling? |

| Answers |
|---|
| Kayla. |
| He's calling Kayla. |

| | |
|---|---|
| 1. Wh- questions with *Who* can be about a subject or an object. In very formal English, *Whom* is used in questions about an object. | **Who** is talking? (*Who* = subject)<br>**Who** are you talking to? (*Who* = object of "to")<br>**Whom** are you talking to? |
| 2. **Remember:** In *Who* questions about a subject, use the singular form of the verb even if the answer is plural. | A: **Who** <u>is</u> studying French?<br>B: *I am. / She is. / They are.* |

**9** Read each question. Is it about a subject or an object? Check (✓) the correct column.

| | Subject | Object |
|---|---|---|
| 1. Who is helping them? | ✓ | ☐ |
| 2. Who is taking the photograph? | ☐ | ☐ |
| 3. Who is he talking to? | ☐ | ☐ |
| 4. Who are you working with? | ☐ | ☐ |
| 5. Who is talking? | ☐ | ☐ |
| 6. Who are they waiting for? | ☐ | ☐ |
| 7. Who is sitting next to Julio? | ☐ | ☐ |
| 8. Who is she calling? | ☐ | ☐ |
| 9. Who is he teaching? | ☐ | ☐ |
| 10. Who is teaching? | ☐ | ☐ |

**10** Read the answer to each question. Then complete the question. Use the present progressive form of the verb in parentheses.

1. A: Who _____ are you studying _____ (study) with?

   B: I'm studying with Fran and Taylor.

2. A: Who _____ (give) the lessons?

   B: Nick Stone. He's an excellent teacher.

3. A: Who _____ (stand) in the hallway?

   B: Alice and Tina.

4. A: Who _____ (sit) behind?

   B: He's sitting behind Anna.

5. A: Who _____ (write) on the board?

   B: Efren and Henri are.

6. A: Who _____ (live) with?

   B: She's living with her parents.

7. A: Who _____ (wait) for?

   B: We're waiting for Professor Carter.

8. A: Who _____ (teach) the class?

   B: Professor Lang is.

**11**  **SPEAK.** Work with a partner. Ask and answer questions with *Who*. Use the words in parentheses. Use short or long answers.

1. (Who / you / sit next to)

2. (Who / sit / in front of you)

3. (Who / wear / jeans today)

4. (Who / I / look at)

Student A: *Who are you sitting next to?*     Student B: *Martin.* OR *I'm sitting next to Martin.*

# PRACTICE

**12**  **LISTEN** and choose the correct answer for each question.

1. a. Yes, they are.     b. In the ocean.     c. Studying sharks.

2. a. Yes, he is.     b. Stephen is.     c. On the mountain.

3. a. No, they aren't.     b. In Thailand.     c. They're trying.

4. a. Yes, he is.     b. Michael.     c. Yes, he does.

5. a. Yes, I am.     b. With my brother.     c. I don't like scary movies.

6. a. Yes, I am.     b. English.     c. In London.

7. a. No, she isn't.     b. In Taipei.     c. Her parents.

8. a. No, she's reading.     b. Yes, they are.     c. Because she's tired.

## 13 WRITE & SPEAK.

**A** Look at the photos and read the captions. Then use the words in parentheses to complete each *Wh-* or *Yes/No* question. Use the present progressive.

PHOTO A

▲ Rescue workers in Sedona, Arizona

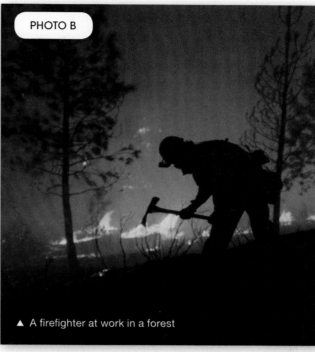
PHOTO B

▲ A firefighter at work in a forest

### Photo A

1. (What / those men / do) __What are those men doing__ ?

2. (Who / stand) _____ on the cliff?

3. (Where / those men / work) _____ ?

4. (they / work / at night in this photo) _____ ?

### Photo B

5. (What / the firefighter / do) _____ ?

6. (Why / the firefighter / do) this _____ ?

7. (the firefighter / wear) special clothing _____ ?

8. (the firefighter / sit) down _____ ?

**B** Work with a partner. Match each question in exercise **A** with the correct answer below. Then take turns asking and answering the questions.

a. _____ A rescue worker.

b. __1__ They're rescuing someone.

c. _____ In Arizona.

d. _____ He's fighting a fire.

e. _____ Yes, they are.

f. _____ Because it's his job.

g. _____ Yes, he is.

h. _____ No, he isn't.

Student A: *What are those men doing?*    Student B: *They're rescuing someone.*

▲ A technician on a wind turbine

## 14 LISTEN, WRITE & SPEAK.

CD2-29

**A** Listen to the conversation. Match each activity to the correct person.

1. Tay _____          a. He climbs wind turbines in his job.

2. Evan _____          b. He wants to climb in Logan Canyon.

3. Jake _____          c. He is working on a project.

**B** Write the correct question for each answer. Use the words in parentheses and the present progressive of each verb.

1. A: Who _____ (call)?                    B: Jake is.

2. A: What _____ (Tay / do)?               B: He's working on a project right now.

3. A: _____ (Evan / live) at home?         B: No, he's not.

4. A: What _____ (do)?                      B: He's working on wind turbines.

5. A: (make) _____ much money?              B: Yes, he's making a lot of money.

6. A: Where _____ (Evan / travel)?          B: All over the world.

7. A: _____ (Tay / joke)?                   B: No, he's serious.

8. A: Where _____ (Evan / work) now?        B: In Greece.

**C** Work with a partner. Look at the photo on page 226. Then write interview questions for the worker in the photo. Use the words in the box to help you.

| Nouns | | Verbs | |
|---|---|---|---|
| helmet | sun | blow | look at |
| rope(s) | wind | climb | look down |
| safety belt | wind turbine | hang | shine |
| | | hold on | turn |
| | | | wear |

What are you doing?

Is the turbine turning?

_____

_____

_____

_____

_____

## 15 APPLY.

**A** Work with a partner. Write questions for other classmates. Use the present progressive. Use the verbs in the box or your own ideas.

| do | live | sit | study | take | write | wear | text | look |
|---|---|---|---|---|---|---|---|---|

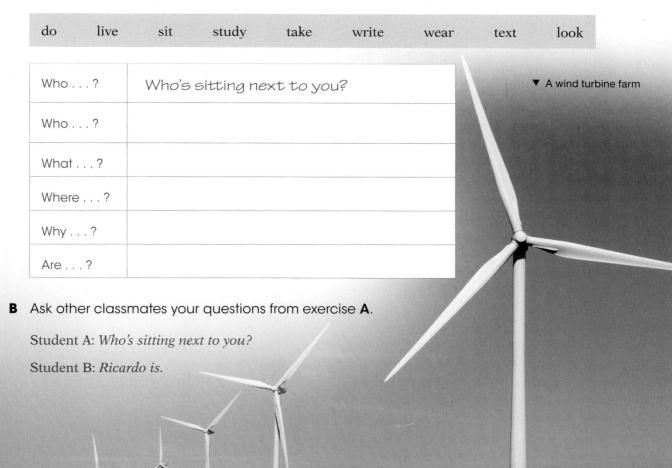

▼ A wind turbine farm

| Who . . . ? | Who's sitting next to you? |
|---|---|
| Who . . . ? | |
| What . . . ? | |
| Where . . . ? | |
| Why . . . ? | |
| Are . . . ? | |

**B** Ask other classmates your questions from exercise **A**.

Student A: *Who's sitting next to you?*

Student B: *Ricardo is.*

## EXPLORE

CD2-30

**1 READ** the article about tornadoes and storm chasers. Notice the verbs in **bold**.

# Tornado!

Rex Geyer **is standing** near the window in his house. He**'s watching** a storm in the distance. The sky **is getting** dark. In the dark clouds, he **sees** a tornado. It**'s moving** directly toward him. He **needs** to get out of the storm's path.[1] It's time to leave his house and drive away.

While Rex **is driving** away from the storm, another car **is driving** *toward* it. A storm chaser **is driving** this car. Most people **run** away from tornadoes. Storm chasers **chase**[2] them. When storm chasers **hear** about tornadoes, they **try** to get near them. Some storm chasers **do** this as a hobby. Others **do** it because they are scientists and engineers. It's part of their research. They **use** weather probes to study tornadoes. Weather probes **measure** the wind and **give** scientists important information about storms. Tornadoes are extremely powerful storms, so storm chasers **have** very dangerous jobs.

[1] **path:** the direction that something or someone moves in     [2] **chase:** follow something or someone quickly

**2 CHECK.** Read each statement about tornadoes and storm chasers. Then circle **T** for *true* or **F** for *false*.

1. Rex is watching the storm on TV.              **T**      (**F**)

2. The storm is moving closer.                    **T**      **F**

3. Storm chasers run away from tornadoes.         **T**      **F**

4. Some storm chasers are scientists.             **T**      **F**

**3 DISCOVER.** Complete the exercises to learn about the grammar in this lesson.

**A** Find these sentences in the article from exercise **1**. Write the missing words.

1. Rex Geyer _____ near the window in his house.

2. The sky _____ dark.

3. Most people _____ away from tornadoes.

4. When storm chasers _____ about tornadoes, they

   _____ to get near them.

**B** Look at the sentences from exercise **A**. Then answer the questions below. Discuss your answers with your classmates and teacher.

1. Which sentences have verbs in the simple present? _____

2. Which sentences have verbs in the present progressive? _____

3. Which verb form talks about general information, not an action in progress?

   a. simple present      b. present progressive

▶ A tornado in Campo, Colorado, USA.

# LEARN

## 7.7 Simple Present vs. Present Progressive

| Simple Present |
| --- |
| I **study** every day. |
| She **calls** her sister once a week. |
| We usually **eat** dinner at 7:00. |
| It **gets** dark early in winter. |

| Present Progressive |
| --- |
| I'**m studying** right now. |
| She'**s calling** her sister right now. |
| We'**re not eating** dinner now. |
| It'**s getting** dark outside. |

| | |
| --- | --- |
| 1. **Remember:** Use the simple present to talk about habits or routines, schedules, and facts. | Habit or Routine: I **walk** to work every day. Schedule: He **leaves** work at 6:00 p.m. Fact: It **doesn't snow** a lot in Rome. |
| 2. **Remember:** Use the present progressive to talk about actions that are in progress now or are in progress at the present time, but maybe not at this moment. | Look out the window! **It's snowing!** Max **is taking** Greek this semester. He'**s not studying** right now. |
| 3. Frequency adverbs and frequency expressions are often used with the simple present. | I <u>always</u> **walk** to work. She **visits** her parents <u>once a month</u>. |
| 4. The present time expressions *now, right now, at the moment, today, this week, this moment, this month,* and *this year* are often used with the present progressive. | A: What **are** you **doing** <u>right now</u>? B: I'**m cooking** dinner. John'**s visiting** his sister <u>this week</u>. |

**4** Circle the correct form of the verb to complete each sentence.

1. Rex **watches** / (**is watching**) a tornado right now.

2. Storm chasers have dangerous jobs. They **study** / **are studying** tornadoes.

3. Right now, **he listens to** / **he's listening to** a tornado report.

4. Take your umbrella. **It rains!** / **It's raining!**

5. Quebec City **gets** / **is getting** a lot of snow in the winter.

6. We **learn** / **'re learning** about storms in class this week.

7. She **gives** / **is giving** the weather report every morning.

8. The weather is perfect today. It's warm, and the sun **shines** / **is shining**.

9. I **read** / **'m reading** a book about tornadoes. It's very interesting.

10. They **watch** / **'re watching** the weather report every night.

**5** Complete each sentence with the simple present or present progressive form of the verb in parentheses.

1. We _____ are having _____ (have) a thunderstorm right now.

2. Look! The tornado _____ (move) toward us!

3. Florida _____ (get) a lot of hurricanes.

4. It _____ (rain). Let's go inside.

5. Tom never _____ (listen) to the weather report.

6. It _____ (rain) almost every afternoon in August here.

7. The wind _____ (blow) very hard today.

8. She _____ (check) the weather online every morning.

9. I always _____ (wear) a hat when it's hot and sunny.

10. They _____ (not hike) today because it's very hot.

## 7.8 Non-Action Verbs

| | |
|---|---|
| 1. Some verbs do not show actions. These *non-action* verbs are not common in the progressive.<br><br>For example: *hear, know, like, own, see, want, be,* and *need.* | I **know** the answer.<br>He **wants** some coffee.<br>I **don't own** a car. |
| 2. Non-action verbs do not describe actions. They describe things such as:<br>  a. emotions<br>  b. thoughts<br>  c. possessions<br>  d. states of being<br>  e. senses | <br><br>a. She **loves** her children.<br>b. Kim **knows** the answer.<br>c. He **owns** a car.<br>d. We **are** happy.<br>e. I **see** Tanya. |
| 3. Some verbs have both an action meaning and a non-action meaning. | He's **having** lunch right now. *(action)*<br>He **has** a car. *(non-action)* |

**REAL ENGLISH**

The verbs *see* and *hear* are *non-action verbs* because we see and we hear automatically; we do not control these actions. The verbs *look (at)*, *watch*, and *listen (to)* are action verbs because we choose to do these actions.

  *I **see** the train.*
  *I'm **watching** a movie with my sister.*

  *I **hear** a strange noise.*
  *We're **listening to** the teacher.*

**6** Read each sentence. Is the underlined verb used as an action verb or a non-action verb? Put a check (✓) in the correct column.

|  | | Action | Non-Action |
|---|---|:---:|:---:|
| 1. | Scientists <u>study</u> tornadoes. | ✓ | ☐ |
| 2. | The tornado <u>is coming</u> towards his house. | ☐ | ☐ |
| 3. | Storm chasers <u>have</u> a dangerous job. | ☐ | ☐ |
| 4. | We'<u>re listening to</u> the weather report right now. | ☐ | ☐ |
| 5. | I <u>hear</u> thunder. | ☐ | ☐ |
| 6. | He <u>knows</u> a lot about tornadoes. | ☐ | ☐ |
| 7. | Hurricanes <u>are</u> very dangerous. | ☐ | ☐ |
| 8. | Tornadoes often <u>destroy</u> houses. | ☐ | ☐ |
| 9. | I <u>don't like</u> storms. | ☐ | ☐ |
| 10. | She <u>reads</u> a lot of books about extreme weather. | ☐ | ☐ |
| 11. | I <u>see</u> dark clouds in the distance. | ☐ | ☐ |
| 12. | My dog <u>is</u> afraid of thunderstorms. | ☐ | ☐ |
| 13. | It'<u>s snowing</u> very hard. | ☐ | ☐ |
| 14. | They usually <u>watch</u> the news at 10:00 p.m. | ☐ | ☐ |

**7** Complete each sentence with the simple present or present progressive form of the verb in parentheses.

1. Toronto _____gets_____ (get) a lot of snow in the winter.

2. Please be quiet. I _____ (listen) to the weather report.

3. The reporter _____ (talk) about the storm right now.

4. They _____ (not like) snow storms.

5. She _____ (not own) a raincoat.

6. I _____ (hear) the wind. It's blowing very hard.

7. The weather in Chicago _____ (be) terrible today.

8. That umbrella _____ (belong) to Lisa.

9. I _____ (look) at the thermometer. It's 32 degrees.

10. I _____ (see) a lot of clouds, but it's not raining.

11. The hurricane _____ (not move) toward Miami.

12. We _____ (check) the weather report online right now.

# PRACTICE

**8** Choose the correct form of the verb to complete each sentence.

## Climate Change

The earth's climate (1) **changes** / **is changing**. The biggest change is in the Arctic. The Arctic (2) **gets** / **is getting** warmer. The ice there (3) **melts** / **is melting**. In the oceans, the water level (4) **rises** / **is rising**. Scientists also often (5) **use** / **are using** the Maldive Islands in the Indian Ocean as an example. The ocean (6) **rises** / **is rising** and (7) **starts** / **is starting** to cover parts of these islands. Scientists (8) **know** / **are knowing** the causes of climate change. Governments (9) **need** / **are needing** to do something, but it is a difficult problem.

▶ A Maldivian island

**9** Complete each sentence with the correct form of the verb in parentheses.

## Weather around the World

Every night we (1) _____ (listen) to the news. We often (2) _____ (hear) reports about bad weather. Some places around the world never (3) _____ (get) enough rain. In other places, it (4) _____ (rain) too much. This often (5) _____ (cause) floods.

Today we (6) _____ (listen) to all the weather reports because they (7) _____ (talk) about a huge snow storm. We almost never (8) _____ (get) snow in this part of the country, but this storm (9) _____ (move) in our direction.

I (10) _____ (need) to get ready for the storm now. I (11) _____ (not like) to drive in the snow at all, so I (12) _____ (want) to go to the supermarket and buy groceries.

**10 EDIT.** Read the paragraph. Find and correct five more errors with action and non-action verbs.

I am looking
Right now I ~~look~~ out the window of my house. I see a lot of dark clouds. A storm comes. The sky gets dark. Now I am hearing the wind. It's raining hard now. I am not liking storms. I'm being afraid of them!

**11 LISTEN & SPEAK.**

CD2-31

**A** Listen to the conversation. Choose the correct answer for each question.

1. Who is talking?            a. News reporters.       b. Weather reporters.

2. What are they talking about?   a. A tsunami.        b. A hurricane.

3. What do they see?            a. Police.            b. Smoke.

**B** Match the items in Columns A and B to make sentences. Then complete each sentence with the simple present or present progressive form of the verb in parentheses.

| Column A | Column B |
|---|---|
| 1. Maria Lopez __is reporting__ (report) _b_ | a. a lot of damage. |
| 2. The storm _____ (cause) _____ | ~~b.~~ from the coast. |
| 3. Alvaro _____ (see) _____ | c. in the fire. |
| 4. He _____ (hear) _____ | d. people to leave their homes. |
| 5. Some people _____ (want) _____ | e. safe. |
| 6. The police _____ (ask) _____ | f. the waves. |
| 7. Houses _____ (burn) _____ | g. the wind. |
| 8. Maria _____ (feel) _____ | h. to stay in their homes. |

**12 APPLY.**

**A** Work with a partner. Plan a news report about an extreme weather event (for example: a bad storm, or very hot or cold weather). Answer the questions in the chart with the information about your news report.

| What's the weather event? | A hurricane |
|---|---|
| What's happening right now? | |
| What are people doing? | |

**B** Practice your weather report from exercise **A**. Partner A is the news reporter at the station. Partner B is the reporter outside. Then role-play your weather report for your classmates.

Charts
7.1–7.8

**1 LISTEN.** Listen to each question. Choose the correct answer.

1. a. Yes, I am.                           b. Stephen is.

2. a. I'm studying.                        b. I study.

3. a. Greg.                                b. To the park.

4. a. Because they like it there.          b. In Oklahoma.

5. a. They're watching the waves.          b. Jen and Makiko.

6. a. I'm not feeling well.                b. With Carol.

7. a. An article.                          b. Because it's interesting.

8. a. Yes, we are.                         b. Yes, they are.

Charts
7.1–7.8

**2 EDIT.** Read the conversation. Find and correct six more errors with the present progressive and simple present.

**Tony:**  Wow. Look at this photo. This man ~~competes~~ *is competing* in a marathon. He runs in the Sahara.

**Kay:**  Why are people wanting to run in the desert?

**Tony:**  They are liking the challenge. That marathon is very, very difficult. It lasts for five or six days. Are you seeing his backpack? He's having all his food in there.

**Kay:**  Do the runners stop at night to sleep?

**Tony:**  That's a good question. I'm not knowing the answer.

◄ A competitor climbs a dune during the Marathon des Sables in the Sahara.

Charts
7.1–7.8

**3** **WRITE & LISTEN.** Complete the interview with the words in parentheses. Use the present progressive or simple present. Then listen and check your answers.

**Alex:** Hello, everyone. Our visitor today is Isabel Lee. Isabel,

(1) _____how are you doing_____ (how / you / do)?

**Isabel:** (2) _____ (I / do) great, Alex.

**Alex:** So, (3) _____ (you / train) for a new event now?

**Isabel:** Yes, (4) _____ (I / train) for a triathlon competition.

**Alex:** Really? Wow. What (5) _____ (you / like) about triathlons?

**Isabel:** (6) _____ (I / enjoy) the challenge. Triathlons are very difficult!

Also, triathlons include three sports: biking, swimming, and running, and

(7) _____ (I / like) all of them a lot!

**Alex:** Interesting. How many bicycles (8) _____ (you / own)?

**Isabel:** (9) _____ (I / have) three. (10) _____ (I / need) all of them

because (11) _____ (bicycles / often / break).

**Alex:** Well, good luck in your next triathlon!

**Isabel:** Thank you.

Charts
7.1–7.8

**4** **SPEAK, WRITE & LISTEN.**

**A** Listen to the conversation about the photo. Check (✓) the words you hear.

1. a. _____ in the Arctic
   b. __✓__ in Norway

2. a. _____ from a mountain
   b. _____ from an airplane

3. a. _____ at the scenery
   b. _____ for a place on
      the ground to land

4. a. _____ a parachute
   b. _____ a tent

▲ A parachutist on an expedition, Spitsbergen Island, Svalbard, Norway

**B** Write three *Wh-* questions and one *Yes/No* question about the photo on page 236. Use the present progressive.

1. ___What is he doing?___
2. _____
3. _____
4. _____
5. _____

**C** Work with a partner. Ask and answer your questions from exercise **B**. Use the words in exercise **A** to help you.

Student A: *What's he doing?*

Student B: *He's hanging from a plane.*

Charts
7.1–7.8

## 5 SPEAK & WRITE.

**A** Choose one of the photos in this unit and write five questions about it. Use the present progressive or simple present. Use the verbs in the box to help you.

| carry | do | feel | happen | have | hold | look at | see | wear |

| I'm looking at the photo on page _____. | |
|---|---|
| What . . . ? | What is she wearing? |
| Is / Are . . . ? | |
| Who . . . ? | |
| Where . . . ? | |
| Why . . . ? | |

**B** Work with a partner. Ask and answer your questions from exercise **A**.

Student A: *What is she wearing?*

Student B: *She's wearing a red jacket and . . .*

# Connect the Grammar to Writing

**1 READ & NOTICE THE GRAMMAR.**

**A** Read the e-mail. Where is the writer, and what is he doing? Discuss with a partner.

Hi everyone,

I'm writing to you from London. Right now I'm sitting in the university library. Some people are studying, but I don't have any homework yet. Most people are walking around and chatting. It's not quiet at all.

I'm not spending all my time in the library. I'm also playing tennis and singing in the school choir. I already know a lot of people. I like it here a lot, but I miss you!

Please write to me soon!

David

### GRAMMAR FOCUS

In the e-mail in exercise **A**, the writer uses the present progressive to describe activities that are happening at the present time.

*I'm **writing** to you from London.*
*Right now I'm **sitting** in the university library.*

**B** Read the e-mail in exercise **A** again. Underline the present progressive. Then work with a partner and compare answers.

**C** Complete the chart with information from the e-mail in exercise **A**. What activities is he doing right now? What activities is he doing, but not right now?

| David's Life in London | |
|---|---|
| Right Now | Not Right Now |
| writing | |

**2  BEFORE YOU WRITE.** Think about the activities in your life. What are you doing right now? What activities are you doing, but not right now? Write your notes in the chart. Use the chart from exercise **1C** as a model.

| My Life in _____ | |
|---|---|
| Right Now | Not Right Now |
| | |

**3  WRITE** an e-mail to a friend or family member. Describe where you are and what you are doing. Use the information from your chart in exercise **2** and the e-mail in exercise **1A** to help you.

> **WRITING FOCUS**    Using *And* to Join Two Verbs
>
> *And* is a conjunction. It joins two similar parts of speech. For example, it joins two nouns or two verbs. Using *and* to join similar activities or activities that are in progress at the same time helps make the writing flow more smoothly and sound more natural.
>
> Two sentences: *People are walking around. They are chatting.*
> One sentence with *and*: *People are walking around **and** chatting.*
>
> **Remember:** Do not repeat the subject and the verb *be* when the subject is doing two actions.
>
> > *Most people <u>are walking</u> around **and** <u>chatting</u>.*
> > *I'm also <u>playing</u> tennis **and** <u>singing</u> in the school choir.*

**4  SELF ASSESS.** Read your e-mail. Underline the present progressive. Circle *and*. Then use the checklist to assess your work.

- [ ] I used the present progressive for activities I am doing now. [7.1, 7.2]
- [ ] I used the simple present for non-action verbs. [7.8]
- [ ] I spelled the verb + *-ing* forms correctly. [7.3]
- [ ] I did not repeat the subject and the verb *be* in sentences with two activities in progress at the same time. [7.1]
- [ ] I used *and* to join two similar activities in progress at the same time. [WRITING FOCUS]

# The Past: Part 1

▶ Highway 101, Oregon, USA

## EXPLORE

CD2-35

**1** **READ** the travel blog about the Atlas Mountains. Notice the words in **bold**.

## Next stop...

A Travel Blog

**June 2**
**The Atlas Mountains**

I'm on the train again. I **wasn't** online **yesterday,** so I have a lot of stories for you today. Our three days in Marrakech **were** great. The city **was** exciting, but it **was** very noisy. It **was** also very hot. **On Wednesday**, it **was** 100 degrees Fahrenheit (38 degrees Celsius)! We visited Djemaa el Fna Square. It's a huge outdoor market with food and entertainment. It **was** a very interesting place.

**On Thursday,** we hired a guide¹ and drove to the Atlas Mountains. The Atlas mountain range is amazing! It's more than 1200 miles (2000 kilometers) long. It crosses Morocco, Algeria, and Tunisia. The weather in the mountains **was** sunny and cool, and there **was** snow on the tops of the mountains.

Our hikes in the mountains **weren't** easy, but the views **were** incredible. Our guide, Simo, **was** great. He **was** helpful and funny. There are some small villages in the Atlas Mountains. The people there **were** very friendly. In one village, we had lunch in a family's home. We had fresh bread with honey and mint tea. It **was** delicious!

Next stop: The Sahara!

¹ **guide:** a person who shows the way and gives information, especially to tourists

**Recent posts:**

- **Atlas Mountains**
- Marrakech!
- Rabat
- Fez
- Tangier
- Seville

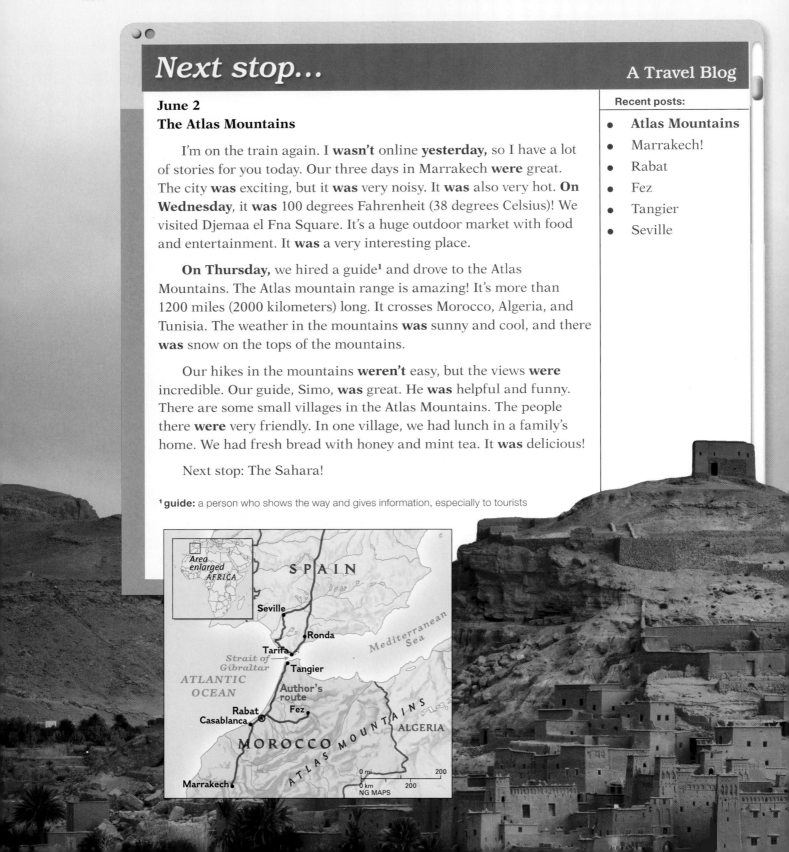

**2 CHECK.** Read each statement about the travel blog. Then circle **T** for *true* or **F** for *false*.

1. On Wednesday it was very hot in Marrakech.          **T**      **F**

2. It was cloudy in the Atlas Mountains.          **T**      **F**

3. The hikes in the mountains were easy.          **T**      **F**

4. Simo wasn't a helpful guide.          **T**      **F**

5. The fresh bread was delicious.          **T**      **F**

**3 DISCOVER.** Complete the exercises to learn about the grammar in this lesson.

**A** Find these sentences in the travel blog from exercise **1**. Write the missing words.

1. I'_____ on the train again.

2. I _____ online yesterday.

3. Our three days in Marrakech _____ great.

4. There _____ some small villages in the Atlas Mountains.

5. Our guide, Simo, _____ great.

**B** Which sentences in exercise **A** talk about the present? Which sentences talk about the past? Discuss with your classmates and teacher.

▼ The village of Ait Benhaddou, Atlas Mountains, Morocco

# LEARN

## 8.1 Simple Past of *Be:* Statements

| Affirmative | | |
|---|---|---|
| Subject | *Be* | |
| I<br>He<br>She<br>It<br>Amy | was | in Miami yesterday. |
| We<br>You<br>They<br>Carl and Ann | were | |

| Negative | | |
|---|---|---|
| Subject | *Be* | |
| I<br>He<br>She<br>It<br>Amy | was not<br>wasn't | in Miami yesterday. |
| We<br>You<br>They<br>Carl and Ann | were not<br>weren't | |

| | |
|---|---|
| 1. The verb *be* has two forms in the past: *was* and *were*. | I **was** sick yesterday.<br>They **were** in Hong Kong last week. |
| 2. The contractions *wasn't* and *weren't* are usually used in conversation and informal writing. | A: Our hike yesterday was wonderful.<br>   It **wasn't** very difficult, and there **weren't** any bugs.<br>B: Nice! |

**4** Complete each statement with *was* or *were.*

1. Our trip _____was_____ very exciting.

2. The city _____ noisy.

3. Our guide _____ friendly.

4. The mountains _____ beautiful.

5. The weather _____ cool and sunny.

6. I _____ tired yesterday.

7. There _____ some villages in the mountains.

8. The people _____ friendly.

9. Our hikes _____ easy.

10. You _____ in the mountains yesterday.

**5 SPEAK.** Work with a partner. Make the sentences from exercise **4** negative.

1. *Our trip wasn't very exciting.*

## 8.2  Past Time Expressions with *Last, Yesterday*, and *Ago*

| | |
|---|---|
| 1. Time expressions with *last, yesterday,* and *ago* tell when an action or event happened in the past. | I was at home **last night**.<br>They weren't in class **yesterday**.<br>He was here ten minutes **ago**. |
| 2. Use time expressions at the beginning or end of a sentence. Do not use time expressions in the middle of a sentence. | ✓ I was in Seoul **last week**.<br>✓ **Last week** I was in Seoul.<br>✗ I was <u>last week</u> in Seoul. |
| 3. Use *last* with *night, week, month,* and *year*. Do not use *the* before *last* in these time expressions. | It was cold **last night**.<br>We were in Beijing **last week**.<br>**Last month** she was in Colombia.<br>There were a lot of people on the tour **last year**.<br><br>✓ I was in my hotel room **last night**.<br>✗ I was in my hotel room <u>the</u> last night. |
| 4. Use *yesterday* alone or with times of day (except *night*). | The weather was beautiful **yesterday**.<br>**Yesterday morning** it was very windy.<br>They were on a tour **yesterday afternoon**.<br><br>✓ He was at home **yesterday evening**.<br>✗ He was at home yesterday <u>night</u>. |
| 5. Use *ago* after a period of time. Do not use *before*. | ✓ **Two weeks ago** they were in Madrid.<br>✓ We were in India **eight months ago**.<br>✗ We were in India <u>before</u> eight months. |

**6** Complete each sentence with *yesterday, last,* or *ago*.

1. I was in New York _____ last _____ night.

2. Two years _____ I was in Tokyo.

3. We were on a tour _____ afternoon.

4. Many years _____ Frank was a tour guide.

5. Mike wasn't in Hong Kong four years _____ .

6. They were on vacation in Turkey _____ week.

7. We were in London three weeks _____ .

8. Airplane tickets weren't this expensive ten years _____ .

9. I was really tired _____ night after the hike.

10. We were at a Moroccan restaurant _____ evening.

# PRACTICE

CD2-36

**7 LISTEN** to each sentence. Is it past or present? Put a check (✓) in the correct column.

| | Present | Past | | Present | Past |
|---|---|---|---|---|---|
| 1. | ☐ | ☐ | 5. | ☐ | ☐ |
| 2. | ☐ | ☐ | 6. | ☐ | ☐ |
| 3. | ☐ | ☐ | 7. | ☐ | ☐ |
| 4. | ☐ | ☐ | 8. | ☐ | ☐ |

## 8 READ, WRITE & SPEAK.

**A** Read the travel plan and Lila's notes about her trip to Guatemala. Then complete the sentences in her journal. Use the past of *be* and the information in Lila's notes.

| Your Visit to Guatemala | Notes . . . |
|---|---|
| **Day 1**<br>Arrive Guatemala City<br>Antigua by bus<br>lunch and dinner at the hotel | short bus ride<br>hotel—very nice;<br>food—not very good |
| **Day 2**<br>Antigua<br>Tour of 18th-century ruins | ruins—beautiful!<br>restaurant food—<br>delicious |
| **Day 3**<br>Bus to Lake Atitlan | scenery—amazing |
| **Day 4**<br>Boat trip around Lake Atitlan | villages—interesting |
| **Day 5**<br>Bus to<br>Chichicastenango<br>("Chi Chi") | drive—not fun!<br>road—very narrow<br>bus driver—friendly;<br>bus ride—scary! |
| **Day 6**<br>Market in Chi Chi<br>Bus back to Guatemala City | prices—very good<br>weather—not good,<br>cool and rainy |
| **Day 7**<br>Tikal by plane | Tikal—crowded |
| **Day 8**<br>Tikal, Guatemala City Depart | Very tired! |

### Journal

**Day 1**
The bus ride _was short_.
The hotel _____
but the food _____

**Days 2-4**
The ruins of Antigua _____
The food at the restaurant _____
The scenery at Lake Atitlan _____

The villages _____

**Days 5-6**
The drive _____ because the
road _____.
The bus driver _____,
but the bus ride _____.

In Chi Chi, the prices _____
The weather _____ because
_____

**Days 7-8**
Tikal _____.
On the last day, I _____,
but it was a great trip!

◀ Lake Atitlan and Toliman volcano, Guatemala, Central America

**B** Work with a partner. Choose two days from Lila's trip and tell your partner about them. Use the information from exercise **A** and some of your own ideas.

*Day 1: The bus ride was short, and the hotel was very nice. The food wasn't very good.*

**C** Discuss these questions with your partner.

1. What do you think? Was this a good trip?

2. Do you prefer to visit cities or small towns? Why?

**9 SPEAK.** Work with a partner. Say sentences with time expressions. Use the past of *be*. Talk about the weather or people using the past.

| an hour ago | yesterday | last week | last year |
|---|---|---|---|

Student A: *Yesterday the weather was good.*          Student B: *I wasn't in this class last year.*

**10 EDIT.** Read the e-mail. Find and correct five more errors with the past of *be* and time expressions.

Hi Marco,

Greetings from Italy! We were in Rome ~~before~~ two days ˄ago. Now we're in Florence. We're having a great time! Yesterday the weather is rainy, so it was a good day to visit the Uffizi. The Uffizi is a huge art museum. We was there for five hours. I was really tired yesterday night. The last week we were in Venice. There weren't many tourists, so it weren't very crowded. It's a beautiful city. Have a great summer, and please say hello to your family.

Todd

**11 LISTEN & SPEAK.**

CD2-37

**A** Read each statement. Then listen to the conversation about a trip. Choose the correct word(s) to complete each sentence.

1. They were on a **skiing** / (camping) trip.

2. Their trip was **yesterday** / **last week** / **a month ago**.

3. Selena **was** / **wasn't** happy about the trip.

4. Nick **was** / **wasn't** happy about the trip.

**B** Listen again. What do Selena and Nick say about each topic? Write **S** if Selena uses the word and **N** if Nick uses it.

| 1. The camping trip | terrible _____ | fun _____S_____ |
| 2. The weather on Friday | warm _____ | wet _____ |
| 3. The weather on Saturday and Sunday | sunny _____ | wet _____ |
| 4. The insects | terrible _____ | not bad _____ |
| 5. The hike | easy _____ | difficult _____ |
| 6. The views | amazing _____ | incredible _____ |

**C** Write three sentences about Selena's ideas and three sentences about Nick's ideas. Use words from the chart in exercise **B**.

**Selena** 1. _The camping trip was fun._____

2. _____

3. _____

**Nick** 1. _____

2. _____

3. _____

**D** Work with a partner. Role-play a conversation between Selena and Nick. Use ideas from exercises **B** and **C**. Student A, take the part of Selena. Student B, take the part of Nick.

Student A: *Our trip was really fun!*     Student B: *No, it wasn't.*

## 12 APPLY.

**A** Talk about your own experience on a trip. Use the topics from the list to help you.

| when | the food | the weather | where | the people | the scenery |

*I was in Costa Rica. The trip was last summer…*

**B** Write six sentences about the place you visited. Use the past of *be*.

1. _I was in. . ._____

2. _____

3. _____

4. _____

5. _____

6. _____

## EXPLORE

**1** **READ** the conversation. Notice the words in **bold**.

## Iceland

| | |
|---|---|
| **Ben:** | Hi, Andy. **How was your vacation?** |
| **Andy:** | It was great. |
| **Ben:** | **Were you in Denmark?** |
| **Andy:** | No, I was in Iceland. |
| **Ben:** | Really? I was there two years ago. |
| **Andy:** | I didn't know that. **Were you on a tour?** |
| **Ben:** | No, I was with my brother. It was a lot of fun. |
| **Andy:** | **Were you there in the summer?** |
| **Ben:** | No, we were there in March. |
| **Andy:** | In March? **How was the weather?** |
| **Ben:** | It was cold, but it was a good time. We saw the Northern Lights. |
| **Andy:** | Wow. **Were they amazing?** |
| **Ben:** | Yeah, they really were. The sky was green and yellow. |
| **Andy:** | Interesting! We didn't see them. |
| **Ben:** | Well, the best time to see them in Iceland is from September to April. **When were you there?** |
| **Andy:** | In July, so there was daylight almost all of the time. |
| **Ben:** | That's right. The sun only sets for a few hours during the summer. **Was that strange?** |
| **Andy:** | Yeah, it was. It was a great trip. I want to go back sometime. |
| **Ben:** | Me, too. |

◄ The Northern Lights over icebergs off the black sand beach of Breiarmerkursandur, Iceland

**2 CHECK.** Circle the correct words to complete each statement.

1. Ben was in Iceland **two months ago** / **two years ago**.

2. He **was** / **wasn't** on a tour.

3. The weather in March was **cold** / **warm**.

4. Andy was in Iceland **in July** / **in March**.

5. Andy's trip was **great** / **terrible**.

**3 DISCOVER.** Complete the exercises to learn about the grammar in this lesson.

**A** Find these questions in the conversation from exercise **1** on page 249. Write the missing words.

1. How _____ your vacation?

2. _____ in Denmark?

3. _____ on a tour?

4. How _____ the weather?

5. When _____ there?

6. _____ that strange?

**B** Look at the questions from exercise **A**. Then choose the correct word to complete the statement below. Discuss your answer with your classmates and teacher.

The subject comes **before** / **after** *was* and *were* in questions.

▼ The fishing village of Djupivogur, Iceland

# LEARN

## 8.3 Simple Past of *Be: Yes/No* Questions

| Yes/No Questions | | |
|---|---|---|
| **Was/Were** | Subject | |
| **Was** | he<br>she<br>it<br>the information | helpful? |
| **Were** | we<br>you<br>they<br>the guides | |

| Short Answers | | | | |
|---|---|---|---|---|
| Affirmative | | | Negative | |
| Yes, | he<br>she<br>it | **was.** | No, | he<br>she<br>it | **wasn't.** |
| | we<br>you<br>they | **were.** | | we<br>you<br>they | **weren't.** |

**Remember:** The verb comes before the subject in *Yes/No* questions with *be*.

**Were** you in Mexico last week?
**Was** the weather nice?

**REAL ENGLISH**

People usually give more information after short answers to *Yes/No* questions.

A: *Were you in Tokyo last week?*
B: *No, I wasn't. I was in Kyoto.*

A: *Was Alice absent yesterday?*
B: *Yes, she was. She was sick.*

**4** Change each statement to a *Yes/No* question. Then complete each short answer.

1. He was with a tour.

   A: _____Was he_____ with a tour?

   B: No, _____he wasn't._____

2. He was in Iceland two years ago.

   A: _____ in Iceland two years ago?

   B: Yes, _____ .

3. They were on vacation last week.

   A: _____ on vacation last week?

   B: No, _____ .

4. The scenery was beautiful.

   A: _____ the scenery beautiful?

   B: Yes, _____ .

5. There were a lot of tourists.

   A: _____ a lot of tourists?

   B: Yes, _____ .

6. It was cold in Iceland.

   A: _____ cold in Iceland?

   B: Yes, _____ .

7. We were there in the winter.

   A: _____ there in the winter?

   B: No, _____ .

8. The Northern Lights were beautiful.

   A: _____ beautiful?

   B: Yes, _____ .

## 8.4　Simple Past of *Be: Wh-* Questions

| Wh-Word | Was / Were | Subject | | Answers |
|---|---|---|---|---|
| Who | was | your guide? | | Carlos. |
| Where | was | Barbara | yesterday? | In Rome. |
| What | was | your guide's name? | | Erik. |
| When | were | you | in Norway? | Last summer. |
| Why | were | they | in Iceland? | Because their aunt lives there. |
| How | was | the weather | in Sydney? | Warm and sunny. |

| | |
|---|---|
| 1. **Remember:** Use *Wh-* questions to ask for specific information. | A: **When** were they in Venice? <br> B: Last month. <br><br> A: **Where** was your hotel? <br> B: Near the airport. |
| 2. **Remember:** When a *Who* question is about a subject, use the singular form of the verb even if the answer is plural. | A: **Who** was on vacation last week? <br> B: Margo and Fabian. |
| 3. **Remember:** In conversation, the answers to *Why* questions often begin with *because*. In writing, use complete sentences to answer *Why* questions. | A: Why was he in Hong Kong last week? <br> B: Because he had a business meeting. <br><br> He was in Hong Kong last week because he had a meeting. |

**5**　Complete each of A's questions with *When, Where, What, How, Who,* or *Why.* Use each of B's answers to help you.

1. A: _____How_____ was your trip?　　　　　B: It was wonderful!

2. A: _____ was your trip?　　　　　　B: Last summer.

3. A: _____ was the flight late?　　　　B: The weather was bad.

4. A: _____ was your hotel?　　　　　　B: Near the airport.

5. A: _____ were you yesterday?　　　　B: I was at the beach.

6. A: _____ was he angry?　　　　　　　B: Because his flight was late.

7. A: _____ weren't you at work last week?　B: I was on vacation.

8. A: _____ was the weather in Hawaii?　　B: It was great.

9. A: _____ was the temperature yesterday?　B: It was 90 degrees.

10. A: _____ was your hotel?　　　　　　B: It was OK.

**6** Put the words in the correct order to make questions.

1. When / in China / he / was   _When was he in China?_____

2. late / Why / the tour bus / was _____

3. in India / was / How / the weather _____

4. the tour / Was / interesting _____

5. your last vacation / was / When _____

6. Where / you / two hours ago / were _____

7. were / last summer / Where / you _____

8. absent / were / Why / our classmates _____

9. last / you / on vacation / week / Were _____

10. you / Where / were / born _____

**7  SPEAK.** Work with a partner. Ask and answer questions 5-10 from exercise **6**.

Student A: *When was your last vacation?*

Student B: *Two months ago.*

# PRACTICE

**8  LISTEN** and choose the correct answer to each question.

CD2-39

| | | | |
|---|---|---|---|
| 1. | a. In November. | b. In Canada. | c. Yes, it was. |
| 2. | a. Last year. | b. In India. | c. No, I wasn't. |
| 3. | a. I was in Montreal. | b. France. | c. Yes, it was great. |
| 4. | a. To Thailand. | b. Great! | c. Yes, it was. |
| 5. | a. They were sick. | b. In Dubai. | c. No, they weren't. |
| 6. | a. In London. | b. Yes, they were. | c. No, it wasn't. |
| 7. | a. My sister. | b. At the hotel. | c. Yes, we were. |
| 8. | a. It was expensive. | b. Near the airport. | c. No, it wasn't. |
| 9. | a. Yes, she was. | b. From Spain. | c. Maria. |
| 10. | a. Warm and sunny. | b. Yes, it was. | c. In Iceland. |

**9** Complete the conversation. Use *Wh-* questions, *Yes/No* questions, and answers. Then listen and check your answers.

**Ann:** Hi, Beth. (1) ___Where were___ you last week? (2) _____ you in California again on business?

**Beth:** No, (3) _____. I was in Africa.

**Ann:** Africa? (4) _____ you in Africa?

**Beth:** I (5) _____ on vacation.

**Ann:** (6) _____ you in Africa?

**Beth:** I (7) _____ in South Africa, Botswana, and Zambia.

**Ann:** (8) _____ you on a safari¹?

**Beth:** Yes, (9) _____. It was amazing. We saw a lot of zebras, some giraffes, and a few lions, too.

**Ann:** Lions? Wow! (10) _____ you afraid?

**Beth:** No, I (11) _____. It was fun and really interesting.

¹ A **safari** is a trip to look at wild animals.

**10 READ, WRITE & SPEAK.**

**A** Read the paragraph about David Livingstone. Then use the words in the box to write *Wh-* questions. The underlined words are the answers.

| what | when | where | who | why |

# DAVID LIVINGSTONE

David Livingstone was (1) a famous traveler. He was from (2) Scotland. He was interested in (3) science, medicine, and nature. He was also very interested in Africa. His first trip (4) to Africa was in 1841. His most famous trip was (5) in 1855. This trip was (6) to the great falls on the Zambezi River. His guides were from the Makololo tribe. The name of the falls was (7) Mosi oa Tunya. Livingstone gave the falls an English name. The English name was Victoria (8) because Victoria was the queen of England.

1. ___Who was David Livingstone?___
2. _____
3. _____
4. _____
5. _____
6. _____
7. _____
8. _____

▲ Victoria Falls between Zambia and Zimbabwe

**B** Work with a partner. Compare your answers from exercise **A**. Then practice asking and answering your questions.

Student A: *Who was David Livingstone?*     Student B: *He was a famous traveler.*

## 11   LISTEN & SPEAK.

CD2-41

**A** Listen to the conversation. Then match each question with the correct answer.

| Column A | Column B |
|---|---|
| 1.  Where was Jackie all summer? _e_ | a.  No, it wasn't. |
| 2.  Where was Neeta in June? _____ | b.  Yes, it was. |
| 3.  Was Neeta's summer great? _____ | c.  For a wedding. |
| 4.  Why was Neeta in India? _____ | d.  It was hot. |
| 5.  Was Jackie's summer fun? _____ | e.  In Springfield. |
| 6.  Why was Jackie's summer boring? _____ | f.  In India. |
| 7.  Who was at the wedding? _____ | g.  Most of her friends were away. |
| 8.  How was the weather in India? _____ | h.  All of Neeta's relatives. |

**B** Work with a partner. Close your books. Ask and answer the questions from exercise **A**.

Student A: *Where was Jackie all summer?*     Student B: *In Springfield.*

## 12   APPLY.

**A** Think of a special event in the past, such as a graduation, a wedding, or a birthday. In your notebooks, use these words as a guide and write notes about the event.

| What?   When?   Where?   Who . . . there?   . . . fun? |
|---|

**B** Work with a partner. Ask and answer questions about your special events. Use the past of *be*.

Student A: *What was the special event?*     Student B: *It was my cousin's graduation.*

Student A: *When was it?*     Student B: *In May.*

### EXPLORE

CD2-42

**1  READ** the article about Andrew Evans' trip. Notice the words in **bold**.

# Antarctic Adventure

Andrew Evans **had** an interesting idea. He **wanted** to travel to Antarctica. He also **wanted** a real adventure, so he **looked** at a map and **planned** a trip from his home in Washington, D.C. all the way to Antarctica.

On January 1, 2010, he **got** on a bus in Washington, D.C. and **started** his adventure. He **traveled** through nine states in the United States and 14 countries. He **took** 40 different buses and **spent** more than a thousand dollars on bus fares. Of course, the road **didn't go** all the way to Antarctica. It **ended** in Ushuaia, Argentina. From there, Andrew **traveled** by ship. Finally, on February 14, 2011, he **arrived** in Antarctica. He was very happy!

Andrew **traveled** for ten weeks. Thousands of people **followed** him online. He **shared** his travel experiences with them. He **took** photographs of the scenery and local people and **posted** them on his website. National Geographic **named** Andrew the *digital nomad*.[1] He's always traveling, and he's always connected to the Internet.

---

[1] **nomad:** a person who travels from place to place

▶ Andrew took this interesting photo when his bus driver stopped for a break on the Salar de Uyuni, the world's largest salt flat, Bolivia.

**2 CHECK.** Read each statement about Andrew Evans' trip to Antarctica. Circle **T** for *true* or **F** for *false*.

1. Andrew Evans wanted an adventure.                                    T     F

2. Andrew Evans started his trip in Florida.                            T     F

3. He traveled on 14 buses.                                             T     F

4. He arrived in Antarctica in March.                                   T     F

5. Andrew shared his travel experiences online.                        T     F

**3 DISCOVER.** Complete the exercises to learn about the grammar in this lesson.

**A** Find these sentences in the article from exercise **1**. Write the missing words.

1. He _____ to travel to Antarctica.

2. Andrew _____ for ten weeks.

3. Thousands of people _____ him online.

**B** Look at the verbs in the sentences from exercise **A**. What ending do all of these verbs have? What does this ending show? Discuss with your classmates and teacher.

# LEARN

## 8.5　Simple Past: Affirmative Statements with Regular Verbs

| Subject | Verb | |
|---|---|---|
| I | hiked | a lot on my vacation. |
| You | arrived | late last night. |
| He | started | his trip in August. |
| She | traveled | to Australia last summer. |
| We | walked | three miles yesterday morning. |
| You | visited | some interesting places in Mexico. |
| They | stayed | at a nice hotel. |

| | |
|---|---|
| 1. Use the simple past to talk about completed actions. | I **finished** my homework this morning.<br>She **worked** until seven-thirty last night. |
| 2. For most regular verbs, add *–d* or *–ed* to the base form of the verb.* | They **lived** here twenty years ago.<br>I **called** Lisa yesterday. |
| 3. The simple past has the same form for all subjects. | I **walked** to the store.<br>He **walked** to the bus stop. |
| 4. Do not use *was* or *were* with another verb in the simple past. | ✓ I visited my grandparents last week.<br>✗ I <u>was visited</u> my grandparents last week. |

*See Chart 8.6 on page 259 for information on spelling rules for *-ed* forms.

**4** Read each sentence and underline the verb. Is it present or past? Put a check (✓) in the correct column.

| | | Present | Past |
|---|---|---|---|
| 1. | Andrew <u>planned</u> a bus trip to Antarctica. | ☐ | ✓ |
| 2. | His trip starts in Washington, D.C. | ☐ | ☐ |
| 3. | The bus goes through the United States. | ☐ | ☐ |
| 4. | He started his adventure in August. | ☐ | ☐ |
| 5. | He traveled for ten weeks. | ☐ | ☐ |
| 6. | Thousands of people followed his adventure. | ☐ | ☐ |
| 7. | They like the stories on his website. | ☐ | ☐ |
| 8. | He posted his photographs online. | ☐ | ☐ |
| 9. | Andrew travels a lot. | ☐ | ☐ |
| 10. | He shares his adventures online. | ☐ | ☐ |

## 8.6 Spelling Rules: -ed Forms

| | | |
|---|---|---|
| 1. For most verbs, add -ed to the base form of the verb. | pack | I pack**ed** my suitcase. |
| 2. For verbs that end in silent e, add -d. | hike | We hike**d**. |
| 3. For one-syllable verbs that end in a consonant + vowel + consonant (CVC*), double the final consonant and add -ed. | plan | They plan**ned** their trip. |
| 4. For two-syllable verbs that end in CVC and have the stress on the second syllable, double the final consonant and add -ed. | prefer | We prefer**red** the first hotel. |
| 5. For two-syllable verbs that end in CVC and have the stress on the first syllable, add -ed but do not double the final consonant. | travel visit order | She travel**ed** from Mexico to Argentina last year. We visit**ed** our grandparents last weekend. I order**ed** a new backpack online. |
| 6. For verbs that end in a consonant + vowel + -w, -x, or -y, add -ed but do not double the final consonant. | follow fix play | We follow**ed** our guide. He fix**ed** our car. They play**ed** tennis on their vacation. |
| 7. For verbs that end in consonant + -y, change the -y to -i and add -ed. | study | I stud**ied** Japanese before my trip. |

\* consonant + vowel + consonant

**5** Write the simple past of each verb in parentheses.

1. I _____carried_____ (carry) my backpack everywhere.

2. She _____ (post) her photos online last night.

3. Jack _____ (order) a new camera before his trip.

4. We _____ (stop) at a nice restaurant for lunch.

5. They _____ (climb) two mountains last week.

6. We _____ (try) several hotels near the airport. They were all full.

7. I _____ (call) the front desk.

8. She _____ (share) her adventures with her friends and family.

9. He _____ (stay) at a small hotel.

10. They _____ (enjoy) the tour yesterday.

11. We _____ (love) the food in India. It was delicious.

12. Sue _____ (visit) a lot of interesting places on the tour.

**6 PRONUNCIATION.** Read the chart and listen to the examples. Then complete the exercises.

| PRONUNCIATION | Past -*ed* Endings |
|---|---|

The -*ed* ending has three sounds: /t/, /d/, and /əd/.

1. Say /əd/ only after verbs that end with /t/ and /d/ sounds.

    want – wanted     need – needed

2. Say /t/ after verbs that end with the sounds /f/, /k/, /p/, /s/, /ʃ/, /tʃ/, and /ks/.

    laugh – laughed     stop – stopped     wash – washed     tax – taxed
    work – worked     kiss – kissed     watch – watched

3. Say /d/ after verbs that end with the sounds /b/, /dʒ/, /g/, /l/, /m/, /n/, /ŋ/, /p/, /r/, /ð/, /v/, and /z/ sounds, and after vowel sounds.

    rub – rubbed     climb – climbed     stir – stirred     play – played
    judge – judged     pin – pinned     bathe – bathed     lie – lied
    bag – bagged     bang – banged     love – loved     show – showed
    pull – pulled     hope – hoped     buzz – buzzed     allow – allowed

See page **A4** for a guide to pronunciation symbols.

**A** Listen to each sentence. What sound do you hear at the end of the underlined verb? Check (✓) the correct column.

| | /t/ | /d/ | /əd/ |
|---|---|---|---|
| 1. My friend Tony and I <u>wanted</u> an adventure. | ☐ | ☐ | ✓ |
| 2. We <u>discussed</u> the trip. | ☐ | ☐ | ☐ |
| 3. We <u>decided</u> to go to Mexico. | ☐ | ☐ | ☐ |
| 4. We <u>looked</u> at a lot of travel websites. | ☐ | ☐ | ☐ |
| 5. We <u>discussed</u> the trip. | ☐ | ☐ | ☐ |
| 6. I <u>reserved</u> the hotel rooms online. | ☐ | ☐ | ☐ |
| 7. We <u>packed</u> our suitcases. | ☐ | ☐ | ☐ |
| 8. We <u>called</u> a taxi. It was time to go! | ☐ | ☐ | ☐ |

**B** Work with a partner. Practice saying the sentences in exercise **A**. Pay attention to the pronunciation of past endings.

Puebla, Mexico, at nightfall

## 8.7 Simple Past Irregular Verbs: Group 1

| Present | Past | Present | Past | Present | Past |
|---------|------|---------|------|---------|------|
| buy | bought | go | went | make | made |
| come | came | have | had | spend | spent |
| do | did | hear | heard | take | took |
| get | got | leave | left | teach | taught |

Many common verbs are irregular* in the past. They do not have -ed endings.

She goes to Italy every summer.
She **went** to Italy last summer.

I always take the bus to work.
I **took** the bus to work yesterday.

*See page **A5** for a list of irregular verbs.

**7** Underline the verb in each sentence. Then write the base form of the verb on the line.

1. Gina <u>went</u> to Indonesia last year. ___go___

2. The trip took five hours. _____

3. They bought some postcards. _____

4. We came home late. _____

5. Unfortunately, I got sick on the trip. _____

6. We had a great time. _____

7. The plane left two hours late. _____

8. I spent a lot of time at the beach. _____

9. We did the mountain hike with a guide. _____

10. I heard a loud noise in the hotel lobby. _____

> ### REAL ENGLISH
>
> The verb *take* is used in many different ways.
>
> **take** a vacation/a trip/a break/a nap
> **take** a test/exam
> **take** a photograph
> **take** the bus/a taxi/the subway/the train
> **take** six hours/a few minutes/a lot of time
>
> They **took** a trip to Austria last summer.
> We **took** the final exam this morning.
> The trip **took** five hours.

**8** Complete each sentence with the past form of the verb in parentheses.

1. The tour _____left_____ (leave) at 8:30 this morning.

2. We _____ (go) to a lot of beautiful places on the tour.

3. She _____ (make) some new friends on her trip.

4. They _____ (have) lunch in a small village yesterday.

5. He _____ (get) a map at the front desk.

6. I _____ (buy) some small gifts for my family at the market.

7. They _____ (spend) ten days in Peru.

8. Our guide _____ (teach) us a few words in Spanish.

**9 SPEAK.** Work with a partner. Make sentences in the past with four of the verbs in the box. Use time expressions.

| buy | do | find | go | have | hear | take |

*I bought a new phone last month.*

# PRACTICE

**10 LISTEN.**

CD2-45

**A** Listen to each sentence. Is it present or past? Put a check (✓) in the correct column.

**Present**      **Past**

1. ☐        ✓

2. ☐        ☐

3. ☐        ☐

4. ☐        ☐

5. ☐        ☐

6. ☐        ☐

7. ☐        ☐

8. ☐        ☐

CD2-45

**B** Listen again and complete each sentence with the verb you hear.

1. We _____ *went* _____ on a trip.

2. She _____ on Monday.

3. He _____ a lot for his job.

4. You _____ at a nice hotel.

5. They always _____ their hotel reservations online.

6. I _____ my camera at the hotel.

7. I really _____ to go to Italy.

8. She really _____ her vacation last summer.

**11** Complete the paragraph. Use the past tense of the verbs in parentheses.

# The Inca Road

The Incas (1) _____ had _____ (have) a huge empire[1] in South America 500 years
ago. They (2) _____ (need) a way to reach all parts of their empire. The

Inca road system (3) _____ (carry) people from one
end of the empire to the other. It (4) _____ (have)
two main roads. One road (5) _____ (go) near the
ocean between Tumbes, Peru and Talca, Chile. The other road
(6) _____ (cross) part of the Andes Mountains
between Quito, Ecuador and Mendoza, Argentina.

Karin Muller, a filmmaker, photographer, and adventurer
from Switzerland, (7) _____ (decide) to make a
film about the Inca Road. She (8) _____ (follow)
the ancient road and (9) _____ (travel)
4000 miles (6440 kilometers). The journey (10) _____ (take) six
months. Along the way, she (11) _____ (try) many new things and
(12) _____ (learn) a lot about the people. She (13) _____ (make)
a film about her journey. She (14) _____ (call) the film *Along the Inca Road*.

[1] An **empire** is a group of nations controlled by one ruler.

**12 EDIT.** Read the paragraph about Hiram Bingham. Find and correct six more errors with
regular and irregular verbs in the simple past.

# Hiram Bingham

                                     studied

Hiram Bingham ~~studyed~~ South American history.

In 1908, he get a job at Yale University in the United

States and tought history. In 1908, he went to Santiago,

Chile, and learned about the lost cities of the Incas.

He was visit the ruins of an ancient Incan city in

Choquequirao. In 1911, he go to Peru. There he heared

about more ruins called "Machu Picchu." He traveled

with two Peruvians along the Urubamba River near

Cusco. There some people showwed them the way to

some very old ruins. It was Machu Picchu!

## 13 LISTEN & SPEAK.

**A**  Listen to Ana and Don talk about their trips to Machu Picchu. Then circle the correct word to complete each statement.

*CD2-46-47*

1. Ana and Sudie's trip **was** / **wasn't** great.

2. Cusco **is** / **isn't** very high in the mountains.

3. Don's trip **was** / **wasn't** great.

**B**  Look at the information in the chart. Then listen again. Is the information about Ana and Sudie or Don? Check (✓) the correct column(s).

*CD2-46-47*

|  | **Ana and Sudie** | **Don** |
|---|:---:|:---:|
| 1. always wanted to go to Machu Picchu | ✓ | ✓ |
| 2. went with a tour group | ☐ | ☐ |
| 3. stayed in Cusco for one night | ☐ | ☐ |
| 4. went by train and bus | ☐ | ☐ |
| 5. hiked on the Inca Trail | ☐ | ☐ |
| 6. had a guide | ☐ | ☐ |
| 7. stayed in a tent | ☐ | ☐ |
| 8. got really sick | ☐ | ☐ |

**C**  Work with a partner. Answer the questions. Use the words in the box to help you.

| three nights | four hours | a hotel | by train and bus | the Inca Trail |
|---|---|---|---|---|
| four days | a guide | a tent | sick | |

1. Why wasn't Don's trip very good?

2. What was fun for the women?

3. What were three differences between the trips?

## 14 APPLY.

**A**  Write about a place you know and your visit there. Use the simple past.

Name of the place: *I went to Copán in Honduras.*

Information about the place: *It's very interesting. The Maya lived there. . .*

The trip: *I went there three years ago. I went by bus with my family. We visited some ancient ruins and a museum. . . .*

**B**  Work with a partner. Share the information about your place and your visit there.

## EXPLORE

CD2-48

**1** **READ** the article about an interesting journey. Notice the words in **bold**.

### Amazon Explorer Ed Stafford

The Amazon River is a very long river. It's almost 4000 miles (6440 kilometers) long. In 2008, Ed Stafford, an adventurer from Great Britain, started a journey down the Amazon River. He **didn't go** by boat. He walked from the beginning to the end of the river! His journey began in the Andes Mountains in Peru and ended in Brazil. It took 859 days.

Ed **didn't travel** alone. He started the trip with a friend, but after three months, his friend **didn't want** to continue. In Peru, Cho Rivera joined him. They traveled together for two years. They **didn't have** an easy journey. It was often difficult and dangerous. They got very sick, and they saw large snakes and other dangerous animals. Finally, on August 9, 2010, Ed and Cho arrived at the end of the Amazon River—the Atlantic Ocean!

▶ Ed Stafford on his 859-day hike down the Amazon River

**2 CHECK.** Circle the correct information to complete each statement.

1. Ed Stafford's journey began in **Peru** / **Brazil**.

2. He started his trip **alone** / **with a friend**.

3. Ed Stafford and Cho Rivera traveled together for **two months** / **two years**.

4. Their journey was **easy** / **difficult**.

5. They arrived at the **Atlantic** / **Pacific** Ocean.

**3 DISCOVER.** Complete the exercises to learn about the grammar in this lesson.

**A** Find these sentences in the article from exercise **1** on page 265. Write the missing words.

1. He _____ by boat.

2. Ed _____ alone.

3. His friend _____ to continue.

**B** Look at the sentences in exercise **A**. CIrcle the correct word to complete each statement. Then discuss your answer with your classmates and teacher.

1. The verbs in these sentences are **present** / **past**.

2. The verbs in these sentences are **affirmative** / **negative**.

▼ Stafford walking through a swamp, Amazon jungle, Peru

# LEARN

## 8.8 Simple Past: Negative Statements

| Subject | Did Not/ Didn't | Base Form of Verb | |
|---------|-----------------|-------------------|---|
| I You He She It We You They | did not didn't | arrive | last Monday. |

| | |
|---|---|
| 1. Remember to use the base form of the verb after *did not/didn't*. Do not use the past form. | ✓ We didn't arrive late.<br>✗ We didn't <u>arrived</u> late.<br><br>✓ They didn't take the bus.<br>✗ They didn't <u>took</u> the bus. |
| 2. The contraction *didn't* is often used in conversation and informal writing. | A: How was the party last night?<br>B: I **didn't go.** |

**4** Underline the verb in each sentence. Then change each verb from affirmative to negative.

1. Ed Stafford's journey <u>started</u> in Brazil.  Ed Stafford's journey ___ *didn't start* ___ in Brazil.

2. He went alone.  He _____ alone.

3. Ed and Cho traveled with a group.  Ed and Cho _____ with a group.

4. They had a guide.  They _____ a guide.

5. They took a bus to Brazil.  They _____ a bus to Brazil.

6. They bought a boat for their journey.  They _____ a boat for their journey.

7. Ed's friend wanted to continue.  Ed's friend _____ to continue.

8. They stayed in nice hotels.  They _____ in nice hotels.

## 8.9 Simple Past Irregular Verbs: Group 2

| Present | Past | Present | Past | Present | Past |
|---------|------|---------|------|---------|------|
| become | became | lose | lost | sell | sold |
| begin | began | know | knew | tell | told |
| drink | drank | meet | met | win | won |
| eat | ate | ride | rode | write | wrote |
| feel | felt | say | said | | |
| give | gave | see | saw | | |

See page **A5** for a list of common irregular verbs.

**5** Complete each sentence with the correct simple past form of the verb in parentheses.

1. We _____ (see) some beautiful scenery on our trip.

2. The tour _____ (begin) at 8:00 a.m.

3. I _____ (write) a blog about my trip.

4. They _____ (eat) a lot of delicious food in Thailand.

5. He _____ (drink) fresh pineapple juice in Costa Rica.

6. Our guide _____ (know) a lot about the ruins.

7. She _____ (meet) some interesting people on her trip.

8. The hotel clerk _____ (give) me a map of the city.

9. We _____ (ride) our bicycles every day on our vacation.

10. Paul and Ellen _____ (win) a trip to Hawaii.

11. We _____ (feel) very tired after the hike yesterday.

12. Victor _____ (lose) his guidebook, so he bought a new one.

## 8.10 Simple Past Irregular Verbs: Group 3

| Present | Past | Present | Past | Present | Past |
|---------|------|---------|------|---------|------|
| cost | cost | fit | fit | hit | hit |
| hurt | hurt | let | let | put | put |
| quit | quit | read | read | shut | shut |

| 1. Some irregular verbs have the same form in the simple present and simple past. | I **cut** my hair every six weeks. (simple present) <br> Meg **cuts** her hair every month. (simple present) <br> I **cut** my hair last week. (simple past) <br> Meg **cut** her hair last month. (simple past) |
|---|---|
| 2. The past of *read* has the same form as the simple present, but the pronunciation is different. | Simple present: read /rid/ <br> Simple past: read /rɛd/ |

See page **A5** for a list of irregular verbs.

**6** Look at the underlined verb in each sentence. Is it present or past? Check (✓) the correct column.

|  | **Present** | **Past** |
|---|:---:|:---:|
| 1. Ahn <u>reads</u> a lot of travel books. | ✓ | ☐ |
| 2. He <u>quit</u> his job to travel. | ☐ | ☐ |
| 3. That trip <u>costs</u> a lot of money. | ☐ | ☐ |

|  | Present | Past |
|---|---|---|
| 4. The trip <u>cost</u> $485. | ☐ | ☐ |
| 5. The tour bus <u>hit</u> a car. | ☐ | ☐ |
| 6. I <u>read</u> an article in the newspaper last week. | ☐ | ☐ |
| 7. He <u>hurt</u> his leg on the hike. | ☐ | ☐ |
| 8. She <u>put</u> the dates for the trip in her calendar. | ☐ | ☐ |
| 9. Lisa usually <u>puts</u> a snack in her backpack every morning. | ☐ | ☐ |
| 10. My sister <u>let</u> me borrow her camera. | ☐ | ☐ |

**7 SPEAK.** Work with a partner. Complete the sentences.

1. I read _____ last week.

2. My _____ cost _____ .

3. I put a / an / some / my _____ in my bag / backpack this morning.

*I read an article about bears last week.*

# PRACTICE

**8** Write the simple past of each verb.

1. write _____
2. put _____
3. become _____
4. hurt _____
5. read _____

6. drink _____
7. shut _____
8. sell _____
9. give _____
10. eat _____

11. lose _____
12. know _____
13. meet _____
14. begin _____
15. tell _____

**9 WRITE & SPEAK.**

**A** Choose five verbs from exercise **8** and write five sentences about yourself.

*I drank four cups of coffee this morning.*

**B** Work with a partner. Share your sentences from exercise **A**.

Student A: *I drank four cups of coffee this morning.*

Student B: *Really? That's a lot!*

---

**REAL ENGLISH**

*Really* is often used in informal conversation to show interest or surprise.

A: *Where were you last week?*
B: *I was on vacation. I went to Peru.*
A: ***Really?*** *How was it?*
B: *Fantastic!*

A: *These flowers cost ten dollars each.*
B: ***Really?*** *That's very expensive!*

**10** Complete the exercises.

**A** Complete the paragraph with the simple past form of the verbs in parentheses.

## Harriet Chalmers Adams

In the early twentieth century, most people (1) ___didn't travel___ (not travel) very much. They usually (2) _____ (not visit) foreign countries. Harriet Chalmers Adams was different. She lived in the United States, and she loved adventure. In 1904, she and her husband (3) _____ (begin) a three-year journey to every country in South America. People (4) _____ (not have) cars at that time. Adams and her husband took trains and boats. They (5) _____ (travel) across the Andes Mountains on horses. She (6) _____ (no go) only to South America. She also (7) _____ (ride) a horse across Haiti.

On her trips, Adams (8) _____ (see) many interesting places and took photographs. In 1907, she (9) _____ (write) her first travel article for *National Geographic Magazine*. She also (10) _____ (sell) her photographs and (11) _____ (write) more than twenty articles. In those days, the National Geographic Society (12) _____ (not let) women join. In 1925, Adams helped start the Society of Women Geographers and (13)_____ (become) its first president.

**B** Read the statements about Harriet Chalmers Adams. Circle **T** for *true* or **F** for *false*.

| | | |
|---|---|---|
| 1. People went on a lot of tours in the early twentieth century. | **T** | (**F**) |
| 2. People didn't visit foreign countries very often. | **T** | **F** |
| 3. Harriet Chalmers Adams didn't travel very often. | **T** | **F** |
| 4. Adams and her husband's journey in South America took three years. | **T** | **F** |
| 5. They drove a car across the Andes Mountains. | **T** | **F** |
| 6. She only traveled in South America. | **T** | **F** |
| 7. Adams didn't have a camera. | **T** | **F** |
| 8. Adams started the Society of Women Geographers in 1907. | **T** | **F** |

**C** Correct the false statements in exercise **B**. Work with a partner. Compare answers.

*People didn't go on a lot of tours in the early twentieth century.*

**11** **EDIT.** Read the travel story. Find and correct six more errors with the simple past.

        *made*
      I ~~make~~ reservations six months ago for a trip to my cousin's wedding. The night before my trip I called a taxi company for a 6:00 a.m. pick-up. The day begin with a terrible rainstorm. The taxi didn't came at 6:00 a.m. I was call the company. Nobody answered the phone, so I got in my car and drove to the airport. Unfortunately, they didn't had any parking places at the parking garage. I parked six miles from the airport. I not get my flight. They put me on a flight to another city, and I rented a car. It costed more, but I didn't miss the wedding. I even arrived an hour early!

**12** **LISTEN & SPEAK.**

CD2-49

**A** Read the statements. Then listen and complete each statement with the affirmative or negative form of the verb in parentheses. Use the simple past.

1. Lee _____ (take) a trip to Alaska.

2. He _____ (go) on a group tour.

3. He _____ (listen) to the guide.

4. He _____ (stay) with the group.

5. He _____ (see) three bears.

6. The bear _____ (see) Lee.

7. The bear _____ (run) after Lee.

8. Lee _____ (take) a photo of the bear.

CD2-49

**B** Listen again and check your answers from exercise **A**. Then close your books and retell the story to a partner.

▲ A black bear and her two cubs

**13** **APPLY.**

**A** In your notebook, use the words to make a list of typical travel problems. Use the simple past.

1. I / get / sick   *I got sick*

2. I / lose / my passport, wallet, etc.

3. Someone / take / my passport, wallet, etc.

4. I / miss / the plane, train, bus, etc.

5. I / get on / the wrong plane, train, bus, etc.

6. I / not bring / the right clothes

7. My luggage / not arrive

**B** Did you have any of the problems from exercise **A** on your last trip? Look at your list from exercise **A**. Check (✓) the problems you had.

**C** Work with a partner. Tell your partner about your experience. Where was it? When? What happened? Use the simple past.

*I was on a beach in France. I went in the water, and someone took my bag. . . .*

Charts
8.1,
8.5–8.10

**1** Complete the article with the correct simple past form of the verbs in the boxes.

## Two Famous Travelers

~~be~~   be   have   leave   live   not return   travel

Marco Polo and Ibn Battata (1) _____were_____ famous travelers. They both

(2) _____ very interesting lives.

Marco Polo (3) _____ in the thirteenth century. He (4) _____ from

Venice, Italy. In 1271, Marco Polo (5) _____ Italy with his father and uncle.

They (6) _____ to Asia. They (7) _____ to Italy for more than 20 years.

be   become   leave   not travel   read   stay   take   travel   write

Ibn Battata (8) _____ born in Morocco in 1304. He (9) _____

Tangier in 1325 and (10) _____ 75,000 miles (120,700 kilometers). The trip

(11) _____ almost 30 years. He often (12) _____ in one place for

several years; he (13) _____ all the time.

Both men (14) _____ books about their travels. Many people

(15) _____ their books, and Marco Polo and Ibn Battata (16) _____

famous.

Charts
8.1,
8.5–8.10

**2 EDIT.** Read the information about Ferdinand Magellan. Find and correct six more errors with the use of the simple past.

    *True or false?* Ferdinand Magellan ~~is~~ the first person
    ^was
to travel around the world.

    *False.* Magellan planed the trip, but he didn't complete
it. Magellan leaved Spain in 1519 with over 200 men on
five ships. Only one of his ships went all the way around
the world. It returnned to Spain in 1522. Eighteen men
are on the ship. Magellan himself was not finish the
journey. He was died in the Philippines in 1521.

▲ Ferdinand Magellan

**3 LISTEN & SPEAK.**

**A** Read each statement. Then listen to the story. Circle **T** for *true* or **F** for *false*.

1. Jason Lewis and Steve Smith wanted to go around the world.          **T**     **F**

2. They didn't want to use "human power."          **T**     **F**

3. Colin Angus did not complete his trip.          **T**     **F**

CD2-50

**B** Read each statement. Then listen again. Is the statement true for Jason Lewis or Colin Angus? Put a check (✓) in the correct column.

|  | Jason Lewis | Colin Angus |
|---|---|---|
| 1. He started in England. |  |  |
| 2. He started in Canada. |  |  |
| 3. He left in 2004. |  |  |
| 4. He went to Alaska. |  |  |
| 5. He went to Australia. |  |  |
| 6. He started the trip with a partner. |  |  |
| 7. He rowed a boat from Alaska to Russia. |  |  |
| 8. His fiancée joined him on the trip. |  |  |
| 9. He crossed the Equator. |  |  |
| 10. He finished his trip in 2007. |  |  |
| 11. He finished first. |  |  |
| 12. He rode a bicycle from Costa Rica to Canada. |  |  |

**C** Work with a partner. Compare your answers from exercise **B**. Then ask and answer questions about the two trips.

**D** Read the statements below with your classmates. Do you agree or disagree? Why?

Jason Smith was the first person to go around the world under human power. Colin Angus did not go around the world.

**4 SPEAK & WRITE.** Work with a partner. Write a story about two students. Complete the first two sentences with two names and the name of a place. In your notebook, write five more sentences to tell about the students' adventure.

*Two students, . . . . and . . . ., wanted an adventure. They planned a trip to . . . .*

**1 READ & NOTICE THE GRAMMAR.**

**A** Read the blog entry. Was this trip a good experience or a bad experience? Discuss with a partner.

# The End of the Trail

October 3

Today was an exciting day. We're in Canada! We reached the end of the Pacific Crest Trail this afternoon. We started at the Mexican border five months ago. We hiked every day, and now here we are!

This was an amazing experience. The scenery was beautiful. We hiked on trails high up in the mountains. It was difficult sometimes, especially when it rained. That wasn't fun at all!

Our friends from California met us at the Canadian border. We are having a great time tonight!

◄ Hikers on the Pacific Crest Trail

**GRAMMAR FOCUS**

In the blog entry in exercise **A**, the writer uses the simple past to talk about experiences in the past.

*Today **was** an exciting day.*
*We finally **reached** the end of the Pacific Crest Trail.*

**B** Read the blog in exercise **A** again. Underline the verbs in the simple past. Then work with a partner and compare answers.

**C** Complete this chart with information from the blog in exercise **A**.

| Information about the Trip | |
|---|---|
| Place | |
| Events and activities | |
| Description of the trip | |

**2** **BEFORE YOU WRITE.** Think of one day on a trip you took. Was it a good experience or a bad experience? Where were you? What happened? Write notes in the chart. Use the chart from exercise **1C** as a model.

| Information about the Trip | |
|---|---|
| Where | |
| Events of the day | |
| Description of the trip | |

**3** **WRITE** a blog entry about your trip. Use the information in your chart in exercise **2** and the paragraph in exercise **1A** to help you.

> **WRITING FOCUS**    Writing Complete Sentences
>
> A complete sentence needs a subject and verb. The subject is a noun or a pronoun.
>
> **Remember:** Complete sentences begin with capital letters and end with periods. Sometimes writers use exclamation marks (!) in informal writing to show excitement or surprise.
>
> *Today was an exciting day. We're in Canada!*

**4** **SELF ASSESS.** Circle the subject in each sentence of your blog entry. Underline the verbs in the simple past. Use the checklist to assess your work.

☐ I used *was* after a singular subject. I used *were* after a plural subject. [8.1]

☐ I used past time expressions correctly. [8.2]

☐ I used the correct spelling of *-ed* forms. [8.6]

☐ I used the correct form of irregular verbs. [8.7–8.9]

☐ There is a subject and verb in each sentence. [WRITING FOCUS]

# The Past: Part 2

► Climbers on Gasherbrum II,
Karakoram Mountain Range,
Pakistan

## EXPLORE

CD3-2

**1 READ** the conversation about Wangari Maathai. Notice the words in **bold**.

# Wangari Maathai

**Brad:** Hey, what are you doing?

**Peter:** I'm reading a book about Wangari Maathai.

**Brad:** Who's she?

**Peter:** She was a professor at the University of Nairobi in Kenya. She won the Nobel Peace Prize in 2004.

**Brad:** **What did she get it for?**

**Peter:** She got it for her work with women in Kenya and other countries in Africa.

**Brad:** **How did she help them?**

**Peter:** They didn't have enough firewood or other resources[1]. She got the idea to plant trees and started an organization called the Green Belt Movement.

**Brad:** So, **did she plant more trees?**

**Peter:** Yes, she did. Wangari Maathai and thousands of other women from rural[2] areas in Kenya planted over 50 million trees. This helped the environment, and it also helped make the women's lives better. Then other countries around the world copied the Green Belt Movement's idea and planted trees, too.

**Brad:** Interesting. **When did she start the Green Belt Movement?**

**Peter:** In the 1970s. She was an amazing woman. She worked her entire life to help people, especially women in Africa. She died in 2011.

[1] **Resources** are things that a country, an organization, or a person has and can use.
[2] A **rural** area or place is in the countryside, not in the city.

▶ Wangari Maathai in the Newlands forest in Cape Town, South Africa, in 2005

▲ Members of the Kiharo-Kahuro Women's Group prepare young trees in rural Kenya. © Green Belt Movement

**2 CHECK.** Choose the correct information to complete each statement.

1. Wangari Maathai was _____.

   a. a farmer          (b.) a professor

2. She lived _____.

   a. in Kenya          b. in the Green Belt

3. She won _____.

   a. the Nobel Peace Prize          b. a race

4. The Green Belt Movement started _____.

   a. in the 1970s          b. in 2011

**3 DISCOVER.** Complete the exercises to learn about the grammar in this lesson.

**A** Find these questions in the conversation from exercise **1**. Write the missing words.

1. What _____ she _____ it for?

2. How _____ she _____ them?

3. So, _____ she _____ more trees?

4. When _____ she _____ the Green Belt Movement?

**B** Look at the questions in exercise **A**. Then choose the correct words to complete each statement. Discuss your answers with your classmates and teacher.

1. *Did* is used to form _____.

   a. questions in the present          b. questions in the past          c. questions in the future

2. We use _____ of the verb after the subject in *Wh-* questions with *did*.

   a. the past form          b. the base form

# LEARN

## 9.1 Simple Past: *Yes/No* Questions and Short Answers

| *Yes/No* Questions | | |
|---|---|---|
| *Did* | Subject | Base Form of Verb |
| Did | I<br>you<br>he<br>she<br>it<br>we<br>you<br>they | help? |

| Short Answers | | | |
|---|---|---|---|
| Affirmative | | Negative | |
| Yes, | I<br>you<br>he<br>she<br>it<br>we<br>you<br>they **did.** | No, | I<br>you<br>he<br>she<br>it<br>we<br>you<br>they **didn't.** |

| | |
|---|---|
| 1. Use *did* to form *Yes/No* questions in the simple past. | **Did** you **call** Scott? |
| 2. Use the base form of the verb after the subject in simple past *Yes/No* questions. | ✓ **Did** you **know** her?<br>✗ **Did** you <u>knew</u> her? |
| 3. **Remember:** Do not use *did* in *Yes/No* questions with *was* or *were*. | ✓ **Were** they students?<br>✗ <u>Did</u> they <u>be</u> students? |

### REAL ENGLISH

The answers to *Yes/No* questions often do not include *Yes* or *No*.

A: *Did it rain last night?*
B: *A little.*

A: *Did you like the movie?*
B: *It was OK.*

**4** Match each *Yes/No* question with the correct short answer.

1. Did you know Wangari Maathai? _d_

2. Did she win the Nobel Prize? _____

3. Did Peter know about Wangari Maathai? _____

4. Did the women in Kenya have a challenge? _____

5. Did Brad know about her? _____

6. Did the Green Belt Movement help the environment? _____

  a. Yes, they did.

  b. No, he didn't.

  c. Yes, she did.

  d. No, I didn't.

  e. Yes, it did.

  f. Yes, he did.

**5** Change each statement to a *Yes/No* question. Then complete each short answer.

1. She won a prize.

   A: _Did she win a prize?_____

   B: Yes, _she did_____.

2. They planted a lot of trees.

   A: _____

   B: Yes, _____.

3. She lived in Kenya.

   A: _____

   B: Yes, _____.

4. He read the book.

   A: _____

   B: No, _____.

5. We knew about her.

   A: _____

   B: No, _____.

6. She grew up in Nairobi.

   A: _____

   B: Yes, _____.

7. He finished the book.

   A: _____

   B: Yes, _____.

8. They learned about the Green Belt Movement.

   A: _____

   B: No, _____.

**6 SPEAK.** Work with a partner. Use the words to make *Yes/No* questions. Then ask and answer your questions.

we / have / homework / last night

you / do / the homework

everybody / come to class / on time / today

Student A: *Did we have homework last night?*        Student B: *Yes, we did.*

## 9.2 Simple Past: *Wh*- Questions

| *Wh*- Word | *Did* | Subject | Base Form of Verb | Answers |
|---|---|---|---|---|
| What | did | I | buy? | A notebook and some pens. |
| Where | did | you | go? | Home. |
| When | did | she | arrive? | Last night. |
| Why | did | he | leave? | He felt sick. Because he felt sick. |
| Who | did | they | visit? | Their uncle. |
| How | did | we | do? | OK. |
| How long | did | it | take? | Five hours. |

| | |
|---|---|
| 1. **Remember:** *Wh-* questions ask for specific information. | A: **Why did** he **arrive** late? B: *Because there was a lot of traffic.* |
| 2. Put *did* before the subject in questions about the past. | ✓ When **did** <u>they</u> finish? ✗ When <u>they did</u> finish? |
| 3. Use the base form of the verb after the subject. Do not use the past form of the verb with *did*. | ✓ A How did <u>they</u> **get** there? ✗ How did they <u>got</u> there? |
| 4. **Remember:** In conversation, the answers to *Why* questions often begin with *because*. In writing, use complete sentences to answer *Why* questions. | A: **Why did** you **scream**? B: *Because I saw a spider on my desk.* |

**REAL ENGLISH**

*What for* is sometimes used in place of *Why* in informal conversations.

A: *Julie went to the doctor.*
B: **What for?**
A: *She hurt her foot.*

**7** Choose the correct answer for each question.

1. Where did she live?

   a. For two years.  (b.) In Africa.

2. When did she win the prize?

   a. In 2010.  b. She did a lot for other people.

3. Where did he go to university?

   a. In London.  b. In 2008.

4. How did you do on the exam?

   a. Yesterday.  b. I passed it.

5. When did you graduate from college?

   a. Last summer.  b. In Moscow.

6. Who did she help?

   a. Her family.  b. Yesterday.

7. What did he win?

   a. A prize.  b. In 2006.

8. Why did he win the prize?

   a. He was an excellent student.  b. Two years ago.

▶ Apollo 11 astronauts Neil Armstrong and Buzz Aldrin placed the American flag on the moon on July 20, 1969.

**8** Look at each sentence. Write a question about the underlined word or phrase.

**Neil Armstrong: The First Man on the Moon**

1. Neil Armstrong's family lived <u>in Ohio, USA</u>. _Where did Neil Armstrong's family live?_

2. He went to college <u>at Purdue University</u>. _____

3. He loved <u>planes</u>. _____

4. He <u>became an astronaut</u> in 1962. _____

5. He got to the moon <u>in a rocket called Apollo 11</u>. _____

6. He traveled to the moon with <u>Buzz Aldrin and Michael Collins</u>. _____

7. They started their trip to the moon <u>on July 16, 1969</u>. _____

8. They landed on the moon on <u>July 20, 1969</u>. _____

9. Armstrong <u>walked on the moon</u> on July 20, 1969. _____

10. Millions of people <u>watched on TV</u>. _____

11. Armstrong won awards <u>because he was the first man on the moon</u>. _____

12. He died <u>on August 25, 2012</u>. _____

**9** **WRITE & SPEAK.** Work with a partner. Use the words to make *Wh-* questions. Then ask and answer your questions.

1. How / you / get to class / today    *How did you get to class today?*

2. When / you / wake up / this morning

3. What / you / eat / for dinner / last night

4. Where / you / go / last weekend

Student A: *How did you get to class today?*    Student B: *I walked.*

### 9.3 Wh- Questions with Who or What

| Who/What Questions about a Subject | | | Answers |
|---|---|---|---|
| Wh- Word | Verb | | |
| Who | went | with you? | Felix. |
| What | happened | to you? | I hurt my hand. |

| Who/What Questions about an Object | | | | Answers |
|---|---|---|---|---|
| Wh- Word | Did | Subject | Base Form of Verb | |
| Who | did | you | ask? | Professor Davis. |
| What | did | they | do? | They went home. |

| | |
|---|---|
| 1. **Remember:** Wh- questions with Who or What can be about a subject or an object. | Question about a Subject: **Who** called? <br> Question about an Object: **Who** did you call? |
| 2. Do not use did when the question is about a subject. | ✓ **What** took so long? <br> ✗ What did <u>take</u> so long? <br><br> ✓ **Who** went on the trip? <br> ✗ Who did <u>go</u> on the trip? |

**10** Read each question. Is it about a subject or an object? Check (✓) the correct column.

| | Subject | Object |
|---|---|---|
| 1. Who won the Nobel Peace Prize last year? | ✓ | ☐ |
| 2. Who was the first person on the moon? | ☐ | ☐ |
| 3. What did the women do? | ☐ | ☐ |
| 4. What happened three years ago? | ☐ | ☐ |
| 5. Who did it? | ☐ | ☐ |
| 6. What did she say? | ☐ | ☐ |
| 7. Who didn't attend the meeting? | ☐ | ☐ |
| 8. Who did you talk to? | ☐ | ☐ |

**11** Put the words in the correct order to make Wh- questions.

1. lived / Who / that / house / in  _Who lived in that house?_____

2. she / did / ask / Who  _____

3. Who / his / were / parents  _____

4. she / did / What / do  _____

5. Who / go / didn't  _____

6. your / life / What / changed  _____

7. they / did / say / What  _____

8. Who / them / helped  _____

# PRACTICE

**12** **LISTEN** and choose the correct answer for each question.

1. a. In 1995.  ⓑ In Paris.
2. a. Three years ago.  b. Yes, he did.
3. a. Very happy.  b. No, I didn't.
4. a. Someone in the library.  b. At the library.
5. a. Two weeks ago.  b. I hurt my arm.
6. a. Yes, she did.  b. She did her homework.
7. a. She got a job there.  b. In 2010.
8. a. I felt sick.  b. At 6:30.

**13** Complete the interview with the correct question words. Then listen and check your answers.

**Interviewer:** OK, so Mr. Nash, (1) _____where_____ were you born?

**Nash:** In Jamaica.

**Interviewer:** (2) _____ did you move to London?

**Nash:** I knew a lot of people there.

**Interviewer:** (3) _____ you always want to be a writer?

**Nash:** No, I really wanted to be a football player!

**Interviewer:** Really? (4) _____ happened?

**Nash:** I broke my ankle and had other injuries.

**Interviewer:** (5) _____ you a good player?

**Nash:** No, I really wasn't very good.

**Interviewer:** (6) _____ taught you to write?

**Nash:** My teachers.

**Interviewer:** (7) _____ did you write your first book?

**Nash:** Ten years ago. No one liked it.

**Interviewer:** (8) _____ did you feel about that?

**Nash:** I felt terrible, of course.

**Interviewer:** (9) _____ didn't people like it?

**Nash:** It really wasn't very good. It was horrible, in fact.

**Interviewer:** (10) _____ you want to give up?

**Nash:** Yes, but I continued to write, and now I'm glad.

**14 SPEAK.** Work with a partner. Ask and answer questions about Mr. Nash from the interview in exercise **13**.

Student A: *Where was he born?*     Student B: *In Jamaica.*

**15 EDIT.** Read the conversations. Find and correct five more errors with simple past questions.

1. **Jim:** Did you grow up in South Africa?

   **Clive:** Yes, I did.

   **Jim:** Did you ever s̶a̶w̶ <sup>see</sup> Nelson Mandela?

   **Clive:** Yes, I went to hear him speak many times.

   **Jim:** Did you read the new book about him?

   **Clive:** No, I didn't. Who did write it?

   **Jim:** I don't remember, but it was really good.

2. **Lily:** When they did win the prize?

   **Jeff:** Last week.

   **Lily:** How they feel?

   **Jeff:** They were very happy, of course.

3. **Amelia:** Were you meet the president?

   **Kyle:** No, I didn't. How about you?

   **Amelia:** I saw her, but I didn't meet her.

   **Kyle:** Who she met with?

   **Amelia:** Photographers and news reporters.

**16 WRITE & SPEAK.**

**A** Write the correct question for the underlined information in each answer.

1. Q: _Where did you grow up?_

   A: I grew up <u>in Riyadh, Saudi Arabia</u>.

2. Q: _____

   A: <u>Yes</u>, my family came from that city.

3 Q: _____

   A: I went to school <u>in Australia</u>.

4. Q: _____

   A: I studied <u>biology</u>.

5. Q: _____

   A: I did <u>well</u> in school.

6. Q: _____

   A: <u>My parents</u> helped me.

7. Q: _____

   A: I lived with <u>my cousin</u> in Sydney.

8. Q: _____

   A: We went <u>to India</u> last year.

**B** Ask and answer questions 1-5 from exercise **A**.

Student A: *Where did you grow up?*        Student B: *I grew up in Izmir, Turkey.*

## 17 LISTEN, SPEAK & WRITE.

CD3-5

**A** Read the statements about Wong How-Man. Then listen and circle **T** for *true* or **F** for *false*.

1. Wong How-Man is from the United States.        **T**        **F**

2. Wong How-Man is a writer and photographer.        **T**        **F**

CD3-5

**B** Listen again. Check (✓) the information you hear about Wong How-Man.

| Name: Wong How–Man | | |
|---|---|---|
| Lived | _✓_ Hong Kong | _____ Beijing |
| Explored | _____ Oceans | _____ Rivers |
| In the 1980s | _____ Led expeditions | _____ Taught classes |
| In 1985 and 2005 | _____ Yangtze River | _____ Mekong River |
| Started | _____ An exploration and research society | _____ A photography school |

**C** Write as many *Yes/No* and *Wh-* questions in the past as you can about Wong How–Man.

*Where did he grow up?*

**D** Work with a partner. Ask and answer your questions from exercise **C**.

Student A: *Where did he grow up?*        Student B: *In Hong Kong.*

## 18 APPLY.

**A** Write questions in the simple past for your classmates. Use the words in the chart.

| Wh- Word | Questions | Notes |
|---|---|---|
| Where | Where did you grow up? | Cali, Colombia (Maria) |
| When | | |
| Why | | |
| How | | |
| What | | |
| Who | | |

**B** Stand up and walk around the classroom. Find six classmates, and ask each person a question from exercise **A**. Write notes in your chart.

**C** Tell your classmates about the students you interviewed in exercise **B**.

*Maria grew up in Cali, Colombia. Hamid rode his bicycle to class today. . . .*

## EXPLORE

CD3-6

**1** **READ** the article about Ernest Shackleton's expedition. Notice the words in **bold**.

# Ernest Shackleton's Expedition

In early August 1914, members of the British Imperial Trans-Antarctic Expedition sailed for Vahsel Bay in Antarctica on a ship called the *Endurance*. Their leader was Ernest Shackleton.

Shackleton and his 27 men were 100 miles from their destination[1] **when ice surrounded[2] their ship.** For the next nine months, the ice moved their ship more than 1000 miles (1609 kilometers). Finally, **before the ice crushed[3] the ship,** the men left it and got onto the ice. The temperature was –16°F (–27°C). The men camped on the ice for several months.

In April, the ice started to melt. It was time for them to try to reach safety. They got in lifeboats[4] and started across the South Atlantic Ocean. After a week of terrible storms, they reached Elephant Island. Unfortunately, no one lived there. **After they rested for a week,** Shackleton and five of his men left Elephant Island in one of the lifeboats. They spent 17 days on the ocean **before they reached South Georgia Island.** There they walked for 36 hours over the mountains and finally reached a town.

Shackleton returned to rescue the other men on August 25, 1916. Everyone on Shackleton's expedition survived.

[1] **destination:** the place that someone is going to
[2] **surround:** to be all around something
[3] **crush:** to push or press hard
[4] **lifeboat:** a small boat used in emergencies

◀ *Endurance,* surrounded by ice

**2 CHECK.** Read each statement. Then circle **T** for *true* or **F** for *false*.

1. Shackleton's ship was called the *Explorer*.                    **T**     **F**

2. They sailed for Vahsel Bay on December 19, 1914.               **T**     **F**

3. Ice surrounded their ship.                                     **T**     **F**

4. The men stayed on the ship.                                    **T**     **F**

5. Nobody on Shackleton's expedition died.                       **T**     **F**

**3 DISCOVER.** Complete the exercises to learn about the grammar in this lesson.

**A** Look at the underlined part of each of these sentences from the article in exercise **1**. Put a check (✓) next to the ones with a subject and a verb.

1. They were 100 miles from their destination <u>when ice surrounded their ship.</u>   ☐

2. <u>Before the ice crushed their ship,</u> the men left the ship and got onto the ice.   ☐

3. <u>After a week of terrible storms,</u> they reached Elephant Island.   ☐

4. <u>After they rested for a week,</u> Shackleton left the island in one of the lifeboats.   ☐

5. They spent 17 days on the ocean <u>before they reached South Georgia Island.</u>   ☐

**B** Discuss your answers from exercise **A** with your classmates and teacher.

# LEARN

## 9.4 Past Time Clauses with *Before* and *After*

She finished school **before she moved to Seoul.**
⎣___Main Clause___⎦ ⎣_____Time Clause_____⎦

She moved to Seoul **after she finished school.**
⎣___Main Clause___⎦ ⎣_____Time Clause_____⎦

| | |
|---|---|
| 1. A clause is a group of words with a subject and a verb. A main clause can stand alone as a complete sentence. | We did our homework before dinner.<br>⎣_____Clause_____⎦ |
| 2. A clause that begins with *before* or *after* is a time clause. A past time clause tells when an action or event happened. | They ate lunch **before they left**.<br>We played soccer **after we ate dinner.** |
| 3. A time clause is not a complete sentence. Do not use a time clause without a main clause. | ✓ They moved to Beirut **after they got married.**<br>⎣____Main Clause____⎦ ⎣___Time Clause___⎦<br>✗ After they got married.<br>⎣____Time Clause____⎦ |
| 4. A time clause can come before or after a main clause. Use a comma when a time clause is at the beginning of the sentence. | After he left work, he went to the gym.<br>He went to the gym after he left work.<br><br>Before he left work, he met with his boss.<br>He met with his boss before he left work. |
| 5. *Before* and *after* show the order of two actions or events. | After they ate dinner, they watched the game.<br>⎣___First Event___⎦ ⎣___Second Event___⎦<br>They ate dinner **before** they watched the game.<br>⎣___First Event___⎦ ⎣___Second Event___⎦ |

### REAL ENGLISH

*Before* and *after* are also prepositions. They can be followed by a noun.

I ate breakfast **before** work.
⎣_Noun_⎦

**After** lunch, we went to the museum.
⎣_Noun_⎦

---

**4** Read each sentence. Which action or event happened first? Which action or event happened second? Write *1* for *first* and *2* for *second* below each action or event.

1. After <u>they reached land</u>, <u>two of the men went for help.</u>

        <u>1</u>             <u>2</u>

2. <u>They reached South Georgia Island</u> after <u>they spent 17 days on the ocean.</u>

        <u>    </u>             <u>    </u>

3. <u>They walked for 36 hours</u> before <u>they reached a town.</u>

        <u>    </u>             <u>    </u>

4. Before <u>the ice crushed the ship,</u> <u>the men moved onto the ice.</u>

           _____              _____

5. <u>He returned to rescue the others</u> after <u>he reached a town.</u>

           _____              _____

6. After <u>Shackleton rescued the other men,</u> <u>he became famous.</u>

              _____               _____

7. <u>Other men reached the South Pole</u> before <u>Shackleton did.</u>

         _____               _____

8. After <u>they rested for a week,</u> <u>he left the island with five of the men.</u>

           _____              _____

**5** Look at the time line for Shackleton's expedition. Then complete each sentence with *before* or *after*.

1. Shackleton and his men saw ice on the ocean ___*before*___ they crossed the Antarctic Circle.

2. _____ they crossed the Antarctic Circle, ice surrounded the ship.

3. _____ ice surrounded the ship, it moved 1000 miles away from the South Pole.

4. _____ they moved onto the ice, the ice carried the ship 1000 miles.

5. They moved from the ship onto the ice _____ ice began to crush the ship.

6. They moved onto the ice _____ the ship broke up.

7. The ship sank _____ the ice started to break up.

8. They got into lifeboats _____ the ice started to break up.

**Shackleton's Expedition**

**August, 1914** —

← Shackleton and his men saw ice in the ocean.

← They crossed the Antarctic Circle.

← Ice surrounded the ship.

← Ice moved the ship 1000 miles.

← Ice began to crush the ship.

← They moved onto the ice.

← The ice started to break up.

← The ship sank.

← They got into lifeboats.

**August, 1916** —

**6** **SPEAK.** Work with a partner. Complete the sentences.

Before class, I _____.     After I got home last night, I _____.

*Before class, I ate breakfast.*

## 9.5 Past Time Clauses with *When*

I made dinner **when I got home.**
| Main Clause | | Time Clause |

They bought an apartment **when they moved to London.**
| Main Clause | | Time Clause |

| | |
|---|---|
| 1. Use *when* + the simple past to talk about an action or event that happened at a point in the past. **Remember:** A time clause is not a complete sentence. Do not use a time clause without a main clause. | ✓ I had a cup of coffee **when I got to work.**<br>✗ When I got to work. |
| 2. Use *when* in a time clause to talk about two actions or events in the past. The action or event in the *when* clause happened first. The action or event in the main clause happened second. | **When** the war started, they left London.<br>First Event — Second Event<br>They left London **when** the war started.<br>Second Event — First Event |
| 3. **Remember:** Use a comma when the time clause comes at the beginning of a sentence. | **When he got to Chicago,** he called us. |

**7** Change each sentence. Begin each sentence with *When*.

1. They celebrated when their team won the World Cup.

   When their team won the World Cup, they celebrated.

2. We had a party when my sister graduated.

   _____

3. He took a photo when he reached the top of the mountain.

   _____

4. Lisa helped me when I had a problem.

   _____

5. My parents were very happy when Neil Armstrong landed on the moon.

   _____

6. Bob texted us when he finished the race.

   _____

7. I called my mother when I heard the good news.

   _____

8. They bought their first house when they moved to Ohio.

   _____

# PRACTICE

**8** Read each sentence. Underline the part of the sentence that shows when the event or action happened. Which of your answers are past time clauses?

1. Emma hurt her leg <u>when she ran in a race last year.</u>   *past time clause*

2. After her injury, Emma wanted to run in another race.

3. Before the next big race, she did special exercises for her leg.

4. She was very nervous before the race.

5. After she ran the first mile, she wasn't nervous.

6. After the fifth mile, she was in first place.

7. When she won the race, everyone said, "Congratulations."

8. After she won the race, she celebrated with her friends and family.

CD3-7 **9** Complete the sentences. Use *before, after,* or *when.* Then listen and check your answers.

## JACQUES COUSTEAU

Jacques Cousteau was a famous ocean explorer. He was born in France in 1910. He learned to swim (1) _____*when*_____ he was four. (2) _____ he was thirteen, he bought his first movie camera. (3) _____ he finished school, he joined the navy.[1] (4) _____ he was 23, Cousteau was in a bad car accident. He almost died. (5) _____ his accident, he went swimming every day in the Mediterranean Sea. (6) _____ the salt water hurt his eyes, he started to wear goggles.[2] This changed his life. (7) _____ he used goggles, he never saw anything underwater. With goggles, he saw a lot of interesting things in the sea. (8) _____ this, he wanted to dive deeper and deeper.

◀ Jacques Cousteau in 1982

[1] **navy:** a country's sailors and fighting ships
[2] **goggles:** plastic glasses that protect the eyes

## 10 LISTEN & WRITE.

**A** Listen to the information about Jacques Cousteau and his family. Match each name on the left with the correct information.

1. Jacques Cousteau _b_
2. Simone _____
3. Emile _____
4. *Calypso* _____

a. an inventor
b. an underwater explorer
c. Cousteau's wife
d. Cousteau's ship

**B** Listen again. Number the events in the correct order.

_____ Met Emile Gagnan

_____ Helped to design an underwater camera

_____ Designed a small submarine, called "a diving saucer"

_1_ Got married

_____ Became famous after his book became a film

_____ Started to lead expeditions

_____ Designed the aqua lung

_____ Bought a ship

_____ Wrote a book

▲ *Calypso* crew members used a crane to launch diving saucer *Denise* during an expedition off the coast of France.

**C** Complete each sentence with information from exercise **B**. Use time clauses with *before, after,* or *when.*

1. Cousteau met Emile Gagnan _after he got married._

2. _____, people had no way to swim under water for long periods of time.

3. Cousteau had a way to film under water _____.

4. _____, he had a way to travel and explore the ocean.

5. _____, it became a film.

6. _____, Cousteau didn't have enough money for his expeditions.

7. _____, he became famous.

8. _____, he taught people about fish and other animals in the ocean.

**11 EDIT.** Read the information about Jacques Cousteau. Add five more commas.

# A Friend of the Ocean

Before Jacques Cousteau wrote *The Silent World*, he wasn't famous. After the book became a movie Cousteau led many expeditions to study the ocean. When he led expeditions a film crew went with him on his ship, the *Calypso*. He made a one-hour television show. It was very popular. When people watched this TV show they learned about the ocean. He had the TV show for nine years. Before it ended Cousteau began to see many changes and problems in the ocean. After he saw these problems he wanted to help the ocean. He started the Cousteau Society and made special television shows about problems in the ocean. Many people joined the Cousteau Society after they saw the television shows. Jacques Cousteau died in 1997 after a long career as an explorer, an inventor, and a friend of the ocean.

**12 LISTEN & WRITE.**

CD3-9-10

**A** Read each statement. Then listen to two conversations. Which statements are true? As you listen to each conversation, check (✓) the correct boxes.

| | Conversation 1 | Conversation 2 |
|---|---|---|
| 1. He had a good experience. | ✓ | ☐ |
| 2. He had a bad expreience. | ☐ | ☐ |
| 3. He felt nervous before he started. | ☐ | ☐ |
| 4. He felt nervous after he started. | ☐ | ☐ |
| 5. His face was red when he started. | ☐ | ☐ |
| 6. He felt sick. | ☐ | ☐ |

**B** Write sentences about the speakers from the conversations in exercise **A**. Use the words in parentheses and *before, after,* or *when*. Add other words if needed.

1. (nervous / started / his presentation)

   In conversation 1, Max _was nervous before he started his presentation._

2. (not nervous / started / the presentation)

   He _____.

3. (practiced / a lot / his presentation)

   Max _____.

4. (fell asleep / finished)

His dog _____.

5. (sick / the game )

In conversation 2, Sidney _____.

6. (left / the game / half-time)

He _____.

7. (scored a goal / he left the game)

His team _____.

8. (not hurt / the game)

His stomach _____.

## 13 APPLY.

**A** Think of a time in your life when you had a challenge. Write notes in the chart.

| What was the challenge? | a presentation |
|---|---|
| When was it? | in high school |
| How did you feel? | |
| What happened? | |

**B** Write about your experience. Use *before, after,* and *when.*

*When I was in high school, I gave a speech. Before the speech, I was very nervous. I did a good job. After the speech, I felt very happy. Everyone liked it.*

_____

_____

_____

_____

_____

**C** Work with a partner. Share your experiences from exercise **B**. Use *before, after,* and *when.*

## EXPLORE

CD3-11

**1** **READ** the article about Tenzing Norgay. Notice the words in **bold**.

# Tenzing Norgay

On May 29, 1953, the leader of a climbing expedition[1] **was waiting** at a camp on Mount Everest. Two of the expedition's climbers, Edmund Hillary and Tenzing Norgay, **were trying** to reach the top of the mountain. They were not the first to try. In fact, this was Tenzing's seventh attempt.

Tenzing Norgay grew up in a very poor family in Nepal. He was a Sherpa. Sherpas are often porters.[2] They carry things for other climbers. When Tenzing was 19, **he was living** in India. He got a job on a climbing expedition. After several expeditions, he became a climber and was no longer a porter.

In 1953, Tenzing met Edmund Hillary when he joined an expedition to climb to the top of Mount Everest. It was a very difficult and dangerous expedition. Once when **they were climbing**, Hillary fell and Tenzing rescued him. Climbers from another expedition **were also trying** to reach the top of Mount Everest, but they failed.

Early in the morning on May 29, 1953, Hillary and Tenzing left their camp and continued their climb up Mount Everest. At 11:30, they reached the top.

[1] **expedition:** a journey usually made by a group for a special purpose
[2] **porter:** a person whose job is to carry things

▼ Tenzing Norgay at the top of Chukhung Peak
  on his way to the top of Mount Everest (1953)

**2  CHECK.** Read each statement. Then circle **T** for *true* or **F** for *false*.

1. Tenzing Norgay and Edmund Hillary were trying to reach the top
   of Mount Everest.                                                    **T     F**

2. Tenzing was a Sherpa.                                               **T     F**

3. This was Tenzing's first attempt.                                   **T     F**

4. Tenzing rescued Hillary.                                            **T     F**

**3  DISCOVER.** Complete the exercises to learn about the grammar in this lesson.

**A** Find these sentences in the article from exercise **1**. Write the missing words.

1. When Tenzing was 19, he _____ in India.
                                       a

2. He _____ a job on a climbing expedition.
           b

3. Once when they _____ , Hillary fell and Tenzing _____ him.
                          c                                              d

4. At 11:30, they _____ the top.
                         e

**B** Look at the verbs in exercise **A**. Then answer these questions. Discuss your answers with your classmates and teacher.

1. Which two verbs talk about an action that was          a   b   c   d   e
   happening for a period of time in the past?

2. Which verb talks about an action that happened         a   b   c   d   e
   when another action was in progress?

▼ Tenzing Norgay and Edmund Hillary
drinking tea after their successful
climb, Mount Everest (1953)

# LEARN

## 9.6 Past Progressive

| Affirmative Statements | | | |
| --- | --- | --- | --- |
| Subject | Was/Were | Verb + -ing | |
| I<br>He<br>She | was | living | in Rio in 2009. |
| You<br>We<br>You<br>They | were | | |

| Negative Statements | | | |
| --- | --- | --- | --- |
| Subject | Was Not/ Were (Not) | Verb + -ing | |
| I<br>He<br>She | was not<br>wasn't | living | in Rio in 2009. |
| You<br>We<br>You<br>They | were not<br>weren't | | |

1. Use the past progressive to talk about an action that was in progress at a specific time in the past.

We **were eating** dinner at 7:30 last night.
She **was working** in Mexico City in 2011.

2. Use the past progressive to talk about an action in the past that was in progress when another action or event happened.

We **were eating** when she **arrived**.
└─ Action in Progress ─┘ └─ Second Action ─┘

---

**4** Read the sentences. Put a check (✓) next to the sentences that have a verb in the past progressive. Then underline the verbs in the past progressive.

1. __✓__ In the early 1950s, many people <u>were trying</u> to climb to the top of Mount Everest.

2. _____ Many Sherpas were porters, but Tenzing Norgay became a climber.

3. _____ One day Hillary and Tenzing were climbing Mount Everest.

4. _____ When Hillary fell, Tenzing rescued him.

5. _____ Tenzing was living in India when he was 19.

6. _____ They were very happy when they reached the top.

7. _____ When they returned to their camp, the other climbers were waiting for them.

8. _____ They were all hoping to reach the top, but Tenzing and Hillary were the first.

**5** Complete each sentence with the past progressive form of the verb in parentheses.

1. Karen and Frank ___were climbing___ (climb) the mountain when the accident happened.

2. Frank _____ (work) as a guide when they first met.

3. In June 2004, we _____ (travel) in Nepal.

4. They _____ (live) in Bangkok at that time.

5. I _____ (not pay attention) when I fell down the stairs.

6. I _____ (sleep) at 11:00 p.m. last night.

7. Carol and Ed _____ (wait) for the train when we saw them.

8. I _____ (drive) home when I heard the news.

9. They _____ (talk) during the entire presentation. It was very rude!

10. We _____ (study) for the exam all last week.

## 9.7   Simple Past vs. Past Progressive

I **was walking** to class when I **heard** a loud noise.
      Past Progressive                      Simple Past

Junko **was riding** her bike when it **started** to rain.
         Past Progressive                       Simple Past

| | |
|---|---|
| 1. **Remember:** Use the simple past for completed actions. | I **called** my parents last night.<br>He **woke up** at 6:00 a.m. this morning. |
| 2. When one event happened while another event was in progress, use the simple past for the second action or event. | I **was watching** the game when my sister **called**.<br>First Action          Second Action |
| 3. Do not use the past progressive with non-action verbs.* | ✓ We **saw** Gemma yesterday.<br>✗ We <u>were seeing</u> Gemma yesterday.<br><br>✓ Efren **knew** the answer.<br>✗ Efren <u>was knowing</u> the answer. |

\* See Chart **7.8** in Unit 7 for more information on non-action verbs.

**6**   Circle the correct form of the verb(s) to complete each sentence.

1. My brother (**started**)/ **was starting** his own business when he was in high school.

2. He **got** / **was getting** the idea when he **helped** / **was helping** our grandmother one day.

3. She **had** / **was having** a new computer at that time.

4. She **wasn't knowing** / **didn't know** anything about computers.

5. She **didn't understand** / **wasn't understanding** a lot of things about her new computer when she **called** / **was calling** him.

6. He **gave** / **was giving** computer lessons to her once a week.

7. One of her friends **came** / **was coming** to our grandmother's house when he **taught** / **was teaching** her.

8. The friend **wanted** / **was wanting** to take lessons, too. Soon my brother **had** / **was having** a lot of students.

# PRACTICE

**7** Complete the paragraph. Use the simple past or past progressive of each verb in parentheses.

## The Paralympic Games

The Paralympic Games are international competitions for athletes with disabilities. The idea for the games (1) _____ (begin) in 1948. At that time, many former soldiers with disabilities from the war (2) _____ (live) in England. Dr. Ludwig Guttmann (3) _____ (work) at a London hospital, and he (4) _____ (want) to help the soldiers. He (5) _____ (organize) an archery competition for people in wheelchairs. Soon there (6) _____ (be) many sport competitions for people with disabilities. Many people (7) _____ (like) Guttmann's idea, and the first Paralympics (8) _____ (take) place in 1960.

**8 LISTEN & SPEAK.**

CD3-12

**A** Listen to the information about the first voyage of the *Titanic*. Complete the sentences.

1. The *Titanic* was going from Southampton in ____England____ to ____New York____.

2. About _____ people were on the ship.

3. There were _____ lifeboats on the ship.

4. The *Titanic* left England on _____ 10, 1912.

5. There were _____ about icebergs.

**B** Circle the correct form of the verb to complete each sentence.

1. The *Titanic* **crossed** / (**was crossing**) the Atlantic Ocean on April 10, 1912.

2. The ship **had** / **was having** space for more lifeboats.

3. It was carrying 20 lifeboats, but it **needed** / **was needing** 64 for the number of passengers on the ship.

4. Other ships **knew** / **were knowing** about the icebergs and sent reports about them.

5. The captain didn't get the reports because he **had** / **was having** dinner with the passengers.

6. The ship **went** / **was going** at full speed when it hit the iceberg.

7. At first, people **didn't believe** / **weren't believing** that the *Titanic* was sinking.

8. The *Titanic* **sank** / **was sinking** on April 15, 1912.

9. Over 1500 people **died** / **were dying**.

10. It **was** / **was being** a terrible event in history.

▼ *Titanic*, Southhampton, England, April 10, 1912

**C** Work in a group. Share your answers to these questions.

1. Did you know about the *Titanic* before this? How did you learn about it?

2. What other facts do you know about the *Titanic*?

3. Did you see the movie, *Titanic*? Did you like it? Why, or why not?

*I knew about the* Titanic *before this. I learned about it in high school . . .*

**9 APPLY.**

**A** Think of another historical event, such as the first moon landing in 1969. Write notes to answer each question about this event.

| Questions | Answers |
|---|---|
| What was the event? | The first man landed on the moon. |
| When did it happen? | |
| Where did it happen? | |
| What happened? | |
| What were people doing when it happened? | |
| How did you learn about it? | |

**B** Work in a group. Share your information from exercise **A** with your classmates.

**C** In your notebook, write about your event. Use the information from your chart in exercise **A**.

Charts
9.1, 9.2,
9.4–9.7

**1 WRITE & SPEAK.**

**A** Complete the sentences. Use the simple past or past progressive. Add a comma if necessary.

1. Before I ate breakfast this morning _____.

2. When I woke up _____.

3. After breakfast I _____.

4. When I was at home last night _____.

5. I was coming to class when _____.

6. I was doing my homework when _____.

7. I started school when _____.

8. Before I was born _____.

**B** Work with a partner. Share your sentences from exercise **A**.

Student A: *Before I ate breakfast this morning, I called my parents.*

Charts
9.1, 9.2,
9.4–9.7

🎧
CD3-13

**2 WRITE, LISTEN, & SPEAK.**

**A** Complete the article with the correct form of each verb in parentheses. Then listen and check your answers.

# Exploration of the Arctic and the Antarctic

The early 20th century was a time of great exploration. Expeditions from several countries (1) ___were trying___ (try) to reach the North and South Poles. Voyages to the Arctic and Antarctic took several years and (2) _____ (be) very dangerous. Many explorers (3) _____ (die) when they (4) _____ (travel). The weather was very cold. Sometimes the temperature was only –20 degrees Fahrenheit (–29 degrees Celsius).

▲ Roald Amundsen

In 1910, several explorers (5) _____ (want) to reach the North Pole. A Norwegian, Roald Amundsen, (6) _____ (be) one of the explorers, but when he (7) _____ (prepare) for his voyage, two explorers from the United States (8) _____ (reach) the North Pole. This was bad news for Amundsen because he wanted to be first.

After the challenge of the North Pole (9) _____ (end), the race for the South Pole (10) _____ (begin). In fact, in 1910, explorers from Germany, France, Japan, Norway, and the United States all (11) _____ (plan) new expeditions to the South Pole. The explorers all (12) _____ (have) the same goal: They (13) _____ (want) to be the first expedition to reach the South Pole.

**B** Write as many questions as you can about the information in exercise **A**. Use the simple past and the past progressive.

*What were expeditions from different countries trying to do in the early 1900s?*

**C** Ask and answer your classmates' questions from **B**.

Student A: *What were expeditions from different countries trying to do in the early 1900s?*

Student B: *They were trying to reach the North and South Poles.*

Charts
9.1–9.7

**3 EDIT.** Read the questions and answers about polar expeditions. Find and correct six more errors with simple past questions and the past progressive.

▶ Robert Peary

## Frequently Asked Questions about Polar Expeditions

**Q:** Who ^was the first man ~~was~~ to the North Pole?

**A:** No one really knows. In 1909, two men from the United States, Robert Peary and Fredrick Cook, both said, "I was the first."

**Q:** Why so many explorers wanted to reach the poles first?

**A:** They were wanting to be famous.

**Q:** Did expeditions continued after explorers reached the North and South Poles?

**A:** Yes, they did.

**Q:** Why they continued?

**A:** Many explorers were scientists. They wanted to learn many things about the poles. When they were returned, they were having a lot of new information.

Charts
9.1–9.7

**4 LISTEN & WRITE.**

CD3-14

**A** Two classmates see each other after many years. Read the information in the chart. Then listen to their conversation. Is the information about Dana or Allen? Put a check (✓) in the correct column(s). Then work with a partner and compare your charts.

|  | Dana | Allen |
|---|---|---|
| Lives in Oklahoma |  | ✓ |
| Is married |  |  |
| Has two daughters |  |  |

CD3-14

**B** Listen again. Number the events in Allen's life in the correct order.

| Allen | Dana |
|-------|------|
| _____ Graduated from high school | _____ Graduated from high school |
| _____ The tornado happened | _____ The tornado happened |
| _____ Graduated from college | _____ Graduated from college |
| __1__ Got a job | _____ Got a job |
| _____ Got married | _____ Got married |
| _____ Had a child | _____ Had a child |

CD3-14

**C** Listen again. Number the events in Dana's life in the correct order. Then compare your answers from exercises **B** and **C** with a partner.

**D** Write about three events in Allen and Dana's lives. Use past time clauses with the past or past progressive and *before, after,* or *when.*

1. (when)  Allen _was living in Oklahoma when Dana saw him._

2. (before) Allen _____.

3. (after)  Allen _____.

4. (when)  Dana _____.

5. (before) Dana _____.

6. (after)  Dana _____.

Charts
9.1–9.7

**5 WRITE & SPEAK.**

**A** Write six important events in your life on the time line.

I was born                                                              now

**B** Work with a partner. Discuss the events in your life. Use the information from your time line from exercise **A** and *before, after,* and *when.* Use the simple past or past progressive.

Student A: *We moved to Germany when I was six.*

Student B: *Really? Do you speak German?*

# Connect the Grammar to Writing

**1 READ & NOTICE THE GRAMMAR.**

**A** Read the biography. What did Florence Nightingale do? Discuss with a partner.

## Florence Nightingale

Florence Nightingale lived in the 1800s. When she was 24, Nightingale studied nursing. After she finished school, she got a job in a hospital. She became the director of the hospital after only three years. When she was 34, Nightingale took a group of nurses to help injured soldiers in Crimea. Before the nurses arrived, the hospital was very dirty. Many soldiers got diseases. After Nightingale arrived with her nurses, the number of deaths went down by 66 percent.

When she returned to England, Nightingale wrote a book about ways to improve hospital care. Her book changed the nursing profession. Her knowledge saved many people's lives.

▲ Florence Nightingale

### GRAMMAR FOCUS

In the biography in exercise **A**, the writer uses past time clauses to show when events happened.

**Remember:** A time clause includes a word such as *before, after,* or *when,* a subject, and a verb.

> **When she was 24,** *Nightingale became a nurse.*
> **After she finished school,** *she got a job in a hospital.*

**B** Read the biography in exercise **A** again. Underline the past time clauses. Then work with a partner and compare answers.

**C** Complete the notes with information about Florence Nightingale's life with information from the biography in exercise **A**.

| Florence Nightingale |
|---|
| 1. _____ lived in the 1800s. _____ |
| 2. (age 24) _____. |
| 3. _____ in a hospital. |
| 4. _____ director of the hospital. |
| 5. (age 34) _____ a hospital in Crimea. |
| Deaths _____. |
| 6. _____ about ways to improve hospital care. |

## 2 BEFORE YOU WRITE.

**A** Choose a person to write about. Complete the chart below with information about that person's life. What did he or she do? What were the important events in his or her life? Use the chart from exercise **1C** as a model.

| |
|---|
| 1. |
| 2. |
| 3. |
| 4. |
| 5. |
| 6. |

## 3 WRITE a biography. Use the information in your chart in exercise 2A and the biography in exercise 1A to help you.

> **WRITING FOCUS    Using *When, Before,* and *After***
>
> Writers use *when, before,* and *after* at the beginning of time clauses to show the sequence of events. They also use *before* and *after* as prepositions.
>
> **Remember:** Use a comma when the time clause is at the beginning of the sentence.
>
> <u>*When she was 24,*</u> *Nightingale studied nursing.* (time clause)
>
> *She became the director of the hospital* **after** *only three years.* (preposition)

## 4 SELF ASSESS. Read your biography. Underline the past time clauses. Then use the checklist to assess your work.

☐  I used the simple past for completed actions and the past progressive for actions that were in progress at a specific time in the past. [9.6, 9.7]

☐  I used main clauses with past time clauses. [9.4, 9.5]

☐  There is a subject and a verb in each time clause. [9.4, 9.5]

☐  I used a comma after a time clause at the beginning of a sentence. [9.4, 9.5]

☐  I used *when, before,* and *after* to show the sequence of events. [WRITING FOCUS]

# Adjectives and Adverbs

◄ A diver has a close encounter with a southern right whale, Auckland Islands, New Zealand.

## EXPLORE

CD3-15

**1** **READ** the article about the fennec fox. Notice the words in **bold**.

# Fennec Foxes

The fennec fox lives in the Sahara and in other parts of North Africa. Everything about this **small** fox helps it in the desert. For example, it is **cream colored**. The fox's **sandy** color helps it hide in the desert. The fennec fox also has very **large** ears. Its ears keep its body **cool**. This is **important** because the desert gets very **hot** during the day.

The fennec fox has **thick** fur. This keeps it warm at night and cool during the day. The **thick** fur on its feet also helps protect it when it walks or runs across the **hot desert** sand.

Several other things help the fennec fox live in the desert. For one thing, it's a **nocturnal** animal, so it's **active** at night. During the day, it lives under the ground in its den.[1] Another thing that helps this fox is its **excellent** hearing. This helps it find and catch **small** animals to eat, such as mice, reptiles, and insects. When the fox hears a **small** animal under the sand, it starts to dig. The fennec fox also doesn't need a lot of water. This is **helpful** because the desert doesn't get much rain. The fennec fox is truly a **desert** animal.

### Related Articles

**What's** the Sahara **like** at night?
**How big is** the Sahara?
**What kinds of** animals live in the Sahara?
**What's** life **like** for nocturnal animals?

[1] **den:** the home of some kinds of animals

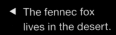
◀ The fennec fox lives in the desert.

▲ A family of fennec foxes

**2  CHECK.** Match the first part of each sentence in Column A with the second part in Column B. Write the letter on the line.

**Column A**

1. The sandy color of its fur ___C___.

2. Its big ears _____.

3. Its thick fur _____.

4. Its excellent hearing _____.

5. The small amount of water it needs _____.

**Column B**

a. helps it in the dry desert

b. keep its body cool

c. helps it hide

d. keeps it warm at night and cool during the day

e. helps it find food

**3  DISCOVER.** Complete the exercises to learn about the grammar in this lesson.

**A**  Find these sentences in the article from exercise **1** on page 310. Write the missing words.

1. Everything about this _____ fox helps it in the desert.

2. The fennec fox also has very _____ ears.

3. The fennec fox has _____ fur.

4. Another thing that helps this fox is its _____ hearing.

5. This is _____ because the desert doesn't get much rain.

**B**  Look at the words you wrote in exercise **A**. What do these words describe? Choose your answer. Then discuss your answer with your classmates and teacher.

These words describe _____ in the sentences.

a. the subjects        b. the verbs        c. the nouns

# LEARN

## 10.1 Modifying Nouns with Adjectives

| Noun | Be | Adjective |
|------|-----|-----------|
| The article | is | interesting. |
| The foxes | are | small. |

| | Adjective | Noun |
|------|-----------|------|
| It's an | interesting | article. |
| They are | small | foxes. |

| | |
|---|---|
| 1. **Remember:** Adjectives describe or modify nouns or pronouns. | The desert is **hot**.<br>She is **friendly**. |
| 2. **Remember:** Adjectives often come after the verb *be* and modify the subject. They can also come before nouns. | They are **nice**.<br>They are **nice** people.<br>That **tall** man over there is Lee's brother. |
| 3. **Remember:** Use *a* or *an* before an adjective + singular noun. Use *a* before a consonant sound. Use *an* before a vowel sound. | She's **a** good student.<br>He's **an** excellent teacher. |
| 4. **Remember:** The form of an adjective does not change. An adjective is the same for singular and plural nouns and pronouns. | ✓ That flower is **beautiful**.<br>✓ Those flowers are **beautiful**.<br>✗ Those flowers are <u>beautifuls</u>. |
| 5. Some adjectives after the verb *be* are followed by specific prepositions. | I'm **afraid** <u>of</u> snakes.<br>I'm **worried** <u>about</u> the test.<br>Sugar isn't **good** <u>for</u> you. |
| 6. Use *very* to make an adjective stronger. | Antarctica is **very** <u>cold</u>.<br>My backpack is **very** <u>heavy</u>. |

### REAL ENGLISH

Like *very, really* makes an adjective stronger. *Really* is less formal than *very*.

*It was **really** <u>cold</u> last night.*
*That movie is **really** <u>funny</u>.*

**4** Underline the adjectives in the paragraph. Draw an arrow from each adjective to the word it modifies.

## Arabian Camels

<u>Arabian</u> camels live in the <u>sandy</u> desert. They are perfect animals for life in this difficult climate. Long eyelashes protect them from blowing sand. They have large feet, so they don't sink into deep sand. They can go for a long time without food or water. They truly are desert animals.

▲ Rothschild giraffes eat from a table at Giraffe Manor in Nairobi, Kenya.

**5** Complete each sentence with an adjective from the box. Add *a* or *an* if necessary. Many answers are possible.

| bad | dangerous | good | intelligent | nice | scary | strong |
|---|---|---|---|---|---|---|
| beautiful | friendly | huge | interesting | noisy | small | tall |

1. Giraffes are very _____tall_____.

2. Cats are _____ pets.

3. A fennec fox is _____ animal.

4. Grizzly bears are _____ animals.

5. A dog is _____ pet.

6. Snakes aren't _____.

7. Ants are _____ insects.

8. An elephant is _____ animal.

9. Sharks are _____.

10. A lion is _____ animal.

**6** **WRITE & SPEAK.** Write four sentences with adjectives about animals. Use the adjectives from exercise **5** and add an article if necessary. Then share your sentences with a partner.

*My dog is a good pet.*          *I don't like cats. They aren't friendly.*

## 10.2 Adjectives with *How* and *What* Questions

| Questions | Answers |
|---|---|
| *How + Be . . . ?* | |
| **How are** you? | I'm fine. |
| **How's** the pizza? | It's good. |
| *How + Adjective + Be . . . ?* | |
| **How tall is** your brother? | Six feet. |
| **How bad was** the storm? | Very bad. |
| *What + Be . . . Like?* | |
| **What's** Boston **like**? | It's great. I love Boston. |
| **What are** your roommates **like**? | They're nice. I like them a lot. |

| | |
|---|---|
| 1. Questions with *How + be*, *How + adjective*, and *What . . . like* ask for descriptions. The answers are often adjectives. | A: **How's** that book?<br>B: It's interesting.<br><br>A: **How cold is** Antarctica?<br>B: It's freezing!<br><br>A: **What's** Rosa's brother **like**?<br>B: He's very funny. |
| 2. **Be careful!** Questions with *What + be . . . like* and *What do/does . . . like* are not the same. | A: **What's** she **like**?<br>B: She's nice. I like her.<br><br>A: **What does** she **like**?<br>B: Tennis and funny movies. |

**REAL ENGLISH**

*What kind of . . .* asks for specific information.

A: **What kind of** music do you like?
B: *Rock music.*

A: **What kind of** ice cream is that?
B: *Chocolate.*

**7** Read each conversation. Then choose the correct word(s) to complete A's question.

1. A: _____ the Sahara Desert like?          (a.) What's          b. What does
   B: It's hot and dry.

2. A: _____ is the Sahara Desert?          a. How big          b. How hot
   B: It's huge!

3. A: _____ the weather like at night there?          a. What's          b. How's
   B: It's cool.

4. A: _____ that article about meerkats?          a. How was          b. What was
   B: It was very interesting.

▲ A family of meerkats

5.  A: _____ meerkats?      a. How big are  b. What is
    B: They're small.

6.  A: What _____ like?      a. is a meerkat  b. are meerkats
    B: They're very friendly.

7.  A: _____ was the test?     a. How long   b. How difficult
    B: Very hard.

8.  A: _____ John like?      a. What does   b. What's
    B: He's funny and smart.

9.  A: How _____ are you?     a. tall     b. old
    B: I'm 21.

10. A: How _____ the weather today?  a. cold    b. 's
    B: It's really cold.

11. A: What _____ your city like?   a. does    b. 's
    B: It's really nice.

12. A: How _____ your family?    a. big is   b. is
    B: There are only four of us.

**8**  **SPEAK.** Work with a partner. Ask and answer questions 10–12 in exercise **7**. Use your own answers, not the answers in the book.

Student A: *How's the weather today?*   Student B: *It's sunny and windy.*

## 10.3 Using Nouns as Adjectives

| | Noun as Adjective | Noun |
|---|---|---|
| He is an | animal | doctor. |
| She is a | tour | guide. |

| | |
|---|---|
| 1. Nouns are often used to describe or modify other nouns. | I made a big salad in a **salad bowl**. (= a bowl for salad) |
| 2. Nouns used as adjectives are similar to adjectives. They are used in the singular, not in the plural. | ✓ She's a **horse** trainer. (= She trains horses.)<br>✗ She's a <u>horses</u> trainer. |
| 3. Some nouns used as adjectives end in *-ing*. | We went on a **camping** trip.<br>It's a huge **shopping** center. |
| 4. With *a* and *an*, nouns used as adjectives follow the same rules as nouns. | She's **a bus** driver.<br>He's **an art** teacher. |

**9**  Underline the noun used as an adjective in each sentence.

1. The <u>desert</u> sand is hot.

2. I need a new pencil case.

3. We live in a tall apartment building.

4. It's a very good English program.

5. That biology class is difficult.

6. The hotel has a swimming pool.

7. Where did I put my math book?

8. This is a great shoe store.

**10**  Complete each sentence. Use nouns as adjectives. Add *a* or *an*.

1. He's a trainer for animals. He's _____*an animal trainer*_____.

2. It's a park for wildlife. It's _____.

3. It's an elephant. It's a baby. It's _____.

4. I'm a driver. I drive a taxi. I'm _____.

5. He's a teacher. He teaches science. He's _____.

6. It's a report. It's about the weather. It's _____.

7. We're students. We go to college. We're _____.

8. It's an assignment. It's for homework. It's _____.

9. They're workers. They work for the government. They're _____.

10. It's a room. It's for exercise. It's _____.

# PRACTICE

**11**  Read the paragraph. Underline the adjectives and circle the nouns used as adjectives. Then draw an arrow to the nouns they modify.

## Saltwater Crocodiles

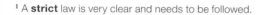

(Saltwater) crocodiles are large animals. They are dangerous, too. On the Adelaide River near Darwin, Australia, they are also tourist attractions. Tour boats take people along the river. The tour guides put small pieces of meat on metal poles. Then they hold the poles out over the side of the boat. The crocodiles jump up and take the meat. Fifty years ago, crocodile hunters killed almost all of the crocodiles. The Australian government passed a strict[1] law to protect these crocodiles, and they are now common in Australia.

[1] A **strict** law is very clear and needs to be followed.

▲ A saltwater crocodile jumps for meat, Adelaide River, Northern Territory, Australia.

**12**  **WRITE & SPEAK.**

**A**  Complete the e-mail with adjectives and nouns used as adjectives from the box. Add *a* or *an* if necessary. Then work with a partner and compare your answers.

| boat | close | ~~exciting~~ | huge | nervous | scary | small | tour |

Hi Jess,

Greetings from Australia! We're are having a wonderful time here. We went on (1) _____an exciting_____ tour today! It was (2) _____ trip on the Adelaide River near Darwin. We saw (3) _____ crocodiles! The crocodiles swam near the boat, and the boat was (4) _____ , so I was a little (5) _____ at first. The (6) _____ guide held some meat up over the crocodiles, and the crocodiles jumped up right next to the boat. One was really (7) _____ to us. It was really (8) _____! That's all for now! Take care.

Paula

**B** Work with a partner. Ask and answer the questions about the information in exercise **A** on page 317.

How was the tour?

What kind of trip did she take?

What were the crocodiles like?

How big was the boat?

Was she nervous?

How close were the crocodiles?

Student A: *How was the tour?*

Student B: *It was exciting.*

## 13 LISTEN & WRITE.

CD3-16

**A** Listen to the information about Brian Skerry. Then write the answers to the questions.

1. What is Brian Skerry's job? _____

2. How does he feel about his job? _____

CD3-16

**B** Look at the words. Then listen again and match each adjective or noun used as an adjective in Column A with the correct noun in Column B. Write the letter on the line.

**Column A**

1. shark ___c___

2. work _____

3. clear _____

4. huge _____

5. rare _____

6. amazing _____

7. underwater _____

8. exciting _____

**Column B**

a. assignment

b. job

c. fin

d. photographer

e. photos

f. kind of shark

g. water

h. shark

◄ An oceanic whitetip shark has white on the top of its fin.

318

▲ An oceanic whitetip shark with a diver in the background

**C** Look at the underlined part of each sentence on the right. Write a question about the underlined word or phrase.

1. _What kind of photographer is Skerry?_     Skerry is an <u>underwater</u> photographer.

2. _____     His job is <u>exciting and dangerous</u>.

3. _____     The shark was <u>very</u> dangerous.

4. _____     The shark was <u>huge</u>.

5. _____     His photographs were <u>amazing</u>.

6. _____     The shark was <u>very</u> close.

7. _____     Whitetip sharks are <u>very</u> rare.

8. _____     The water was <u>very clear and blue</u>.

**D** Work with a partner. Ask and answer your questions in exercise **C**.

## 14 APPLY.

**A** Work with a partner. Choose one of the jobs listed. Then write an interview for a person with that job. Use questions with *How + be, How + adjective, What . . . like,* and *What kind of . . .?*

tour guide on the Adelaide River     underwater photographer     wild animal photographer

Student A: *What do you do?*     Student B: *I'm a tour guide on the Adelaide River.*

**B** Role-play your interview from exercise **A** for your classmates.

## EXPLORE

CD3-17

**1** **READ** the news article about a gorilla encounter. Notice the words in **bold**.

Uganda

# Gorilla Encounter[1]

In Uganda, 300 gorillas move around **freely** in Bwindi Impenetrable[2] National Park. The park **carefully** controls the number of visitors. Tourists usually follow guides through the forests to see the gorillas, but one morning, a family of gorillas walked into the tourists' camp. A wildlife photographer, John King, wanted to photograph them. He sat down next to a path and waited **patiently**. The gorillas walked **slowly** past King. Then one gorilla **suddenly** stopped and sniffed[3] him. It touched his hair **lightly**. He sat **quietly** and looked down. The gorillas all sat behind King and looked at him.

King didn't **seem afraid**. In fact, he **looked happy**. Later, he said, "These gorillas were interacting with me just like I was one of their own, and it happened completely **naturally**. Who knows why it happened?" Maybe it was his black shirt and silver hair. The big male silverback gorillas have black and silver fur, so perhaps they thought he was a gorilla!

[1] **encounter:** an unplanned meeting
[2] **impenetrable:** hard or impossible to enter or pass through
[3] **sniff:** to smell something

**2 CHECK.** Read the statements. Circle **T** for *true* or **F** for *false*.

1. Gorillas are in cages in the Bwindi Impenetrable National Park.  T  (F)

2. A family of gorillas came out of the forest into a camp.  T  F

3. The gorillas were afraid of the photographer.  T  F

4. He enjoyed this experience.  T  F

5. He thinks the gorillas were interested in his camera.  T  F

**3 DISCOVER.** Complete the exercises to learn about the grammar in this lesson.

**A** Find these sentences in the news article from exercise **1**. Write the missing words.

1. The park _____ controls the number of visitors.

2. He sat down next to the path and waited _____.

3. The gorillas walked _____ past King.

4. Then one gorilla _____ stopped and sniffed him.

5. It touched his hair _____.

**B** Look at the words you wrote in exercise **A**. What do these words describe? Circle your answer. Then discuss your answer with your classmates and teacher.

These words describe _____ in the sentences.    a. nouns    b. verbs    c. adjectives

# LEARN

## 10.4 Adjectives vs. Adverbs of Manner

| | |
|---|---|
| 1. **Remember:** Adjectives describe or modify nouns or pronouns. Adverbs of manner describe or modify action verbs. | I'm **careful**.<br>Adjective<br>I drive **carefully**.<br>Adverb<br>I always **drive carefully**.<br>(*Carefully* describes *drive*.) |
| 2. Do not use an adverb to modify a noun. | ✓ She is happy.<br>✗ She is happily. |
| 3. Do not use an adverb before an object. | ✓ I **carefully** drove my new car.<br>✗ I drove carefully my new car. |
| 4. To form adverbs of manner, add *-ly* to most adjectives.* | beautiful      beautifully<br>Adjective     Adverb |
| 5. *Well* is the adverb form of the adjective *good*. | She's a **good** driver.   She drives **well**.<br>Adjective        Adverb |

*See page **A3** for more information on spelling rules for adverbs.

**4** Underline the adverb in each sentence. Draw an arrow to the verb it describes.

1. The park carefully controls the number of visitors.

2. The gorillas move freely in the park.

3. John King sat beside the path and waited patiently.

4. The gorillas walked slowly past King.

5. One of the gorillas touched his hair lightly.

6. King sat quietly.

7. I read the news article quickly.

8. We did the exercise carefully.

**5** Look at the underlined adjectives. Then complete each sentence with the correct adverb.

1. That bird is very loud. It sings very _____ loudly _____.

2. The gorillas were quick. They ran _____.

3. The scientists are very careful. They work _____.

4. The photographer has a good camera. It works _____.

5. Everyone was silent. We sat _____.

6. She was very <u>calm</u>. She walked very _____ and watched the bear.

7. Those tourists were very <u>rude</u>. They acted very _____.

8. Our guide was very <u>clear</u>. He explained everything very _____.

**6  SPEAK.** Work with a partner. Use two of the adverbs from exercise **5**. Say sentences about yourself.

Student A: *I wake up slowly.*

Student B: *I walk to the bus quickly.*

## 10.5 Linking Verbs + Adjectives

| Subject | Linking Verb | Adjective |
|---------|-------------|-----------|
| I | am | warm. |
| Jonathan | looks | tired. |

| | |
|---|---|
| 1. Linking verbs connect, or link, subjects and adjectives. The adjective modifies the subject.<br><br>*Be, become, feel, get, look, seem, smell, sound, stay,* and *taste* are linking verbs. | We **are** hungry.<br>The sky **became** cloudy.<br>He **feels** happy. |
| 2. Some verbs can be action verbs or linking verbs; for example: *get, feel, look, smell, sound,* and *taste.* | The flower **smells** good. (*smell* = linking verb)<br>Noun    Adjective<br>I **smelled** the flower. (*smell* = action verb) |

**REAL ENGLISH**

The adjectives *afraid, asleep, alone,* and *awake* are only used after the verb *be.* They are never used before nouns.

✓ The baby's **asleep**.
✗ The <u>asleep</u> baby.

*I was **awake** at 4:00 a.m.*
*We weren't **afraid**.*
*Joe is **alone** in his office right now.*

**7** Underline the linking verbs in these sentences. Then circle the adjectives and adverbs. Draw an arrow back to the words they modify.

1. The gorillas <u>were</u> (interested) in the photographer.

2. He didn't seem afraid. In fact, he acted bravely.

3. She looked happy as she looked at the photographs.

4. I love these flowers. They smell wonderful.

5. I had a headache last night. I felt fine this morning.

6. Most people feel nervous when they make presentations.

7. Please taste this soup. Does it taste OK?

8. I need to buy some warm clothes. The weather is getting cold.

9. You sound upset. Did something happen?

10. I'm very tired today. I didn't sleep well last night.

**8 SPEAK.** Work with a partner. Complete the sentences with linking verbs. Use your own ideas.

1. I'm _____ *cold* _____ .

2. I feel _____ .

3. _____ (*name of classmate*) seems _____ .

4. _____ (*name*) looks _____ .

5. _____ (*food*) tastes _____ .

## 10.6 Adverbs and Adjectives with the Same Form

| 1. Some adjectives and adverbs have the same form: *early, fast, hard, late* | He's a **fast** runner. (*fast* = adjective)<br>He runs **fast**. (*fast* = adverb) |
|---|---|
| 2. **Remember:** Some adjectives end in *–ly*: *lonely, ugly, friendly.* | She's a **friendly** person. |

**REAL ENGLISH**

In everyday conversation and informal writing, we use *slow* as an adjective and adverb. In formal writing, we use *slowly*.

**Informal:** He does everything slow.
**Formal:** He does everything slowly.

**9** Look at the <u>underlined</u> word in each sentence. Is it an adjective or an adverb? Check (✓) the correct column.

|  | **Adjective** | **Adverb** |
|---|:---:|:---:|
| 1. The homework was <u>hard</u>. | ✓ | ☐ |
| 2. Marcy seems very <u>friendly</u>. | ☐ | ☐ |
| 3. Drive <u>slowly</u>. The roads are icy tonight. | ☐ | ☐ |
| 4. They were driving <u>fast</u> when they saw the police car. | ☐ | ☐ |
| 5. Julie won the race <u>easily</u>. | ☐ | ☐ |
| 6. We worked <u>hard</u> and finished on time. | ☐ | ☐ |

|  | **Adjective** | **Adverb** |
|---|---|---|
| 7. When you're feeling <u>lonely</u>, please call me. | ☐ | ☐ |
| 8. The horse didn't look <u>fast</u>, but it won the race. | ☐ | ☐ |
| 9. Walk <u>fast</u>, OK? We're late! | ☐ | ☐ |
| 10. Sorry I'm late. The bus was really <u>slow</u>. | ☐ | ☐ |
| 11. I have an <u>early</u> class. | ☐ | ☐ |
| 12. The train was <u>late</u> this morning. | ☐ | ☐ |

## PRACTICE

**10** Circle the correct words to complete the story. Then work with a partner and compare answers.

# A Helpful Chimpanzee

Geza Teleki is a primatologist. He studies chimpanzees. One day he saw some chimps go into the woods (1) **quick / quickly**. He was (2) **curious / curiously**, so he followed them. He followed the chimpanzees for several hours in the woods. Then the chimpanzees stopped and began to eat fruit from the trees. Teleki (3) was **hungry / hungrily**. His stomach was making (4) **loud / loudly** noises. The fruit looked (5) **good / well**. He wanted to eat some, too. He tried to reach the fruit in the trees, but it wasn't (6) **easy / easily**. The fruit was very (7) **high / highly** in the trees. Teleki tried to use a stick to knock the fruit from the tree, but it didn't work very (8) **good / well**. He didn't get any fruit. One of the young chimps was watching him (9) **careful / carefully**. The chimp picked a piece of fruit from the tree and gave it to him. Teleki was very surprised. The young chimp understood Teleki's problem and helped him solve it. They are very (10) **intelligent / intelligently** animals.

◄ A young chimpanzee in the Tai Forest, Tai National Park, Ivory Coast, Africa

**11** Work with a partner. Complete each sentence with a verb and an adverb from the box.

| Verbs | | | | Adverbs | | | |
|-------|------|-------|------|----------|------|--------|--------|
| arrive | read | study | yell | carefully | fast | loudly | softly |
| drive | speak | swim | walk | early | hard | quickly | slowly |

1. When I'm late for work or class, I _____ walk fast. _____

2. When I'm talking to someone in a noisy place, I _____ .

3. When I see a shark at the beach, I _____ .

4. When I have a big test, I _____ .

5. When I'm reading a test question, I _____ .

6. When I'm talking to someone in the library, I _____ .

7. When I'm going to the airport for an international flight, I _____ .

8. When I'm in my car and it's raining or snowing, I _____ .

**12** **EDIT.** Read the safety tips. Find and correct six more errors with adverbs or adjectives and linking verbs.

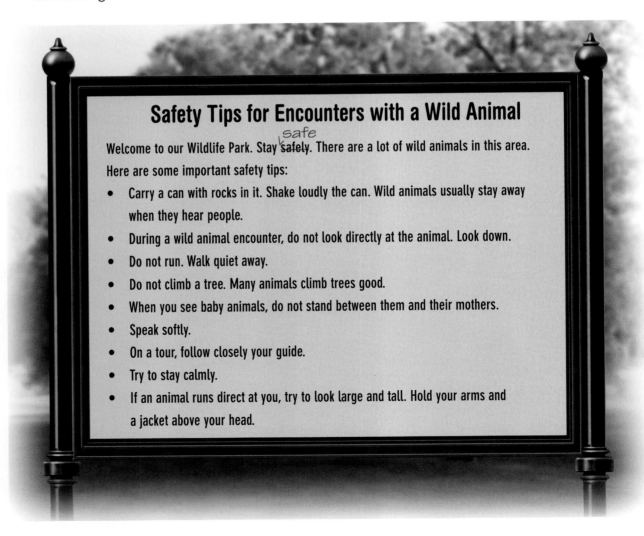

## Safety Tips for Encounters with a Wild Animal

Welcome to our Wildlife Park. Stay ~~safely~~ safe. There are a lot of wild animals in this area. Here are some important safety tips:

- Carry a can with rocks in it. Shake loudly the can. Wild animals usually stay away when they hear people.
- During a wild animal encounter, do not look directly at the animal. Look down.
- Do not run. Walk quiet away.
- Do not climb a tree. Many animals climb trees good.
- When you see baby animals, do not stand between them and their mothers.
- Speak softly.
- On a tour, follow closely your guide.
- Try to stay calmly.
- If an animal runs direct at you, try to look large and tall. Hold your arms and a jacket above your head.

▲ Jambo the gorilla at the Jersey Zoo (now the Durrell Wildlife Park), Jersey, Channel Islands

## 13 LISTEN & SPEAK.

CD3-18

**A** Listen to a true story about an unusual animal encounter. Then choose the correct answer.

1. Where did this story happen?   a. In a wildlife park.   b. In the wild.

2. Did the gorilla hurt the boy?   a. Yes.   b. No.

CD3-18

**B** Listen again. Read the statements. Circle **T** for *true* and **F** for *false*.

| | | |
|---|---|---|
| 1. The boy didn't want to see the gorillas. | T | **(F)** |
| 2. He wanted to get very close to the gorillas. | T | F |
| 3. He hit his head hard when he fell. | T | F |
| 4. A 400-pound gorilla named Jambo quickly ran over to the child. | T | F |
| 5. Jambo touched the boy gently on the back. | T | F |
| 6. Jambo sat next to the boy and yelled loudly. | T | F |
| 7. Jambo ran away quickly. | T | F |
| 8. The zookeepers moved slowly. | T | F |

**C** Work with a partner. Compare your answers from exercise **A**. Then correct the false statements to make them true.

1. The boy ~~didn't want~~ <sub>wanted</sub> to see the gorillas.

**D** Work in a group. Discuss these questions.

1. How did the boy feel before he fell?

2. How did he feel when he woke up?

3. How did Jambo act with the boy?

4. Did Jambo's actions surprise you?

▲ A common house mouse searches for a snack.

## 14 APPLY.

**A** Think about an encounter with an animal. Write notes in the chart about the experience. Use the questions in the chart to help you.

| | |
|---|---|
| What kind of animal was it? Describe it. Use adjectives. | a little mouse |
| How did you feel? Use adjectives. | |
| Describe the experience. Was it funny, exciting, scary? Use adjectives. | |
| What happened? Use adverbs. | |

**B** In your notebook, write about this animal encounter. Use adjectives and adverbs to make your story interesting.

I moved into a new apartment. When I turned on the oven for the first time, a little mouse ran out from behind the stove. I was really scared. I screamed loudly and . . .

**C** Work in a group. Share your stories with your classmates.

## EXPLORE

CD3-19

**1  READ** the article about the Iberian lynx. Notice the words in **bold**.

# Save the Iberian Lynx

Is the world **big enough** for both humans and wild animals? Cities are expanding[1] **very quickly** into the countryside. When human activity is **too close** to wild animal habitats,[2] it causes problems for the animals.

This is the case with the Iberian lynx in Spain, for example. People started to move into the lynx's native habitat in the mountains. They cut down trees and grew olives on the hillsides. This forced the lynx into smaller areas in the mountains. Now the Iberian lynx is almost extinct; only a few hundred are still alive. They live **too far** from each other to grow in number.

Is it **too late** to save the Iberian lynx? People in Spain have a plan. They are removing olive trees in the mountains and planting native trees. They want to grow a forest **big enough** for the lynx to live in. They hope the forests will grow **quickly enough** to save the Iberian lynx.

[1] **expand:** get bigger
[2] **habitat:** the area in which an animal or plant usually lives

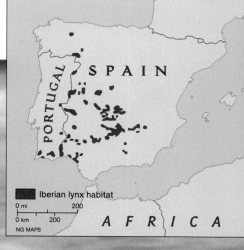

▲ An Iberian lynx in motion. Wildlfe experts in Spain track the Iberian lynx with the help of a special collar.

**2 CHECK.** Choose the correct answer for each question.

1. What happened to the lynx's habitat?    a. animals moved in    ⓑ people moved in

2. How many Iberian lynx are there?    a. a few hundred    b. a few thousand

3. Where do Iberian lynx live?    a. in the desert    b. in the mountains

4. What is the plan to help the lynx?    a. plant trees    b. make new farms

**3 DISCOVER.** Complete the exercises to learn about the grammar in this lesson.

**A** Find these sentences in the article from exercise **1** on page 329. Write the missing words.

1. Cities are expanding _____ into the countryside.

2. When people move _____ to wild animal habitats, it causes problems for the animals.

3. Is it _____ to save the Iberian lynx?

4. They want to grow a forest _____ for the lynx to live in.

**B** Look at your answers from exercise **A**. Choose the correct answer to the question below. Then discuss your answer with your classmates and teacher.

Which word has a negative meaning?    a. too    b. very    c. enough

◄ Close-up of an Iberian lynx

# LEARN

## 10.7  *Too/Very* + Adjective or Adverb

| ***Too* + Adjective or Adverb** |
|---|
| I don't want to go outside. It's **too cold**. (*too* + adjective) |
| I didn't understand them. They spoke **too quickly**. (*too* + adverb) |

| ***Very* + Adjective or Adverb** |
|---|
| I don't want to go outside. It's **very cold** (*very* + adjective) |
| They finished the assignment early. The worked **very quickly**. (*very* + adverb) |

| | |
|---|---|
| 1. *Too* has a negative meaning. It means "more than necessary." Use *too* + adjective or adverb when there is a problem or a negative result. | The hotel is **too noisy**. (Negative result: We can't sleep at night.) He was driving **too fast**. (Negative result: He got a ticket.) |
| 2. **Remember:** Use *very* to make an adjective or adverb stronger. *Very* does not mean the same thing as *too*. It does not have a negative meaning. | ✓ The people were **very friendly**. ✗ The people were <u>too</u> friendly. ✓ We studied **very hard**. ✗ We studied <u>too</u> hard. |

**4**  Circle the correct word to complete each sentence.

1. People are moving (too) / **very** close to the lynx's habitat. It's causing problems for the animals.

2. The Iberian lynx is a **too** / **very** beautiful animal.

3. The lynx's habitat is **too** / **very** small. The animals don't have enough space.

4. The article about the Iberian lynx was **too** / **very** interesting.

5. The information was **too** / **very** helpful.

6. Everyone in our class is **too** / **very** nice. It's a great class.

7. I didn't finish the assignment last night. It was **too** / **very** long.

8. Amy is **too** / **very** smart. She always gets good grades.

**5**  **SPEAK.** Work with a partner. Complete each sentence with *too* or *very* and an adjective.

The weather today is . . .      *The weather today is very nice.*

This city is . . .

My friends are . . .

## 10.8 Adjective or Adverb + *Enough*

| | Adjective/ Adverb | Enough | |
|---|---|---|---|
| It's | cold | enough | for gloves and a hat today. |
| He did | well | | to pass the course. |

| | |
|---|---|
| 1. After an adjective or an adverb, *enough* means "to a necessary or satisfactory extent." | We voted this year. We are **old enough**. <br> I missed the bus. I did**n't** run **fast enough**. |
| 2. Put *enough* after adjectives and adverbs. | ✓ This room is <u>big</u> **enough** for our meeting. <br> ✗ This room is <u>enough big</u> for our meeting. |
| 3. *Enough* is often followed by an infinitive. | He's tall **enough** <u>to touch</u> the ceiling. <br> I'm not strong **enough** <u>to lift</u> that heavy box. |

**6** Complete each sentence with the word(s) in parentheses and *enough*.

1. Our classroom is _____*not big enough*_____ (not big) for all the students.

2. He didn't speak _____ (loudly) during his presentation. It was difficult to hear him.

3. She didn't explain the information _____ (clearly). We didn't understand.

4. They didn't do _____ (well) to pass the test.

5. He doesn't do his homework _____ (carefully). He makes a lot of mistakes.

6. It's _____ (not warm). Please turn up the heat.

7. I can't hear the music. It's _____ (not loud). Please turn it up.

8. It feels _____ (cold) to snow!

9. Is your sister _____ (old) to live alone?

10. She's _____ (not old) to drive.

**7** Work with a partner. Complete each sentence with *enough* or *not enough* and an adjective.

I am . . .
This classroom is . . .
This building is . . .

*I'm not tall enough to play basketball.*

# PRACTICE

**8** Match each sentence in Column A with a sentence in Column B. Write the letter on the line.

**Column A**

1. He's not studying hard enough. _g_
2. She's running very fast. _____
3. It's raining too hard. _____
4. He's reading very carefully. _____
5. It's not warm enough. _____
6. He's working too hard. _____
7. It's too hot in here. _____
8. You're driving too slowly. _____

**Column B**

a. Please turn up the heat.
b. He needs to relax and take a vacation.
c. Come on. Hurry up!
d. Let's stay home.
e. Let's open the window.
f. She's winning the race.
g. His grades are terrible.
h. He wants to understand the information.

**9** Complete the conversation with *too, very,* or *enough* and the adjectives in parentheses. Then listen and check your answers.

**Ethan:** Look. This is (1) _____very interesting_____ (interesting). There's a new exhibit at the zoo.

**Emma:** I don't like to go to zoos. I feel (2) _____ (sad) when I see the animals in those little cages.

**Ethan:** Me, too. The areas for the animals aren't (3) _____ (big), especially for the large animals such as lions and tigers.

**Emma:** Yeah, I agree with you, but zoos want to show the animals. When the exhibits are (4) _____ (large), sometimes people don't see any animals. The animals usually don't stay (5) _____ (close) to the windows of the exhibit, so it's difficult to see them.

**Ethan:** You're right. That's (6) _____ (true). The animals are often (7) _____ (far) from the windows for anyone to see them.

**Emma:** My friends and I want to go on a safari someday. In Africa, animal parks are (8) _____ (big) for the animals. The animal parks help protect the animals.

**Ethan:** I know, but safaris are (9) _____ (expensive).

**Emma:** That's true. They're (10) _____ (expensive) for me right now. Maybe someday!

**10 EDIT.** Read the news article. Find and correct five more errors with *too, very,* or *enough*.

## ZOO NEWS

# The City Zoo

The City Zoo is planning to expand. Right now the zoo isn't ~~enough~~ large ᵥenough for all of the animals. Many animal exhibits are too small. There isn't enough land to expand on this site. The zoo tried very hard to buy more land in the city, but the land was enough expensive. Last week, the zoo bought the old Cherry Hill Farm. "We are too happy about this," says the zoo director. "The Cherry Hill Farm is too large. The property is big enough for us to build a new zoo." Plans for the new exhibits are too exciting. They include natural habitats. These are enough big for the animals.

▲ A child watches a polar bear at a zoo exhibit.

**11 LISTEN & SPEAK.**

CD3-21-23

**A** Listen to the conversations. Match each topic with the correct conversation.

Conversation 1 _____        a. A bear

Conversation 2 _____        b. A new exhibit for night animals

Conversation 3 _____        c. The weather

CD3-21-23

**B** Listen again. The speakers in the conversations do not always agree with each other. After you listen, work with a partner and make sentences for each conversation. Use *very, too, enough,* and the words in the boxes.

**Conversation 1**

| cold | hard | warm | windy |
|------|------|------|-------|

**Mindy:**     We're having a picnic at the zoo. Do you want to come with us?

**Eduardo:**   Isn't it _____ and cold? The wind is blowing _____ to eat outside.

**Mindy:**     No, it isn't. It's _____ to eat outside.

**334** ADJECTIVES AND ADVERBS

**Conversation 2**

| crowded | dark | hot | interesting | slowly |
|---------|------|-----|-------------|--------|

**Sam:** It's a beautiful exhibit. It's _____.

**Liz:** I didn't like it. It was _____.

**Sam:** Of course it was. It has to be _____ for the animals. They're nocturnal. When it's light, they go to sleep.

**Liz:** I know, but it was also _____, and it was _____. There were too many people in there, and everyone was walking _____. I didn't like it at all.

**Conversation 3**

| big | huge | small |
|-----|------|-------|

**Marta:** Isn't that bear cute?

**David:** Well, grizzly bears are _____ to be cute.

**Marta:** This exhibit isn't really _____ for a huge bear, is it?

**David:** You're right. It's _____.

▲ The slender loris is a nocturnal animal. It lives in forests in Sri Lanka and southern India.

**C** With your partner, practice saying the conversations in exercise **B**.

**12 APPLY.**

**A** Work in a small group. Share your answers to these questions.

1. What animals are interesting to you? Why?

2. What do you think about zoos? Are the animal exhibits big enough? Do the animals live freely enough? Do zoos help or hurt animals? How?

3. Why do you like or dislike zoos?

**B** Write four or five sentences to explain your answer to question 3 in exercise **A**.

_____

_____

_____

_____

_____

_____

_____

Charts
10.1,
10.4–10.8

**1** Circle the correct words to complete the paragraph.

## A Dangerous Situation

Mattias Klum is a famous photographer. He takes (1)(**beautiful**)/ **beautifully** photographs of animals. Once when he was in Borneo, he saw a king cobra. The cobra was lying (2) **quiet** / **quietly** near a small river. King cobras are very (3) **dangerous** / **dangerously** snakes. Klum wanted to take a photograph of the cobra, but he wasn't (4) **quick** / **quickly** enough to get a (5) **good** / **well** photograph.

Klum (6) **quick** / **quickly** ran along the river and tried to find a (7) **good** / **well** place to take a photograph. He jumped into the river, and then he saw the cobra. It was in the water moving (8) **direct** / **directly** in front of him. It was very (9) **close** / **closely** to Klum. The cobra raised its head out of the water and tried to bite him. Klum used his camera to protect his legs. It was a very (10) **dangerous** / **dangerously** situation for Klum. His (11) **quick** / **quickly** action worked (12) **good** / **well**. The snake didn't bite him, and he took some (13) **amazing** / **amazingly** photographs of the cobra.

▲ A king cobra

Charts
10.1,
10.3–10.7

**2** **EDIT.** Read the e-mail. Find and correct six more errors with adjectives and adverbs.

| From: | Davis, Pam |
| To: | Martin, Judy |
| Subject: | Dugong |

Hi Judy,

I had an amaze~~~v-ing~~~ day today. I saw a dugong. It was huge! The water was clearly and quiet. It wasn't very deeply. I saw perfectly the dugong. It was moving slowly along the bottom and it was eating the seagrass. Every few minutes it swam up and quick put its nose out of the water. It seemed very gently. No one was afraid of it. There aren't many dugongs anymore. They're endangered. I was luckily to see one!

Pam

▲ A dugong

**3  LISTEN, WRITE & SPEAK.**

**CD3-24**

**A**  Dugongs are endangered animals. Why? Listen and check (✓) the reasons you hear.

1. __✓__ the supply of seagrass       5. _____ nets on large fishing boats

2. _____ the water temperature        6. _____ the number of baby dugongs

3. _____ hunters                      7. _____ disease

4. _____ large tour boats

**CD3-24**

**B**  Complete each sentence with information from the listening. Add a verb and use the word in parentheses with *too, very,* or *enough.* Then listen again and check your answers.

1. The supply of seagrass __is not large enough__ (large).

2. Seagrass _____ (slowly).

3. Hunters _____ them _____ (easily) because
   dugongs _____ (slowly).

4. Fishing boats _____ dugongs _____ (frequently)
   because dugongs _____ (fast).

5. The number of dugongs _____ (quickly).

**4  READ & SPEAK.**

**A**  Work with a partner. Partner A, read the information about giant pandas on this page. Partner B, read the information about Mexican gray wolves on page **A7**. Then close your books. Tell your partner about the animal. Use adjectives, adverbs, *too, very,* and *enough.*

**Partner A**

## Giant Pandas

Giant pandas are black and white bears. They are very shy. In Chinese, their name means "Large Bear-Cat." In the past, they lived in China, Myanmar, and North Vietnam. Now they only live in a small area of China. Giant pandas are very rare. They are endangered because people moved into their habitats, so their habitats are not big enough for them.

# Connect the Grammar to Writing

## 1 READ & NOTICE THE GRAMMAR.

**A** Read the paragraph. How does the writer feel about snakes? What encounters did she have with snakes? Discuss with a partner.

### My Feelings about Snakes

I am afraid of snakes. In my hometown, there are a lot of huge snakes. They are very dangerous. One time, I almost stepped on a snake when I was walking in my yard. I was walking slowly, so I didn't step directly on it, but it was very scary. Another time, I went on a camping trip, and a big snake crawled into our tent. Fortunately, I saw it before it got dark. Of course, I screamed loudly, and my father ran quickly to help. That was my last camping trip.

### GRAMMAR FOCUS

In the paragraph in exercise **A**, the writer uses adjectives and nouns used as adjectives to modify nouns and pronouns. The writer also uses adverbs to modify verbs.

I am **afraid** of snakes.
Adjective

I was walking **slowly**, so I didn't step **directly** on it.
Adverb · · · · · · · Adverb

**B** Read the paragraph in exercise **A** again. Underline the adjectives and the nouns used as adjectives. Circle the adverbs of manner. Then work with a partner and compare answers.

**C** Write notes in the chart to answer the questions about the information in the paragraph in exercise **A**.

| What is the topic of the paragraph? | The writer's feelings about snakes. |
|---|---|
| How does the writer feel about them? | |
| Why? What encounters or experiences did the writer have with snakes? | |

**2 BEFORE YOU WRITE.** Complete the chart with information about an animal you feel strongly about. Use the questions to write notes about your ideas. Use the chart from exercise **1C** as a model.

| | |
|---|---|
| What is the topic of your paragraph? | My feelings about _____ |
| How do you feel about it / them? | |
| Why do you feel this way? Write about an encounter or experience. | |

**3 WRITE** a paragraph. Use the information in your chart in exercise **2A** and the paragraph in exercise **1A** to help you.

---

**WRITING FOCUS**  Using Adverbs and Adjectives to Add Interest

Writers use adjectives and adverbs to add interest to their writing.

GOOD: *In my hometown, there are a lot of snakes.*

BETTER: *In my hometown, there are a lot of **huge** snakes. They are very **dangerous**.*

GOOD: *I screamed, and my father ran to help.*

BETTER: *I screamed **loudly**, and my father ran **quickly** to help.*

---

**4 SELF ASSESS.** Read your paragraph. Underline the adjectives. Circle the adverbs of manner. Then use the checklist to assess your work.

- ☐ I used adjectives and nouns used as adjectives to describe nouns and pronouns. [10.1, 10.3]
- ☐ I used adverbs to describe action verbs. [10.4, 10.6]
- ☐ I used adjectives (not adverbs) after linking verbs. [10.5]
- ☐ I used adjectives and adverbs to add interest to my writing. [WRITING FOCUS]

# Modals: Part 1

▲ BASE jumper Miles Daisher during a jump from the New River Gorge Bridge on Bridge Day, October 22, 2009, Fayetteville, West Virginia, USA

### EXPLORE

CD3-25

**1 READ** the article about Yves Rossy. Notice the words in **bold**.

## *Look! I can fly!*

The passengers on a plane in Switzerland were surprised when they looked out the windows. A man was flying next to the plane!

The passengers were not imagining[1] things. Yves Rossy, or "Jetman," **can fly**. Rossy wears a large V-shaped wing with very small jet engines on it. A helicopter takes Rossy up. Then he falls back first out of the helicopter. When he starts the jet engines in his wing, he **can go** between 200 and 300 miles per hour (between 320 and 480 kilometers per hour)!

Rossy's wing is about six feet (two meters) wide. It weighs 120 pounds (55 kilograms). With the wing, he **can fly** for eight minutes. He **can't fly** any longer than that because there isn't enough fuel[2] for the engines. When he wants to land, he opens his parachute.[3] On one flight, he had some trouble: He **couldn't open** his parachute. Finally, at 1500 feet (457 meters) above the ground, he **was able to open** it and landed safely.

[1] **imagine:** to picture something in your mind
[2] **fuel:** a substance such as oil or gasoline that is burned to provide energy
[3] **parachute:** something that helps people float slowly to the ground from high in the air

DISCUSS THIS ARTICLE

**D.J. Butler**
Interesting! **Where can I learn** to fly?
July 17, 10:21 AM

**Arlene Sargeant**
**Can anyone buy** a wing like this?
July 17, 10:40 AM

**Sarah8201**
**Why couldn't he open** his parachute? That's really scary!
July 17, 10:42 AM

◀ "Jetman" Yves Rossy over Lake Lucerne, Switzerland

**2** **CHECK.** Read the statements. Circle **T** for *true* or **F** for *false*.

1. Yves Rossy uses a big wing with small jet engines to fly.      **T**      **F**

2. Rossy flies very fast with his jet wing.      **T**      **F**

3. Rossy flies for 200 minutes.      **T**      **F**

4. The wing uses all the fuel in 80 minutes.      **T**      **F**

5. Rossy lands with a parachute.      **T**      **F**

**3** **DISCOVER.** Complete the exercises to learn about the grammar in this lesson.

**A** Find these sentences in the article from exercise **1**. Write the missing words.

1. Yves Rossy, or "Jetman," _____.

2. He _____ any longer than that because there isn't enough fuel for the engines.

3. On one flight, he had some trouble: He _____ his parachute.

**B** Look at the sentences from exercise **A**. Then choose the correct word to complete each statement. Discuss your answers with your classmates and teacher.

1. We use *can* and *can't* to show _____.      a. ability      b. necessity

2. *Could* and *couldn't* show possibility in the _____.      a. present      b. past

3. The verb after *can* or *could* _____ a final *-s*.      a. has      b. doesn't have

# LEARN

## 11.1 Can/Could for Ability and Possibility: Statements

| Affirmative | | |
|---|---|---|
| Subject | Can/ Could | Base Form of Verb |
| I<br>You<br>He<br>She<br>It<br>We<br>You<br>They | **can**<br><br>**could** | <br><br>fly. |

| Negative | | |
|---|---|---|
| Subject | Can't/ Couldn't | Base Form of Verb |
| I<br>You<br>He<br>She<br>It<br>We<br>You<br>They | **can't**<br>**cannot**<br><br>**couldn't**<br>**could not** | <br><br>fly |

| | |
|---|---|
| 1. Use *can* to talk about present and future ability or possibility. Use *could* to talk about ability or possibility in the past. | **I can speak** Spanish. (present)<br>We **can** talk later. (future)<br>My grandfather **could run** ten miles when he was young. (past) |
| 2. *Can* and *could* are modals. A modal verb changes the meaning of the main verb. *Can* and *could* add the meaning of ability or possibility to the main verb. | He **can** <u>speak</u> German.<br>I **can't** <u>speak</u> German.<br>I **couldn't** <u>speak</u> German before this class. |
| 3. Use the base form of the verb after *can* and *could*.<br><br>*Can* and *could* keep the same form for all subjects. | ✓ I **can ride** a bicycle.<br>✓ She **could ride** a bicycle.<br>✗ She can <u>rides</u> a bicycle.<br>✗ She could <u>to ride</u> a bicycle. |
| 4. *Can't* and *couldn't* are used in speaking and informal writing. *Cannot* and *could not* are used in formal writing. | I **can't** ice skate.<br>She **couldn't** drive.<br>Children under 15 **cannot** drive.<br>We **could not** understand him. |

**4** Complete each sentence with *can, can't, could,* or *couldn't* and the verb in parentheses.

1. Rossy _____*can fly*_____ (fly) with special jet wings.

2. The jet wing uses a lot of fuel, so Rossy _____ (stay) in the air for more than eight minutes.

3. You _____ (learn) more about Rossy online.

4. One time, Rossy _____ (open) his parachute. That was scary!

5. A long time ago people _____ (travel) by plane.

6. The plane _____ (leave) because the weather was bad.

7. Some planes _____ (go) very long distances now.

8. The pilot _____ (see) very far because it was very cloudy.

**5 PRONUNCIATION.** Read the chart and listen to the examples. Then complete the exercises.

CD3-26

| PRONUNCIATION | *Can/Can't* |
| --- | --- |

Pay attention to the vowel sounds in *can* and *can't*.

In affirmative statements with *can* + verb, *can* is usually pronounced /kən/, and the main stress of the sentence is on the ability that follows.

I can speak Spanish. = I /kən/ speak Spanish.    He can swim = He /kən/ swim.

Main Stress                                                                                          Main Stress

In negative statements, *can't* is usually pronounced /kænt/, and it is stressed to emphasize the lack of an ability.

I can't speak Arabic. = I /kænt/ speak Arabic.    He can't ski. = He /kænt/ ski.

Main Stress                                                                                          Main Stress

See page **A4** for a guide to pronunciation symbols.

CD3-27

**A** Listen to each sentence. Do you hear *can* or *can't*? Check (✓) the correct column.

|  | **Can** | **Can't** |  |  | **Can** | **Can't** |
| --- | --- | --- | --- | --- | --- | --- |
| 1. | ☐ | ✓ | | 6. | ☐ | ☐ |
| 2. | ☐ | ☐ | | 7. | ☐ | ☐ |
| 3. | ☐ | ☐ | | 8. | ☐ | ☐ |
| 4. | ☐ | ☐ | | 9. | ☐ | ☐ |
| 5. | ☐ | ☐ | | 10. | ☐ | ☐ |

**B** Work with a partner. Complete the sentences.

1.  I can _____.

2.  I can't _____.

Student A: *I can speak three languages.*

Student B: *I can't ice skate.*

▶ An ice skater on frozen Canyon
Ferry Lake, Montana, USA

## 11.2 *Can/Could* for Ability and Possibility: Questions

### Yes/No Questions

| Can/Could | Subject | Base Form of Verb |
|---|---|---|
| Can Could | you he she they | swim? |

### Short Answers

| | Affirmative | | | Negative | |
|---|---|---|---|---|---|
| Yes, | I he she they | can. could. | No, | I he she they | can't. couldn't. |

### Wh- Questions

| Wh- Word | Can/Could | Subject | Base Form of Verb |
|---|---|---|---|
| Who | | | ask? |
| What | | I | make? |
| When | | you | talk? |
| Where | can | he | meet? |
| How | could | she | find it? |
| How far | | we | run? |
| How fast | | you | fly? |
| How many languages | | they | speak? |

### Answers

| |
|---|
| The librarian. |
| Goulash and pasta. |
| Tomorrow afternoon at three. |
| At the coffee shop. |
| Ask at the front desk. |
| Three miles. |
| Two hundred miles per hour. |
| Four. |

| | |
|---|---|
| 1. *Can* and *could* come before the subject in *Yes/No* questions and most information questions. | **Can** <u>you</u> speak Korean? Where **can** <u>we</u> get some coffee? How **could** <u>he</u> do that? |
| 2. Use *How far* to ask questions about distance. | A: **How far** can you swim? B: About a mile. |
| 3. Use *How fast* to ask questions about speed. | A: **How fast** can it go? B: Eighty miles per hour. |
| 4. **Remember:** *Wh-* questions with *Who* or *What* can be about a subject or an object. | Questions about a Subject: **Who can speak** Russian? (**Igor** can.) **What can happen?** (**Anything** can happen.) Questions about an Object: **Who can** we **ask?** (We can ask **Mary**.) **What can** she **play?** (She can play **tennis**.) |

**6** Change each statement into a *Yes/No* question. Then complete the short answer for each question.

1. I can ice skate.

   A: <u>Can you ice skate?</u>

   B: Yes, <u>I can</u>.

2. I can ski.

   A: _____

   B: No, _____.

3. We could understand the article.

   A: _____

   B: No, _____.

4. She can play the piano.

A: _____

B: Yes, _____ .

5. He could sing very well.

A: _____

B: No, _____ .

6. I can drive a car.

A: _____

B: Yes, _____ .

7. My brother can cook.

A: _____

B: Yes, _____ .

8. They could swim.

A: _____

B: No, _____ .

**7** Read each statement. Write a *Wh-* question about the underlined information.

1. A marathon runner can run <u>26.2 miles</u>. _____How far can a marathon runner run?_____

2. That plane can fly <u>400 miles per hour</u>. _____

3. Astronauts can <u>travel into space</u>. _____

4. <u>The teacher</u> can help me. _____

5. I can speak <u>three</u> languages. _____

6. We can play <u>tennis</u>. _____

7. You can see the Northern Lights <u>in Iceland</u>. _____

8. They can meet <u>at 2:00</u>. _____

9. They can get to Paris <u>by boat or plane</u>. _____

10. He could swim <u>a mile</u> when he was younger. _____

**8** **SPEAK.** Ask your classmates questions about the activities in the box. Use *Can you . . . ?* Write the names of students who say *Yes* next to each activity. Do not use a student's name more than once.

Student A: *Can you ride a horse?*        Student B: *Yes, I can.*

| | |
|---|---|
| ice skate _____ | ski _____ |
| speak Arabic _____ | play the piano _____ |
| ride a horse _____ | drive a car _____ |
| cook _____ | swim _____ |

## PRACTICE

**9** Complete the paragraph with *can, can't, could, couldn't* and the verb in parentheses.

### Frequently Asked Questions: The Amphicar

**What is an Amphicar?**

An Amphicar is a very unusual car. (1) It ___can travel___ (travel) on the road or in the water.

**What is the history of the Amphicar?**

A man named Hans Trippel made the first Amphicar in Berlin, Germany in 1962.
It (2) _____ (go) 70 miles per hour (112 kilometers per hour) on the road, but in the water
it (3) _____ only _____ (go) seven mph (11 kph). That didn't worry four Englishmen
who in 1965 took two Amphicars across the English Channel! Everyone was surprised that the
cars (4) _____ (do) this. In the 1960s, people (5) _____ (buy) an Amphicar for about $3000.
Now, you (6) _____ (not buy) a used Amphicar for less than $30,000. Trippel's company sold
almost 4000 cars, but it closed in 1968. The car (7) _____ (not pass) the new air pollution[1] tests.

**Can you find Amphicars anywhere now?**

Yes, you can. In many places, Amphicar owners have "swim-ins." They usually meet at a lake
where they (8) _____ (drive) into the water together.

---

[1] **pollution:** the process of making water, air, or land dirty and dangerous

▼ A 1964 Amphicar on the River Thames near Staines, England in 1998

**10** **EDIT.** Read the conversation about flying cars. Find and correct five more errors with *can, can't, could,* or *couldn't.*

| | |
|---|---|
| **Dad:** | Here's an interesting ad. It says, "Yes, cars can ~~flies~~ fly!" |
| **Daughter:** | That's crazy. Cars can't to fly! |
| **Dad:** | Well, I saw a flying car when I was a child. |
| **Daughter:** | Really? Could it flies? |
| **Dad:** | Yes, but it couldn't goes very fast. |
| **Daughter:** | Where you can drive it? You can't drive a car with wings on the highway. |
| **Dad:** | Sure you can. The wings fold up, and you can to drive it on the highway. |

**11** Look at each answer. Write a question about the underlined phrase.

## Frequently Asked Questions: Flying Cars

1. **Q:** _Can cars really fly?_

   **A:** <u>Yes</u>, cars really can fly!

2. **Q:** _____

   **A:** <u>Yes</u>, companies could build flying cars more than fifty years ago.

3. **Q:** _____

   **A:** The flying cars can travel <u>on roads and in the air</u>.

4. **Q:** _____

   **A:** <u>No</u>, they can't take off from the highway. You need a flat place with no other cars, such as an airport.

5. **Q:** _____

   **A:** The cars can go <u>100 miles per hour</u>.

6. **Q:** _____

   **A:** The cars can carry <u>two people</u>. They're very small.

7. **Q:** _____

   **A:** You can fit <u>two suitcases</u>. Not all flying cars have this much room, but a couple of them do.

8. **Q:** _____

   **A:** You can learn more about them <u>online</u>.

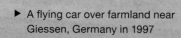

▶ A flying car over farmland near Giessen, Germany in 1997

## 12 LISTEN, WRITE & SPEAK.

**A** Look at the photos and the information about three flying cars. Then listen to information about these flying cars. Write the name of each flying car.

| SkyRunner | Transition® | PAL-V |
|---|---|---|

1. Name: _____

   Air speed: _____ mph (185 kph)

   Distance: 490 miles (787 km)

   Passengers: 2

   Other: the wings fold

2. Name: _____

   Air speed: _____ mph (177 kph)

   Distance: _____ miles (563 km)

   Passengers: _____

   Other: flies like a tiny helicopter;

   drives like a _____

3. Name: _____

   Air speed: 55 mph (88 kph)

   Distance: 200 miles (321 km)

   Passengers: _____

   Other: a parasail

**B** Listen again. Complete the chart in exercise **A** with information about each flying car.

**C** Write sentences about each flying car. Use information from the chart in exercise **A**. Use *can* or *can't*.

1. The Transition can fly 115 miles per hour.
2. _____
3. _____
4. _____
5. _____
6. _____

**D** Work with a partner. Ask and answer questions about the flying cars.

Student A: *Can the SkyRunner fly 115 miles per hour?*

Student B: *No, it can't.*

## 13 APPLY.

**A** Work in a group with four or five students. You are at a flying car show. Choose one of the roles below.

Student A wants to buy a flying car.

Student B wants to buy a flying car.

Student C is a salesperson for the Transition®.

Student D is a salesperson for the SkyRunner.

Student E is a salesperson for the PAL-V.

**B** Role-play a conversation at the flying car show. Students A and B ask Students C, D, and E questions about their flying cars. Students C, D, and E answer the questions about their cars. Which car do you want to buy?

Student A: *How far can the SkyRunner fly?*

Student D: *It can fly 200 miles.*

Student C: *The Transition® can fly 490 miles.*

Student B: *How fast can the PAL-V fly?*

Student E: *It can fly 110 miles per hour.*

**C** Which car do Students A and B want to buy? Why? Write three sentences about each student.

Abdul likes the Transition® because he can drive it on the road and keep it at his house. It can fly . . .

Beatrice likes the SkyRunner because . . .

## EXPLORE

CD3-29

**1 READ** the article about Winter the dolphin. Notice the words in **bold**.

# Winter the Dolphin

One day, a fisherman in Florida saw a dolphin in the water. When he got close to it, he **was able to see** the dolphin's problem. Lines from a crab trap[1] were wrapped around the dolphin's tail and mouth. The dolphin **wasn't able to get** free from the lines. The fisherman called for help, and a rescue team took the dolphin to an aquarium. However, the people at the aquarium **weren't able to save** its tail.

This was a big problem because dolphins use their tails to move through the water. With no tail, the dolphin **wasn't able to swim** very well. The little dolphin named Winter was in danger. The people at the aquarium **didn't know how to keep** Winter strong. Then, Kevin Carroll and Dan Strzempka heard about Winter's problem. They **knew how to help**. Their company made artificial[2] legs and arms for people. They **were able to** make a new tail for Winter.

It wasn't easy, but they did it! With the artificial tail, Winter **was able to move** through the water like a dolphin again.

[1] **trap:** a device to catch something, for example, an animal
[2] **artificial:** made by a person, not by nature

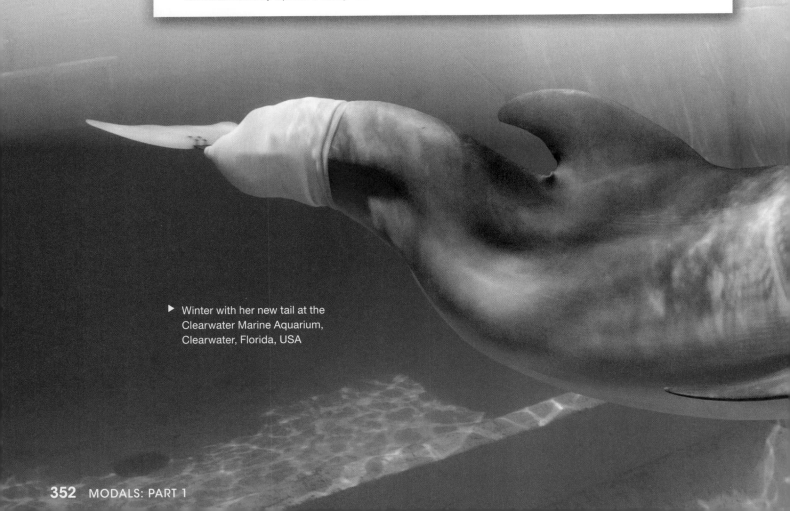

▶ Winter with her new tail at the
Clearwater Marine Aquarium,
Clearwater, Florida, USA

**2  CHECK.** What is the correct order of these events in the article from exercise **1**? Write numbers 1–5 next to each sentence.

_____ A rescue team took the dolphin to an aquarium.

_____ The dolphin got an artificial tail.

_____ A fisherman saw the dolphin.

_____ The dolphin lost its tail.

_____ Kevin Carroll and Dan Strzempka helped the dolphin.

**3  DISCOVER.** Complete the exercises to learn about the grammar in this lesson.

**A**  Find these sentences in the article from exercise **1**. Write the missing words.

1.  The dolphin _____ get free from the lines.

2.  However, the people at the aquarium _____ save its tail.

3.  With the artificial tail, Winter _____ move through the water like a dolphin again.

**B**  Look at the sentences from exercise **A**. What do these words tell us? Choose your answer. Then discuss your answer with your classmates and teacher.

1.  We use *wasn't able to* when _____.

    a.  something wasn't necessary          b.  something wasn't possible

2.  The verb after *be able to* _____ the base form.

    a.  is                                  b.  isn't

# LEARN

## 11.3 Be Able To

### Affirmative Statements

| Subject | Be Able To | Base Form of Verb | |
|---|---|---|---|
| I | am able to<br>was able to | | |
| He<br>She | is able to<br>was able to | fix | their car. |
| You<br>We<br>They | are able to<br>were able to | | |

### Negative Statements

| Subject | Be Not Able To | Base Form of Verb | |
|---|---|---|---|
| I | 'm not able to<br>wasn't able to | | |
| He<br>She | isn't able to<br>wasn't able to | fix | their car. |
| You<br>We<br>They | aren't able to<br>weren't able to | | |

### Yes/No Questions

Is he **able to fix** their car?
Was he **able to fix** their car?

Are they **able to help**?
Were they **able to help**?

### Short Answers

| Affirmative | | Negative | |
|---|---|---|---|
| Yes, he | is.<br>was. | No, he | isn't.<br>wasn't. |
| Yes, they | are.<br>was. | No, they | aren't.<br>weren't. |

| | |
|---|---|
| 1. To talk about ability or possibility, use *be able to*. It has the same meaning as *can*. | I'm **able to swim**. = I can swim.<br>Are you **able to swim**? = Can you swim? |
| 2. To talk about abilities and inabilities in the past, use *was able to* or *were able to*. | He **was able to meet** with us yesterday.<br>We **weren't able to finish** the assignment. |
| 3. To form the negative of *be able to*, put *not* after *be*. | ✓ I'm **not able to talk** right now.<br>✗ I <u>don't</u> able to talk right now.<br><br>✓ I **wasn't able to answer** all the questions.<br>✗ I <u>didn't</u> able to answer all the questions. |

**4** Change each sentence from the present to the past.

1. The dolphin isn't able to swim.     The dolphin _____wasn't able to swim_____.

2. The fisherman is able to help.     The fisherman _____.

3. The rescuers aren't able to save its tail.     The rescuers _____ its tail.

4. The two men are able to make a new tail.     The two men _____ a new tail.

5. The dolphin is able to move normally.     The dolphin _____ normally.

6. We are able to see dolphins in Florida.     We _____ dolphins in Florida.

7. The dolphin is able to swim very well.     The dolphin _____ very well.

8. We aren't able to see the aquarium.     We _____ the aquarium.

**5** Write *Yes/No* questions about abilities in the past. Use the words in parentheses and *be able to*. Then complete the short answer.

1. (you / swim)

   A: When you were a child, <u>were you able to swim?</u>

   B: Yes, <u>     I was     </u>.

2. (you / understand / that question)

   A: _____

   B: No, _____.

3. (you / finish / your homework)

   A: _____

   B: Yes, _____.

4. (the students / finish / the test)

   A: _____

   B: No, _____.

5. (Fred / go / to the movies)

   A: _____

   B: No, _____.

6. (your parents / go / with you)

   A: _____

   B: Yes, _____.

7. (you / fall asleep / last night)

   A: _____

   B: No, _____.

8. (you / hear / the bell)

   A: _____

   B: No, _____.

9. (they / do / the exercise)

   A: _____

   B: Yes, _____.

10. (she / find / her book)

    A: _____

    B: Yes, _____.

11. (Oleg / talk to / his teacher)

    A: _____

    B: No, _____.

12. (you / see / anything)

    A: _____

    B: No, _____.

**6** **WRITE & SPEAK.** List three things you were not able to do in the past, but are able to do now. Then share your sentences with a partner. Use the verbs in the box or your own ideas.

| buy | go | read | understand |
|-----|-----|------|------------|
| drive | play | speak | use |

I wasn't able to speak English before I came here.

I wasn't able to drive when I was fifteen.

## 11.4  *Know How To*

| Affirmative Statements |
| --- |
| He **knows how to read** a map. |
| They **know how to ski.** |

| Negative Statements |
| --- |
| He **doesn't know how to fly** a plane. |
| They **don't know how to skate**. |

| Yes/No Questions |
| --- |
| **Do** you **know how to ski**? |
| **Does** he **know how to skate**? |

| Short Answers | |
| --- | --- |
| Affirmative | Negative |
| Yes, I **do.** | No, I **don't.** |
| Yes, he **does.** | No, he **doesn't.** |

| | |
| --- | --- |
| 1. *Know how to* means you have a skill or ability to do something from practice or experience. It is similar to *can*. | I **know how to** swim. = I can swim.<br>**Do** you **know how to** swim? = Can you swim? |
| 2. Use *do/does* to make this expression negative or interrogative. | A: **Do** you **know** how to fix a car?<br>B: No, I **don't.** |
| 3. The past of *know* is irregular: *knew*. Use *knew how to* to talk about a skill or ability in the past. | I **knew** how to read before I started school. |
| 4. Use *can*, not *know how to*, when an ability does not come from practice or experience. | ✓ I **can** open the door for you.<br>✗ I <u>know how to</u> open the door for you.<br><br>✓ Fish **can** swim.<br>✗ Fish <u>know how to</u> swim. |

### REAL ENGLISH

*Learn how to* is used to talk about an ability or skill we don't have, but want to learn.

I want to **learn how to** ski. Do you know where I can take lessons?

**7**  Change each affirmative statement to a negative statement.

1. They know how to play tennis.  <u>*They don't know how to play tennis.*</u>

2. I know how to fly a plane. _____

3. He knows how to speak Chinese. _____

4. We know how to solve the problem. _____

5. She knows how to cook. _____

6. I knew how to swim. _____

7. They knew how to help. _____

8. We knew how to find the answer. _____

9. Ted knows how to fix your computer. _____

10. Lori knew how to get there. _____

**8** Use the words in parentheses to write *Yes/No* questions. Use *know how to* in the present.

1. (you / fly a plane) <u>Do you know how to fly a plane?</u>

2. (your son / ride a bicycle) _____

3. (they / dance the tango) _____

4. (you / play the guitar) _____

5. (he / scuba dive) _____

6. (they / take good photographs) _____

7. (I / play golf) _____

8. (she / fix a car) _____

9. (he / make cookies) _____

10. (you / use this vending machine) _____

**9** **SPEAK.** Work with a partner. Ask and answer questions about ability. Use *know how to* and the words in the box.

| | | | |
|---|---|---|---|
| cook | fly a plane | play tennis | ride a horse |
| drive a car | make coffee | play the piano | surf |

Student A: *Do you know how to surf?*

Student B: *No, I don't.*

# PRACTICE

**10** Match each question in Column A with the correct answer in Column B. Write the letter on the line.

**Column A**

1. Were you able to read before you started school? <u>b</u>

2. Do you know how to ride a motorcycle? _____

3. Does a dolphin know how to swim? _____

4. Does your grandmother know how to use a computer? _____

5. Were people able to fly in the nineteenth century? _____

6. Was I able to finish the last lesson? _____

7. Are dogs able to talk? _____

8. Do babies know how to walk? _____

**Column B**

a. No, I don't.

b. No, I wasn't.

c. Yes, you were.

d. No, they don't.

e. Yes, she does.

f. No, they weren't.

g. No, they aren't.

h. Yes, it does.

**11** **EDIT.** Read the questions and answers about doctors in the past. Find and correct five more errors with *be able to* and *know how to*.

> ## Ask the Doctor
>
> **Q:** When people were sick in the old days, were doctors able ⌄to help them?
>
> **A:** In the past, many people died because doctors didn't able to save them. Doctors didn't know to help very sick people.
>
> **Q:** Were women able to being doctors?
>
> **A:** In some countries, they did. But in most countries, women weren't able to be doctors. They wasn't able to go to medical school.

**12** **LISTEN & SPEAK.**

**A** Listen to the information about Sophie Germain. Then choose the correct answers.

1. When did Sophie Germain live?
   - a. in the 1900s
   - b. in the 1800s
   - c. in the 1700s

2. Why was her life difficult?
   - a. Education for women was not common.
   - b. She wasn't a good student.

**B** Listen again. What things was she able to do? Put a check (✓) next to the activities.

1. ☐ study math when her parents were awake
2. ☐ study late at night
3. ☐ attend college
4. ☐ write to a professor
5. ☐ sign her letter "Sophie Germain"
6. ☐ learn math from a college professor
7. ☐ solve difficult math and physics problems
8. ☐ help people build tall buildings

**C** Work with a partner. Ask and answer *Yes/No* questions about Sophie Germain. Use *be able to* and *know how to*.

Student A: *Was she able to go to college?*     Student B: *No, she wasn't.*

**13** **APPLY.** Work in a group. How is life different for women now? Ask and answer questions about the activities in the box. Use *Were women able to . . .* and *Are women able to . . .*

| become doctors | become the leader of the country | drive cars | vote |
| buy houses | have jobs outside the home | wear pants | |

Student A: *Are women able to vote in the United States?*

Student B: *Yes, they are now. They weren't able to vote before 1920.*

## EXPLORE

CD3-31

**1   READ** the article about athletes with disabilities. Notice the words in **bold**.

# Challenges for Athletes

In 1904, George Eyser competed in gymnastics in the Olympics. He won three gold medals, two silver medals, and a bronze medal. He was a great athlete, **but** he was also an unusual athlete. As a child, he lost his leg in a train accident, **so** he had an artificial leg. It was made of wood.

Eyser isn't the only athlete with a physical disability to compete in the Olympics. Im Dong Hyun is almost blind, **but** he won gold medals in archery with his team from South Korea. Natalia Partyka from Poland was born with only one arm, **but** she competed in the Olympics in table tennis.

Many more athletes with disabilities compete in the Paralympic Games. These take place every four years in the winter and summer. The first Games were in 1960, **and** 400 athletes from 23 countries competed. Now, more than 4000 athletes from more than 160 countries compete. Like George Eyser, these athletes focus on the competition, not on their disabilities.

▲ Hannah Cockroft of Great Britain on her way to her second gold medal at the 2012 Summer Paralympic Games in London, England

**2 CHECK.** Read the statements. Circle **T** for *true* or **F** for *false*.

1. George Eyser won seven medals in the Olympics.     **T**     **F**

2. Eyser had only one arm.     **T**     **F**

3. Im Dong Hyun's team won gold medals.     **T**     **F**

4. The Paralympic Games are only in the summer.     **T**     **F**

5. In the first Paralympic Games, 400 athletes competed.     **T**     **F**

**3 DISCOVER.** Complete the exercises to learn about the grammar in this lesson.

**A** Find these sentences from the article from exercise **1** on page 359. Write the missing words.

1. He was a great athlete, _____ he was also an unusual athlete.

2. As a child, he lost his leg in a train accident, _____ he had an artificial leg.

3. The first Games were in 1960, _____ 400 athletes from 23 countries competed.

**B** Look at the sentences and words you wrote in exercise **A**. Then choose the correct word to complete each statement. Discuss your answers with your classmates and teacher.

1. Use _____ to add information.     a. and     b. but     c. so

2. Use _____ to show a contrast or add surprising information.     a. and     b. but     c. so

3. Use _____ to show a result.     a. and     b. but     c. so

▼ David Weir of Great Britain wins the gold medal in the men's 1500-meter T54 final at the 2012 Summer Paralympic Games in London, England.

# LEARN

## 11.5 And, But, So

I can speak Spanish, **and** I also speak a little Italian.
Independent Clause · Independent Clause

She can't read Farsi, **but** she can speak it.
Independent Clause · Independent Clause

I lived in Costa Rica, **so** I can understand Spanish.
Independent Clause · Independent Clause

| | |
|---|---|
| 1. *And, but,* and *so* are often used to connect two sentences or independent clauses.<br><br>**Remember:** A clause is a word group with a subject and a verb. An independent clause can stand alone as a complete sentence. | He was a very fast runner. He won a lot of races.<br>He was a very fast runner, **so** he won a lot of races.<br><br>Larry ran very fast, **but** he didn't win the race.<br>Independent Clause · Independent Clause |
| 2. Put a comma before *and, but,* or *so* when you connect two independent clauses. | Pablo plays soccer, **and** he likes tennis, too.<br>I can play the piano, **but** I'm not very good.<br>Mina felt sick yesterday, **so** she didn't run in the race. |
| 3. Use *and* to add information. | I ran in the race, **and** I finished it in 35 minutes. |
| 4. Use *but* to show a contrast or add surprising information. | They tried hard, **but** their team didn't win. |
| 5. Use *so* to show a result. | She broke her leg, **so** she couldn't run in the race. |

### REAL ENGLISH

In conversation, we often use parts of sentences.

*But I like it.*
*So we did it.*

This is not correct in writing. Use complete sentences in writing.

*My science class is difficult, but I like it.*
*Our teacher gave us homework, so we did it.*

**4** Connect the two sentences. Use the word in parentheses.

1. He didn't win. He did very well. (but) ___He didn't win, but he did very well.___

2. He had an artificial leg. He could walk. (so) _____

3. He was in an accident. He lost his leg. (and) _____

4. She had an artificial leg. She could run very fast. (but) _____

5. She entered the race. She won. (and) _____

6. The Games were very popular. Tickets sold fast. (so) _____

7. Ava is strong. She's not fast. (but) _____

8. They were very fast. They won a lot of races. (so) _____

**5** Circle the correct word to complete each sentence.

1. We lost the game, **and** / **but** we had fun.

2. He ran in the marathon, **and** / **but** he did very well.

3. We read an article about sports, **and** / **so** it was very interesting.

4. She didn't understand the assignment, **and** / **so** she asked her teacher for help.

5. They want to learn French, **but** / **so** they're taking classes twice a week.

6. I don't have any sisters, **but** / **and** I have two brothers.

7. Anil missed the bus, **but** / **so** he was late for work.

8. My history class is difficult, **and** / **but** I like it a lot.

**6  SPEAK.** Work with a partner. Complete the sentences.

I can speak English, but I …
English grammar is difficult, but …
The weather today is good/terrible, so …
Today we're sitting in class, and …

*I can speak English, but I can't speak Chinese.*

## 11.6  Contrasts after *But*

| Affirmative Clause | But | Negative Clause | | Negative Clause | But | Affirmative Clause |
|---|---|---|---|---|---|---|
| We're ready, | | they aren't. | | We aren't ready, | | they are. |
| I was there, | | she wasn't. | | I wasn't there, | | she was. |
| He plays tennis, | but | I don't. | | He doesn't play tennis, | but | I do. |
| We can speak Korean, | | they can't. | | We can't speak Korean | | they can. |
| They could go, | | we couldn't. | | They couldn't go | | we could. |

| | |
|---|---|
| 1. The clause after *but* is often shortened. | I'm ready for the race, <u>but</u> **he isn't**. (= I'm <u>ready for the race</u>, but he isn't <u>ready for the race</u>.) <br><br> She plays soccer, <u>but</u> **her brother doesn't**. (= She <u>plays soccer</u>, but her brother doesn't <u>play soccer</u>.) <br><br> We can't speak French, <u>but</u> **they can**. (= We can't <u>speak French</u>, but they can <u>speak French</u>.) |
| 2. Do not shorten the clause after *but* if the verb is different from the verb in the first clause. | ✓ I'm <u>studying</u>, **but** my brother is <u>working</u>. <br> ✗ I'm studying, but <u>my brother is</u>. |

**7** Circle the correct word to complete each sentence.

1. I can ski, but my parents **can** / **can't**.

2. My brother likes baseball, but I **do** / **don't**.

3. We watched the game, but she **did** / **didn't**.

4. He doesn't compete in races, but his brother **does** / **doesn't**.

5. He's an athlete, but they **are** / **aren't**.

6. I wasn't in the race, but my friends **were** / **weren't**.

7. Marie wasn't able to finish the race, but I **was** / **wasn't**.

8. I don't know how to swim, but he **does** / **doesn't**.

9. She finished the race, but I **did** / **didn't**.

10. We're tired today, but she **is** / **isn't**.

**8** Complete each sentence with the correct affirmative or negative form of *be, do,* or *can.*

1. That exercise isn't difficult, but this one _____ is _____ .

2. My sister is a very good athlete, but I _____ .

3. We can't go, but they _____ .

4. He knows her, but I _____ .

5. Claudia can't speak Arabic, but Noor _____ .

6. I ate breakfast, but you _____ .

7. She likes to go shopping, but I _____ .

8. They didn't get lost, but we _____ .

**9** **SPEAK.** Work with a partner. Make sentences about some differences between you and your partner. Use *but* and the correct form of *be, do,* and *can.*

| am (not)/is (not) | do/does | |
|---|---|---|
| can | like/like to | _____ (your idea) |

*I like to wake up early, but Cara doesn't.*

*Monica can speak Portuguese, but I can't.*

*I'm married, but Antonio isn't.*

*I don't play soccer, but Ahmed does.*

# PRACTICE

**10** Match the beginning of each sentence in Column A with the correct ending in Column B.

**Column A**

1. I can't speak Spanish, but __d__.

2. Yesterday Ed and Al went to work, but _____.

3. I can speak Chinese, so _____.

4. Last year, she didn't run the marathon, but _____.

5. My brother is a fast runner, but _____.

6. Anita can swim very well, and _____.

7. He hurt his arm, so _____.

8. She was tired after the race, so _____.

9. I went to the game last night, and _____.

10. The game was very exciting, and _____.

**Column B**

a. this year she did

b. he can't play tennis

c. today they didn't

d. I can speak Italian

e. she went to bed early

f. we had great seats

g. I saw Peter and Jun there

h. he couldn't finish the race

i. I want to go to Hong Kong to study

j. she can scuba dive, too

**11** Complete the conversations with *and, but,* and *so.* Then listen and check your answers.

**Conversation 1**

**Andres:** I really want to play in the game tomorrow, (1) _____but_____ I can't.

**Jill:** Why not?

**Andres:** Well, I was practicing yesterday, (2) _____ I hurt my foot.

**Jill:** That's too bad. Ted is sick, (3) _____ he can't play either.

**Conversation 2**

**Yuri:** Terry won the bike race yesterday, (4) _____ we're having a party for her. Are you free on Friday night?

**Liam:** That's great, (5) _____ I have plans for dinner with my parents. What time is the party?

**Yuri:** The party's at 8:00, (6) _____ it's at Carol's house.

**Liam:** Oh, well, we usually eat dinner at 6:00, (7) _____ Carol lives near me, (8) _____ I can go to the party after dinner.

**Conversation 3**

**Jason:** It's noon, (9) _____ I'm thinking about lunch. Do you want to join me?

**Ed:** Sorry. I just finished breakfast, (10) _____ I'm not hungry.

**Jason:** Hi, Mark. Ed isn't hungry, (11) _____ I am. How about lunch?

**Mark:** Oh, I'm sorry. That sounds good, (12) _____ I have a lot of work today.

**12** **EDIT.** Read the paragraph about Aimee Mullins. Find and correct five more errors with the use of *but, and,* and *so.*

# Aimee Mullins

When Aimee Mullins was born, she didn't have bones in part of her legs,
~~but~~ <sub>so</sub> she couldn't walk. The doctors talked to her parents, so they decided
to amputate¹ part of her legs. Some people have trouble with artificial
legs, and Mullins doesn't. She learned to walk with them, but they were a
normal part of her life. In high school, Aimee played softball, and in college
she competed in many track and field events. In the Paralympics, she ran
100 meters in 17.01 seconds, so she jumped 3.14 meters in the long jump.
Aimee Mullins has a physical disability, and that doesn't slow her down.

¹ **amputate:** to cut off surgically

**13** **LISTEN & WRITE.**

CD3-33-35

**A** Listen to information about three famous people. What were their challenges and achievements? Put a check (✓) in the correct column.

| | | Walt Disney | Bruce Hall | Beethoven |
|---|---|:---:|:---:|:---:|
| Challenges | • couldn't hear | ☐ | ☐ | ☐ |
| | • couldn't see | ☐ | ☐ | ☐ |
| | • had very little money | ✓ | ☐ | ☐ |
| Achievements | • artist and businessperson | ☐ | ☐ | ☐ |
| | • underwater photographer | ☐ | ☐ | ☐ |
| | • music composer | ☐ | ☐ | ☐ |

**B** Work with a partner. Write three sentences about each famous person from exercise **A**. Use the words from list A and list B with *and, but,* and *so.*

1. Walt Disney

**List A**

family / poor

not be / a good student

start / a company

**List B**

get / a job

leave / high school

do / very well

(so) _Walt Disney's family was poor, so he got a job._

(and)_____

(and)_____

2. Bruce Hall

**List A**

be blind
hear about stars
learn to scuba dive

**List B**

be / a photographer
not see / them
take / underwater photographs

▲ An example of Bruce Hall's underwater photography

(but) _____

(but) _____

(so) _____

3. Beethoven

| **List A** | **List B** |
| --- | --- |
| be / a great musician | write / music |
| become / a composer | lose / his hearing |
| become / deaf | continue to write / music |

(and)_____

(but) _____

(but) _____

## 14  APPLY.

**A**  Work in a small group. Discuss these questions.

1. Think of three or four people who had challenges in their lives. They can be famous people or people you know. Who are these people? What challenges did they face?

*Michael J. Fox is an actor. He got a disease, but he didn't stop acting.*

2. What did he or she do about this challenge or situation?

*Michael J. Fox started an organization to make money for research about his disease . . .*

**B**  Write five or six sentences about one of the people from exercise **A** and his or her challenges. Use *and, but,* and *so* in your sentences.

**C**  Share your sentences with your classmates.

Charts
11.1–11.4

**1** Complete the conversations. Use words from the box. There are two possible answers for some of the sentences. You can use the words more than once.

| | | |
|---|---|---|
| can | Can you | know how to |
| can't | Do you know how to | don't know how to |

1. A: Excuse me. (1) __Can you / Do you know how to__ read Chinese?

   I (2) _____ read this street sign.

   B: I'm sorry. I (3) _____ read Chinese either.

2. A: This door is stuck! I (4) _____ open it.

   B: Let me try. No, I (5) _____ open it either. Is it locked?

3. A: (6) _____ fix computers? My computer isn't working.

   I (7) _____ turn it on.

   B: Yes, I (8) _____ fix some computer problems.
   Let me look at it.

4. A: (9) _____ solve this math problem?

   I (10) _____ do it.

   B: No, I'm sorry. I (11) _____ do it either.

Charts
11.1–11.3

**2 READ & SPEAK.**

**A** Read the story about National Geographic photographer, Alison Wright. Underline the forms of *be able to* and *could/couldn't*.

# Alison Wright

Alison Wright is a photographer and writer. She travels to remote villages, places far away from cities and airports. She takes photographs of the people there and writes about their lives. Several years ago, she was traveling on a bus on a remote mountain road in Laos when a truck hit the bus. She was able to get out of the bus, but she had a broken back and many other injuries. She couldn't move, and she wasn't able to breathe very well. No one could help her because she was very far away from any doctors or hospitals. She waited for ten hours. Finally, someone came by in a small truck and saw her. He put her in the back of his truck and drove for eight hours to a small hospital in Thailand. A doctor there was able to save her life, but she had serious injuries. She returned to her home in the United States and had more than 20 operations. When she left the hospital, she couldn't walk very well, and she wasn't able to travel. However, she didn't give up. She became stronger and exercised every day because she had a dream: she wanted to climb Mount Kilimanjaro. Four years later, she did it. She was able to climb Mount Kilimanjaro!

**B** Work with a partner. Compare your answers from exercise **A** on page 367.

**C** Role-play an interview between Alison Wright and a reporter. Partner A is the reporter. Partner B is Alison Wright. Use information in the story and your imagination.

Reporter: *Where was the accident?*

Alison: *In Laos.*

Reporter: *Were you able to breathe?*

Alison: *Yes, I was, but I couldn't breathe very well.*

Charts
11.5–11.6

**3** **EDIT.** Read the paragraph about Bethany Hamilton. Find and correct seven more mistakes with *and*, *but*, and *so*.

# Bethany Hamilton

    Bethany Hamilton grew up in Hawaii, ~~but~~ <sup>and</sup> she was an excellent surfer. She won many competitions, but she was the number 1 surfer for the 13-year-old age group. One day, she was on her surfboard with one arm in the water, but a shark bit her. People nearby took her to the hospital, so doctors couldn't save her arm. She lost her arm, so she got back on her surfboard one month after the shark attack. Most people can't surf with one arm, and Bethany can. She entered a competition four months after the attack, so she won fifth place. A year later, she entered a national competition, and she won! Bethany faced a huge challenge when she lost her arm, and she didn't give up.

▶ Bethany Hamilton at Super Girl Pro (2013), Oceanside, California, USA

**4 LISTEN & SPEAK.**

**A** Listen to the conversation. Then complete the sentences.

1. Tami and Richard tried to get away from the hurricane, but ___they couldn't___.

2. Most waves don't turn a boat upside down, but _____.

3. When Tami woke up the next day, she thought Richard was on the boat, but

   _____.

4. Tami tried to find Richard, but _____.

5. Tami survived the hurricane, but _____.

6. Many people don't know how to use the sun for location, but _____.

7. Tami wanted to use the engine, but _____.

8. Most people don't sail again after a terrible experience, but _____.

CD3-36

**B** Listen again. Then work with a partner. Use *and, but,* or *so* to combine the sentences.

1. Tami wanted to see the ~~world. She~~ *world, so she* helped people sail their boats across the ocean.

2. A hurricane was coming. Tami and Richard didn't know.

3. The hurricane was moving toward them. They changed direction.

4. A huge wave turned the boat over. It caused a lot of damage in the boat.

5. Tami looked for Richard. She didn't find him.

6. Tami's trip to Hawaii took 41 days. She survived.

7. It was a terrible experience. Tami still likes to sail.

8. Tami is a brave woman. She's a good sailor.

**C** Work with a partner. Discuss these questions.

1. Can you imagine a trip across an ocean in a sailboat? Why, or why not?

2. What surprised you about this story?

## 1 READ & NOTICE THE GRAMMAR.

**A** Read the story. What was the challenge? Discuss with a partner.

### My Cousin's Challenge

My cousin got very sick when she was 14 years old. She was in the hospital for two weeks, and she couldn't go to school for a month. She wasn't able to sit up, so she couldn't do any homework. When she finally went back to school, she didn't know how to do any of the math problems, and she was behind in all her courses.

Before my cousin got sick, she wasn't really a very good student, but she decided to change. She studied every weekend, and she also studied with a tutor after school. Finally, she was able to catch up with the other students. She studied hard every day, and after high school she went to a very good university. I am very proud of her.

### GRAMMAR FOCUS

In the story in exercise **A**, the writer uses *couldn't* and *be able to* to describe abilities or inabilities in the past.

She **couldn't** go to school for a month.
She **wasn't able to** sit up.

**B** Read the story in exercise **A** again. Underline the modals and expressions that show ability or inability. Then work with a partner and compare answers.

**C** Complete the chart with information from the story in exercise **A**. What challenges did the writer's cousin face? What actions helped her with this challenge?

| My Cousin's Challenge | |
| --- | --- |
| Challenges | Actions |
| got sick<br>was in the hospital | |

**2 BEFORE YOU WRITE.** Think of a person who faced a challenge (you or another person). What challenge did this person face? What actions helped this person with the challenge? Write notes in the chart. Use the chart in exercise **1C** as a model.

| _____ **Challenge** | |
|---|---|
| Challenges | Actions |
| | |

**3 WRITE** a paragraph about this person's challenge. Use the information from your chart in exercise **2** and the story in exercise **1A** to help you.

---

**WRITING FOCUS**    Combining Sentences with *And, But,* and *So*

Writers use *and, but,* and *so* to join two independent clauses. This helps show the relationship between ideas and adds variety to their writing.

*She was in the hospital for two weeks,* **and** *she couldn't go to school for a month.*

*She wasn't able to sit up,* **so** *she couldn't do any homework.*

*Finally, she was able to go back to school,* **but** *she had a hard time.*

---

**4 SELF ASSESS.** Read your story. Underline *and, but,* and *so.* Then use the checklist to assess your work.

- ☐ I used the base form of the verb after *can/can't* and *could/couldn't.* [11.1–11.2]
- ☐ I used the correct forms of *be able to.* [11.3]
- ☐ I used *know how to* when I wrote about a skill from practice or experience. [11.4]
- ☐ I used a comma before *and, but,* and *so.* [11.5]
- ☐ I used *and, but,* and *so* to join two independent clauses and add variety to my sentences. [WRITING FOCUS]

# Comparative and Superlative Adjectives

▲ Horseshoe Bend on the Colorado
River, near Page, Arizona, USA

## EXPLORE

**1** **READ** the article about Mount Everest and K2. Notice the words in **bold**.

# Two Amazing Mountains

Two mountains in the Himalayas are very well known around the world: Mount Everest and K2. Mount Everest is **more famous than** K2 because it's the highest mountain in the world. However, K2 is **more difficult** to climb and **more dangerous**. In fact, very few climbers reach the top of K2. About 20 percent of all climbers die in their attempt.

What makes K2 **more challenging**[1] **than** Mount Everest? First, the weather on K2 is often **worse than** on Mount Everest. High winds, storms, and heavy snow make the climb very difficult. K2 is also **steeper than** Mount Everest. The climb to the top typically takes ten days **longer** as well. It usually takes 75 days to climb K2. The average expedition to climb Mount Everest is about 65 days.

[1] **challenging:** very difficult

▶ An expedition climbs K2.

**2** **CHECK.** Read the list of adjectives in the chart. Which mountain does each adjective describe? Check (✓) the correct column. Then compare your answers with a partner.

| Adjective | Mount Everest | K2 |
|---|---|---|
| higher | ✓ | |
| more famous | | |
| more difficult | | |
| more challenging | | |
| steeper | | |
| more dangerous | | |

**3** **DISCOVER.** Complete the exercises to learn about the grammar in this lesson.

**A** Find these sentences in the article from exercise **1**. Write the missing words.

1. Mount Everest is _____ K2 because it's the highest mountain in the world.

2. However, K2 is _____ to climb and _____ .

3. What makes K2 _____ Mount Everest?

4. First, the weather on K2 is often _____ on Mount Everest.

**B** Look at these sentences from exercise **A**. What do these words show? Circle **T** for *true* or **F** for *false* for each statement below. Then discuss your answers with your classmates and teacher.

1. These words show differences between two things.     **T**     **F**

2. These words show how two things are similar.     **T**     **F**

# LEARN

## 12.1 Comparative Forms of Short Adjectives

| | Be | Comparative Adjective | Than | |
|---|---|---|---|---|
| Ted | is | older | | his brother. |
| Lucia | | younger | than | Katya. |
| Planes | are | faster | | buses. |

| | |
|---|---|
| 1. Use a comparative adjective + *than* to talk about the difference between two people, places, or things. | Eduardo is **taller than** Joe.<br>Brazil is **larger than** Colombia.<br>My computer is **smaller than** my notebook. |
| 2. *Than* is not necessary when the second item in the comparison is understood by both the speaker and the listener. | A: Do you prefer this hotel or the Grand Hotel?<br>B: The Grand Hotel. It's **nicer.** |
| 3. For short adjectives (one syllable), add -*er* to the end of the adjective. | old → old**er**<br>new → new**er**<br>high → high**er** |
| 4. When a short adjective ends in CVC*, double the final consonant and add -*er*. | big → big**ger**<br>fat → fat**ter** |
| 5. When a short adjective ends in -*e*, add -*r*. | nice → nice**r** |
| 6. Some adjectives have irregular comparative forms. | good → **better**<br>bad → **worse**<br>far → **farther** |

*consonant + vowel + consonant

**REAL ENGLISH**

*One* is often used with comparatives to avoid repeating the noun, or when the noun is understood by both the speaker and the listener.

*This house is older than that* **one**. *(one = house)*

A: *Is this table OK?*
B: *That* **one***'s bigger. Let's sit there.*

---

**4**  Complete each sentence with the comparative form of the adjective in parentheses. Add *than* when necessary.

1. Mount Everest is _____*higher than*_____ (high) K2.

2. K2 is _____ (low) Mount Everest.

3. K2 is _____ (steep) Mount Everest.

4. The weather on K2 is _____ (bad) on Mount Everest.

5. The weather on Mount Everest is _____ (good) the weather on K2.

6. The climb to the top of Mount Everest is _____ (short) the climb to the top of K2.

7. The climb to the top of K2 is _____ (hard) the climb to the top of Mount Everest.

8. Expeditions to the top of Mount Everest are long, but expeditions to the top of K2 are _____ (long).

**5 SPEAK.** Compare people in your class. Use the comparative form of the adjectives in the box.

| tall | short | old | young |
|------|-------|-----|-------|

*Junko is taller than Sonia.*

## 12.2 Comparative Forms of Long Adjectives

|  | *Be* | Comparative Adjective | *Than* |  |
|--|------|----------------------|--------|--|
| This hotel | is | more famous | | that one. |
| The new store | | more expensive | than | the old store. |
| The brown shoes | are | more comfortable | | the blue ones. |

| 1. For long adjectives (two or more syllables), put *more* before the adjective to make the comparative form. | modern → **more modern** <br> careful → **more careful** <br> expensive → **more expensive** |
|---|---|
| 2. When a long adjective ends in consonant + -y, change the -y to -i and add -er. | easy → eas**ier** <br> pretty → prett**ier** <br> friendly → friendl**ier** |
| 3. Some short adjectives are used with *more than*. | Soccer is **more fun** <br> **than** golf. |

**REAL ENGLISH**

Add -er to some two-syllable adjectives to make the comparative form.

*quiet → quiet**er*** <br> *simple → simpl**er*** <br> *narrow → narrow**er***

**6** Complete each sentence with the comparative form of the adjective in parentheses.

1. (interesting) The movie about Mt. Everest was _more interesting than_ the book.

2. (expensive) Paris is _____ Lisbon.

3. (quiet) Quebec City is _____ Mexico City.

4. (beautiful) The beach is _____ the city.

5. (sunny) Miami is _____ Seattle.

6. (crowded) Mumbai is _____ Toronto.

7. (relaxing) A vacation in Hawaii is _____ a vacation in New York City.

8. (busy) People in big cities are _____ people in small towns.

9. (noisy) Bangkok is _____ Boston.

10. (scary) The climb to the top of K2 is _____ the climb to the top of Mount Everest.

**7 WRITE & SPEAK.** Use the adjectives from the box to compare two places or things. Then share your sentences with a partner.

| crowded | expensive | famous | interesting | pretty |
|---------|-----------|--------|-------------|--------|

Istanbul is more interesting than Orlando.
My sunglasses were more expensive than my shoes.

## 12.3 Questions with Comparatives

| Yes/No Questions | | | | Short Answers |
|------|---------|-------------------------|---------|---------------|
| Be | Subject | Comparative Adjective | | |
| Is | Brazil | larger than | Canada? | No, it isn't. |
| Are | planes | faster than | trains? | Yes, they are. |

| Questions with *Which* and *Who* | | | | Answers |
|-------------|-------|-----|----------------------------------------------|---------------|
| Wh-Word | Noun | Be | | |
| Which | café | is | better? | The Bistro. |
| | shoes | are | more expensive, the red ones or the blue ones? | The blue ones. |
| Which | | is | bigger, Tokyo or Osaka? | Tokyo. |
| Who | | is | older, you or your sister? | My sister. |

| | |
|---|---|
| 1. **Remember:** The verb comes before the subject in *Yes/No* questions with *be*. | **Is** <u>Mount Everest</u> higher than K2? <br> **Are** <u>you</u> taller than your brother? |
| 2. *Wh-* questions with *Which* or *Who* are often about a subject. | **Which** mountain is higher? <br> **Who** is taller, you or your brother? |

**8** Put the words in the correct order to make *Yes/No* questions and questions with *Which*.

1. higher / is / Which / mountain

   Which mountain is higher? _____

2. hotel / is / Which / cheaper

   _____

3. Which / difficult / more / course / is

   _____

4. new / your / bigger / Is / apartment

   _____

5. your / new / Is / farther away / apartment

_____

6. worse / is / rain or snow / Which

_____

7. closer / Which / is / bus stop / to your house

_____

8. neighborhood / Which / safer / is

_____

**9** Read each statement. Write a question about the <u>underlined</u> word(s) or phrase(s).

1. <u>Monaco</u> is smaller than <u>Grenada</u>.

   _____Which is smaller_____ , _____Monaco_____ *or* _____Grenada_____ ?

2. <u>No</u>, Australia isn't bigger than Russia.

   _____ ?

3. <u>The bus</u> is more convenient than <u>the subway</u>.

   _____ , _____ *or* _____ ?

4. <u>My parents' house</u> is nicer than <u>my apartment</u>.

   _____ , _____ *or* _____ ?

5. <u>My brother</u> is older than <u>my sister</u>.

   _____ , _____ *or* _____ ?

6. <u>No</u>, my city isn't larger than New York.

   _____ ?

7. <u>English</u> is more difficult than <u>my language</u>.

   _____ , _____ *or* _____ ?

8. <u>Shopping online</u> is more fun than <u>shopping in a store</u>.

   _____ , _____ *or* _____ ?

**10 SPEAK.** Work with a partner. Ask and answer questions 6–8 from exercise **9**. Use your own answers, not the answers in the book.

Student A: *Is your city larger than New York City?*

Student B: *Yes, it is. Mexico City is huge!*

# PRACTICE

**11** **WRITE, READ & SPEAK.**

**A** Complete the conversation with the comparative form of the adjectives in parentheses.

**Kay:** Guess what? We're going to Rome in January!

**Alex:** Rome, Italy? In the middle of winter? Isn't it (1) ___*better*___ (good) to go there in the summer?

**Kay:** Maybe, but airfares are much (2) _____ ( low) in the winter.

**Alex:** Well, sure. They're (3) _____ (cheap) because no one wants to go there then.

**Kay:** That's true. In the summer, it's a lot (4) _____ (crowded). I like to go to places in the winter when it's (5) _____ (quiet). I like the off season.

**Alex:** Yes, but the off season is usually (6) _____ (cold) and (7) _____ (rainy), too.

**Kay:** That's OK. Even in the rain, no city is (8) _____ (interesting) than Rome!

**B** Work with a partner. Read the conversation from exercise **A**. Then discuss these questions.

1. Why is Kay going to Rome now?

2. What do you think? Is it better to go to a place in the off season? Why, or why not?

3. Do you go to places in the off season? Where?

**12** **EDIT.** Read the questions and answers on the travel site about Edinburgh, Scotland. Find and correct five more errors with comparative adjectives.

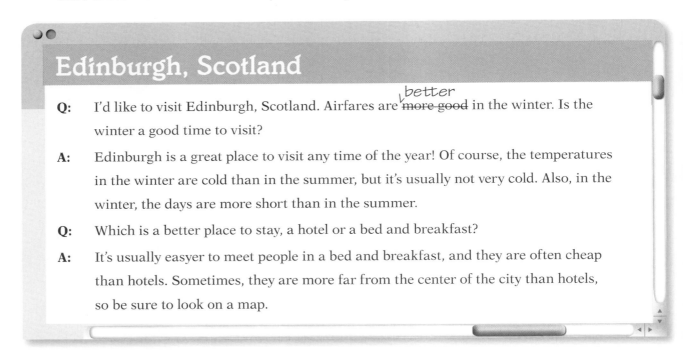

## Edinburgh, Scotland

**Q:** I'd like to visit Edinburgh, Scotland. Airfares are ~~more good~~ *better* in the winter. Is the winter a good time to visit?

**A:** Edinburgh is a great place to visit any time of the year! Of course, the temperatures in the winter are cold than in the summer, but it's usually not very cold. Also, in the winter, the days are more short than in the summer.

**Q:** Which is a better place to stay, a hotel or a bed and breakfast?

**A:** It's usually easier to meet people in a bed and breakfast, and they are often cheap than hotels. Sometimes, they are more far from the center of the city than hotels, so be sure to look on a map.

## 13 READ, WRITE & SPEAK.

**A** Read the information in the chart. Then use the adjectives from the box below to write sentences comparing the two mountains.

|  | **Mount Everest** | **Mount Kilimanjaro** |
|---|---|---|
| 1. Height | 29,035 feet | 19,340 feet |
| 2. Difficulty | 4 out of 5* | 1 out of 5* |
| 3. Length of expedition | 65 days | 8 days |
| 4. Weather | bad | not usually bad |
| 5. Number of climbers per year | 400+ | 20,000+ |

(* Scale: 1 = easy; 5 = very difficult)

| bad | crowded | dangerous | difficult | high | long | popular |
|---|---|---|---|---|---|---|

*Mount Everest is higher than Mount Kilimanjaro.*

**B** Work with a partner. Compare your sentences from exercise **A**.

**C** Ask and answer questions about the differences between Mount Everest and Mount Kilimanjaro. Use the information from exercises **A** and **B**.

Student A: *Which mountain is higher?*     Student B: *Mount Everest.*

## 14 SPEAK & LISTEN.

**A** Work with a partner. Look at the photos. How are the two places different?

Phuket, Thailand

Prague, Czech Republic

**B** Listen and complete the chart with information about Phuket and Prague.

| | **Phuket** | **Prague** |
|---|---|---|
| Description | Tropical beaches, mountains, jungle | Beautiful city with many historical buildings |
| Average rainfall each year | _____ inches (160 cm) | _____ inches (50 cm) |
| Good weather | February to April | July and August |
| Average high temperature | _____ °F (33°C) | _____ °F (21°C) |
| Tourists | _____ million each year | _____ million each year |
| Tourist activities or attractions | Beaches, scuba diving, swimming, safaris | Historic places such as the Old Town Square, Prague Castle, and the Charles Bridge, museums, cafés, and parks |

**C** Work with a partner. Ask and answer questions about Phuket and Prague. Use the comparative form of the adjectives from the box.

| | | | |
|---|---|---|---|
| close | exciting | hot/warm | old |
| cold/cool | fun | interesting | relaxing |
| entertaining | historic | modern | sunny/rainy |

Student A: *Which place is colder?*        Student B: *Prague.*

Student A: *Is Phuket colder than Prague?*        Student B: *No, it isn't. Prague is colder than Phuket.*

**D** Work in a group. You just won a free trip to one of the places from exercise **A**. You can go camping in Phuket, or you can go to a very luxurious hotel in Prague. Which trip do you want to take? Why? Discuss your ideas.

Student A: *I want to go to Prague and stay in a hotel.*

Student B: *Me, too. A hotel is nicer than a tent.*

Student C: *I don't. I want to go to a beach in Phuket. It's more relaxing.*

## 15  APPLY.

**A** Compare two places you know. Write five sentences in your notebook.

Mexico City is bigger than Miami, Florida.

Mexico City is more crowded than Miami.

**B** Work with a partner. Share your sentences from exercise **A**. Then ask and answer questions about your places. Use *Yes/No* questions and questions with *which*.

Student A: *Which city is more expensive?*

Student B: *Miami.*

## EXPLORE

**1** **READ** the article about the National Museum of Anthropology. Notice the words in **bold**.

# The National Museum of Anthropology

The National Museum of Anthropology[1] (Museo Nacional de Antropología) in Mexico City is **the largest** museum in Mexico, and it is one of **the most interesting** museums in the world. As you walk through the exhibits, you learn about the history of ancient[2] cultures in Mesoamerica: the area from central Mexico through Belize, Guatemala, El Salvador, Honduras, Nicaragua, and northern Costa Rica. Each room in the museum has artifacts[3] from a different region and culture.

The museum has **the biggest** collection in the world of artifacts from life before the Spanish arrived in the Americas. Two of **the most famous** artifacts in this museum are the huge Aztec sunstone and a beautiful jade[4] mask.

The museum doesn't just have exhibits about ancient cultures. There are also exhibits about life in different parts of Mexico today. A visit to this museum is **the best** way to learn about Mexican culture, both old and new.

[1] **anthropology:** the study of people and their cultures
[2] **ancient:** very old
[3] **artifacts:** objects used by people a very long time ago
[4] **jade:** a green or white stone used for jewelry or ornaments

◄ Jade death mask of Mayan King Pakal, National Museum of Anthropology, Mexico City, Mexico

**2  CHECK.** Read the questions. Circle *Yes* or *No*.

1. Is the National Museum of Anthropology the largest museum in Mexico?　　**Yes**　　**No**

2. Is it one of the most interesting museums in the world?　　**Yes**　　**No**

3. Does it have many artifacts from life before the Spanish arrived in the Americas?　　**Yes**　　**No**

4. Does the museum only have artifacts from Mexico?　　**Yes**　　**No**

**3  DISCOVER.** Complete the exercises to learn about the grammar in this lesson.

**A** Find these sentences in the article from exercise **1** on page 383. Write the missing words.

1. The National Museum of Anthropology in Mexico City is _____ _____ museum in Mexico, . . .

2. . . . and it is one of _____ _____ _____ museums in the world.

3. The museum has _____ _____ collection of artifacts from life before the Spanish arrived in the Americas.

**B** Look at the sentences from exercise **A**. What do these words show? Circle **T** for *true* or **F** for *false* for each statement. Then discuss your answers with your classmates and teacher.

1. We use these words to talk about differences between two things.　　**T**　　**F**

2. We use these words to talk about how one thing is different from many others.　　**T**　　**F**

◀ Stone of the Sun (Aztec Calendar), National Museum of Anthropology, Mexico City, Mexico

# LEARN

## 12.4 Superlative Forms of Short Adjectives

| | *The* | Superlative Adjective | |
|---|---|---|---|
| That's | | newest | building in the city. |
| This is | the | largest | classroom in the building. |
| Benny's is | | closest | restaurant to our office. |

| | |
|---|---|
| 1. The superlative form shows that one person, place, or thing is different from others in some way. | Roberto is **the tallest** student in our class. <br> That's **the oldest** building in the city. |
| 2. For short adjectives (one syllable), add -*est* to the adjective to make the superlative form. | young → the young**est** <br> old → the old**est** |
| 3. When a short adjective ends in CVC*, double the consonant and add -*est*. | big → the big**gest** <br> thin → the thin**nest** |
| 4. When a short adjective ends in -*e*, add -*st*. | nice → the nice**st** |
| 5. *The* comes before a superlative adjective. | ✓ Dilma is **the youngest** student in our class. <br> ✗ Dilma is <u>youngest</u> student in our class. |
| 6. Some adjectives have irregular superlative forms. | good → **the best** <br> bad → **the worst** <br> far → **the farthest** |

*consonant + vowel + consonant

**4** Complete each sentence with the correct superlative form of the adjective in parentheses.

1. It is ___the largest___ (large) museum in Mexico.

2. The museum is _____ (good) way to learn about history and culture.

3. It has _____ (big) collection of artifacts from Mesoamerica.

4. The Uffizi Gallery in Florence, Italy, is one of _____ (old) museums in the world.

5. _____ (cheap) way to get to the museum is by subway.

6. This is _____ (small) room in the museum, but the exhibit is very interesting.

7. That museum has one of _____ (nice) restaurants in the city.

8. _____ (fast) way to get to the museum is by taxi.

> **REAL ENGLISH**
>
> The superlative form is very common after *one of*. Use a plural noun after *one of* + superlative.
>
> He's **one of the youngest** <u>people</u> in the school.
> That's **one of the most famous** <u>restaurants</u> in Rome.

## 12.5 Superlative Forms of Long Adjectives

| | The Most | Adjective | |
|---|---|---|---|
| This is | the most | beautiful | park in Paris. |
| That is | | expensive | hotel in the world. |

1. For long adjectives (two or more syllables), put *the most* before the adjective to make the superlative form.

modern → **the most modern**
useful → **the most useful**
beautiful → **the most beautiful**

2. When a long adjective ends in consonant + -*y*, change the -*y* to -*i* and add -*est*.

easy → eas**iest**
pretty → prett**iest**
friendly → friendl**iest**

**5** Complete each sentence with the superlative form of the adjective in parentheses.

1. (modern) The United Arab Emirates has ___the most modern___ cities in the world.

2. (expensive) The Ginza in Tokyo is one of _____ places to shop.

3. (beautiful) Central Park is _____ park in New York City.

4. (interesting) The history exhibit was _____ part of the museum.

5. (famous) The Louvre is _____ museum in the world.

6. (crowded) That's _____ street in the city.

7. (helpful) This guide book is _____.

8. (exciting) Seoul is the _____ city in South Korea.

▼ People walk by a modern building in Seoul, South Korea.

**6 SPEAK.** Work with a partner. Talk about places in your country such as cities, buildings, and museums. Use the superlative form of the words in the box and your own ideas.

| beautiful | crowded | exciting | famous | interesting | ugly |
|-----------|---------|----------|--------|-------------|------|

*Times Square is one of the most famous places in New York City.*

## 12.6 Questions with Superlatives

| Yes/No Questions | | | |
|------|---------|-------------|-----|
| *Be* | Subject | Superlative | |
| Is | that store | **the best** | place to shop? |
| Are | they | **the most difficult** | units in the book? |

| Short Answers |
|---------------|
| No, it isn't. |
| Yes, they are. |

| Questions with *Who/What* | | | |
|-------|------|-------------|-----|
| Who/What | *Be* | Superlative | |
| Who | are | **the most interesting** | students in our class? |
| What | is | **the best** | place to shop? |

| Answers |
|---------|
| Ed and Sue are. |
| The Bistro. |

| | |
|---|---|
| 1. **Remember:** The verb comes before the subject in *Yes/No* questions with *be*. | **Is** <u>this museum</u> the best one? <br> **Are** <u>you</u> the oldest person in your family? |
| 2. **Remember:** The word order in a question does not change when a question with *Who* or *What* asks about a subject. | <u>Who</u> **is** the youngest person in the class? <br> <u>What</u>**'s** the hottest place on Earth? |

**7** Use the words in parentheses to write questions with the superlative.

1. (Who / old person) _____Who is the oldest person_____ in your family?

2. (What / good place) _____ to study?

3. (this supermarket / cheap) _____ ?

4. (What / interesting museum) _____ to visit?

5. (Who / your good friend) _____ ?

6. (Which city / big) _____ in your country?

7. (you / young) _____ in your family?

8. (What / nice restaurant) _____ in this city?

**8 SPEAK.** Work with a partner. Ask and answer questions from exercise **7**.

Student A: *Who's the oldest person in your family?*

Student B: *My grandmother. She's 90.*

# PRACTICE

**9** Complete the paragraph with the superlative form of the adjectives in parentheses.

## The Most Famous Canals of the World

China's Grand Canal is among (1) ___the oldest___ (old) and one of (2) _____ (long) canals in the world, but there are interesting canals in many parts of the world. The Canal du Midi in southern France is also one of (3) _____ (early) canals. (4) _____ (important) canals today for shipping are the Suez Canal and the Panama Canal. (5) _____ (busy) canal in the world is the Kiel Canal in Germany. About 35,000 ships pass between the North Sea and the Baltic Sea through this canal every year. One of (6) _____ (new) canals in the world is the Narmada Canal in India. Some canals aren't used for shipping any more, but they are popular destinations for tourists. (7) _____ (good) way to see the canals is on a boat, of course! (8) _____ (popular) canals for cruises are in France and Great Britain.

**10** **EDIT.** Read the information. Find and correct five more errors with the superlative form of adjectives.

## The Best Place to . . .

Every year National Geographic asks some of ^the most adventurous explorers for their ideas about the best places to have exciting experiences. Here are some of their favorites.

- The better place to surf in the world is the Mentawai Islands in Indonesia.
- Most challenging place to kayak is the Yarlung Tsangpo River in the Himalayan Mountains.
- The more difficult downhill ski race is Hahnenkamm in Austria.
- One of the hardest trip is across the entire Sahara Desert in North Africa.
- The most amazing place to scuba dive is in the Galápagos Islands in Ecuador.
- The taller mountain in South America is Aconcagua in Argentina.

▶ A surfer in the Mentawai Islands, Indonesia

▲ The driest place in the world

**11** **SPEAK.**

**A** Work with a partner. Partner A, look at this page. Partner B, look at page **A7**.

**B** Ask Partner B questions to complete the chart. Then answer B's questions.

Partner A: *What is the biggest art museum in the world?*

Partner B: *What do you think?*

Partner A: *I think it's the Louvre.*

Partner B: *No, the Metropolitan Museum is the biggest. It's in New York.*

## Geography Trivia

| Big art museum? Metropolitan Museum | High waterfall? _____ | Small country? _____ |
|---|---|---|
| The largest country in the world is Russia. | Dry place? _____ | The biggest desert in the world is the Sahara. |
| The largest islands in the world are Australia and Greenland. | The smallest ocean in the world is the Arctic. | Long river? _____ |

**12** **LISTEN & SPEAK.**

CD3-41-43

**A** Listen to the conversations. What activity do the speakers want to do? Match each conversation with the correct topic. Write the letter on the line.

Conversation 1 _____          a. look at wildlife

Conversation 2 _____          b. go shopping

Conversation 3 _____          c. visit museums

CD3-41-43

**B** Listen again. Match each place with its attraction. Write the letter on the line.

1. Zurich _____          a. wildlife

2. The Galápagos Islands _____          b. a shopping street

3. Berlin _____          c. museums

**C** Complete the statements with information from the listening. Use the superlative form of the adjectives in the box.

| big | expensive | famous | good | rich | unusual |
|-----|-----------|--------|------|------|---------|

1. Berlin _has some of the best museums in Europe._

2. The Louvre in Paris _____.

3. The Hermitage Museum _____.

4. The Galápagos Islands _____.

5. Zurich _____.

6. _____ shop at these very expensive places.

**D** Compare your sentences from exercise **C** with a partner.

**E** Work with a partner. What is the best place in your area to do the activities listed?

| eat lunch | go for a walk | look at wildlife | shop for clothes |
| enjoy a beautiful view | live | ride a bicycle | shop for groceries |

*The best place to shop for clothes is . . .*

## 13 APPLY.

**A** Work with a partner. Write a "Top-ten" list for a visitor to your city. Think about restaurants, parks, stores, museums, and so on. Use the superlative form of the adjectives in the box or your own ideas. Use each adjective only once.

| amazing | famous | interesting | old |
| beautiful | good | large | popular |
| cheap | high | modern | small |
| expensive | historical | new | dangerous |

**Top-Ten List**

San Francisco, California
1. The most beautiful park is Golden Gate Park.

**B** Share your list with your classmates.

## EXPLORE

CD3-44

**1** **READ** the article about Frank Gehry. Notice the words in **bold**.

# Frank Gehry: An Unusual Architect

Modern architecture is changing the look of our cities. Frank Gehry, a Canadian architect, is making us think about architecture in new ways.

It's easy to spot[1] a Gehry building. When you see one, you immediately think, "**Whose** crazy idea was that?"

Gehry's buildings are unique.[2] Most buildings have straight lines, but not Gehry's. **His** have curved lines. Also, most buildings have soft colors such as gray, brown, or white, but not Gehry's. **His** are bright and surprising. For example, the Experience Music Project (EMP) museum in Seattle, Washington, is red, gold, and purple!

Gehry's most popular building is the Guggenheim Museum in Bilbao, Spain.

Some people love Gehry's style, but others don't like it at all. **Whose** opinion do _you_ agree with?

[1] **spot:** to find with your eyes; to see or notice
[2] **unique:** one of a kind

▲ The Guggenheim Museum in Bilbao, Spain, designed by Frank Gehry

▶ Cleveland Clinic Lou Ruvo Center for Brain Health by Frank Gehry, Las Vegas, Nevada, USA

**2 CHECK.** What makes Gehry's buildings different from other buildings? Complete the chart below with the descriptions from the box.

| bright colors | curved lines | soft colors | straight lines | surprising colors |

| Gehry's Buildings | Other Buildings |
|---|---|
| curved lines | |
| | |
| | |

**3 DISCOVER.** Complete the exercises to learn about the grammar in this lesson.

**A** Find these sentences in the article on page 391. What does *His* mean in each sentence? Choose the correct answer for each sentence.

1. <u>His</u> have curved lines.

    a. Gehry         b. Gehry's buildings         c. most buildings

2. <u>His</u> are bright and surprising.

    a. Gehry         b. most buildings         c. the colors of Gehry's buildings

**B** Discuss your answers from exercise **A** with your classmates and teacher.

# LEARN

## 12.7 Possessive Pronouns

| | Possessive Adjective | Noun |
|---|---|---|
| That is | my | |
| | your | |
| | his | |
| | her | car. |
| | our | |
| | your | |
| | their | |

| | Possessive Pronoun |
|---|---|
| That car is | mine. |
| | yours. |
| | his. |
| | hers. |
| | ours. |
| | yours. |
| | theirs. |

| | |
|---|---|
| 1. Use a possessive pronoun in place of a possessive adjective + noun. | A: Is this your phone?<br>B: It's **her phone**. = It's **hers**. |
| 2. When a possessive pronoun replaces a singular noun, use the singular form of the verb. | This is my **book**. **Hers** is on the desk.<br>These are my **keys**. **His** are on the desk. |
| 3. Do not put a noun after a possessive pronoun. | ✓ The book is **mine**.<br>✗ That is mine book. |

### REAL ENGLISH

Possessive pronouns are often used to make comparisons.

*Edgar's house is bigger than **mine**.*
*My car is older than **yours**.*

---

**4** Read the sentences. Circle the possessive pronouns. Then draw an arrow back to the noun that each possessive pronoun replaces.

1. Their buildings are traditional, but (his) are not.

2. His colors are bright and surprising, but theirs are different.

3. Our architecture is very different from theirs.

4. San Francisco is my favorite city. What's yours?

5. His apartment is bigger than hers.

6. That notebook isn't his. He took my notebook by mistake.

7. Is that my phone or yours?

8. Please call me on John's phone. I left mine at home. Here's his number.

**5**  Change the <u>underlined</u> words in each sentence to a possessive pronoun.

1. This isn't my house. It's <u>my parents' house</u>. _____*theirs*_____

2. I like this apartment. It's more convenient than <u>my apartment</u>. _____

3. My city is modern. <u>Your city</u> is very old. _____

4. I told her about my country, and she told me about <u>her country</u>. _____

5. I like this neighborhood better than <u>their neighborhood</u>. _____

6. My husband's favorite restaurant is Vito's. <u>My favorite restaurant</u> is
   Café India. _____

7. Takeshi's class is in Room 203. <u>Our class</u> is in Room 205. _____

8. Here's my address. What's <u>your address</u>? _____

## 12.8  *Wh-* Questions with *Whose*

| Questions with *Whose* | | | Answers |
| --- | --- | --- | --- |
| *Whose* | Noun | | |
| | car | did you take? | We took Sara's car. |
| Whose | idea | was it? | It was mine. |
| | book | is this? | It's Brent's. |

| | |
| --- | --- |
| 1. We often use *Whose* + noun for questions about possession. | A: **Whose computer** is this? <br> B: It's Gemma's. |
| 2. It is not necessary to state the noun when it is understood by both the speaker and the listener. | A: Look at that beautiful car in the parking lot. <br> B: **Whose** is it? <br><br> A: **Whose** are these? <br> B: They're mine. |
| 3. **Be careful!** *Whose* and *Who's* (*Who is*), sound the same. | A: **Whose** apartment is best for the party? <br> B: Tom's is. <br><br> A: **Who's** your favorite classmate? <br> B: Tom is. |
| 4. Be careful about the word order in questions with *Whose* + noun. | Question about a Subject: <br> A: <u>Whose car</u> **goes** faster? <br> B: Carl's does. <br><br> Question about an Object: <br> A: Whose car **did** <u>you</u> **take**? <br> B: We took Sally's. |

**6** Complete each question with *Whose* or *Who's*.

1. _____Whose_____ apartment is bigger, yours or mine?

2. _____ city is warmer in January, yours or Kareem's?

3. _____ your teacher?

4. _____ class are you in?

5. _____ backpack is this?

6. _____ the student from Australia?

7. _____ next?

8. _____ sitting behind Tara?

9. _____ book is this?

10. _____ jacket is on the chair?

**7** Read each statement. Make a question about the <u>underlined</u> words.

1. It was <u>Helen's</u> idea. _____Whose idea was it?_____

2. Those are <u>Ali's</u> glasses. _____

3. It's <u>Linda's</u> notebook. _____

4. <u>My</u> apartment is closer than Jane's. _____

5. It's <u>Greg's</u> turn. _____

6. That's <u>Susan's</u> pen. _____

7. That's <u>my</u> phone. _____

8. <u>Julie's</u> car is behind ours. _____

9. We used <u>John's</u> computer. _____

10. I borrowed <u>David's</u> book. _____

**8** **SPEAK.** Work with a partner. Point to things in the room. Ask and answer questions with *Whose*.

Student A: *Whose is this?*

Student B: *It's Hiro's.* OR *It's mine.*

# PRACTICE

**9**  Circle the correct words to complete the conversation.

**Felix:**  (1)(**Our**) / **Ours** class is ending soon. Let's have a party.

**Alicia:**  Good idea, but (2) **who's** / **whose** apartment is big enough for (3) **our** / **ours** whole class? (4) **My** / **Mine** isn't. It's too small. How about (5) **your** / **yours** ? Is it big enough? You live with (6) **your** / **yours** cousin, right?

**Felix:**  Yes, but (7) **our** / **ours** place isn't big enough either. There isn't even enough space for (8) **our** / **ours** furniture!

**Alicia:**  How about Camila's apartment? She lives with her sister. I think (9) **their** / **theirs** place is pretty big.

**Felix:**  Yeah, it's big enough, but (10) **their** / **theirs** apartment isn't very close.

**Alicia:**  True. How about Lenny's? His apartment is closer.

**Felix:**  Oh, good idea!

**Alicia:**  Do you want to ask him?

**Felix:**  Well, he's really more (11) **your** / **yours** friend, not (12) **my** / **mine**. I don't know him very well.

**Alicia:**  Yeah, but (13) **who's** / **whose** idea was this party anyway, huh?

**Felix:**  OK, OK. I'll ask him.

**10**  **EDIT.** Read the conversation. Find and correct five more errors with possessive pronouns and questions with *Whose*.

**Meg:**  I just finished the design for our architecture class a few minutes ago. Did you finish ~~your~~ yours yet?

**Toshi:**  Yes, I finished mine last night. Juan and Tony finished their last week. They're always ahead of everyone else.

**Meg:**  Did they show you theirs?

**Toshi:**  No, they didn't want to show it to me because my wasn't finished yet.

**Meg:**  I'm sure their is good. Their designs are always really good. Who's design is that over there?

**Toshi:**  Oh, that's Ana's.

**Meg:**  Whose Ana?

**Toshi:**  She's Diana's roommate. Her designs are always very unusual.

## 11 LISTEN & SPEAK.

CD3-45

**A** Look at the photos. Then listen to the description of each building. Match the buildings to their architects. Write the letter on the line.

_____ 1. Zaha Hadid

_____ 2. Jacques Herzog and Pierre de Meuron

_____ 3. Frank Gehry

**B** Complete the paragraph about the buildings in exercise **A**. Use *his, her, hers, their,* and *theirs.*

### Three Different Designs

These three buildings, by different architects, are great examples of modern architecture. (1) _____ designs are all unusual. Gehry's building is different from the others because he uses bright colors and different shapes. Hadid's building has a traditional shape, and some people say (2) _____ design is easier to look at than Gehry's. (3) _____ has smooth lines and curves, while (4) _____ doesn't. Herzog and de Meuron's building is famous for its unique shape. Unlike Gehry's and Hadid's buildings, (5) _____ has no straight lines, and the outside of (6) _____ building has white letters all over it.

**C** Take a survey. Ask five classmates the questions in the chart and take notes on their answers. Use *his, hers,* or *theirs* in your questions and answers.

| Classmate's Name | Whose building do you like? | Whose building don't you like? |
|---|---|---|
|  |  |  |
|  |  |  |
|  |  |  |
|  |  |  |
|  |  |  |

Student A: *Whose building do you like?*

Student B: *Zaha Hadid's building is my favorite. I like hers because . . .*

**D** Look at your notes from exercise **C**. Which building was the most popular? Report to the class.

## 12 APPLY.

**A** Art museums are often in very unusual buildings. In your notebook, draw a design for a modern art museum. Think about these questions when you draw your design.

Is the design modern or traditional?       Are the windows large or small?

Does it have curved or straight lines?       Are the colors bright or soft?

**B** Work in a group. Discuss and compare your designs from exercise **A**. Decide on the best one. Use *mine, yours, his, hers,* or *theirs* in your discussion.

Student A: *Let's look at yours first.*

Student B: *Yours is good. It's better than mine, but I really like Helen's.*

Student C: *Yes, I like hers, too.*

**C** In your notebook, write five sentences about the designs from exercise **B**. Compare your design with your classmates' designs.

My design is more traditional than Helen's.

Hers is more modern. It's very unusual.

Mine has . . .

Charts
12.1–12.6

**1  READ, WRITE & SPEAK.**

**A** Read the information in the chart. Then complete each sentence with the comparative or superlative form of the adjective in parentheses.

| The Largest Pyramids in Egypt | | | |
|---|---|---|---|
| | The Red Pyramid | The Great Pyramid | The Pyramid of Khafre |
| Name of Pharaoh | Sneferu | Khufu | Khafre |
| Original height | 341 feet | 480.6 feet | 471 feet |
| Size | 59.7 million cubic feet | 91.1 million cubic feet | 78 million cubic feet |
| Year built | around 2581 B.C. | around 2560 B.C. | around 2532 B.C. |

# The Pyramids

One of (1) ___the most famous___ (famous) places in the world is in Egypt. It's the site of the Pyramids of Giza. Many people go there to see the Great Pyramid. The Great Pyramid is, of course, (2) _____ (large) pyramid in Egypt. It is also (3) _____ (tall). Khufu's son, Khafre, also built a pyramid in Giza. It is (4) _____ (small) than the Great Pyramid, but it looks (5) _____ (tall) because it's on a hill.

The (6) _____ (popular) pyramids in Egypt are the Pyramids of Giza, but many people also visit the Red Pyramid, the pyramid for Khufu's father, in Dahshur. Some people say the Red Pyramid is (7) _____ (good) than the Great Pyramid because it's a quiet place to visit. It's (8) _____ (far) from Cairo, so there aren't a lot of tourists there.

The Red Pyramid is (9) _____ (old) true pyramid in the world. It is also (10) _____ (small) of all of the Egyptian pyramids. It is definitely an interesting pyramid to visit.

**B** Work with a partner. Ask and answer five questions about the pyramids. Use *Yes/No* questions and *Wh-* questions with *Which* and *Whose*. Use the information in the chart in exercise **A**.

Student A: *Whose pyramid was the largest?*

Student B: *Khufu's. Whose pyramid was the smallest?*

**2 EDIT.** Read the information about the Anasazi cliff dwellings. Find and correct five more errors with the comparative and superlative forms of adjectives.

## The Anasazi Cliff Dwellings

Mesa Verde National Park in Colorado has <sub>the</sub> most interesting ruins in the United States. They are ancient cliff dwellings—homes in cliffs. They belonged to the Anasazi people. The Anasazi were Native Americans. They were some of the earlyest people in North America. They lived in the Mesa Verde area from 600 to 1300. The Mesa Verde National Park has 600 cliff dwellings. There were two types of rooms in the dwellings. *Kivas*, or round rooms, were for families, so they were largest than the other kind of room.

▲ Ruins of the Anasazi Cliff Palace, Mesa Verde National Park, Colorado

Next to Mesa Verde National Park is the Ute Mountain Tribal Park. Mesa Verde is crowded than Ute Park, so Ute Park is sometimes a best park to visit. It also has beautiful cliff dwellings. It's one of the most interesting place to visit in North America.

Charts
12.1–12.2,
12.5–12.6

**3 LISTEN, WRITE & SPEAK.**

**A** Listen to the conversation. Then choose the correct answer for each question.

CD3-46

1. What are they discussing?  a. hotels near Mesa Verde  b. tours of Mesa Verde

2. Do they make a final decision?  a. Yes.  b. No.

CD3-46

**B** Listen again. Complete the chart with information about the ways to visit Mesa Verde. Write **NI** if no information is given.

| Type | Length | Cost | Other Information |
|---|---|---|---|
| Bus tour | 4 hours | | |
| Van tour | | | |
| Jeep tour | | | |
| Car rental | | | |

**C** Write sentences about the ways to visit Mesa Verde. Use comparatives and superlatives of the adjectives in parentheses.

1. (long)

    The bus tour is longer than the jeep ride.

    The van tour is the longest.

2. (cheap)

    _____

    _____

3. (comfortable)

    _____

    _____

4. (fun)

    _____

    _____

5. (educational)

    _____

    _____

6. (expensive)

    _____

    _____

**D** Work with a partner. Ask and answer questions about the ways to visit Mesa Verde.

Student A: *Which tour is the longest?*     Student B: *The van tour.*

**4 APPLY.** Work with a partner. Discuss these questions.

1. From exercise **3**, what do you think is the best way to see Mesa Verde? Why?

    *The best way to see Mesa Verde is by jeep because. . . . The bus tour is more . . . , but it's . . .*

2. What's the most famous historical site in your area? What are some ways people can visit it (bus tour, walking tour, and so on)? What is the best way to visit it? Why?

    *_____ is the most famous site in _____. You can visit it on a bus tour or on a walking tour. The best way to visit it is a bus tour because . . .*

## 1  READ & NOTICE THE GRAMMAR.

**A**  Read the comparison. What two places does the writer compare? Discuss with a partner.

### Two Beaches

I like to go to two different beaches in Hawaii, Waimea and Waikiki. Waimea is my favorite. It is <u>farther</u> from my home <u>than</u> Waikiki is, but it is one of the most beautiful beaches on the whole island.

Sometimes the waves in Waimea are very big. Then I go to Waikiki because it's a safer place to swim. The waves at Waikiki are always smaller than the waves at Waimea. Waikiki Beach is more crowded than Waimea, but it is closer to my home, so it's more convenient. I'm very lucky to live in Hawaii.

▲ Waimea Beach, Oahu, Hawaii, USA

**B**  Read the comparison in exercise **A** again. Underline the comparative and superlative adjectives. Then work with a partner and compare answers.

**C**  Complete the chart with information from the comparison in exercise **A**. What are the differences between Waikiki and Waimea?

| Two Beaches | |
|---|---|
| Waimea | Waikiki |
| farther from home | |

### GRAMMAR FOCUS

In the comparison in exercise **A**, the writer uses comparative and superlative adjectives to describe how the beaches are different from each other and from other beaches.

**Remember:** Use comparative adjectives to compare two things. Use superlative adjectives to compare three or more things.

*It is **farther** from my home **than** Waikiki is, but it is **one of the most beautiful beaches** on the whole island.*

# Write a Comparison between Two Places

**2 BEFORE YOU WRITE.** Choose two places to compare. How are these places different from each other? Complete the chart with the differences between the two places. Use the chart from exercise **1C** as a model.

| Two Places | |
| --- | --- |
| _____ (place 1) | _____ (place 2) |
| | |

**3 WRITE** a comparison between two places. Use the information from your chart in exercise **2** and the paragraph in exercise **1A** to help you.

> **WRITING FOCUS**    Pronouns
>
> Writers use pronouns to refer to something a second time and not repeat the same noun. This helps make their sentences and paragraphs more interesting and helps make them sound more natural.
>
> With no pronouns:
>
> _I go to two different beaches in Hawaii, Waikiki, and Waimea. Waimea is my favorite. Waimea is farther from my home than Waikiki, but Waimea is one of the most beautiful beaches on the whole island._
>
> With pronouns:
>
> _I go to two different breaches in Hawaii, Waikiki and Waimea. Waimea is my favorite. **It** is farther from my home than Waikiki, but **it** is one of the most beautiful beaches on the whole island._

**4 SELF ASSESS.** Read your comparison. Underline the comparative and superlative adjectives. Then use the checklist to assess your work.

- [ ] I used the comparative adjectives correctly. [12.1–12.3]
- [ ] I used the superlative adjectives correctly. [12.4–12.6]
- [ ] I used a plural noun after _one of the_ (adjective) + _-est_. [REAL ENGLISH]
- [ ] When I referred to a noun for the second time, I used a pronoun. [WRITING FOCUS]

# UNIT 13 Customs and Traditions

# Modals: Part 2

▼ Lanterns float into the night sky during the Yee Peng Festival in Chiang Mai, Thailand.

# EXPLORE

**1 READ** the e-mails about advice for a trip to Japan. Notice the words in **bold**.

Tokyo, Japan

**Subject: A Business Trip to Tokyo**

Hi Taka,

I'm going to Tokyo next week to meet with some clients.[1] Do you have any advice for me? This is my first trip to Japan. **Should I take** anything special with me? What's your schedule like this week? I'd like to take you to lunch. Are you free on Thursday?

Peter

[1] **client:** a customer

---

Hi Peter,

Thursday isn't good for me. How about Friday? Here's some advice in the meantime[2].

You **should take** some small gifts for your clients. I usually buy something from a gift shop. They don't have to be expensive.

Don't forget your business cards! In Japan, people exchange[3] business cards when they first meet, so be prepared. Keep them in your jacket. You **shouldn't keep** them in your wallet or in the pocket of your pants. When you present your card, you **should hold** it with both hands. When you get business cards from people at a meeting, you **should place** each card carefully on the table in front of you when you sit down. More advice at lunch.

Best,
Taka

[2] **in the meantime:** in the period between two events
[3] **exchange:** give and take

▼ Sunset, Tokyo, Japan

▲ Business people bow to each other at the Tokyo Stock Exchange.

**2 CHECK.** Look at each action in the chart. Does Taka think it is a good idea or a bad idea? Put a check (✓) in the correct column.

|    |                                                                     | Good idea | Bad idea |
|----|---------------------------------------------------------------------|-----------|----------|
| 1. | Take small gifts for clients.                                       | ✓         |          |
| 2. | Forget your business cards.                                         |           |          |
| 3. | Keep business cards in the pocket of your pants.                    |           |          |
| 4. | Hold your business card with both hands.                            |           |          |
| 5. | Put business cards in front of you on the table at a meeting.       |           |          |

**3 DISCOVER.** Complete the exercises to learn about the grammar in this lesson.

**A** Find these sentences in the e-mails from exercise **1**. Write the missing words.

1. You _____*should take*_____ some small gifts for your clients.

2. You _____ them in your wallet or in the pocket of your pants.

3. When you present your card, you _____ it with both hands.

4. When you get business cards from people at a meeting, you _____ each card carefully on the table in front of you when you sit down.

**B** Look at your answers from exercise **A**. What do these words tell us? Choose the correct words to complete each statement. Then discuss your answer with your classmates and teacher.

1. We use *should* and *shouldn't* to _____.

   a. discuss a problem

   b. give advice

2. The verb after *should* _____.

   a. changes form

   b. is the base form of the verb

# LEARN

## 13.1 *Should* for Advisability: Statements

| Affirmative Statements | | |
|---|---|---|
| Subject | *Should* | Base Form of Verb |
| I<br>You<br>He<br>She<br>It<br>We<br>You<br>They | should | wait. |

| Negative Statements | | |
|---|---|---|
| Subject | *Shouldn't* | Base Form of Verb |
| I<br>You<br>He<br>She<br>It<br>We<br>You<br>They | shouldn't<br>should not | wait. |

| | |
|---|---|
| 1. Use *should* and *shouldn't* to give advice. | You **should study** for the test.<br>You **shouldn't go** to a party the night before a test. |
| 2. *Should* is a modal. Use the base form of the verb after *should* and *shouldn't*. | ✓ He **should stay** home.<br>✗ He should <u>to</u> stay home. |

**4** Use *should* or *shouldn't* and the verb in parentheses to complete each sentence.

1. (buy) I _____should buy_____ a small gift.

2. (have) He _____ his business cards ready.

3. (not keep) You _____ your cards in your pants pocket.

4. (bring) Everyone _____ a lot of business cards.

5. (not be) We _____ late for the meeting.

6. (read) We _____ more about the history of the city.

7. (ask) He _____ his Japanese friends for advice.

8. (learn) She _____ some Japanese words.

**5** **WRITE & SPEAK.** Write three sentences about yourself. Use *should* or *shouldn't* and the verbs from the box or your own ideas. Then share your sentences with a partner.

| | | | | |
|---|---|---|---|---|
| do | eat | go to bed | sleep | study |
| drink | exercise | practice | speak | walk |

Student A: *I shouldn't speak Spanish in class.*

Student B: *I should exercise every day.*

## 13.2 *Should* for Advisability: Questions

| Yes/No Questions | | |
|---|---|---|
| *Should* | Subject | Base Form of Verb |
| Should | she we | leave? |

| Short Answers | | |
|---|---|---|
| | Subject | *Should/ Shouldn't* |
| Yes, | she | should. |
| No, | we | shouldn't. |

| Wh- Questions | | | | |
|---|---|---|---|---|
| Wh- Word | *Should* | Subject | Base Form of Verb | |
| What | | I | bring? | |
| Where | | she | stay? | |
| When | should | he | leave? | |
| Why | | you | arrive | early? |
| Who | | we | ask? | |
| How | | they | get | there? |

| Answers |
|---|
| Some small gifts. |
| At the Grand Hotel. |
| At 3:00. |
| Because it's polite. |
| Paola. |
| By subway. |

*Should* comes before the subject in *Yes/No* questions and in most information questions. | Should <u>she</u> try again?<br>What should <u>we</u> tell her?

**6** Use the words in parentheses to make *Yes/No* questions and *Wh-* questions with *should*.

1. A: _____Should I bring_____ (I / bring) a gift?  B: Yes, you should.

2. A: _____ (we / shake / hands)?  B: Yes, we should.

3. A: _____ (When / I / be) there?  B: At around 10:30.

4. A: _____ (What / he / wear)?  B: A suit.

5. A: _____ (they / call) the office?  B: Yes, they should.

6. A: _____ (Who / she / ask)?  B: Her manager.

7. A: _____ (How / we / get) there?  B: By subway.

8. A: _____ (Where / we / meet)?  B: In the coffee shop.

9. A: _____ (she / be) on time?  B: Yes, she should.

10. A: _____ (Why / we / arrive) early?  B: It's the custom.

# PRACTICE

CD4-3

**7** Complete the statements and questions in the conversation. Use *should* or *shouldn't* and the words in parentheses. Then listen and check your answers.

**Sidney:** Do you know much about German culture? I'm going to Berlin on a business trip next month.

**Darcy:** I know one thing. (1) _____You shouldn't be_____ (you / not / be) late! Germans are very punctual.

**Sidney:** That's right. (2) _____ (I / be) on time for my meetings. (3) _____ (I / take) gifts with me?

**Darcy:** That's a good question. I don't know. (4) _____ (You / ask) Greta. She's from Germany.

**Sidney:** You're right! In fact, if I'm not mistaken, I think she's from Berlin! What else (5) _____ (I / ask) her?

**Darcy:** Well, (6) _____ (you / wear) formal clothes, or is it OK to dress informally?

**Sidney:** Good idea. Also, (7) _____ (I / call) people by their first names? I know in some countries it's better to use Mr. and Ms.

**Darcey:** Right. That's important. (8) _____ (You / look for) information about German business customs online. You can probably find a lot of helpful information there.

**Sidney:** That's true. Thanks. Maybe (9) _____ (I / buy) a guidebook, too. Well, (10) _____ (we / hurry). It's time for our meeting with the director.

▼ Potsdamer Platz, the financial district of Berlin, Germany

## 8 READ, WRITE & SPEAK.

**A** Read each situation. Then put the words in the correct order to make questions.

### Situation 1

Chris Mackenzie owns a company in Canada. She sells her products in many other countries. She got an e-mail from a new international client. The e-mail began, "Dear Mr. Mackenzie."

1. (explain / Should / the mistake / she)  <u>Should she explain the mistake?</u>

### Situation 2

Chris usually shakes hands at business meetings. She knows this is not common in her client's country.

2. (she / greet / How / them / should) _____

### Situation 3

Chris and her assistant Tim Hubbard arrive at the meeting. The client offers them coffee.

3. (Should / say / "No, thank you"/ they) _____

4. (should / When / they / talk about / business) _____

### Situation 4

Something surprises Chris. When she asks her client questions, he answers Tim. When her client asks questions, he asks Tim, not Chris.

5. (she / Should / say something) _____

**B** Work with a partner. Discuss the questions from exercise **A**.

Student A: *Should she explain the mistake?*        Student B: *Yes, she should.*

## 9 LISTEN & WRITE.

**A** Read the chart. Then listen to advice about doing business in South Africa, Thailand, and the United States. Where is each piece of advice important? Check (✓) the correct column(s).

| | Activities | South Africa | Thailand | USA |
|---|---|---|---|---|
| 1. | Arrive exactly on time or early for a meeting. | | | ✓ |
| 2. | Take time to talk about topics such as health or family before you "talk business." | | | |
| 3. | Don't put someone's business card in your pocket. | | | |
| 4. | Don't use your left hand to give something. | | | |
| 5. | Don't touch someone's head or pass anything above someone's head. | | | |
| 6. | Don't show the bottom of your foot. | | | |

**B** Make sentences about the information from the chart in exercise **A**. Use *should* or *shouldn't*.

1. In the United States, <u>you should be exactly on time or early for a meeting</u>.

2. In South Africa, _____.

3. In South Africa, _____.

4. In Thailand, _____.

5. In Thailand, _____.

6. In Thailand, _____.

## 10 APPLY.

**A** What are some important business customs in your country? Think of customs for greetings, introductions, conversations, meetings, or gifts. Write sentences with *should* or *shouldn't*.

1. <u>In my country, you shouldn't ask people about their salary.</u>

2. _____

3. _____

4. _____

5. _____

**B** Work in a group. Share your sentences from exercise **A**. Are any of your customs similar?

▲ Morning rush hour at Grand Central Station, New York City, USA

# EXPLORE

CD4-5

**1   READ** the blog about some unusual laws. Notice the words in **bold**.

## You can't do that here!
### Strange Laws from around the World          Tuesday, August 8

When a government makes a law, we usually understand the reason. For example, in Greece, women **can't wear** high heels[1] at historic sites because high heels may damage the ancient steps. That makes sense, but **why can't** women **wear** high heels in the beach town of Carmel, California, in the United States? On the Isle of Capri in Italy, you **can wear** sandals with high heels, low heels, and anything in between, but you **can't wear** *noisy* sandals! What's the reason for that?

Here are some other unusual laws from around the world.

- In Florida, USA, single women **cannot parachute** on Sundays.
- In Victoria, Australia, you **can't change** a light bulb. Only an electrician **can do** that.
- In Vermont, USA, women **can have** false[2] teeth, but they **have to** get permission in writing from their husbands.
- In Moscow, Russia, you **can't drive** a dirty car.
- In Singapore, you **can't sell** gum.
- In France, you **can't name** a pig Napoleon.

▼ Female skydiver

**3 COMMENTS**

POSTED BY MAC

Funny! **Do** people **have to follow** these laws now?
April 27, 4:56 P.M.

POSTED BY BRAD

This isn't true. People **can change** their own light bulbs in Australia. They **don't have to call** an electrician anymore. That's crazy!
April 28, 12:05 A.M.

POSTED BY RALPH

I heard something strange about England. You **have to be** careful when you put a stamp with a king or queen on a letter. The stamp **can't be** upside down. Is this really a law?
April 28, 12:30 A.M.

[1] **high heels:** a kind of shoes for women that make them taller
[2] **false:** not real

**2 CHECK.** Complete each law in the left-hand column with the correct phrase on the right. Write the letter on the line.

1. Single women can't parachute on Sundays _____.

   a. in Australia

2. Only an electrician can change a light bulb _____.

   b. in Florida

3. You can't drive a dirty car _____.

   c. in France

4. You can't name a pig Napoleon _____.

   d. in Russia

5. Women can't have false teeth without permission from their husbands _____.

   e. in Vermont

**3 DISCOVER.** Complete the exercises to learn about the grammar in this lesson.

**A** Find these sentences in the blog in exercise **1** on page 413. Write the correct words.

1. On the Isle of Capri in Italy, you _____ *can wear* _____ sandals with high heels, low heels, and anything in between, but you _____ *noisy* sandals.

2. In Florida, USA, single women _____ on Sundays.

3. In Moscow, Russia, you _____ a dirty car.

**B** Look at your answers from exercise **A**. Then choose the correct answer to complete the statement. Discuss your answer with your classmates and teacher.

We use *can, can't,* and *cannot* to talk about _____.

a. difficult situations        b. advice        c. rules and laws

▼ A shoemaker's workshop, Capri, Italy

# LEARN

## 13.3 *Can/May* for Permission

### Affirmative Statements

| Subject | *Can* | Base Form of Verb | |
|---|---|---|---|
| I<br>She<br>They | can | park | there. |

### Negative Statements

| Subject | *Can't* | Base Form of Verb | |
|---|---|---|---|
| I<br>She<br>They | can't<br>cannot | park | there. |

### Yes/No Questions

| *Can/May* | Subject | Base Form of Verb | |
|---|---|---|---|
| Can | I<br>we | leave | early today? |
| May | | | |

### Short Answers

| |
|---|
| Sure. |
| Yes, of course. |
| Sorry, not today. |

### Wh- Questions

| Wh-Word | Can/Can't | Subject | Base Form of Verb | |
|---|---|---|---|---|
| When | can | we | begin | the test? |
| Where | can | I | use | my phone? |
| Why | can't | he | drive? | |

### Answers

| |
|---|
| In a few minutes. |
| Outside or in the hallway. |
| Because he's too young. |

| | |
|---|---|
| 1. Use *can* and *can't* to talk about permission. Use *can* to request or give permission. Use *can't* to refuse a request for permission. | They **can** enter now. We're ready.<br>You **can't** come in now. I'm sorry. |
| 2. **Remember:** *Can, can't,* and *may* are modals. Use the base form of the verb with *can, can't,* and *may*. | You **can** <u>leave</u> early today.<br>We **can't** <u>use</u> our phones in class.<br>**May** I <u>sit</u> here? |
| 3. **Remember:** *Can, can't,* and *may* come before the subject in questions. | **May** I have some tea?<br>Where **can** I park? |
| 4. Use *may* to ask for permission. *May* is more formal than *can. May* is most often used with *I* and *we*. | **May I** have a cookie?<br>**May we** take photos in the museum? |
| 5. Use short answers to agree to requests for permission. | A: **Can** I take this chair?<br>B: Sure. / Of course. |
| 6. Use *Sorry* or *I'm sorry, . . .* (and give a reason) to refuse requests for permission. | A: **Can** I borrow your laptop tonight?<br>B: I'm sorry, it's not working. |

> **REAL ENGLISH**
>
> *Could* is also used to ask for permission. It is more polite than *can,* but not quite as formal as *may.* We do not use *could* in the answer.
>
> A: **Could** *I leave early today?*
> B: *Sure. / OK. / Yes, you can leave right after the test.*

**4** Complete the statements. Use *can* or *can't* and the words in parentheses.

1. <u>You can't drive</u> (You / not drive) a dirty car in Russia.

2. In Australia, _____ (people / change) their own light bulbs. They don't need to call an electrician.

3. In the United States, _____ (people / vote) when they are 18 years old.

4. _____ (You / not travel) to many countries without a passport.

5. In France, _____ (people / bring) their dogs to restaurants.

6. _____ (You / not park) here. The sign says, "No Parking."

7. _____ (You / not take) photos in the museum.

8. _____ (We / drink coffee) in class. Our teacher says it's OK.

**5** Complete each question or request. Use *can* or *may* and the words in parentheses.

1. A: <u>May I sit</u> (I / sit) here?
   B: Yes, of course you can.

2. A: _____ (my brother / come), too?
   B: Sure, he's welcome to join us.

3. A: _____ (I / have) a piece of cake?
   B: No, sorry. It's for the party.

4. A: _____ (I / bring) a friend to the party?
   B: Of course.

5. A: _____ (When / we / eat) the cookies?
   B: After dinner.

6. A: _____ (I / take) one of these magazines?
   B: Sure. They're free.

7. A: _____ (Where / we / park)?
   B: Across the street.

8. A: _____ (Why / we / not go) to that restaurant?
   B: Because we're wearing shorts. It's a very formal restaurant.

## 13.4 *Have To* for Necessity: Statements

| Affirmative | | | | Negative | | |
|---|---|---|---|---|---|---|
| Subject | *Has To/ Have To* | Base Form of Verb | | Subject | *Doesn't Have To/ Don't Have To* | Base Form of Verb |
| He She It | has to | stay. | | He She It | doesn't have to | stay. |
| I You We You They | have to | | | I You We You They | don't have to | |

| | |
|---|---|
| 1. To say that something is necessary, use *has to* or *have to*. *Have to* and *need to* mean the same thing. | I **have to** go. She **has to** work today. |
| 2. *Have to* is a modal. Use the base form of the verb after *has/have to* and *doesn't/don't have to*. | We **have to leave** at six-thirty. She **doesn't have to go**. |
| 3. To say that something is not necessary, use *doesn't have to* or *don't have to*. | I **don't have to** go. He **doesn't have to** pay. |
| 4. *Had to* and *didn't have to* are the past forms of *have to*. | She **had to** leave early. We **didn't have to** work yesterday. |
| 5. **Be careful!** *Have to* and *have* do not mean the same thing. | I **have to** get a job. (= It is necessary to get a job.) I **have** a job. (= I work.) |

**6** Complete each sentence with the affirmative or negative of *have to*.

1. We're late! We _____have to hurry_____ (hurry).

2. I can't talk right now. I _____ (catch) the bus.

3. I _____ (work) late tonight. My boss needs this report tomorrow.

4. This is important. He _____ (come) with us.

5. The concert is free. We _____ (not pay).

6. That restaurant is never crowded. We _____ (not make) a reservation.

7. The test is tomorrow. We _____ (study).

8. I don't want to stay up late tonight. I _____ (get up) early tomorrow.

**7** **WRITE & SPEAK.** List some things that you *have to do* or *don't have to do* today. Then share your sentences with a partner.

Student A: *I have to go to the doctor.*          Student B: *I don't have to cook dinner tonight.*

## 13.5 *Have To* for Necessity: Questions

| Yes/No Questions | | | |
|---|---|---|---|
| Do/Does | Subject | *Have To* | Base Form of Verb |
| Do | you | have to | go? |
| Does | she | | |

| Short Answers | | |
|---|---|---|
| | Subject | Do/Don't Does/Doesn't |
| Yes, | I | do. |
| No, | she | doesn't. |

| Wh- Questions | | | | |
|---|---|---|---|---|
| Wh-Word | Do/Does | Subject | *Have To* | Base Form of Verb |
| When | do | you | have to | leave? |
| What | | we | | write? |
| Where | | they | | go? |
| Who | does | he | | call? |
| Why | | she | | study? |

| Answers |
|---|
| Soon. |
| A short paragraph. |
| To the post office. |
| His manager. |
| She has a test tomorrow. |

| | |
|---|---|
| Use the auxiliary* verb *do* or *does* before the subject in questions with *have to*. | **Do** <u>you</u> **have to** work this weekend?<br>**When does** <u>he</u> **have to** leave?<br><br>✓ **What** do you **have to** buy?<br>✗ What <u>have you</u> to buy? |

\* Auxiliary verbs are sometimes called helping verbs. *Do, be,* and modals are auxiliary verbs.

**8** Look at each statement. Write a question about the <u>underlined</u> information.

1. He has to wear a suit <u>because he has a meeting</u>. *Why does he have to wear a suit?*

2. Nasir has to leave <u>at 3:00</u>. _____

3. <u>Yes</u>, you have to ask your manager. _____

4. She has to go <u>to Hong Kong</u> next week. _____

5. <u>No</u>, I don't have to study tonight. _____

6. <u>Yes</u>, we have to bring our books to class. _____

7. We have to bring <u>our student IDs</u> to the exam. _____

8. I have to call <u>Professor Clark</u> after class. _____

9. <u>No</u>, Lily doesn't have to give her presentation today. _____

10. Rosa <u>has to give her presentation</u> tomorrow. _____

**9 SPEAK.** Work with a partner. Ask and answer questions about things you have to do. Ask two *Yes/No* questions and two *Wh-* questions.

Student A: *Do we have to do homework tonight?*

Student B: *No, we don't.*

Student A: *What do you have to do after class?*

Student B: *I have to go to the grocery store.*

## PRACTICE

CD4-6

**10** Complete the article with the correct forms of *can* and *have to*. Then listen and check your answers.

# Wedding Customs around the World

Customs for marriage are different around the world. For example, in some countries, arranged marriages are common. In an arranged marriage, young people (1) _____*can't*_____ choose their own husbands or wives. They (2) _____ marry the person their family chooses. In other societies, young people (3) _____ get their parents' approval before they marry. They (4) _____ make their own decisions. What is the custom in your country? (5) _____ you choose your husband or wife, or are arranged marriages common?

Wedding ceremonies are also different around the world. For example, in China, couples (6) _____ do research to decide on a lucky day for their wedding. A wedding (7) _____ begin on the half hour because the hands on the clock are moving up. The bride has a choice for the color of her dress; she (8) _____ wear red, but red is a lucky color for weddings. In some countries such as Panama, the groom (9) _____ give the bride 13 coins. In Sweden, the bride (10) _____ put a gold coin from her mother in one shoe and a silver coin from her father in the other shoe.

◀ A bride and groom pose for a wedding photo, Shanghai, China.

## 11 EDIT, WRITE & SPEAK.

**A** Find and correct five more errors with *can* and *have to*.

Dear Wedding Advisor,

    Can my bride make all the decisions about our wedding, or does she ~~has~~ <sup>have</sup> to think about my family's ideas, too? My fiancée, Sally, wants to get married on a beach in Hawaii. My mother is very unhappy about this. She says: "You can't to get married on a beach! The wedding can't be in Hawaii. You has to get married close to home. Sally haves to think about our family, too." Sally disagrees. She says: "A wedding can be anywhere. It hasn't to be indoors. It's my wedding, so I should to decide. My opinion should be the most important."

    Please help! Who is right, my fiancée or my mother?

Jeff

**B** Complete the chart with Jeff's mother's opinions and Sally's opinions from exercise **A**.

| Jeff's Mother's Opinions | Sally's Opinions |
| --- | --- |
| A wedding can't be on a beach. | A wedding can be anywhere. |

**C** Work with a partner. Discuss these questions.

1. What is your opinion?
2. What should Jeff do?

## 12 LISTEN & SPEAK.

**A** Listen to the information about Indian weddings. Match each word with the correct definition. Write the letter on the line.

1. mehndi _____
2. henna _____
3. sari _____
4. garlands _____

a. strings of flowers

b. an event where women put henna designs on their skin

c. traditional Indian clothing for women

d. dye that colors the skin

▲ A bride and groom eat traditional sweets at their wedding, Gujurat, India.

CD4-7

**B** Listen again. Then complete the sentences. Use *have to* or *don't have to* and words from the box.

| do | exchange | put | ~~wait~~ | walk | wear |
|----|----------|-----|----------|------|------|

1. You can't wash henna off your skin. You _____ have to wait _____ for it to wear off.

2. A new bride _____ housework until the henna wears off.

3. A bride _____ red, but most brides do wear red or red and white.

4. The bride and groom _____ garlands of flowers.

5. The groom _____ a red mark on the bride's forehead.

6. The bride and groom _____ around the fire.

## 13 APPLY.

**A** Work with a partner. What are wedding ceremonies like in your country? Complete these sentences and add two more sentences of your own.

In (*name of country*) _____, the bride (has to / doesn't have to) wear _____ .

The groom (has to / doesn't have to) _____ .

The wedding ceremony (has to be / doesn't have to be) _____

_____

_____

**B** Ask and answer questions about wedding customs in your partner's country.

*Does the bride have to wear a certain color?*     *What does the groom have to wear?*

## EXPLORE

CD4-8

**1**   **READ** the conversation about customs. Notice the words in **bold**.

Vanuatu

# Disappearing Cultures

| | |
|---|---|
| **Olivia:** | Your lecture was very interesting. **Could I ask** you a question? |
| **Dr. Park:** | Of course. |
| **Olivia:** | Are cultural differences disappearing¹? People are becoming more similar because of movies, the Internet, and travel, right? |
| **Dr. Park:** | Yes, cultures are becoming more similar because of these things, but there are still areas that have little contact with the outside world. |
| **Olivia:** | **Can you give** me an example? I'd like to learn more about this. |
| **Dr. Park:** | Sure. One example is Vanuatu in the South Pacific. There are still traditional tribes in the very remote² areas of the mountains. |
| **Olivia:** | That's interesting. I'd really like to go there. **Could you tell** me more about it? |
| **Dr. Park:** | Well, sure. It's a very interesting place, but tourists aren't always good for places such as Vanuatu. When tourists go to see traditional cultures, life in the village changes. Traditions become tourist attractions. |
| **Olivia:** | Interesting. I didn't think about that. |
| **Dr. Park:** | Do you want to do some research on this topic? |
| **Olivia:** | Definitely. **Could you recommend** some articles? |
| **Dr. Park:** | **I'd be happy to. Would you like to meet** next week to talk about it? |
| **Olivia:** | Sure. Thanks. |

¹ **disappear:** to go away over time
² **remote:** far away and hard to reach

▶ Men perform a traditional dance with spears, Ekasup Village, Vanuatu.

▲ Men from a different part of Vanuatu perform a traditional dance in brightly colored costumes.

**2 CHECK.** Read the questions. Circle *Yes* or *No*.

1. Are cultural differences disappearing?      (a.) Yes.     b. No.

2. Are people and cultures becoming more similar because of movies, the Internet, and travel?      a. Yes.     b. No.

3. Is Vanuatu in Africa?      a. Yes.     b. No.

4. Does tourism change the culture of tribes?      a. Yes.     b. No.

5. Does Dr. Park want to do some research on this topic?      a. Yes.     b. No.

**3 DISCOVER.** Complete the exercises to learn about the grammar in this lesson.

**A** Look at the questions from the conversation in exercise **1**. Notice the words in **bold**. Then circle **T** for *true* or **F** for *false* for each statement.

**Could I ask** you a question?    **Can you give** me an example?    **Could you recommend** some articles?

1. These words are polite.      **T**     **F**

2. These words show something is possible.      **T**     **F**

3. We use these words to request something.      **T**     **F**

**B** Discuss your answers from exercise **A** with your classmates and teacher.

# LEARN

## 13.6 *Can You/Could You/Would You* for Polite Requests

| Can/Could/ Would | Subject | Base Form of Verb | |
|---|---|---|---|
| Can | | | |
| Could | you | help | me? |
| Would | | | |

| Answers |
|---|
| Sure. No problem. |
| OK. Just a minute. |
| I'm sorry, but I can't right now. |

| | |
|---|---|
| 1. Use *can*, *could*, and *would* to make polite requests. | **Can you open** the door? <br> **Could you open** the door? <br> **Would you open** the door? |
| 2. Use *can*, *could*, or *would* before the subject in polite requests. | **Can** <u>you</u> help me with my homework? <br> **Could** <u>you</u> carry this for me? <br> **Would** <u>you</u> close that window? |
| 3. *Could* is more polite than *can*. To make a request more polite, use *please* after the subject (*you*) or at the end of the request. | **Could** you help me? <br> **Can** you help me, <u>please</u>? |
| 4. Use *can't* to refuse a request even when the request uses *could* or *would*. | A: **Could** you help me with this exercise? <br> B: Sorry. I **can't** right now. |
| 5. To refuse a request, we usually explain or apologize. | I'm sorry. I **can't** right now. <br> I **can't** do it right now. I'm late for class. |

### REAL ENGLISH

*Thanks anyway* is often used as a response when someone refuses a request. It is usually used when the person wanted to help but couldn't.

A: *I'm having trouble with this exercise. Could you help me?*
B: *Sorry. I'm having trouble with it, too.*
A: *OK.* ***Thanks anyway.***

---

**4** Rewrite each imperative to make it a polite request.

1. Give me some ideas for my project. _Could you give me some ideas for my project?_

2. Explain the answer, please. _____

3. Tell me about the article. _____

4. Please repeat the question. _____

5. Show me that website. _____

6. Help me with the assignment. _____

7. Do some research for me. _____

8. Recommend some books about your country. _____

**5** Work with a partner. Ask and answer the requests from exercise **4**. Accept the requests for items 1–4. Politely refuse the requests for items 5–8.

Student A: *Would you give me some ideas for my project?*

Student B: *Sure.*

Student A: *Thanks.*

## 13.7 *Can I/Could I/Would You Like* for Polite Offers

| Can/Could/Would | Subject | Base Form of Verb | | Answers |
|---|---|---|---|---|
| Can | I | get | you some coffee? | Sure. Thanks. |
| Could | I | carry | your suitcase for you? | Thanks, that would be great. |
| Would | you | like | some help? | No thanks. I'm fine. |

| | |
|---|---|
| 1. Use *can* or *could* to offer to do something for someone. | **Can** I help you with that? <br> **Could** I get you some more coffee? |
| 2. Use *would you like* to make an offer. | **Would you like** another piece of cake? |
| 3. Respond to an offer with *thank you* or *thanks* to accept or with *no thanks* to refuse. | Sure. **Thanks.** <br> **Thank you.** I'd like that. <br> **No thanks.** I'm fine. |

**6** Complete each request. Use the verb in parentheses and *Can I* or *Would you.*

1. (help)  A: _____Can I help_____ you?  B: Yes. I'd like some information.

2. (make)  A: _____ a suggestion?  B: OK. What is it?

3. (like)  A: _____ to look at a map?  B: Oh, you have a map? Thanks.

4. (help)  A: _____ you with your bags?  B: Yes, thank you.

5. (like)  A: _____ a free movie ticket?  B: Sure! Thanks.

6. (get)  A: _____ you anything?  B: No thanks. I'm fine.

7. (like)  A: _____ a ride to the party?  B: Thanks. I'd like that.

8. (give)  A: _____ you a ride to the party?  B: No, but thanks. I'm going later.

**7 SPEAK.** Work with a partner. Practice the conversations in exercise **6**.

Student A: *Can I help you?*  Student B: *Yes, I'd like some information.*

# PRACTICE

**8** Complete each conversation with a request or an offer from the box. Write the letter on the line.

| | |
|---|---|
| a. Can I get it for you? | e. Could you get me a cup of coffee? |
| ~~b.~~ Can I help you with directions? | f. Would you like me to close the window? |
| c. Can I help you with it? | g. Would you like me to introduce you? |
| d. Really? Can you send me the link, please? | h. Would you wait five minutes? I'd like to go with you. |

1. A: I'm lost.

   B: _b_

2. A: I found a good online travel site.

   B: ____

3. A: It's cold in here.

   B: ____

4. A: I'm ready to leave.

   B: ____

5. A: I can't reach that book on the shelf.

   B: ____

6. A: I don't know them.

   B: ____

7. A: I'm having trouble with this.

   B: ____

8. A: I'm going to the coffee shop.

   B: ____

**9** **SPEAK.** Work with a partner. Practice the conversations in exercise **8**. Add an affirmative response to each conversation.

Student A: *I'm lost.*

Student B: *Can I help you with directions?*

Student A: *Sure.*

**10** **WRITE, LISTEN & SPEAK.**

**A** Read the conversations. Underline any requests or offers that are not polite. Then rewrite them in your notebooks to make them polite.

**Conversation 1**

**Jessie:** You always tell me such interesting things about Panama. I'd like to go there sometime. <u>Give me some suggestions for places to see.</u>

*Could you give me some suggestions for places to see?*

**Felipe:** Oh. What do you want? The names of my favorite places?

**Jessie:** Yes. Tell me the name of a hotel, too.

**Felipe:** Sure. Let me know if you have any other questions.

**Jessie:** Great. Thanks, Felipe!

### Conversation 2

**Agent:** Hello. Adventure Travel Company. Do you want help?

**Hans:** Yes, I want some information about tours to the South Pacific.

**Agent:** Hold on for a minute.

**Hans:** OK.

**Agent:** Hello, I'm back. Now give me your name.

**B** Listen and check your answers from exercise **A**.

**C** Work with a partner. Practice the conversations from exercise **A**.

**11 APPLY.** Work with a partner. Read the situations. Then role-play a request and an offer in each situation.

1. You see a tourist (*your partner*) on the street. The tourist seems confused. Offer to help.

   Student A: *Would you like some help?*

   Student B: *Yes, thanks. I'm lost. Could you help me find the Martin Hotel?*

   Student A: *Sure. I can show you.  / Oh, I'm sorry. I don't know that hotel.*

2. You are at the airport. You missed your plane. Your partner is the customer service agent for the airline.

3. You are interested in a trip to Japan. Your partner is a travel agent.

4. You are on a plane. You want to put your suitcase above your seat. It is very heavy. Your partner is another passenger on the plane.

5. You are at home. A friend comes to see you.

6. You're in class. You and your partner are both students. You forgot your book.

7. You are in a very crowded cafeteria. You are sitting by yourself at a table. Your partner is walking around and looking for a place to sit.

Charts
13.1, 13.3,
13.4, 13.6,
13.7

**1** Complete the conversation below. Use words from the box. You can use some words more than once.

| can | can't | could | have to | should | would |
|-----|-------|-------|---------|--------|-------|

**Driver:** Excuse me. Are you lost? (1) _____Would_____ you like some help?

**Tourist:** Oh, hello! (2) _____ I ask you a question? We're trying to get to the waterfall, but I don't see a bus.

**Driver:** There aren't any buses today, so you (3) _____ go by taxi. I drive a taxi, so I (4) _____ take you there.

**Tourist:** Oh, really? That's great. (5) _____ you tell me the price?

**Driver:** Sure. Here's my card with the price. The waterfall is amazing. You

(6) _____ definitely see it.

**Tourist:** Yes, I know! I've come all this way, so I (7) _____ leave without a visit to see it.

**Driver:** That's true. Here's my car. (8) _____ I help with your bags?

**Tourist:** Thanks!

Charts
13.1–13.4,
13.6, 13.7

**2** **EDIT.** Read the e-mails. Find and correct six more errors with offers, requests, *should, can,* and *have to.*

Papua
New
Guinea

---

Hi Patricia,

After you told me about your trip to Papua New Guinea, I decided to plan a trip there, too! Could you ~~to~~ give me some tips? Here are some questions.

- Have I to get a visa?
- Where I should stay?
- What about clothing? Can women wear shorts?

Thanks for any suggestions!

Best,
Donna

---

Hi Donna,

That's exciting! Papua New Guinea is amazing! Could you like to have lunch next week? I have a lot of information for you. Yes, you have to get a visa. I went with a tour group. I think you should to go with a tour group, too. On a tour, you haven't to worry about hotels or transportation. Also, would like you to borrow some guide books? I have a few really good ones. See you soon!

Patricia

---

CD4-10

**3  LISTEN, WRITE & SPEAK.**

**A** Read the statements. Then listen to the conversation about the Huli Wigmen in Papua New Guinea. Circle **T** for *true* or **F** for *false*.

1. The Huli women grow their hair long for wigs.          **T**      **Ⓕ**

2. Visitors can learn about Huli traditions.              **T**      **F**

3. The Huli women don't have to work hard.                **T**      **F**

4. The Huli men and women live together.                  **T**      **F**

5. The Huli people do dances for visitors.                **T**      **F**

CD4-10

**B** Listen again. Then complete each sentence about the Huli with *can/can't, should/shouldn't,* or *have to/don't have to.*

1. Huli women _____ *don't have to* _____ make wigs.

2. For strong hair, Huli men _____ eat special food.

3. When they are growing their hair, the boys _____ run or go near fires.

4. Visitors _____ give the Huli people money.

5. The men _____ wear wigs all the time.

6. There are special buildings for men. Women _____ go inside them.

7. Huli women _____ do most of the work.

8. Huli men _____ work.

▲ Huli boy, Papua New Guinea

**C** In your notebook, write *Yes/No* questions and *Wh-* questions about the Huli. Use *should, can, have to,* and information from exercise **B**.

**D** Work with a partner. Ask and answer your questions from exercise **C**.

Student A: *Should visitors give the Huli some money?*

Student B: *Yes, they should.*

# Connect the Grammar to Writing

## 1 READ AND NOTICE THE GRAMMAR.

**A** Read the e-mail. What does the writer want? Discuss with a partner.

Dear Ms. Glenn,

I have to take my daughter to her school, so I can't meet with you this morning. I'm very sorry. Could you meet with me after class tomorrow?

I'm having trouble with questions, especially questions with *who*. Can you help me with this? I'm also having trouble with the present progressive. Would you please show me some more examples?

Thank you.

Best,
Carlos Santos

### GRAMMAR FOCUS

In the e-mail in exercise **A**, the writer uses *can, could,* and *would* to make polite requests.
**Could you** meet with me after class?

**B** Read the e-mail in exercise **A** again. Underline the polite requests. Then work with a partner and compare answers.

**C** Complete the chart with information from the e-mail in exercise **A**. What requests does the writer make?

| Requests |
|---|
| Could you meet with me after class tomorrow? |

**2 BEFORE YOU WRITE.** Think of a situation when you need to write a request for information: for example, advice about a course, help with a computer problem, or permission to miss a class. What kind of information do you need? What do you want to do? Complete the chart with your requests. Use the chart from exercise **1C** as a model.

| Requests |
|---|
|  |

**3 WRITE** a request for information or permission. Use two or three polite requests. Use the information from your chart in exercise **2** and the e-mail in exercise **1A** to help you.

> **WRITING FOCUS**    Using Polite Language to Make Requests
>
> Writers use the modals *could* and *would* to make polite requests. Requests with *would* and *could* are more polite than requests with imperatives because they are less direct.
>
> Imperatives:
>   *Meet with me after class.*
>   *Help me with this.*
>   *Show me some more examples.*
>
> Polite requests:
>   **Could** *you meet with me after class?*
>   **Can** *you help me with this?*
>   **Would** *you please show me some more examples?*

**4 SELF ASSESS.** Read your request. Underline the polite requests. Then use the checklist to assess your work.

☐   I used *Could you* or *Would you* to make polite requests. [13.6]

☐   I used *may* or *can* to request permission. [13.3]

☐   I put *can, could,* and *would* before the subjects in my requests. [13.6, 13.7]

☐   I used polite language to make requests. [WRITING FOCUS]

# Education and Learning

# The Future

◀ A child touches an image on a wall designed for people with seeing disabilities, Franklin D. Roosevelt Memorial, Washington, DC.

## EXPLORE

CD4-11

**1 READ** the conversation about an unusual school. Notice the words in **bold**.

# An Unusual College Experience

**Professor Mills:** OK, Hannah, here's your final exam. You did very well. **Are** you **going to take** another math course next semester?

**Hannah:** No, **I'm not**. **I'm not going to be** on campus next semester. **I'm spending** a semester at sea.

**Professor Mills:** At sea?. . . Do you mean on a boat? That sounds more like a vacation than a semester at college.

**Hannah:** No, really, it's not a vacation. **I'm going to take** two biology courses and courses on modern Southeast Asian history and Chinese art history, too.

**Professor Mills:** Where does the ship go?

**Hannah:** From Australia to Indonesia, Singapore, and then Malaysia. Then, **I'm going to do** community service¹ for a couple of weeks at the end.

**Professor Mills:** Where **are** you **going to do** that?

**Hannah:** In Indonesia. **I'm working** at a medical clinic² there.

**Professor Mills:** What's your major?³ Are you planning to be a doctor?

**Hannah:** No. I'd like to get a job in a medical field, but **I'm not going to be** a doctor.

**Professor Mills:** Well, have a good semester.

**Hannah:** Thanks!

¹ **community service:** unpaid work to help people
² **clinic:** a small hospital
³ **major:** the main subject that a student is studying

▲ Nowadays students can take courses on boats like this one.

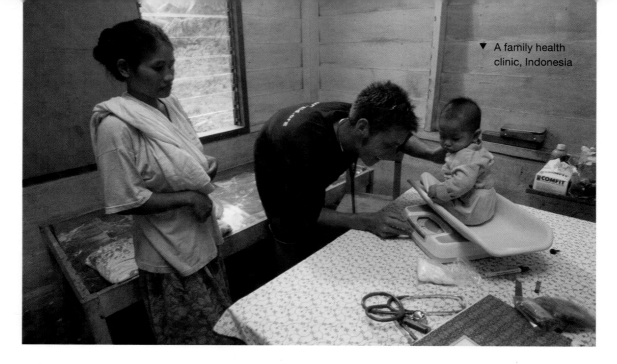

▼ A family health clinic, Indonesia

**2 CHECK.** Look at the list of activities in the chart. Does Hannah plan to do these activities in the future? Check (✓) *Yes* or *No* for each activity.

| Activity | Yes | No |
|---|---|---|
| 1. Study on campus next semester | | |
| 2. Take a math course | | |
| 3. Take two biology courses | | |
| 4. Do community service | | |
| 5. Work at a medical clinic in Indonesia | | |
| 6. Be a doctor | | |

**3 DISCOVER.** Complete the exercises to learn about the grammar in this lesson.

**A** Find these statements and questions in the conversation in exercise **1**. Write the missing words.

1. _____ you _____ another math course next semester?

2. I _____ on campus next semester.

3. I _____ a semester at sea.

4. I _____ two biology courses and courses on modern South East Asian history and Chinese art history, too.

5. Then, I _____ community service for a couple of weeks at the end.

6. Where _____ you _____ that?

**B** Look at the sentences from exercise **A**. Choose the correct word to complete the statement. Then discuss your answer with your classmates and teacher.

The actions in exercise **A** are _____ .     a. past     b. present     c. future

## 14.1 Future with *Be Going To*: Statements

| Affirmative | | | |
|---|---|---|---|
| Subject | *Be* | *Going To* | Base Form of Verb |
| I | am<br>'m | | |
| He<br>She<br>It | is<br>'s | going to | move. |
| We<br>You<br>They | are<br>'re | | |

| Negative | | | |
|---|---|---|---|
| Subject | *Be Not* | *Going To* | Base Form of Verb |
| I | am not<br>'m not | | |
| He<br>She<br>It | is not<br>'s not<br>isn't | going to | move. |
| We<br>You<br>They | are not<br>'re not<br>aren't | | |

| | |
|---|---|
| 1. Use *be going to* + the base form of the verb to talk about:<br>  a. future plans;<br>  b. a prediction or something you feel certain about in the future | a. **I'm going to study** in Japan next year.<br>b. I think Ed**'s going to like** his new job.<br>I listened to the weather report. It**'s going to rain** this afternoon. |
| 2. Future time expressions can come at the beginning or end of a sentence. | **I'm going to visit** my sister <u>this weekend</u>.<br>It**'s going to snow** <u>tonight</u>.<br><u>Next semester</u> she**'s going to take** Chinese. |
| 3. Do not use *the* in future time expressions with *next*. | ✓ **I'm going to study** in Mexico <u>next year</u>.<br>✗ I'm going to study in Mexico <u>the</u> next year. |

**4** Complete each sentence with the correct form of *be going to* and the verb in parentheses.

1. (have) Hannah _____is going to have_____ an interesting experience next semester.

2. (be) It _____ a lot of fun.

3. (study) She _____ on a ship.

4. (take) The students _____ biology courses.

5. (travel) They _____ to different countries.

6. (do) I _____ community service for a couple of weeks.

7. (not be) She _____ on campus.

8. (graduate) We _____ May.

**5 SPEAK.** Work with a partner. Discuss your study plans. Use *be going to*.

(take / not take) another English course

(study / not study) another language

## 14.2 Future with *Be Going To*: Questions

| Yes/No Questions | | | | |
|---|---|---|---|---|
| *Be* | Subject | *Going to* | Base Form of Verb | |
| Are | you | going to | leave | tonight? |
| Is | she | | | |

| Short Answers | | | | |
|---|---|---|---|---|
| | Affirmative | | Negative | |
| Yes, | I am. | No, | I'm not. | |
| | she **is**. | | she **isn't**. | |

| Wh- Questions | | | | | | Answers |
|---|---|---|---|---|---|---|
| Wh- Word | *Be* | Subject | *Going to* | Base Form of Verb | | |
| When | is | she | going to | leave? | | In a couple of hours. At 2:00. |
| How | is | he | going to | get | there? | By bus. He's going to walk. |
| What | are | you | going to | take | next? | Biology and math. I'm not sure yet. |
| Who | are | we | going to | meet | tomorrow? | Our new clients are from Los Angeles. |

| | |
|---|---|
| 1. *Be* comes before the subject in *Yes/No* questions and in most information questions. | **Are** <u>you</u> **going to go** to the library? When **are** <u>you</u> **going to do** your homework? |
| 2. **Remember:** *Wh-* questions with *Who* or *What* can be about a subject or an object. The word order is different. | Questions about a Subject: Who **is going to do** it? What **is going to happen** tomorrow? <br><br> Questions about an Object: Who **are** <u>you</u> **going to ask**? What **are** <u>they</u> **going to do** tomorrow? |

**6** Look at each sentence. Write a question about the <u>underlined</u> word or phrase.

1. They're going to <u>register for their courses</u>. ___*What are they going to do?*___

2. <u>Yes</u>, I'm going to be on campus tomorrow. _____

3. She's going to study <u>math</u> next semester. _____

4. <u>No</u>, I'm not going to take French next semester. _____

5. I'm going to get there <u>by bus</u>. _____

6. <u>Yes</u>, our teacher's going to give us a test tomorrow. _____

7. This course is going to end <u>in two weeks</u>. _____

8. I'm going to <u>do my homework</u> tonight. _____

9. I'm going to go on vacation <u>in June</u>. _____

10. <u>No</u>, it's not going to rain tonight. _____

**7** **SPEAK.** Work with a partner. Ask and answer questions 6–10 in exercise **6** on page 437. Use your own answers, not the answers in the book.

Student A: *Is our teacher going to give us a test tomorrow?*

Student B: *No, she isn't.*

## 14.3 Future with Present Progressive

| Statements | |
|---|---|
| Present Progressive | Future Time Expression |
| I'm leaving | tomorrow. |
| She isn't working | on Monday. |
| They're coming | next week. |

| Yes/No Questions | |
|---|---|
| Present Progressive | Future Time Expression |
| Are you leaving | tomorrow? |
| Is she coming | tonight? |

| Short Answers | | | |
|---|---|---|---|
| Affirmative | | Negative | |
| Yes, | I am. | No, | I'm not. |
| | she is. | | she isn't. |

| Wh- Questions | | Answers |
|---|---|---|
| Present Progressive | Future Time Expression | |
| What are you doing | tonight? | I'm working. |
| When is she leaving | tomorrow? | In the afternoon. |
| Where are they going | next week? | To Seoul. |

| | |
|---|---|
| 1. Use the present progressive to talk about plans already made for the near future.<br><br>The present progressive is commonly used with these verbs to talk about the future: *arrive, leave, fly, drive, meet, stay, visit, come, take,* and *get.* | They have their train tickets. They**'re arriving** on Monday.<br><br>**I'm visiting** my parents this weekend. |
| 2. Time expressions and context show present or future meaning. | **Time Expressions**<br>**I'm taking** French <u>this semester</u>. *(present)*<br>**I'm taking** French <u>next semester</u>. *(future)*<br><br>**Context**<br>Al's my friend. He**'s studying** art. *(present)*<br>When **are** you **leaving**? *(future)* |

**8** Complete each statement with the present progressive for future. Underline the future time expressions.

1. Jeff _____isn't taking_____ (not take) courses on campus <u>next semester</u>.

2. We _____ (start) classes next week.

> **REAL ENGLISH**
>
> With schedules, the simple present often has a future meaning.
>
> *Class **ends** at 10:30 today.*
> *The plane **leaves** at 9:00 tomorrow morning.*

3. My parents _____ (come) to visit in a couple of weeks.

4. My brother _____ (not start) college this year.

5. I _____ (study) in India next year.

6. The university _____ (not offer) that course next semester.

7. Suzy _____ (graduate) in June.

8. We _____ (not go) to the party tomorrow night.

**9** Use the words in parentheses to complete each question with the present progressive for future.

1. _____ (you / take) a history course next semester?

2. _____ (When / Pedro / give) his presentation?

3. _____ (we / start) classes next week?

4. _____ (Who / teach) this class next semester?

5. _____ (Where / she / study) next year?

6. _____ (she / arrive) tomorrow?

7. _____ (Why / he / leave) tonight?

8. _____ (How / you / get) there?

**10** **SPEAK.** Work with a partner. Make sentences about the future. Use the words from the box and the present progressive.

| After class I . . . | Tomorrow . . . | . . . tonight. |

*After class I'm meeting my friends.*

# PRACTICE

**11** **LISTEN** to each statement or question. Is it present or future? Check (✓) the correct column.

| | Present | Future | | Present | Future |
|---|---|---|---|---|---|
| 1. | ☐ | ✓ | 6. | ☐ | ☐ |
| 2. | ☐ | ☐ | 7. | ☐ | ☐ |
| 3. | ☐ | ☐ | 8. | ☐ | ☐ |
| 4. | ☐ | ☐ | 9. | ☐ | ☐ |
| 5. | ☐ | ☐ | 10. | ☐ | ☐ |

**12** **EDIT.** Read the announcement. Find and correct six more errors with *be going to* and the present progressive for future.

## News from the Study Abroad Office

• **NEW PROGRAM**

               *is going to have*

Our college ~~having~~ a new program next fall. Five students are going to go to Scotland in September.

They going to study at the University of Edinburgh. They stay in dormitories on campus.

Everyone is very excited about this new program.

• **PROGRAM CANCELLATION**

We are not send students to study in Turkey this year. We only received one application for the

program. However, we offer it again next year.

• **NEW OFFICES**

We moving to the new Student Union Building on August 1, so the office not going to be open

from July 30 until August 1.

▼ A view of Edinburgh, Scotland

**13** Complete the conversations with the correct form of *be going to* or the present progressive for future and the verbs in parentheses.

1. **Nate:** (1) _____ (you / take) Spanish again next semester?

   **Ellen:** No, (2) _____ (I / take) Italian instead.

   **Nate:** Really? Why (3) _____ (you / do) that?

   **Ellen:** (4) _____ (I / study) in Rome next year, so I want to learn some Italian.

   **Nate:** Wow! (5) _____ (you / love) Rome. It's an amazing city!

2. **Julie:** Look at these dark clouds. (6) _____ (It / rain).

   (7) _____ (I / go) inside to get some coffee. Would you like to join me?

   **Dora:** Oh, thanks, but I can't. (8) _____ (I / meet) my sister.

   (9) _____ (We / go) to a movie this afternoon.

   **Julie:** What (10) _____ (you / see)?

   **Dora:** I forget the name. It's a new foreign film. My sister really wants to see it.

**14 SPEAK.** Role-play a conversation with your partner. Choose one of the topics from the box or your own idea. Use *be going to*. Include at least two questions.

| the weather | plans for the weekend | plans for next semester |
|---|---|---|

Student A: *What are you going to do this weekend?*     Student B: *I'm going to visit my sister.*

## 15 LISTEN, WRITE & SPEAK.

CD4-13

**A** Listen to the discussion about three students' plans after graduation. Look at the activities in the chart. Who is going to do each activity? Check (✓)the correct column.

| Activities | Sonya | Trey | Mylo |
|---|---|---|---|
| 1. Go to college next year | | ✓ | |
| 2. Do community service | | | |
| 3. Get a job and save money | | | |
| 4. Go to India | | | |
| 5. Teach | | | |

**B** Use the words to write *Yes/No* questions and *Wh-* questions with *be going to* about the students' plans from exercise **A**.

1. What / Trey / do / next year   _What is Trey going to do next year?_

2. When / they / graduate _____

3. Where / Trey / study _____

4. Sonya / go / to college next year _____

5. Who / work _____

6. Why / Mylo / visit India _____

▶ Mehrangharh Fort and Jaswant Thada mausoleum overlooking Jodhpur, Rajasthan, India

▲ Students at a school near
Amboseli National Park,
Rift Valley Province, Kenya

7. What / Sonya / teach in Kenya _____

8. What / Sonya / do in Nairobi _____

9. Where / Sonya / live in Kenya _____

10. Mylo and Sonya / go to college _____

**C** Work with a partner. Ask and answer the questions from exercise **B**.

## 16 APPLY.

**A** Work in a group. What do you think about these students' plans? Discuss these questions.

1. Who is going to have the most interesting experience? Why?

2. Which experiences are going to help the students find a job in five or six years?

3. How about you? Do you know anyone who is going to do anything similar?

**B** In your notebook, write your answers to questions 1 and 2 in exercise **A**. Write at least two sentences for each item.

## EXPLORE

CD4-14

**1**   **READ** the article about the Internet and the future of education. Notice the words in **bold**.

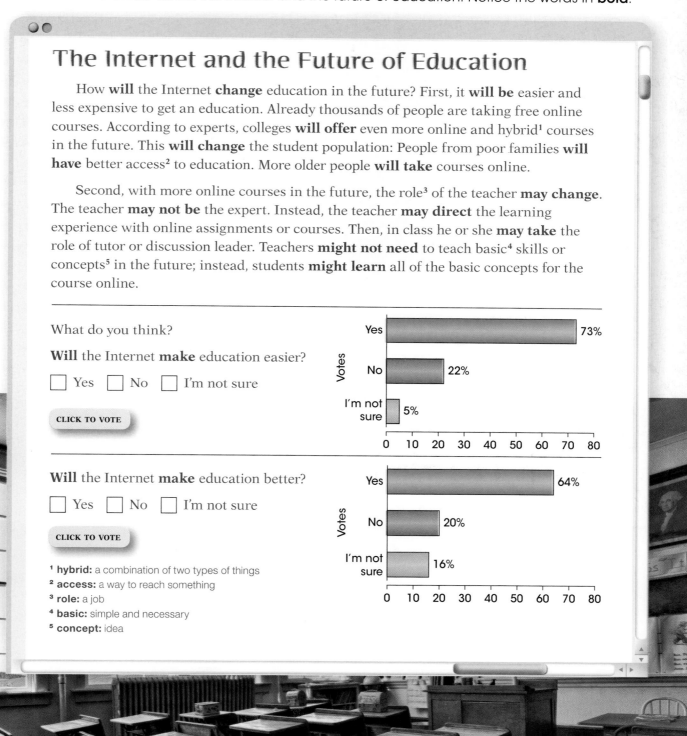

### The Internet and the Future of Education

How **will** the Internet **change** education in the future? First, it **will be** easier and less expensive to get an education. Already thousands of people are taking free online courses. According to experts, colleges **will offer** even more online and hybrid[1] courses in the future. This **will change** the student population: People from poor families **will have** better access[2] to education. More older people **will take** courses online.

Second, with more online courses in the future, the role[3] of the teacher **may change**. The teacher **may not be** the expert. Instead, the teacher **may direct** the learning experience with online assignments or courses. Then, in class he or she **may take** the role of tutor or discussion leader. Teachers **might not need** to teach basic[4] skills or concepts[5] in the future; instead, students **might learn** all of the basic concepts for the course online.

What do you think?

**Will** the Internet **make** education easier?

☐ Yes ☐ No ☐ I'm not sure

CLICK TO VOTE

Votes: Yes 73% | No 22% | I'm not sure 5%
(scale 0 10 20 30 40 50 60 70 80)

**Will** the Internet **make** education better?

☐ Yes ☐ No ☐ I'm not sure

CLICK TO VOTE

Votes: Yes 64% | No 20% | I'm not sure 16%
(scale 0 10 20 30 40 50 60 70 80)

[1] **hybrid:** a combination of two types of things
[2] **access:** a way to reach something
[3] **role:** a job
[4] **basic:** simple and necessary
[5] **concept:** idea

▲ A classroom from the early 1900s, Molson Schoolhouse Museum, Molson, Washington, USA

**2 CHECK.** Match each topic in Column A with the correct information in Column B. Write the letter on the line.

**Column A**

1. The Internet ___d___

2. Education _____

3. People _____

4. Teachers _____

5. Colleges _____

**Column B**

a. take more free courses

b. be cheaper

c. assign online materials

d. make education easier and cheaper

e. offer more online and hybrid courses

**3 DISCOVER.** Complete the exercises to learn about the grammar in this lesson.

**A** Find these sentences in the article from exercise **1** on page 443. Write the missing words.

1. First, it _____ easier and less expensive to get an education.

2. Second, with more online courses in the future, the role of the teacher _____.

3. The teacher _____ the expert.

4. Teachers _____ to teach basic skills or concepts in the future; instead, students _____ all of the basic concepts for the course online.

**B** Look at the sentences in exercise **A**. Notice the verbs. Then look at the statements below and circle **T** for *true* and **F** for *false*. Discuss your answers with your classmates and teacher.

a. The sentence with *will* is about the present.        **T**     **F**

b. The base form of the verb comes after *will (not)*,    **T**     **F**
   *may (not)*, and *might (not)*.

# LEARN

## 14.4 Future with *Will:* Statements

| Affirmative | | | |
|---|---|---|---|
| Subject | *Will* | Base Form of Verb | |
| I | | | |
| You | | | |
| He | | | |
| She | will | need | help. |
| It | 'll | | |
| We | | | |
| You | | | |
| They | | | |

| Negative | | | |
|---|---|---|---|
| Subject | *Will Not/ Won't* | Base Form of Verb | |
| I | | | |
| You | | | |
| He | | | |
| She | will not | need | help. |
| It | won't | | |
| We | | | |
| You | | | |
| They | | | |

| | |
|---|---|
| 1. *Will* is a modal. Use the base form of the verb after *will*. | The test **will be** easy. |
| 2. Use *will*: | |
|   a. to make predictions |   a. In 2060, all classes **will be** online. |
|   b. to talk about things you are certain about in the future |   b. In five years, I**'ll be** 30. |
|   c. for promises and offers |   c. I**'ll call** you tonight.<br>    A: It's cold in here.<br>    B: I**'ll close** the window. |
|   d. for decisions you make at the time of speaking |   d. A: I'm going to the coffee shop.<br>    B: I**'ll go** with you. |
| 3. Do not use *will* to talk about future plans. Use *be going to*. | ✓ We're **going to visit** our grandparents this weekend.<br>✗ We <u>will visit</u> our grandparents this weekend. |
| 4. *Won't* is the contraction of *will not*. | Sam **won't** be at the party. He's sick. |
| 5. The contractions *'ll* and *won't* are used in conversation and informal writing. | We**'ll** be at home at around eight o'clock tonight.<br>Don't worry. You **won't** need your coat on the plane. |

**4** Complete each sentence with *will* or *won't* and the verb in parentheses.

1. In the future, many more people

   _____ (take) courses online.

2. This course _____ (be) online

   next semester.

3. They _____ (send) me

   information about the course soon.

4. Online courses _____ (make) education cheaper.

**REAL ENGLISH**

*Probably* is often used with *will* to talk about something in the future that is not certain. *Probably* goes between *will* and the base form of the verb in the affirmative and before *won't* in the negative.

*It'll* **probably** *rain tomorrow.*
*We* **probably** *won't get our tests back tomorrow.*

5. Professors _____ (not teach) courses in the future.

6. Professor Patel _____ (send) the assignment tomorrow.

7. I _____ (help) you with the assignment after class.

8. Don't ask Brett. He _____ (not know) the answer.

9. Professor Lee _____ (tell) us about the test tomorrow.

10. It's 11:00. The library _____ (not be) open.

11. Do you have Megan's number? I _____ (call) her now.

12. We _____ (get) our grades on Monday.

**5** Complete the conversations with *'ll* or *won't* and the words in parentheses. Then listen and check your answers.

CD4-15

1. **Berta:** Bye! (1) _____ I'll see _____ (I / see) you in class tomorrow.

   **Jess:** OK. It's raining, and I think (2) _____ (there / be) a lot of traffic on your way home, so be careful.

   **Berta:** OK, (3) _____ (I / drive) slowly.

2. **Tasha:** Your cold sounds terrible. Have some hot tea with lemon. (4) _____ (It / make) you feel better.

   **Kim:** Please don't worry about me. (5) _____ (I / be) fine.

   **Tasha:** OK, but get some sleep and feel better!

   **Kim:** OK. Thanks. (6) _____ (I / call) you tomorrow.

3. **Cory:** Why are you studying now for next week's vocabulary test? (7) _____ (You / not remember) all the words next week.

   **Sid:** There are a lot of words on the list. I'm studying a few each day. (8) _____ (It / help) me remember them.

   **Cory:** Well, I guess (9) _____ (I / do) the same thing, but I don't have a list of all of the words.

   **Sid:** (10) _____ (I / e-mail) you my list.

   **Cory:** OK. Thanks!

**6 SPEAK.** Work with a partner. Talk about things you are certain about in the future. Use *will, 'll, won't,* and the words listed.

On Sunday . . .

After class . . .

In ten years . . .

*On Sunday we'll be happy because we don't have class.*

## 14.5 Future with *Will*: Questions

| Yes/No Questions | | |
|---|---|---|
| *Will* | Subject | Base Form of Verb |
| Will | it | help? |
| | they | |

| Short Answers | | | | | |
|---|---|---|---|---|---|
| Affirmative | | | Negative | | |
| Yes, | it | will. | No, | it | won't. |
| | they | | | they | |

| Wh- Questions | | | |
|---|---|---|---|
| Wh-Word | *Will* | Subject | Base Form of Verb |
| Where | will | he | be? |
| When | | we | meet? |
| How | | they | know? |
| What | | you | say? |
| Who | | you | ask? |
| Why | | she | laugh? |

| Answers |
|---|
| At home. |
| After class. |
| We'll tell them. |
| Nothing. |
| Sasha. |
| Because it's a funny story. |

| | |
|---|---|
| 1. Do not use the contraction *'ll* in short answers. | ✓ Yes, **I will.**<br>✗ Yes, **I'll.** |
| 2. **Remember:** *Why* is often used with negative questions. | **Why won't** she like it? |
| 3. **Remember:** *Wh-* questions with *Who* or *What* can be about a subject or an object. | Questions about a Subject:<br>**Who will be** there?<br>**What will happen** next?<br><br>Questions about an Object:<br>**Who will you go** with?<br>**What will they** do? |

**7** Look at each sentence. Write a question about the <u>underlined</u> word or phrase.

1. <u>No</u>, we won't be late for class. _____ *Will we be late?* _____

2. <u>Yes</u>, the teacher will be there at 9:00. _____

3. We'll get our tests back <u>tomorrow</u>. _____

4. <u>No</u>, the test won't be difficult. _____

5. <u>Yes</u>, of course I'll help you. _____

6. They'll talk to <u>the professor</u>. _____

7. <u>Susan</u> will take notes. _____

8. The lecture will be <u>in Room 306</u>. _____

9. <u>No</u>, I won't be absent tomorrow. _____

10. <u>Yes</u>, there will be a final exam. _____

**8** Work with a partner. Ask and answer questions 9–10 in exercise **7**. Use your own answers, not the answers in the book.

Student A: *Will you be absent tomorrow?*

Student B: *Yes, I will. I have a doctor's appointment.*

## 14.6 Possibility with *Might/May*

| Affirmative Statements | | | |
|---|---|---|---|
| Subject | *Might/ May* | Base Form of Verb | |
| I | | | |
| You | | | |
| He | | | |
| She | might may | have | a test tomorrow. |
| We | | | |
| You | | | |
| They | | | |

| Negative Statements | | | |
|---|---|---|---|
| Subject | *Might Not/ May Not* | Base Form of Verb | |
| I | | | |
| You | | | |
| He | | | |
| She | might not may not | have | a test tomorrow. |
| We | | | |
| You | | | |
| They | | | |

| | |
|---|---|
| 1. Use *might* or *may* to talk about possibility in the present or future. | Present Possibility: Sue isn't here. She **may** be sick. You **might** be right. Future Possibility: Sue isn't sure about tomorrow. She **may** come. I **might** go to the game tonight. I'm not sure yet. |
| 2. Use *might* or *may* for actions or events that are possible in the future. Use *will* for actions or events that are certain in the future. | They **might** win. (= It's possible.) They **will** win. (= It's certain.) |
| 3. *Might* and *may* are modals. Use the base form of the verb after *might* and *may*. | ✓ It **might** rain. ✗ It might <u>rains</u>. |
| 4. There is no negative contraction for *might* or *may*. | ✓ He **might not** have time. ✗ He <u>mightn't</u> have time. ✓ We **may not** go. ✗ We <u>mayn't</u> go. |
| 5. Do not use *may* and *might* for questions about possibility. | ✓ Is it going to rain this afternoon? ✗ **May/might** it rain this afternoon? |
| 6. **Be careful!** *Maybe* and *may be* are not the same. *Maybe* is an adverb. It comes before the subject and verb. *Maybe* is used in conversation and informal writing. | Bring a jacket. It **may be** very cold there. It's snowing. **Maybe** we won't have class tomorrow. |

**9** Complete each sentence with *may* or *might* and the verb in parentheses. Use *may* for 1–4. Use *might* for 5–8.

1. (study) I _____ may study _____ at the library tonight.

2. (not come) She _____ to class tomorrow.

3. (have) We _____ a quiz tomorrow.

4. (rain) It _____ tonight.

5. (be) Your idea _____ better. Let's try it.

6. (not be) This _____ the best way to solve the problem.

7. (not go) I _____ to the party. I'm not sure yet.

8. (take) The homework _____ a long time.

**10** Choose *may be* or *maybe* to complete each sentence.

1. There _____ a test next week.

   ⓐ may be          b. maybe

2. _____ we'll be classmates again in another course.

   a. May be          b. Maybe

3. The new vocabulary words _____ on the quiz.

   a. may be          b. maybe

4. Trudy's not here. _____ she didn't know about the change in classrooms.

   a. May be          b. Maybe

5. Look at that traffic. We _____ late for class.

   a. may be          b. maybe

6. I'm not sure yet, but I _____ take an art class next semester.

   a. may          b. maybe

7. Are you feeling sick? _____ you should stay home.

   a. May be          b. Maybe

8. The weather forecast says it _____ sunny later.

   a. may be          b. maybe

**11** **SPEAK.** Work with a partner. Talk about possibilities in the future. Use the words from the box.

| might | may | may be |
|---|---|---|
| might not | may not | maybe |

*My parents might visit me next month.*

# PRACTICE

**12** Complete the exercises.

**A** Circle the correct word(s) to complete the announcement.

## Announcement

We are happy to announce some exciting changes at the college. Next year, all first-year courses (1) **will** / **might** be online. Many people want to know, "How (2) **this will** / **will this** change the college?"

This change (3) **may be** / **will** help the college in many ways. First-year students (4) **aren't** / **won't** need to come to campus. This (5) **maybe** / **may** save them both time and money. The college will also (6) **saves** / **save** money because it (7) **won't** / **doesn't** spend as much money on classrooms and instructors. There (8) **maybe** / **may be** more students because of this plan. In two years, the college will (9) **reviews** / **review** the success of the online program. More courses (10) **may be** / **maybe** online in the future.

**B** Use the words to write *Yes/No* questions and *Wh-* questions with *will* or *won't.*

1. When / online classes / start ___When will online classes start?___

2. the change / help / the college _____

3. Who / not need / to come to campus _____

4. When / the college / review the online program _____

5. the college / spend less on classes _____

6. classes / be / more expensive _____

7. the college / need / more instructors _____

8. more students / take / online classes _____

**C** Work with a partner. Ask and answer the questions from exercise **B**. Use *will/won't, may,* and *maybe.* For your answers to 6–8, use your own ideas.

Student A: *When will online classes start?*          Student B: *They'll start next year.*

**13** **EDIT.** Read the conversation. Find and correct seven more errors with *will, won't, may, maybe,* and *might.*

**Kerry:** Hey, did you hear the news? Next year a lot of our courses ⌄will be online.

**Justin:** Really? That's great! It'll be easier for me. I mightn't need to come to campus as often. Will many first-year courses be online?

**Kerry:** Yes, they'll. We won't has those huge lecture classes anymore, the ones with 600 students. Students will listening online. In a few years, all classes maybe online.

**Justin:** Online classes, that's interesting. Everyone might has more free time.

**Kerry:** That's true. May be I won't have any 8:30 classes!

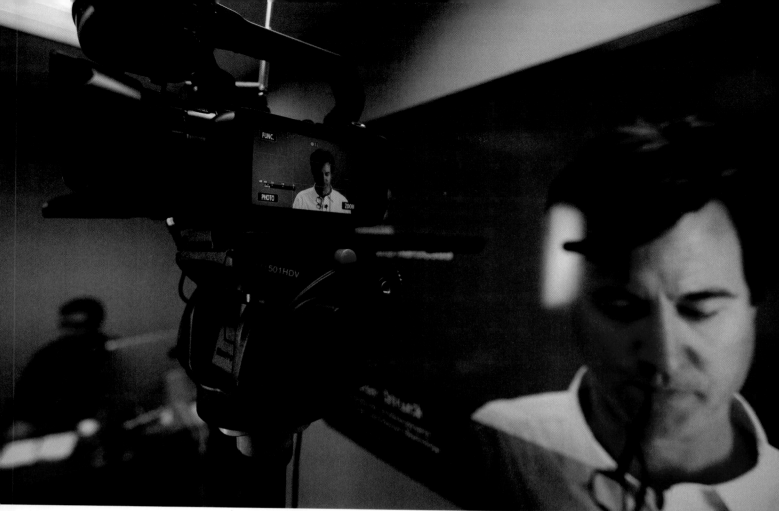

▲ A professor prepares to record a lecture for an online course.

## 14   LISTEN & SPEAK.

CD4-16

**A**   Listen to the conversation about online classes. Circle each correct answer.

1.  Who is positive about online classes?         a. Keesha         b. Craig

2.  What course are they talking about?           a. Math           b. Spanish

CD4-16

**B**   Listen again. Complete the notes on Craig's opinions and ideas about online classes.

| Craig's Opinions and Ideas |
| --- |
| 1. Students ___won't learn as much___ online. |
| 2. The college _____ teachers. |
| 3. Some teachers _____ their jobs. |

**C**   Work with a partner. Does Keesha agree or disagree with Craig's opinions and ideas? In your notebook, write her opinions and ideas about online classes.

## 15   APPLY. Answer these questions. Discuss your answers with a partner.

1.  What is your opinion about online courses? Why?

2.  What is your experience with online courses?

3.  Do you think you might take an online course in the future? Why, or why not?

## EXPLORE

CD4-17

**1 READ** the article about color and tests. Notice the words in **bold**.

# Color and Test Scores

**Mother:** Good morning. I just made coffee. Would you like some breakfast?

**Son:** Thanks, Mom. I'll just have coffee. I'll be late **if I have breakfast.** I have my final exam today for math.

**Mother:** Oh, don't wear that red shirt **if you have an exam.** I read something about this last week. **When people see red before a test,** they get lower scores.

**Son:** Seriously?

**Mother:** Yes, really. They did some research about it. In the research study, everyone got the same test, but the test booklet[1] had three different covers. Some of the covers were red, some were green, and some were black. The people with the red covers got lower scores.

**Son:** Wow! I wonder why.

**Mother:** Think about it. We use red **when we want to show danger**, right? Teachers use it **when they grade papers.** Maybe red makes us nervous.

**Son:** Yeah, but I'm in a hurry. **If I change my shirt,** I'll miss my bus. Hmmm. Maybe this is a good idea. **When the other students see my red shirt,** maybe they'll get nervous. Then *they'll* get lower scores, and *I'll* get the highest grade in the class.

**Mother:** I hope so. Good luck!

[1] **booklet:** a small book with a paper cover

**2 CHECK.** Read the statements. Circle **T** for *true* or **F** for *false*.

1. The son has time for breakfast.                                    **T**      **F**

2. He's wearing a red shirt.                                          **T**      **F**

3. His mother did research about the color red.                       **T**      **F**

4. People get higher scores when they see red before a test.          **T**      **F**

5. The son has time to change his shirt.                              **T**      **F**

**3 DISCOVER.** Complete the exercises to learn about the grammar in this lesson.

**A** Find these sentences in the conversation on page 452. Write the missing words.

1. I'll be late **if** I _____ breakfast.

2. **When** people _____ red before a test, they get lower scores.

3. **If** I _____ my shirt, I'll miss my bus.

4. **When** the other students _____ my red shirt, maybe they'll get nervous.

**B** Look at the sentences from exercise **A**. Choose the correct word(s) to complete each statement. Then discuss your answers with your classmates and teacher.

1. Each sentence has _____.

    a. one clause          b. two clauses

2. The verb after *if* is in the _____.

    a. present          b. future          c. present or future

3. The verb after *when* is in the _____.

    a. present          b. future          c. present or future

## 14.7  *If* Clauses

> **If I have time before class,** I usually get some coffee.    *(habit or fact)*
>     *If Clause*        *Main Clause*
>
> **If I don't understand,** I'll ask the teacher.    *(condition with future result)*
>     *If Clause*        *Main Clause*

| | |
|---|---|
| 1. Sometimes an activity or event depends on something else. This is a condition. | You'll get a good grade **if you study hard.** <br>                   *Condition* <br><br> **If it snows**, the buses are always late. <br> *Condition* |
| 2. An *if* clause shows a condition. The main clause shows a result. | **If you study hard**, you'll get a good grade. <br>   *Condition*           *Result* <br> **If I don't feel better**, I'm going to stay home. <br>     *Condition*         *Result* <br> **If you don't study**, you might fail the test. <br>     *Condition*         *Result* |
| 3. For habits or facts, use the simple present in the *if* clause. Use the simple present in the main clause. | Habit: If I **have** time before class, I usually <u>go</u> to the coffee shop. <br><br> Fact: **If I eat too many sweets,** I <u>feel</u> sick. |
| 4. For future conditions, use the simple present in the *if* clause. Use the future in the main clause. | If I **go** to bed  late, I'<u>ll be</u> tired tomorrow. <br> If we **don't leave** now, we'<u>ll be</u> late. <br><br> ✓ If we **miss** our plane, I'<u>ll call</u> you. <br> ✗ If we <u>will miss</u> our plane, I'll call you. |
| 5. When the *if* clause is at the beginning of the sentence, use a comma. | **If Professor Wang teaches the course,** I'll take it. <br> I'll take the course if Professor Wang teaches it. |

**4**   Underline the *if* clause in each sentence. Add a comma if necessary.

1.  <u>If I have breakfast</u>, I'll be late for my exam.

2.  Don't wear that red shirt if you have an exam.

3.  If he has a test he studies hard.

4.  If you study hard you'll get a good grade.

5.  You can borrow a pencil if you don't have one.

6.  If I don't understand the assignment I'll call you.

7.  If they have questions they should ask the professor.

8.  If the weather is nice we walk to class.

**5**   Complete each condition or result with the verb in parentheses.

1.  If I _____*don't have*_____ (not have) a test tomorrow, I'll go out with my friends.

2.  If he _____ (finish) the assignment, he'll come with us.

3. If you _____ (not understand) the homework, you should ask the teacher.

4. If I _____ (get) good grades, I'll get into a good university.

5. If she _____ (study) engineering, she'll get a good job.

6. If I _____ (not take) notes in class, I don't remember anything.

7. If we _____ (be) late for class, our teacher gets angry.

8. If we _____ (not leave) soon, we'll be late for class.

**6  SPEAK.** Work with a partner. Use these sentence beginnings to talk about your plans.

If I have a lot of homework, . . .          If we don't have a lot of homework, . . .

If it rains on Saturday, . . .          If the weather is nice this weekend, . . .

*If I have a lot of homework tonight, I'll stay up late.*

## 14.8  Future Time Clauses with *Before, After,* and *When*

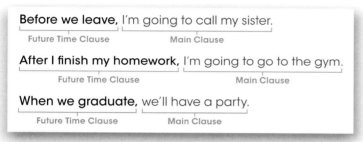

| | |
|---|---|
| 1. **Remember:** A time clause tells when an action or event will happen. It tells the order of events. | **After I watch the news,** I'm going to cook dinner. |
| 2. Future time clauses often begin with *before, after,* or *when.* Use *after* and *when* for the first action or event. Use *before* for the second action or event. | **After** he eats dinner, he's going to watch TV. <br> *First Event* *Second Event* <br> **When** he finds a job, he'll be very happy. <br> *First Event* *Second Event* <br> **Before** I go to class, I'm going to eat lunch. <br> *Second Event* *First Event* |
| 3. Use simple present in the future time clause, and future in the main clause. | When I **get** home, I**'ll call** you. <br> *Future Time Clause* *Main Clause* |
| 4. Time clauses with *when* are also used to talk about facts or habits. | Fact: **When a baby is hungry**, it cries. <br> Habit: **When I get home,** I watch the news. |
| 5. To talk about facts or habits, use the simple present in the time clause and the main clause. | Ken **listens** to music when he **exercises**. <br> *Main Clause* *Time Clause* <br> When I **drink** coffee at night, I **can't sleep**. <br> *Time Clause* *Main Clause* |
| 6. Use a comma after the time clause when it comes at the beginning of the sentence. | **Before he goes,** he'll call you. <br> **After I send this e-mail,** I'm going to call Lisa. <br> **When I have a cold,** I drink tea with honey. |

**7** Read each sentence. Which *event* or *action* will happen first? Circle **a** or **b**. Add a comma if necessary.

1. When everyone gets here we'll begin.
   ⓐ        b

2. The teacher grades homework after class ends.
   a                b

3. When I graduate my parents will be very happy.
   a                b

4. I might take a trip after I finish this course.
   a                b

5. Let's have a party after we finish our exams.
   a                b

6. Before we leave I'll call you.
   a        b

7. She'll tell you her plans when you talk to her.
   a                b

8. When she gets home she takes her dog for a walk.
   a                b

**8** Look at Lara's "To Do List." Then complete the sentences with *when, after,* or *before.*

1. _____ When _____ Lara calls Tomoko, she's going to ask her for her lecture notes.

2. _____ she calls Tomoko, she's going to go to the library.

3. _____ she goes to the library, she'll start the research for a psychology paper.

4. She'll go to the library _____ she meets Polly and Brittany for dinner.

5. She plans to go to the college bookstore _____ she has dinner.

6. _____ she's at the bookstore, she'll buy more paper.

7. She plans to study _____ she goes to the bookstore.

8. She's going to do her math homework _____ she studies vocabulary.

**TO DO LIST**

A.M. - Call Tomoko & ask for lecture notes
11-3: Go to library to start research for psychology paper
6:30 - Meet Polly & Brittany for dinner
After dinner:
    college bookstore: buy more paper
    finish math homework
    study vocabulary

**9** **SPEAK.** Work with a partner. Talk about your plans. Use the words from the box.

Before I go home today, . . .          After I get home, . . .          After I have lunch tomorrow, . . .
When I get home tonight, . . .        When I get up tomorrow, . . .

*Before I go home today, I'm going to go to the library.*

## PRACTICE

**10**  Match each result on the right with the correct condition on the left.

1. If I have a lot of homework tonight, I __h__.

2. If I don't have a lot of homework at night, I _____.

3. If you miss a lot of classes, you _____.

4. If I feel sick, I _____.

5. If the teacher is sick, we _____.

6. If you're tired, _____.

7. If you have any trouble, I _____.

8. If you don't finish this now, you _____.

a. 'll help you

b. can do it tonight for homework

c. won't go to class

d. drink some coffee

e. usually watch a movie

f. might not have class

g. won't do well in the course

h. won't go out with my friends

**11**  Complete the exercises.

**A**  Circle the correct verb to complete each sentence.

# Rewards for Good Grades

How important are rewards in learning? Will children get better grades if they (1) **receive** / **will receive** something special for them? (2) **Will they study** / **Are they studying** harder if they (3) **get** / **will get** rewards?

Consider this example: Greta is taking a test tomorrow. Her father says to her, "Greta, if you (4) **will get** / **get** an A on your next test, I (5) **give** / **will give** you $20." Greta answers, "OK, Dad. If you are going to give me $20, (6) **I'll get** / **I get** an A."

There are several problems with this situation. After Greta (7) **is getting** / **gets** a few rewards, she'll probably expect them. If she (8) **gets** / **will get** a lot of rewards, she won't learn to do things on her own. Last, if she (9) **doesn't get** / **will get** rewards, she might not try to get good grades anymore.

Experts have advice for parents:

- Explain why good grades are important. Say, "If you (10) **will get** / **get** good grades, you (11) **are getting** / **are going to get** a good job in the future.

- Focus on effort, not grades. When your child (12) **works** / **will work** hard, say, "You worked hard. I'm proud of you."

Think carefully before you give your child a reward for good grades!

**B** Use the information from exercise **A** on page 457 and your own ideas to complete the sentences. Add commas if necessary.

1. Good grades are important. If children get good grades, <u>they'll get into good colleges.</u>

2. Some parents give their children rewards when _____.

3. If children get rewards _____.

4. Parents should think about some experts' advice before _____.

5. Children may not work hard on their own after _____.

6. If children understand why good grades are important _____.

7. If children work hard in school _____.

8. When I have children, I _____ if they get good grades.

**C** Work with a partner. Discuss this question.

*What do you think? Should parents give their children rewards for good grades? Why, or why not?*

## 12 LISTEN & SPEAK.

CD4-18

**A** Read each statement. Then listen to the conversation. Choose the correct words to complete each sentence.

1. David is going to _____ soon.

   a. take a course     b. go to college

2. Martha is going to _____.

   a. study business     b. decide later about her future

CD4-18

**B** Listen again and complete the sentences from the conversation in exercise **A**. Add commas if necessary.

1. Why are you taking the course before _____<u>you need it?</u>_____

2. Then I'm going to take another course before _____ the exam.

3. _____ a good score on the entrance exam, I won't get into a good university, and then _____ a good job.

4. If you're smart, _____ on the test. If _____ you won't.

5. If _____ you can do a lot better.

6. When _____ I'll figure it out.

7. _____ I'm going to work in my family's store.

8. If _____ for my father, everyone will be upset.

**C** Work in a group. Discuss these questions.

1. Do test prep courses help students get better scores? Why, or why not?

2. When should students take test prep courses?

## 13 APPLY.

**A** Work with a group. You are members of a committee to recommend changes in your education system, school, or program. Complete the chart with the changes you recommend and your reasons.

| Changes | Reasons |
| --- | --- |
| 1. We should make classes cheaper. | 1. If classes are cheaper, students will take more classes. They'll learn more. |

**B** Share your ideas with your classmates. Then discuss. Which ideas do you like? Which ideas will never happen? Why?

*I like Group A's first idea. If we make classes cheaper, students will take more classes and learn more.*

Charts
14.1, 14.3,
14.4,
14.6–14.8

**1** Circle the correct verb to complete each sentence in the advertisement.

# The Outdoor English Experience

Outdoor English is a great new way to study English! At Outdoor English, you (1) **are learning** / **will learn** English and hike and camp in the mountains. When you (2) **arrive** / **will arrive** at Outdoor English, you (3) **are having** / **will have** two days of English lessons. You (4) **will also learn** / **are also learning** camping skills before you (5) **start** / **will start** your adventure. For example, (6) you **are learning** / **will learn** how to set up a tent, cook over a campfire, and stay safe in the mountains.

Then, you and your team members (7) **will hike and camp** / **are hiking and camping** in the mountains for a week with an experienced mountain guide. Your guide (8) **will be** / **maybe** your English teacher, too! After you (9) **will spend** / **spend** a week in the mountains, you (10) **return** / **will return** to share stories of your adventures with the other teams. This is an experience that you (11) **are never forgetting** / **are never going to forget**, and it is a great way to learn English!

Charts
14.1–14.8

**2** **EDIT**. Read the conversation. Find and correct six more errors with *will/won't, be going to,* and the future with present progressive.

| | |
|---|---|
| **Hal:** | Hi, Adam. What are you doing? |
| **Adam:** | Hey, Hal. I'm ~~make~~ <sup>making</sup> a packing list. |
| **Hal:** | Where you are going? |
| **Adam:** | I going to the Andes Mountains next month. |
| **Hal:** | Wow. Are you going there for vacation? |
| **Adam:** | No, I'm going to study Spanish. |
| **Hal:** | Really? Are you going stay with a family? |
| **Adam:** | No. I'm go with this unusual language program I found online. It combines hiking and camping trips with Spanish classes. After I will get there, I'll meet the other students in the program and the guides. Then, we're going to go on a two-week camping trip. The guides are Spanish teachers, too. |
| **Hal:** | That sounds amazing! I'm sure you going to have a great time and learn a lot! |

**3  LISTEN, WRITE & SPEAK.**

**A**  Look at Ali's plans in the chart. Then listen to the conversation. Which plans is he sure about? Which plans is he unsure about? Check (✓) the correct column.

| Plans | Sure | Not Sure |
|---|---|---|
| 1. Take more English courses | | |
| 2. Study English for eight more months | | |
| 3. Take the English test in May | | |
| 4. Go to university next September | | |
| 5. Get married | | |

CD4-19

**B**  Listen again. Complete the flow chart for Ali's plans.

**Long-Term Goal:** Be a _____

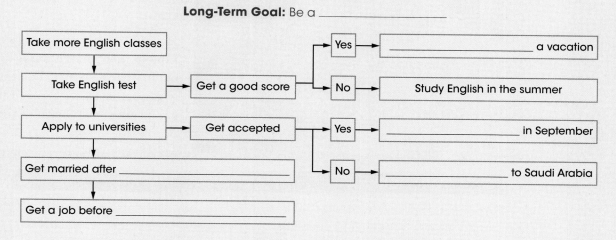

**C**  In your notebook, write about Ali. Use the words given and the information in exercise **B**.

1.  When / Ali / finish / his English course

    *When Ali finishes his English course, he'll take a test.*

2.  If / he / not get / high score

3.  If / he / get / high score

4.  If / he / get accepted

5.  If / he / not get accepted / to a university

6.  After / he / finish university

7.  Before / he / get married

**4  SPEAK.**

**A**  Make a chart with your plans for the future. Use the chart in exercise **3B** as a model.

**B**  Work with a partner. Share your charts from exercise **A**. Ask each other questions about your plans for the future. Then share the information about your partner with the class.

*Martin is going to go back to France. After he graduates, he's going to look for a job in marketing . . .*

# Connect the Grammar to Writing

**1 READ AND NOTICE THE GRAMMAR.**

**A** Read Binh's personal statement. What are some of her plans for the future? Discuss with a partner.

## My Plans for the Future

Right now, I'm a student at a community college. I'm going to be a nurse. Next semester, I'm starting a nursing program. When I finish it, I'm going to take a test to get my nursing license. If I pass, I'll apply for a job in a hospital. If I don't pass the test, I'll take a test preparation course and take the test again.

After I work for a couple of years, I might take more nursing courses and get a four-year degree. If I do that, I'll be able to get better nursing jobs. I think this is a good career plan because there will always be jobs for nurses.

### GRAMMAR FOCUS

In her personal statement in exercise **A**, the writer uses different verb forms and modals to talk about her future plans.

> I**'m going to be** a nurse.
> Next semester, I**'m starting** a nursing program.

**B** Read the personal statement in exercise **A** again. Underline the verb forms and modals that the writer uses to talk about her future plans. Then work with a partner and compare answers.

**C** Complete the chart with information about the writer's personal statement.

**Binh's long-term goal:** Be a nurse

**Reasons for goal:** _____

**Plans:**

1. start a nursing program _____

2. _____

3. _____

4. _____

5. _____

**2 BEFORE YOU WRITE.** Complete the chart with ideas and information about your long-term goal and future plans. Use the chart from exercise **1C** as a model.

**My long-term goal:** _____

**Reasons for goal:** _____

**Plans:** _____

_____

_____

_____

_____

**3 WRITE** a personal statement. Use the information from your chart in exercise **2** and the personal statement in exercise **1A** to help you.

> **WRITING FOCUS**     Using *If* Clauses and Time Clauses
>
> Writers use *if* clauses to show a condition. They use time clauses with *when, before,* and *after* to show the order of events.
>
> **Remember:** Use a comma when the *if* clause or time clause is at the beginning of the sentence.
>
> **If I pass,** I'll apply for a job as a nurse in a hospital.
> **When I finish it,** I'm going to take a test to get my nursing license.

**4 SELF ASSESS.** Read your personal statement. Underline the verb forms and modals that talk about the future. Then use the checklist to assess your work.

☐   I used *be going to* or present progressive to talk about future plans. [14.1, 14.3]

☐   I used *will* or *won't* for predictions and things I am certain about in the future. [14.4]

☐   I used *may* or *might* to express possibility in the future. [14.6]

☐   I used *if* clauses to talk about conditions in the future. [14.7, WRITING FOCUS]

☐   I used future time clauses with *before, after,* and *when* to talk about the order of actions and events in the future. [14.8, WRITING FOCUS]

## 1 Spelling Rules for Regular Plural Nouns

| | |
|---|---|
| 1. Add -s to most nouns. | student-students<br>teacher-teachers<br>pen-pens |
| 2. Add -es to nouns that end in -ch, -s, -sh, and -x. | watch-watches<br>class-classes<br>dish-dishes<br>box-boxes |
| 3. Add -s to nouns that end in a vowel + -y. | boy-boys<br>day-days |
| 4. Change the -y to -i and add -es to nouns that end in a consonant + -y. | city-cities<br>country-countries |
| 5. Add -s to nouns that end in a vowel + -o. | video-videos<br>radio-radios |
| 6. Add -es to nouns that end in a consonant + -o.<br><br>Exceptions: photo → photos<br>piano → pianos | potato-potatoes<br>tornado -tornadoes |

## 2 Common Irregular Noun Plurals

| Singular | Plural | Explanation |
|---|---|---|
| man<br>woman<br>tooth<br>foot<br>goose | men<br>women<br>teeth<br>feet<br>geese | Vowel change |
| sheep<br>fish<br>deer | sheep<br>fish<br>deer | No change |
| child<br>person<br>mouse | children<br>people<br>mice | Different word forms |
| No singular form | belongings<br>clothes<br>groceries<br>glasses<br>jeans<br>pajamas<br>pants<br>scissors<br>shorts | |

## 3 Simple Present Spelling Rules: -s and -es Endings

| | |
|---|---|
| 1. Add -s to most verbs. | like-like**s**<br>sit-sit**s** |
| 2. Add -es to verbs that end in-*ch*, -*s*, -*sh*, -*x*, or -*z*. | catch-catch**es**<br>miss-miss**es**<br>wash-wash**es**<br>mix-mix**es**<br>buzz-buzz**es** |
| 3. Change the -*y* to -*i* and add -*es* when the base form of the verb ends in a consonant + -*y*. | cry-cr**ies**<br>carry-carr**ies** |
| 4. Do not change the -*y* *to* -*i* when the base form ends in a vowel + -*y*. | pay-pay**s**<br>stay-stay**s** |
| 5. Some verbs are irregular in the third-person singular form of the simple present. | be-**is**<br>go-**goes**<br>do-**does**<br>have-**has** |

## 4 Spelling Rules for the -*ing* Form of Verbs

| | |
|---|---|
| 1. Add -*ing* to the base form of most verbs. | eat-eat**ing**<br>do-do**ing**<br>speak-speak**ing**<br>carry-carry**ing** |
| 2. Verbs that end in a consonant and silent -*e*: Drop the -*e* and add -*ing*. | ride-rid**ing**<br>write-writ**ing** |
| 3. One-syllable verbs that end in CVC*: Double the final consonant and add -*ing*. | stop-stop**ping**<br>sit-sit**ting** |
| Do not double the final consonant for verbs that end in -*w*, -*x*, or -*y*. | show-show**ing**<br>fix-fix**ing**<br>stay-stay**ing** |
| 4. Two-syllable verbs that end in CVC and have the stress on the first syllable: Add -*ing*, but do not double the final consonant. | listen-listen**ing**<br>travel-travel**ing** |
| 5. Two-syllable verbs that end in CVC: Double the final consonant only if the last syllable is stressed, and add -*ing*. | begin-begin**ning**<br>refer-refer**ring** |

*consonant + vowel + consonant

## 5 Spelling Rules for the -*ed* Form of Verbs

| | |
|---|---|
| 1. Add -*ed* to the base form of most verbs that end in a consonant. | start-start**ed**<br>talk-talk**ed** |
| 2. Add -*d* if the base form of the verb ends in -*e*. | dance-danc**ed**<br>live-liv**ed** |
| 3. One-syllable verbs that end in CVC*: Double the final consonant and add -*ed*.<br><br>Do not double the final consonant of verbs that end in -*w*, -*x*, or -*y*. | stop-stop**ped**<br>rob-rob**bed**<br><br>follow-follow**ed**<br>fix-fix**ed**<br>play-play**ed** |
| 4. Change the -*y* to -*i* and add -*ed* when the base form ends in a consonant + -*y*.<br><br>Do not change the -*y* when the verb ends in a vowel + -*y*. | cry-cr**ied**<br>worry-worr**ied**<br><br>stay-stay**ed** |
| 5. Two-syllable verbs that end in CVC and have the stress on the first syllable: Add -*ed*, but do not double the final consonant. | travel- travel**ed**<br>visit-visit**ed**<br>order-order**ed** |
| 6. Two-syllable verbs that end in CVC: Double the final consonant when the second syllable is stressed, and add -*ed*. | prefer-prefer**red**<br>refer-refer**red** |

*consonant + vowel + consonant

## 6 Spelling Rules for Adverbs Ending in -*ly*

| | Adjective | Adverb |
|---|---|---|
| 1. Add -*ly* to the end of most adjectives. | careful<br>quiet<br>serious | careful**ly**<br>quiet**ly**<br>serious**ly** |
| 2. Change the -*y* to -*i* and add -*ly* to adjectives that end in a consonant + -*y*. | easy<br>happy<br>lucky | eas**ily**<br>happ**ily**<br>luck**ily** |
| 3. For many adjectives that end in -*e*: Keep the -*e* and add -*ly*. | nice<br>free | nice**ly**<br>free**ly** |
| 4. For adjectives that end with a consonant followed by -*le*: Drop the final *e* and add -*y*. | simple<br>comfortable | sim**ply**<br>comforta**bly** |
| 5. For most adjectives that end in -*ic*: Add -*ally*. | basic<br>enthusiastic | basic**ally**<br>enthusiastic**ally** |

## 7 Spelling Rules for Comparative and Superlative Forms

|  | Adjective | Comparative | Superlative |
|---|---|---|---|
| 1. One-syllable adjectives and adverbs: Add -er to form the comparative. Add -est to form the superlative. | tall<br>fast | taller<br>faster | the tallest<br>the fastest |
| 2. Adjectives that end in -e: Add -r to form the comparative, and -st to form the superlative. | nice | nicer | the nicest |
| 3. Two-syllable adjectives and adverbs that end in -y: Change the -y to -i before adding -er or -est. | easy<br>happy | easier<br>happier | the easiest<br>the happiest |
| 4. One-syllable adjectives and adverbs that end in CVC*: Double the final consonant before adding -er or -est. | big | bigger | the biggest |
| 5. Some adjectives have irregular comparative and superlative forms. | good<br>bad | **better**<br>**worse** | **the best**<br>**the worst** |

*consonant + vowel + consonant

## 8 Guide to Pronunciation Symbols

| Vowels | | | | Consonants | | |
|---|---|---|---|---|---|---|
| Symbol | Key Word | Pronunciation | | Symbol | Key Word | Pronunciation |
| /a/ | hot<br>far | /hat/<br>/far/ | | /b/ | boy | /bɔɪ/ |
| /æ/ | cat | /kæt/ | | /d/ | day | /deɪ/ |
| /aɪ/ | fine | /faɪn/ | | /dʒ/ | just | /dʒʌst/ |
| /aʊ/ | house | /haʊs/ | | /f/ | face | /feɪs/ |
| /ɛ/ | bed | /bɛd/ | | /g/ | get | /gɛt/ |
| /eɪ/ | name | /neɪm/ | | /h/ | hat | /hæt/ |
| /i/ | need | /nid/ | | /k/ | car | /kar/ |
| /ɪ/ | sit | /sɪt/ | | /l/ | light | /laɪt/ |
| /ou/ | go | /gou/ | | /m/ | my | /maɪ/ |
| /ʊ/ | book | /bʊk/ | | /n/ | nine | /naɪn/ |
| /u/ | boot | /but/ | | /ŋ/ | sing | /sɪŋ/ |
| /ɔ/ | dog<br>four | /dɔg/<br>/fɔr/ | | /p/ | pen | /pɛn/ |
| /ɔɪ/ | toy | /tɔɪ/ | | /r/ | right | /raɪt/ |
| /ʌ/ | cup | /kʌp/ | | /s/ | see | /si/ |
| /ɛr/ | bird | /bɛrd/ | | /t/ | tea | /ti/ |
| /ə/ | about<br>after | /əˈbaut/<br>/ˈæftər/ | | /tʃ/ | cheap | /tʃip/ |
|  |  |  | | /v/ | vote | /vout/ |
|  |  |  | | /w/ | west | /wɛst/ |
|  |  |  | | /y/ | yes | /yɛs/ |
|  |  |  | | /z/ | zoo | /zu/ |
|  |  |  | | /ð/ | they | /ðeɪ/ |
|  |  |  | | /θ/ | think | /θɪŋk/ |
|  |  |  | | /ʃ/ | shoe | /ʃu/ |
|  |  |  | | /ʒ/ | vision | /ˈvɪʒən/ |

Source: The *Newbury House Dictionary plus Grammar Reference, Fifth Edition*, National Geographic Learning/Cengage Learning, 2014

## 9   Common Irregular Verbs

| Base Form of Verb | Simple Past | Base Form of Verb | Simple Past | Base Form of Verb | Simple Past |
|---|---|---|---|---|---|
| be | was, were | get | got | say | said |
| become | became | give | gave | see | saw |
| begin | began | go | went | sell | sold |
| bend | bent | grow | grew | send | sent |
| bite | bit | hang | hung | set | set |
| blow | blew | have | had | shake | shook |
| break | broke | hear | heard | shut | shut |
| bring | brought | hide | hid | sing | sang |
| build | built | hit | hit | sink | sank |
| buy | bought | hold | held | sit | sat |
| catch | caught | keep | kept | sleep | slept |
| choose | chose | know | knew | speak | spoke |
| come | came | lead | led | spend | spent |
| cost | cost | leave | left | stand | stood |
| cut | cut | lend | lent | steal | stole |
| dive | dived/dove | let | let | swim | swam |
| do | did | lose | lost | take | took |
| draw | drew | make | made | teach | taught |
| drink | drank | meet | met | tear | tore |
| drive | drove | pay | paid | tell | told |
| eat | ate | put | put | think | thought |
| fall | fell | quit | quit | throw | threw |
| feed | fed | read | read | understand | understood |
| feel | felt | ride | rode | wake | woke |
| fight | fought | ring | rang | wear | wore |
| find | found | rise | rose | win | won |
| fly | flew | run | ran | write | wrote |
| forget | forgot | | | | |

## Unit 3, Lesson 2, Exercise 15, Page 95

Partner B's Schedule

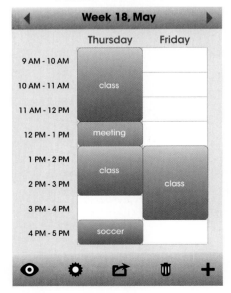

## Unit 5, Lesson 2, Exercise 12B, Page 161

**B** Partner B, look at the ingredients on the list below. Answer your partner's questions about the ingredients. Put a check (✓) next to the ingredients you need to buy. Then write the amount of each ingredient you need to buy on your shopping list.

Partner A: *Do we have **one and a half pounds of ground beef**?*

Partner B: *No, we don't. We have **one pound**.*

Ingredients in Our Kitchen

- a bottle of olive oil ☐
- 1 pound of ground beef ☐
- a head of garlic ☐
- a small onion ☐
- 1 can of tomato paste ☐
- a jar of Italian seasoning ☐
- a container of salt ☐
- a bag of sugar ☐

Shopping List

½ pound of ground beef

**C** Check with your partner. Are your shopping lists the same?

## Unit 6, Review the Grammar, Exercise 4, Page 203

**Partner B**

### Mexican Gray Wolf

Mexican gray wolves are small wolves with long thick fur. They are very rare. In the past, they lived in parts of Mexico and the United States. Now they only live in the United States. These wolves are not dangerous to people, but they eat farm animals when they don't have enough food. Because of this, farmers and hunters killed many of the Mexican gray wolves. Now these wolves are very rare.

## Unit 12, Lesson 2, Exercise 11B, Page 389

**B**  Use your chart to answer Partner A's questions. Then ask Partner A questions to complete the chart.

Partner A: *What is the biggest art museum in the world?*

Partner B: *What do you think?*

Partner A: *I think it's the Louvre.*

Partner B: *No, the Metropolitan Museum is the biggest. It's in New York.*

## Geography Trivia

| | | |
|---|---|---|
| small/ ocean?<br>_____ | The longest river in the world is the Nile. | big/ desert?<br>_____ |
| The highest waterfall in the world is Angel Falls (in Venezuela). | The biggest art museum in the world is the Metropolitan Museum of Art (New York). | The smallest country in the world is the Vatican. |
| large/ country?<br>_____ | The driest place in the world is the Atacama Desert in Chile. | large/ islands?<br>_____ |

**action verb:** a verb that shows an action.
- ➤ He **drives** every day.
- ➤ They **left** yesterday morning.

**adjective:** a word that describes or modifies a noun or pronoun.
- ➤ She is **friendly**.
- ➤ Brazil is a **huge** country.

**adverb:** a word that describes or modifies a verb, an adjective, or another adverb.
- ➤ He eats **quickly**.
- ➤ She drives **carefully**.

**adverb of manner:** an adverb that describes the action of the verb. Many adverbs of manner are formed by adding -ly to the adjective.
- ➤ You sing **beautifully**.
- ➤ He speaks **slowly**.

**affirmative statement:** a statement that does not have a verb in the negative form.
- ➤ My uncle lives in Portland.

**article:** a word that is used before a noun: a, an, the.
- ➤ I looked up at **the** moon.
- ➤ Lucy had **a** sandwich and **an** apple for lunch.

**auxiliary verb:** (also called helping verb) a verb used with the main verb. Be, do, have, and will are common auxiliary verbs when they are followed by another verb. Modals are also auxiliary verbs.
- ➤ I **am** working.
- ➤ He **won't** be in class tomorrow.
- ➤ She **can** speak Korean.

**base form of the verb:** the form of the verb without to or any endings, such as -ing, -s, or -ed.
- ➤ **eat, sleep, go, walk**

**capital letter:** an uppercase letter.
- ➤ **N**ew **Y**ork, **M**r. **F**ranklin, **J**apan

**clause:** a group of words with a subject and a verb. See dependent clause and main clause.
- ➤ We watched the game. (one clause)
- ➤ We watched the game after we ate dinner. (two clauses)

**comma:** a punctuation mark that separates parts of a sentence.
- ➤ After he left work, he went to the gym.
- ➤ I can't speak Russian, but my sister can.

**common noun:** a noun that does not name a specific person, place, or thing.
- ➤ man, country, book, help

**comparative adjective:** the form of an adjective used to talk about the difference between two people, places, or things.
- ➤ I'm **taller** than my mother.
- ➤ Canada is **larger** than Mexico.

**comparison:** a statement of the similarities or differences between things, ideas, or people.
- ➤ Mexico City is more crowded than Buenos Aires.

**conditional:** a structure used to talk about an activity or event that depends on something else.
- ➤ **If the weather is nice on Sunday,** we'll go to the beach.

**conjunction:** a word used to connect information or ideas. And, but, or, and because are conjunctions.
- ➤ He put cheese **and** onions on his sandwich.
- ➤ I wanted to go, **but** I had too much homework.

**consonant:** the following letters are consonants: b, c, d, f, g, h, j, k, l, m, n, p, q, r, s, t, v, w, x, y, z.

**contraction:** two words combined into a shorter form.
- ➤ did not $\longrightarrow$ **didn't**
- ➤ I am $\longrightarrow$ **I'm**
- ➤ she is $\longrightarrow$ **she's**
- ➤ we will $\longrightarrow$ **we'll**

**count noun:** a noun that names something you can count. They are singular or plural.
- ➤ I ate an **egg** for breakfast.
- ➤ I have six **apples** in my bag.

**definite article:** the; it is used before a specific person, place, or thing.
- ➤ I found it on **the** Internet.
- ➤ **The** children are sleeping.

**dependent clause:** a clause that cannot stand alone as a sentence. It must be used with a main clause.
- ➤ I went for a walk **before I ate breakfast**.

**direct object:** a noun or pronoun that receives the action of the verb.
- ➤ Aldo asked a **question**.
- ➤ Karen helped **me**.

**exclamation point:** a punctuation mark that shows emotion (anger, surprise, excitement, etc.) or emphasis.
- ➤ We won the game!
- ➤ Look! It's snowing!

**formal:** language used in academic writing or speaking, or in polite or official situations rather than in everyday conversation or writing.
- ➤ *Please do not take photographs inside the museum.*
- ➤ *May I leave early today?*

**frequency adverb:** an adverb that tells how often something happens. Some common adverbs of frequency are *never, rarely, sometimes, often, usually,* and *always.*
- ➤ *I **always** drink coffee in the morning.*
- ➤ *He **usually** leaves work at six o'clock.*

**frequency expression:** an expression that tells how often something happens.
- ➤ *We go to the grocery store **every Saturday.***
- ➤ *He plays tennis **twice a week.***

**future:** a verb form that expresses an action or situation that has not happened yet. *Will, be going to,* the present progressive, and the simple present are used to express the future.
- ➤ *I **will call** you later.*
- ➤ *We're **going** to the movies tomorrow.*
- ➤ *I'm **taking** French next semester.*

**helping verb:** see *auxiliary verb.*

**if clause:** a clause that begins with *if* and expresses a condition.
- ➤ ***If you drive too fast,** you will get a ticket.*

**imperative:** a verb form that gives an instruction or command. Use the base form of the verb to form the imperative.
- ➤ ***Turn** left at the light.*
- ➤ ***Don't use** the elevator.*

**indefinite article:** *a* and *an;* they are used before singular count nouns that are not specific.
- ➤ *We have **a** test today.*
- ➤ *She's **an** engineer.*

**indefinite pronoun:** a pronoun that refers to people or things that are not specific or not known. *Someone, something, everyone, everything, no one, nothing,* and *nowhere* are common indefinite pronouns.
- ➤ ***Everyone** is here today.*
- ➤ ***No one** is absent.*
- ➤ *Would you like **something** to eat?*

**independent clause:** see *main clause.*

**infinitive:** an infinitive is *to* + the base form of a verb.
- ➤ *He wants **to see** the new movie.*

**informal:** language that is used in everyday conversation and writing.
- ➤ *Who are you talking to?*
- ➤ *We'll be there at eight.*

**information question:** see *Wh-* question.

**irregular adjective:** an adjective that does not change form in the usual way .
- ➤ *good* ⟶ *better*
- ➤ *bad* ⟶ *worse*

**irregular adverb:** an adverb that does not change form in the usual way.
- ➤ *well* ⟶ *better*
- ➤ *badly* ⟶ *worse*

**irregular verb:** a verb form that does not follow the rules for regular verbs.
- ➤ *swim* ⟶ *swam*
- ➤ *have* ⟶ *had*

**main clause:** (also called *independent clause*) a clause that can stand alone as a sentence. It has a subject and a verb.
- ➤ *I **heard the news** when I was driving home.*

**measurement word:** a word used to talk about a specific quantity of something.
- ➤ *We need to buy a **box** of pasta and a **gallon** of milk.*

**modal:** an auxiliary verb that adds additional meaning to a verb, such as ability or possibility. *May, might, can, could, will, would,* and *should* are common modals.
- ➤ *Julie **can** speak three languages.*
- ➤ *He **may** be at the office. Call him.*

**negative statement:** a statement that has a verb in the negative form.
- ➤ *I **don't have** any sisters.*
- ➤ *She **doesn't drink** coffee.*

**non-action verb:** a verb that does not describe an action. Non-action verbs indicate states, senses, feelings, or ownership. They are not common in the progressive.
- ➤ *I **love** my grandparents.*
- ➤ *They **have** a new car.*

**non-count noun:** a noun that names something that cannot be counted.
- ➤ *Carlos drinks a lot of **coffee.***
- ➤ *I need some **salt** for the recipe.*

**noun:** a word that names a person, a place, or a thing.
- ➤ *They're **students.***
- ➤ *It's an excellent **hospital.***

**object:** a noun or pronoun that receives the action of the verb.
> ➤ *Mechanics fix **cars**.*

**object pronoun:** a word that takes the place of a noun as the object of the sentence: *me, you, him, her, it, us, them*.
> ➤ *Rita is my neighbor. I see **her** every day.*
> ➤ *Can you help **us**?*

**past progressive:** a verb form used to talk about an action that was in progress at a specific time in the past.
> ➤ *He **was watching** TV when the phone rang.*

**period:** a punctuation mark that is used at the end of a statement. It is also called "a full stop."
> ➤ *She lives in Moscow**.***

**phrase:** a group of words that does not have a subject or a verb.
> ➤ *He lives **near the train station**.*

**plural noun:** a noun that names more than one person, place, or thing.
> ➤ *He put three **boxes** on the table.*
> ➤ *Argentina and Mexico are **countries**.*

**possessive adjective:** an adjective that shows ownership or relationship (*my, your, his, her, its, our, their*). It is used with a noun.
> ➤ ***My** car is green.*
> ➤ ***Your** keys are on the table.*

**possessive noun:** a noun that shows ownership or a relationship.
> ➤ ***Leo's** apartment is large.*
> ➤ *The **girls'** books are on the table.*

**possessive pronoun:** a pronoun that shows ownership or relationship: *mine, yours, his, hers, its, ours, theirs*. Possessive pronouns are used in place of a possessive adjective + noun.
> ➤ *My sister's eyes are blue. **Mine** are brown. What color are **yours**?*

**preposition:** a word that describes the relationships between nouns. Prepositions describe space, time, direction, cause, and effect.
> ➤ *I live **on** Center Street.*
> ➤ *We left **at** noon.*

**pronoun:** a word that takes the place of a noun or refers to a noun.
> ➤ *The teacher is sick today. **He** has a cold.*

**proper noun:** a noun that names a specific person, place, or thing .
> ➤ ***Maggie** lives in a town near **Dallas**.*

**punctuation:** the use of specific marks to make ideas within writing clear, such as commas (,), periods (.), exclamation points (!), and question marks (?).
> ➤ *John plays soccer, but I don't.*
> ➤ *She's from Japan.*
> ➤ *That's amazing!*
> ➤ *Where are you from?*

**quantifier:** a word that describes the quantity of a noun.
> ➤ *We need **some** potatoes for the recipe.*
> ➤ *I usually put **a little** milk in my coffee.*

**question:** a sentence that asks for an answer.
> ➤ *Is she a teacher?*

**question mark:** a punctuation mark (?) that is used at the end of a question.
> ➤ *Are you a student**?***

**regular:** a noun, verb, adjective, or adverb that changes form according to standard rules.
> ➤ *apple → apples*
> ➤ *talk → talked, talking*
> ➤ *small → smaller*
> ➤ *slow → slowly*

**sentence:** a thought that is expressed in words, usually with a subject and verb. It begins with a capital letter and ends with a period, exclamation point, or question mark.
> ➤ *Karen called last night.*
> ➤ *Don't eat that!*

**short answer:** an answer to a *Yes/No* question.
> ➤ *A: Did you do the homework?*
> ➤ *B: **Yes, I did.**/ **No, I didn't.***

**simple past:** a verb form used to talk about completed actions.
> ➤ *Last night we **ate** dinner at home.*
> ➤ *I **visited** my parents last weekend.*

**simple present:** a verb form used to talk about habits or routines, schedules, and facts.
> ➤ *He **likes** apples and oranges.*
> ➤ *Toronto **gets** a lot of snow in the winter.*

**singular noun:** a noun that names only one person, place, or thing.
> ➤ *They have a **son** and a **daughter**.*

**statement:** a sentence that gives information.
> ➤ *My house has five rooms.*
> ➤ *He doesn't have a car.*

**stress:** we use stress to say a syllable or a word with more volume or emphasis.

**subject:** the noun or pronoun that is the topic of the sentence.
- ➤ *Patricia is a doctor.*
- ➤ *They are from Iceland.*

**subject pronoun:** a pronoun that is the subject of sentence: *I, you, he, she, it,* and *they.*
- ➤ *I have one brother. He lives in Miami.*

**superlative:** the form of an adjective or adverb used to compare three or more people, places, or things.
- ➤ *Mount Everest is the highest mountain in the world.*
- ➤ *Evgeny is the youngest student in our class.*

**syllable:** a part of a word that contains a single vowel sound and is pronounced as a unit.
- ➤ *The word pen has one syllable. The word pencil has two syllables (pen-cil).*

**tense:** the form of the verb that shows the time of the action.
- ➤ *He sells apples.* (simple present)
- ➤ *They sold their car.* (simple past)

**time clause:** a clause that tells when an action or event happened or will happen. Time clauses are introduced by conjunctions, such as *when, after, before,* and *while.*
- ➤ *I'm going to call my parents after I eat dinner.*
- ➤ *I called my parents when I got home.*

**time expression:** a phrase that tells when something happened or will happen. Time expressions usually go at the end or beginning of a sentence.
- ➤ *Last week I went hiking.*
- ➤ *She's moving next month.*

**verb:** a word that shows action, gives a state, or shows possession.
- ➤ *Tori called me last night.*
- ➤ *She is my classmate.*
- ➤ *She has three daughters.*

**vowel:** the following letters (and some combinations of the letters) are vowels: *a, e, i, o, u,* and sometimes *y.*

**Wh- question:** (also called *information question*) a question that asks for specific information, not an answer with *"Yes"* or *"No."* (See also *Wh-* word.)
- ➤ *Where do they live?*
- ➤ *What do you usually do on weekends?*

**Wh- word:** a word such as *Who, What, When, Where, Why,* or *How* that is used to begin a *Wh-* question (information question).
- ➤ *Why are you crying?*
- ➤ *When did they leave?*

**Yes/No question:** a question that can be answered by *"Yes"* or *"No."*
- ➤ A: *Do you live in Dublin?*    B: *Yes, I do. / No, I don't.*
- ➤ A: *Can you ski?*    B: *Yes, I can. / No, I can't.*

Note: All page references in blue are in Split Edition B.

**194:** ©UIG via Getty Images; **196–197:** ©Marcio Jose Bastos Silva/Shutterstock; **199:** ©Marjie Lambert/MCT/Newscom; **201:** © John Greim/age fotostock; **203:** L ©Justin Horrocks/Getty Images; **204:** ©Aspen Photo/Shutterstock; **206–207:** ©Henn Photography/Getty Images; **208–209:** Photograph by Brano Beliancin; **211:** ©Jimmy Chin/National Geographic Creative; **213:** ©Jimmy Chin/National Geographic Creative; **214 left:** © Skip Brown/National Geographic Creative, **middle:** © technotr/iStockphoto, **right:** ©Joe McBride/Getty Images; **215:** ©Bill Hatcher/National Geographic Creative; **216 left and right:** ©Skip Brown/National Geographic Creative; **218:** ©Stephen Alvarez/National Geographic Creative; **219:** ©Stephen Alvarez/National Geographic Creative; **221:** ©Brian J. Skerry/National Geographic Creative; **225 left:** ©John Burcham/National Geographic Creative, **225 right:** Chris Johns/ National Geographic Creative; **226:** ©F1online digitale Bildagentur GmbH/Alamy; **227:** ©Andrew Zarivny/Shutterstock; **228–229:** ©Cultura Science/Jason Persoff Stormdoctor/Getty Images; **233:** ©Lorenzo Mondo/Shutterstock; **235:** ©AFP/Getty Images; **236:** ©Gordon Wiltsie/National Geographic Creative; **238:** ©Don Bayley/Getty Images; **240–241:** ©Phil Schermeister/National Geographic Creative; **242–243:** ©Doug Pearson/Getty Images; **246 :** ©Martin Engelmann/age fotostock; **249:** ©Johnathan Ampersand Esper/Getty Images; **250:** ©Doin Oakenhelm/Shutterstock; **255:** ©Annie Griffiths Belt/National Geographic Creative; **256–257:** ©Andrew Evans/National Geographic Creative, **256 inset:** Brian Gratwicke/Andrew Evans/National Geographic Creative; **260:** ©Florian Kopp/imagebro/age fotostock; **263 top:** ©Karin Muller/National Geographic Creative, **263 bottom:** ©Hiram Bingham/National Geographic Creative; **265:** ©Keith Ducatel/AFP/Getty Images/Newscom; **266:** ©Pete Mcbride/Getty Images; **271:** ©UIG via Getty Images; **272:** ©DEA/G. DAGLI ORTI/Getty Images; **274:** ©Danita Delimont/Getty Images; **276–277:** ©Cory Richards/National Geographic Creative; **278:** ©Nic Bothma/EPA/Landov; **279:** ©The Green Belt Movement; **283:** ©NASA; **288:** © Royal Geographical Society (with IBG); **293:** ©AF archive/Alamy; **294:** ©Luis Marden/National Geographic Creative; **295:** ©Martin Strmiska/Alamy; **297:** © Royal Geographical Society (with IBG); **298:** © Royal Geographical Society (with IBG); **302:** ©GL Archive/Alamy; **303:** Classic Image/Alamy; **304:** ©Hulton Archive/Getty Images; **306:** ©Hulton Archive/Getty Images; **308–309:** ©Brian J. Skerry/National Geographic Creative; **310:** ©INTERFOTO/Alamy; **311:** © Brahim MNII/Alamy; **312:** ©Laszlo Halasi/Shutterstock; **313:** ©Robin Moore/National Geographic Creative; **315:** ©AnetaPics/Shutterstock; **317:** ©Rex Features via AP Images; **318:** ©Brian J. Skerry/National Geographic Creative; **319:** ©Brian J. Skerry/National Geographic Creative; **320:** Courtesy of Jonathan Rossouw & John J King II; **320 background:** ©winnieapple/Shutterstock; **321:** ©Guenter Guni/Getty Images; **325:** ©Michael Nichols/National Geographic Creative; **327:** ©Courtesy of Wildlife Conservation Trust; **328:** ©Roel Hoeve/Foto Natura/Getty Images; **329:** ©Marcelo del Pozo/REUTERS; **330:** Pete Oxford/Getty Images; **334:** ©Paul Sutherland/National Geographic Creative; **335:** ©Konrad Wothe/Getty Images; **336 top:** ©Rebecca Hale/National Geographic Creative, **middle:** © Indiapicture/Alamy, **bottom:** ©David Courtenay/Getty Images; **337:** ©Hung Chung Chih/Shutterstock; **338:** ©Joel Sartore/National Geographic Creative; **340–341:** ©Dustin Ghizzoni and John Jurko II; **342–343:** ©Unimedia Europe/Unimediaimages Inc/Unimedia Europe/Newscom; **345:** ©Cameron Lawson/National Geographic Creative; **348:** ©Dave Hill Mirrorpix/Newscom; **349:** ©Axel Seidemann/AP Images; **350 top:** ©UNIMEDIA/SIPA/Newscom, **middle:** ©AFP/Getty Images, **bottom:** ©CB2/ZOB/WENN.com/Newscom; **352–353:** ©Clearwater Marine Aquarium; **359:** ©Matthew Lloyd/Getty Images; **360:** ©AFP/Getty Images; **365:** ©Phil Cole/Getty Images; **366:** ©Bruce Hall; **367:** ©Alison Wright/National Geographic Creative; **368:** ©Brian A. Witkin/Shutterstock; **370:** ©Pankaj & Insy Shah/Getty Images; **372–373:** ©Frans Lanting/National Geographic Creative; **374–375:** ©Tommy Heinrich/National Geographic Creative; **381 top:** ©Adisa/Shutterstock, **bottom:** ©Taylor Kennedy-Sitka Productions/National Geographic Creative; **383:** ©Kenneth Garrett/National Geographic Creative; **384:** ©De Agostini/Getty Images; **386:** ©EschCollection/Getty Images; **388:** ©Paul Kennedy/Getty Images; **389:** ©Prisma Bildagentur AG/Alamy; **391:** ©Maremagnum/Getty Images; **392:** © Robert Harding World Imagery/Alamy; **397 top right:** ©VIEW Pictures Ltd/Alamy, **top left:** ©Novarc Images/Alamy, **bottom:** ©Richard Nowitz/National Geographic Creative; **399:** ©Nickolay Vinokurov/Shutterstock; **400:** ©Ira Block/National Geographic Creative; **402:** ©Liysa/Getty Images; **404–405:** ©chattakan kosol. www.facebook.com/yodapix; **406:** ©vladimir zakharov/Getty Images; **407:** ©XPACIFICA/National Geographic Creative; **410:** ©Sean Pavone/Shutterstock; **412:** © David Grossman/Alamy; **413:** ©O Furrer/age fotostock; **414:** ©Jorge Royan/Alamy; **419:** ©XPACIFICA/National Geographic Creative; **421:** ©Scotty Robson Photography/Getty Images; **422:** ©Danita Delimont/Alamy; **423:** ©Thierry Falise/Getty Images; **427:** ©AchimHB/Thinkstock; **429:** ©Timothy Allen/Getty Images; **430:** ©David Gilder/Shutterstock; **432–433:** ©Joe Geinert/National Geographic Creative; **434:** ©Greg Pease/Getty Images; **435:** ©Peter Charlesworth/Getty Images; **440:** ©Kyle Smith Photography/Getty Images; **441:** ©Boris Stroujko/Shutterstock; **442:** ©Cultura Travel/Philip Lee Harvey/Getty Images; **443:** ©Pete Ryan/National Geographic Creative; **444:** © Aurora Photos/Alamy; **451:** ©Matt Slocum/AP Images; **452:** © keith morris/Alamy; **453:** ©Roy Mehta/Getty Images; **457:** ©Evgeniya Porechenskaya/Shutterstock; **459:** ©Tetra Images–Erik Isakson/Getty Images; **460:** ©Heeb Christian/Prisma/SuperStock; **462:** © sturti/iStockphoto; **A7:** © Nagel Photography/Shutterstock.

## MAP

**11, 18, 28, 42, 50, 56, 97, 118, 131, 154, 163, 178, 184, 193, 208, 218, 233, 242, 249, 256, 289, 320, 329, 374, 383, 406, 422, 428:** National Geographic Maps

## ILLUSTRATION

**9, 10, 25, 27, 33, 34, 37, 52, 53, 55, 63, 65, 73, 95, 108, 127, 161, 162, 169, 173, 202, 203, 217, 246, 305, 326, 390, 443, 456, 461:** Cenveo Publisher Services